WHO ARE WE NOW?

Who Are

**Christian Humanism
and the Global Market
from Hegel to Heaney**

We Now?

N ICHOLAS B OYLE

University of Notre Dame Press
Notre Dame and London

Essays in Part 1 appeared in *New Blackfriars* and *Magdalene College Magazine and Record*, no. 34 (1989–90): 57–59. Lines from Yeats are reprinted with the permission of A. P. Watt Ltd on behalf of Michael Yeats and with the permission of Simon & Schuster from *The Collected Works of W. B. Yeats*, Volume 1: *The Poems*, revised and edited by Richard J. Finneran. Copyright 1928 by Macmillan Publishing Company; copyright renewed © 1956 by Georgie Yeats. Lines from Wallace Stevens, "Sunday Morning" and "Men Made Out of Words" are printed with permission of Faber and Faber Ltd and Alfred A. Knopf Inc, from *Collected Poems* by Wallace Stevens. Copyright 1954 by Wallace Stevens. Lines from *Four Quartets* by T. S. Eliot are reprinted by permission of Faber and Faber Ltd and of Harcourt Brace & Co for American rights.

Copyright 1998 by
University of Notre Dame Press
Notre Dame, Indiana 46556

Paperback 1999
ISBN 0-268-01958-4

Manufactured in the United States of America

Library of Congress Cataloging-in-Publication Data

Boyle, Nicholas.
    Who are we now? Christian humanism and the global market from
    Hegel to Heaney / Nicholas Boyle.
        p.   cm.
    Includes bibliographical references and index.
    ISBN 0-268-01033-1 (cloth : alk paper)
        1. World politics—1989–   2. Postmodernism.   3. Intellectual
    life—20th century. I. Title.
    D860.B69   1998
    306—dc21   97-19754
                                                    CIP

Book design by Will Powers
Set in Charlotte and Frutiger
by Stanton Publication Services, Inc.

for Faith and Rockley
and in memory of Hugh

Contents

Acknowledgments

This book has been in the making for over ten years. Throughout that time my wife Rosemary has kept the project going, has typed more than half of the manuscript, and has been an informative consultant on the relations between local and central government and the legal structures of the European Union. Her criticisms and suggestions have shaped much of the text. She also put up with my long absences during 1994–95 when I was a Fellow of the Institute of Advanced Study in Berlin. In that remarkable place, where the global market's global mind holds weekly seminars, I found the impetus and the facilities to formulate my argument and to write three of my chapters. I am grateful to the Institute, to its staff, and to its Director, Wolf Lepenies, for an opportunity without which the book would probably never have been finished. Among the many Fellows who helped my thoughts along I must mention particularly Hilary Putnam, Yehuda Elkana, and Ramachandra Guha, to whom I am grateful for comments, discussion, and encouragement. Another institution I am happy to be able to thank for making the book possible is *New Blackfriars*, the journal of the English Dominicans, the original publisher of four chapters which now appear in revised form by permission of the editors. The theological critique of culture and society has perhaps always been something of a Dominican specialty, and *New Blackfriars* has proved its only lasting vehicle among British periodicals. My thanks are also due to the editor of *Magdalene College Magazine and Record* for permission to reprint some material which first appeared there.

Many individuals have helped me with suggestions, information, or practical interventions, among them Neil Ascherson, Simon Barrington-Ward, Peter Collier, Paul Connerton, the late Lord Grimond, Stephen Houlgate, Michael Moriarty, and Martin Swales. If some of the good advice I have received, from these and others, has been ignored, and for no good reason, the responsibility for the result is mine, and I ask their indulgence. I am particularly grateful to Peter and Prue Rowe and to Jack and Kathleen McConnell for their hospitality; to Nicholas Walker, an inexhaustible source of tactfully deployed learning, for his assistance when I came to write about Heidegger; to Jim Devlin and Karen Bernhardt-Devlin for consulting services; and to Charles Gordon, who first saw the possibility of a link with the University of Notre Dame Press. Eamon Duffy has been an unfailing support, especially when spirits were low, and first suggested that I should write on a number of the topics I have treated.

It will be apparent from Chapters Seven and Eight what I think one owes to one's parents and therefore why—if a reason were needed—I have dedicated this book to mine.

N.B.

Cambridge, Probus, Gortin, Berlin

WHO ARE WE NOW?

Foreword

Are we something more than consumers and, if so, what? Are we as individuals still defined by our nationhood, our gender, our religious and cultural affiliations? Is a Christian perspective possible on a secular world? Can literature and philosophy make sense of individual lives any more? Post-Modernists have some penetrating views on these matters, but why is Post-Modernism politically reactionary, and what role will there be in the future for the intellectual class in which it has taken root? Is the world now more diverse and pluralist, as Post-Modernists assert, or is it becoming progressively more unified? What if anything can make it more secure? What was it exactly that came to an end in 1989 (assuming history didn't)? Does the nation-state have a future and what kind of international order is in the making? Why has the recent spate of privatization and market-related reforms been accompanied by a remorseless growth in the power and pretensions of state bureaucracy? Why is European policy so divisive an issue for right-wing politicians? What makes Germany and Britain different and why are they getting more like each other? Why do memories of the Second World War so obsess the British?

These are the principal questions dealt with in this book and they are all in their way questions about identity—the people we think we are and the nations or groups we think we belong to, the ultimate purposes we think we have and the ultimate constraints upon us that we acknowledge. The book was born of an urgent necessity. I believe that for some decades Britain and its people have been going through a historic crisis, which must inevitably undo the British national identity constructed over the last three centuries. I believe also that the unpalatable truths which, as a result, we in Britain have had to admit can help to explain the general crisis, of which the British crisis is only a small part, and which became apparent with revolutionary suddenness in 1989. Much of what I have to say is meant as an experiment in the global thinking which was made possible and necessary by the spectacular collapse of the perspectives imposed by a generation of Russian-American rivalry. In these suddenly wider skies the thunderclouds seem more distant but also more incalculable, and so in the end more threatening. The world has become less divided, but more disparate, its order seems less draconian but more precarious, and possibly more impervious to rational control. But I do not wish simply to be another of the ancestral voices prophesying war. I believe fervently that we have choices, and that it matters that we should choose the paths most likely to lead to justice and to peace. Only if we do so shall we be rewarded with a sense of political, cultural, and personal identity which can take the place of the false certainties of the national and imperial age that is now behind us.

Three challenges derive, I think, from the great upheaval of 1989. There is a challenge, first and last, of course, in the realm of political practice. Have economics now wholly displaced politics? Is there anything we can do? Or should we just accept that our most relevant contribution to world order is to sit back and buy over our mobile telephone the goods we most want at the price we can best afford? Is the management of social policy, for example, best left to bonus-driven administrators disciplined by the internal markets of vast quangos*? The revolutions which put an end to the Communist empire, far from being an unambiguous triumph for "liberal democracy," showed up in their aftermath the uneasy match between the political values and institutions of the non-communist world and its

---

* For the benefit of the non-British reader, I should explain that 'quango' is an acronym for 'quasi-autonomous non-governmental organization'.

economic system. The subject peoples of Eastern Europe and Central Asia voted for Western politics as a means to Western prosperity and the linkage proved not to be automatic. On the contrary, at various points in the Far East economic success has long been fostered by means of benevolent autocracy. The unseemly haste with which the British strove to impose on Hong Kong some last-minute "democratic" reforms before handing the colony over to another autocracy (no doubt less benevolent) merely showed up the concepts and institutions in question as little more than an ideological fetish of rich Westerners. As there are plenty of voices in the Western societies themselves saying that a political structure—"the state"—is redundant altogether and all conflicts can be settled by "the market," it is not surprising that there should have been a worldwide decline of confidence in political institutions, national and international, from local education authorities to the United Nations. In several of the following essays I shall put forward reasons for thinking that there is a political dimension to our life which is not reducible to the economic and which indeed is essential to the functioning of the market in the first place. To think of ourselves purely as consumers is to mis-read fundamentally the most important social developments of the last hundred years. We are, I shall argue, producers too, and this fact is systematically kept from our minds by "the market" itself and by its intellectual fellow-travelers.

The second challenge, therefore, is historical. We have to adjust our understanding of the great conflicts of the twentieth century so that the Seventy-Five Years' War, as we may call it, from 1914 to 1989, appears as a single episode in a larger story which began around 1870. It is not just a quaintly amusing historical coincidence that after the year of revolutions the boundaries and animosities of pre-1914 Europe should have re-emerged, as it were from cold storage. In the last third of the nineteenth century a world order, which is our own, began to establish itself—an international market, with globalizing tendencies. In 1989 the immensely destructive process in which that new order eliminated the political units characteristic of the preceding period—namely the European empires—came to an end. (Though some further decomposition of the longest-lasting of the empires, the Russian, is still to be expected.) But the battle-lines drawn up in the years after 1914, and defended with so much blood and thought, have determined attitudes so deeply, especially among the victims of the process, such as the British, that we are only gradually beginning to reawaken and take stock. A profound change has come over the European middle class, the bearer of the traditions of nationhood. I shall propose that we see the middle class as divided into two quite different camps, which have over the centuries developed quite different self-justifications, of which Britain and Germany provide clearly contrasting examples. But it is part of the current and general crisis that none of these self-definitions of the middle class any longer holds good.

Third, then, middle-class or not, we face a challenge to our sense of identity. The end of the empires has brought with it many new nationalisms but the concept of the nation is even less convincing than that of liberal democracy. The British, for example, are more uncertain whether they are really English (and their flag the cross of St. George, as disinterred for football matches) than they were in 1923, when their United Kingdom was founded. And if we are not citizens of our nation, who are we? It becomes ever more difficult, in a "flexible" labor market, to define ourselves in terms of the job we do, or even, in an age of "social mobility," in terms of the person to whom we are married.

A feeling that individually and collectively we no longer know who we are accounts for a very general unease among people who would not describe themselves as intellectuals, but it has also led post-structuralists and other theorists of post-modernism into oracular and wordily uncommunicative utterances on the subject of identity, and has influenced poets and novelists too. Political claims for the privileged status of particular religious or cultural traditions are equally difficult to resist and to credit, indeed they can really be made only to those who do not believe them. Authorial claims to belong to some such "ethnicity" assort uncomfortably with denials of the coherence of the self or of the authority of authors. It all sounds phoney, which only proves that the problem is genuine. The new world order has undermined all the old certainties but we do not yet seem to know where we stand in it, or even, very clearly, what it is.

The essays in this volume move from politics through history to poetry and make up something of a personal quest. They were written on various occasions over the last ten years but always with the same set of questions in mind and always sustained by the belief that these different branches of humane study grow, in the end, from the same theological stem. They begin with an anguished conspectus of what the 1980s seemed to be doing to the Britain in which I had been formed: this is the one essay which I have left almost exactly as it was first published. Most of it seems to me to stand up well even today. It drew attention to the ramifications of the ideology of consumerism, to the loss of the intermediate institutions of our civil society, and to the importance of European and constitutional issues, at a time when all these were less evident than they are now. To have tried to improve or correct it would have impaired its status as a commentary from within on the dark days when the Soviet empire still seemed intact, when in Britain budget after budget was whipping blinded home-owners and businessmen through the mortgage offices towards the pit of negative equity, and when Mrs. Thatcher had yet to make the Bruges speech which revealed her party's potentially lethal division over the European Union.

The remaining essays in the first section are the attempts of a British, and European, observer, after the great turning-point in 1989, to gain a viewpoint on his local circumstances from which they could be seen as part of a world process. It is not just my personal and professional concern with Germany which causes me to concentrate on the German contribution to understanding these matters. Germany is a hugely important fact in twentieth-century history and its intellectual influence is underrated and misunderstood. During the Weimar Republic it went through a dress-rehearsal of what is now a worldwide drama, the shock of transition to a post-imperial economic order. The dominant figure in this period was undoubtedly Heidegger, the forefather of the post-modern movement of deconstructionism.

In the second group of essays I make use of different aspects of German history and thought to illuminate the political implications of a Post-Modernist stand. Heidegger's intellectual successors can do no more than he to resist the destructive (even if essentially transient) forces of fascism, which continue to threaten us in new guises and old.[1] Profound though the insights may be of Post-Modernists such as Foucault, Derrida, and Lyotard, and of their (more or less sympathetic) Marxist critics such as Jameson and Eagleton, these thinkers seem to me limited by their inadequate reflection on their own relation, as individuals and as a class, to the economic system of which we are all—willing—parts. Their work is too often distorted by a leaning to cultural pessimism and political quiescence, to collaboration, that is, with the forces which imposed themselves on us in Britain under the name of Thatcherism. I do not think we can learn from them who we are, or what it is right for us to do.

If I turn in the final section to literary theory and literary practice, it is because literature is the place where all the questions—philosophical, religious, political, and economic—intersect. It is also the place where they come closest, I believe, to whatever can nowadays be called " ordinary" or "general" experience. However universal their themes, poets can discuss them satisfactorily only in terms drawn from their own time and place and life. It was in such personal and local terms, by trying to understand the British phenomenon of Thatcherism, that I first met the larger issues dealt with here, and in the end it is from poets that I hope for confirmation that I have understood. No one knows better than the poet that you can grasp your time only in the words your time has given you.

It should be evident that this book is not an academic treatise in political science. I have tried to address a reader with general interests in social and intellectual history, in philosophy and literature, who faces personal perplexities similar to my own. These are essays in critique of certain aspects of contemporary culture: attempts not so much to discover facts as to change ideas. We can look at things another way and—I believe—more coherently. Although the method is literary and philosophical, rather than that of the social scientist, it leads me to make some political and economic observations, since one of my main assumptions is that literature and philosophy have to be seen in a political and economic context. "One of the virtues of literary studies," remarks F. R. Leavis, in direct contradiction of what was to become one of the central tenets of deconstructionism, "is that they lead constantly outside themselves."[2] If works of literature are understood as living embodiments of a reaction to particular historical circumstances, they can still serve, even in a secular society, as vehicles of a communicable wisdom about our identity and our duty.

I write as a liberal Catholic humanist. I do not object to labels when it is necessary to apply them: they may not tell you the contents of the luggage but they tell you where it is intended to go. It is however important that the address should be correct. I am not saying that I am a "liberal Catholic"—that sectarian designation has little relevance to the questions discussed here. I understand "liberal" in a political sense, to refer to one who is not a conservative, who thinks change is inevitable and often for the better, but who has a more open view of the future than the socialist, and holds that human freedom is a more ingenious and effective problem-solver than any dictatorial schemer. Freedom, however, is not an individual matter. We create our freedoms in the institutions we jointly construct: there can be no freedom of expression until there are media of communication through which it can be exercised, no political freedoms until there are legislative and executive bodies with rules and constitutions that incorporate them. Freedom—this is perhaps Hegel's most fundamental insight—is not something we are born with, but something we make. Similarly talk of "rights" is always talk of the institutions, however speculative, that might enforce them. (The Chinese government is perfectly correct to think that criticism of its "human rights record" is interference in Chinese internal affairs by foreign powers—like the Euroskeptic, however, that government is of course wrong to think such interference a bad thing.) The Vatican once roundly and regularly condemned "human rights" as an invention of the French Revolution. Its recent conversion to propagating them through international diplomacy is nevertheless wholly consistent with an ancient Catholic view: that the unity of the human moral conscience can be expressed only through the utterances of a religious authority which has at the same time a recognized standing in the secular, temporal, world. The tradition of Catholic humanism, of the cathedral-builders and St. Thomas, Erasmus and Bolzano, Acton and Chesterton, is, as I see it, inspired by the belief that all areas of human life must be reached by the good news and can be bearers of it, and that that is in the nature of the good news itself. To see them as they really are is to see them as the gospel shows them. We do not have to pretend we are not part of the post-modern, economic, political, and cultural system in order to discover our ultimate purpose and identity. We have only to understand the system correctly and acknowledge the obligations which understanding imposes. For that reason even those who do not see or share the theological presuppositions on which these essays are based may I hope be able to learn something from them. It is my central thesis that we all make up one world, even if we are only gradually coming to recognize it.

I
At the Turn of the Times

1 Understanding Thatcherism
(1988)

A year ago, in an editorial, *New Blackfriars* was complaining that the theological understanding of what Mrs. Thatcher had been doing to Britain had "hardly even begun."

The complaint could have been generalized. To judge by the standard of the public debate at the 1987 General Election, any in-depth understanding of Thatcherism, despite the decade of evidence on which it could draw, was non-existent. Even now it is still in its infancy. A government which claims to have wrested intellectual supremacy from the left and to be full of ideas, and which is if anything rather pleased with itself when its opponents accuse it of sacrificing something or other on the altar of ideology, has nonetheless provoked no coherent theoretical critique to speak of from its public opponents, hardly anything other than mesmerized horror.

Is it the indisputable authority of seemingly unending power that has reduced the critical mind to silence? Or is Mrs. Thatcher perhaps right? Has a philosopher-queen inaugurated a republic in which all the questions of political economy, having been answered, no longer need to be asked? Hardly. The massive paradoxes of the Thatcher years—their blatancy must partly account for the opposition's bewilderment—demand explanation, and, like any explanation of human affairs, that explanation will of course have a theological dimension. I am not, though, a theologian. Surely, however, the launching of a really satisfactory "theological critique" of Thatcherism at least partly depends on the opening up of a rather more general discussion of Thatcherism, and what I am offering here is a contribution to this.

I am not, though, a political philosopher or an economist, either. I am professionally concerned with looking at things from a non-British—as it happens, a German—point of view. That may give its own perspective to my thoughts about the policies of the present British government, and so, I hope, help others to understand better than I do.

Paradoxes and Power

I have already spoken of Thatcherism's "massive paradoxes." The first and most obvious paradox is that Thatcherism has won three general elections in a row and is if anything more firmly established in power than ever and yet, regarded simply as a doctrine, is devoid of intellectual substance. There is here a formidable political achievement, without parallel in this century, but it is not an achievement that anyone would think of attributing to the intellectual powers of Mrs. Thatcher's cabinets. Even in the sphere proper to them they have not shown evidence of long-sightedness either in foreign affairs, in European co-operation and defense, for example, or in domestic matters: on the contrary, the government has been remarkable for its lack of interest in the implications of what it has been doing for the British constitution. Even at the most basic level, it neglects systematically to consider the legacy it is leaving to another government of a different political complexion which may well wish to use parliamentary powers to direct and reorganize local government, or ministerial powers to suppress and control information or interfere with educational institutions, in such a way as to vitiate much of what the present administration has done. The government and the Conservative party do of course have their more or less independent think tanks, but the proposals that emerge from these seem often to concentrate on being polemically radical about minutiae and averse even to formulating broader considerations than those of the accountant. And there have for some time been a number of university philosophers willing to feed the mouth that bites them and give support to the present government, but it is important not to confuse a libertarian critique of Marxist and other authoritarian forms of the state with an argument in favor of Thatcherism.

For the second and perhaps most substantial paradox about this strange -ism is that those who profess it were elected to power having promised to reduce government, while the attempt to execute this promise has led to an unprecedented increase in central government's scope and pretensions. For those who are fortunate enough to be employed, taxation has overall increased (unless one is very prosperous indeed), and those who are not so fortunate are subject to an increasing array of government pressures to change their skills, move their homes, or join government-organized labor-gangs. The extension of the Inland Revenue's System of Pay As You Earn (PAYE) has turned thousands more employers into unpaid tax-collectors. Thanks to frequent changes of interest rates government's overwhelming financial power is felt in every household, and by an artificial restriction of funds or by the enormously increased use of earmarked grants, government-dependent bodies are deprived of autonomy and turned into agencies for the immediate execution of whatever happens to be the current wish of the relevant ministry. Local authorities, universities, and broadcasting organizations have all been brought under this financial "discipline," which is somehow never distinct from policy considerations, i.e., from doing what the government wants. Police authorities have already been, school governors shortly will be, encouraged to put themselves in a direct relationship with their ministry should there be local obstacles to their carrying out central policy. Even the Church of England has been rebuked by the Home Secretary for not doing its bit towards keeping down the crime rate. There is a German word for this process of bringing all the agencies of society into line with government intentions—now more or less transparently avowed in the admission that the current administration is seeking to found an "enterprise culture," as if founding any kind of culture were a proper task for government—but it is a word familiar to an English audience from another context: Gleichschaltung. Had a Labour government abolished Conservative-controlled metropolitan authorities and the Inner London Education Authority (ILEA),

we should certainly have been told that a Marxist, or National Socialist, revolution was taking place and that a dictatorship on the
East European model was being set up.

It is important not to trivialize this feature of Thatcherism in
practice by attributing it to the personality of the Prime Minister,
or to her "style." It is a political phenomenon of the deepest significance and inseparable, as we shall see, from the concept of individual political and economic freedom which is the basis of the
ambition to reduce the role of government. Nor must the analyst be
deceived by the prevailing vocabulary into thinking that privatiza-
tions, council house sales, and so on have anything much to do
with freedom or a reduction of social control. Just as the privatized
industrial colossus becomes a commodity on the world market-
place, so the new council-house owner is enthralled to his build-
ing-society, itself increasingly likely to be part of an international
financial concern, and in both cases the accountant's "discipline"
takes the place of the bureaucrat's. The people of Britain are free to
choose between competing bus-companies on routes that are prof-
itable but unable to travel at all, if they lack a car, on those that are
not. They may call themselves owners of their own homes provided
they pay more in mortgage repayments, maintenance, and their
own time and labor than they ever did to rent. We shall be free in
the future no doubt to arrange our own health insurance, but no
one will be allowed to be free of anxiety about their health. The
contradiction in Thatcherism between the vocabulary of liberation
from government on the one hand, and the reality of increased government activity and a narrowing definition of personal choice on
the other, is fundamental.

It may of course be that only a particular kind of personality
could impose this new contradiction on the British social and political system with such rapidity that it is not inappropriate to speak of
a Thatcher revolution. And this is the third paradox. Mrs. Thatcher
offers us (with no option to refuse it) a revolution. I think that offer
is genuine, though the lady in the market stall knows neither the
true nature nor the origin of her goods, and might be shocked to
think that Thatcherism comes from the same foreign factory as Ja-
cobinism or Leninism. But this offer is combined with an appeal to
the Victorian past and with nationalist or imperialist gestures, with
a pretense, that is, of being a *conservative* policy. It will not do to ac-

cept these gestures at face value and dismiss Thatcherite conservatism as simply reactionary—that is to overlook the true modernity of the new creed. Equally it is not a significant criticism—though it is an accurate one and one which for polemical purposes it may from time to time be necessary to make—that Mrs. Thatcher has got Victorian values wrong, and they weren't like that at all. The contradiction here is between the internationalism that is intrinsic to Thatcherite economic practice and the nationalism which is an essential part of its appeal and self-definition: "putting *Britain* back on its feet again." And again it is between an economic and social stance that was occasioned, and even necessitated, by the end of Empire, and a political and military consciousness that ignores the end of Empire entirely. The Thatcherite account of the last forty years of British politics has much to say about domestic economic and welfare policy but nothing about the dissolution of the imperial order, at home, as well as abroad, in which I believe the immediate origins of Thatcherism lie. The absence of a policy (even an out-and-out backing for the Orange card) in Northern Ireland is highly symptomatic.

Returning to the first of these three paradoxes, it is easy to say that the reason why Mrs. Thatcher came to power and stays there is simple. That it is the same as the reason why Thatcherism has needed no significant intellectual content of its own. She needs no political philosophy of her own because in the eyes of the electorate there is no coherent or plausible political philosophy opposing her. But Thatcherism plainly is something, even if it is not an ideology, and its success is not to be explained simply by the impotence or maladroitness of its political opponents. Something important and different has been happening in British society since 1979, or at any rate since the repudiation of the Clegg awards and their ethos. The Conservative party under Mrs. Thatcher have been riding the bow-wave thrown up by a bigger vessel of which however they can give little or no description and from which indeed they avert their gaze. Hegel gives the name of "the cunning of Reason" to the principle that politicians, even great ones, while pursuing aims limited by—and perhaps only attainable through—their own passions or personalities or deluded understandings, can nonetheless be the instruments of greater processes than they are themselves able to grasp. We shall eventually have to ask how cunning Reason is being in subjecting us to Thatcherism. But first we must look a little more closely at the second paradox.

The State and the Institutions

I do not suppose that the members of Mrs. Thatcher's cabinet are much given to reading Hegel's *Philosophy of Right*. If they were they might be in a better position to understand the paradox that the more they attempt to reduce government the more they increase its direct interference in the lives of British citizens. Never before in peacetime can ministers, by their personal decisions to use central powers to regulate public spending, interest rates, and to a certain extent the sterling exchange rate, have intervened so drastically in the lives of millions of households to cow, harass, or punish them with unemployment or the threat of it. The centrally promulgated criminal law, and so also the police force, have been widely deployed in areas they previously touched little if at all: industrial relations and financial transactions in the City of London. Government's relatively limitless resources of money and influence have been used to prevent publication of information which, rationally or irrationally, ministers wished to suppress, doing this often in ways embarrassingly reminiscent of totalitarian regimes, opposition to which now furnishes their party with so much of its *raison d'être*. Most clearly of all, the last nine years have seen a sustained assault by the organs of state on all the intermediate social organizations, the autonomous and semi-autonomous institutions, the constitutional checks and balances, that lie between central government and individual citizens, that protect them from direct, and always potentially arbitrary, central interference, that give shape and substance and continuity to their lives, a focus for loyalty and a place of engagement with other citizens that is not simply an extension of the market-place—the fabric of society, in short, or, as Hegel calls it, "civil society."

It is principally local government that has been the object of this assault, through a reduction in its resources, the centrally influenced disposition of what remains, and the restriction, through privatization requirements and the new Education Bill, of its area of competence. Devolution, even in the milder form of the financial autonomy that would be secured by a local purchase or income tax, could not be a deader dodo. But other areas of corporate public life, not under central control, and branded "vested interests," have felt the chill wind of disapproval that blows from Westminster: notably the trade unions, the BBC, the universities, and now even the Church. Most significant, perhaps, has been the attack on the professions: one, that of the stockbroker, has been summarily abolished, lawyers have been told to advertise and compete, teachers to teach according to contract, and it is shortly to be the turn of doctors too. All this is not just a matter of limiting corruption, abuse, and gross inefficiency, which in a balanced constitution is a perfectly proper function for central government. The case of the professions is significant because it shows that Thatcherism is indeed hostile to the whole range of social institutions that are not part of the state, and not simply to those that exercise quasi-governmental functions. A profession is by definition a corporation that restricts its membership by other than market considerations, and professional standards are standards imposed not by the market but by the opinion of fellow-professionals. You cannot have professional standards without professional restrictive practices and an assault on restrictive practices is an assault on the professional institutions themselves.

The distinction between civil society and the state, so straightforwardly made in *The Philosophy of Right,* is not one of which Thatcherism is aware: it uses the one word "public" to refer to anything other than the supposed desires of the individual (usually called a "consumer"). Freedom is the freedom to satisfy those desires and anything other than the market is a restriction of that freedom. Thatcherism is thus able to present its assault on the social fabric as a reduction in public control, as an increase in freedom for the individual, and as an act of self-sacrifice.

Thatcherism has no theory of the public, social world as a medium in which people exist and which shapes their lives; it has no theory of the constitution, of institutions, or of social, as distinct from economic, behavior. The organs of central government are simply instruments for putting into practice "our ideas," and otherwise there exist only consumers, the meeting of whose quantifiable desires is the one task government should set itself. The classic questions of constitutional theory are simply ignored: the distinction between legislature and executive, already under serious threat in Britain for many years, has largely disappeared, as cabinets have come to be as tightly disciplined as parliamentary majorities and ministerial powers of regulation have increased, and even the distinction from the judiciary is coming into question. The need for restrictions to prevent the abuse of ministerial power is neither admitted nor discussed, nor does Thatcherism allow, either in practice or in theory, for the existence of other parties and the importance, indeed the necessity, that governments should change from time to time. (The British constitution gives such absolute powers to Parliament, from which the only protection is delay, that it is essential that governments should have a limited life if tyranny is to be avoided.) It is perhaps not surprising that Thatcherism shows no interest in electoral reform: it is more remarkable that it ignores both reform of the House of Lords into an effective second chamber restraining the powers of the Commons and the promulgation, in some form, of a Bill of Rights.

That institutions have another function besides providing a service, that they are a source of identity, and not only for their members, is also lost on Thatcherism, which is therefore strangely puzzled about the definition of the British nation. There was a time when to be British was to belong to a nation characterized by certain institutions, to belong to the nation of the bobby, the BBC, the National Health Service, the firewatchers of the Blitz, Anglican vicars, the British Museum, bowler hats and rolled umbrellas, and so on *ad lib*. Because such identity is neither quantifiable nor marketable—quite apart from what has been done to some of these institutions since 1979—it does not register on the Thatcherite consciousness, and in the last election campaign the symbol of British identity for the Conservative party was, together with an emblematic dog like a company mascot, a set of statistics of economic performance. The possibility of being proud of belonging to a nation, a town, a school, a team, a fire brigade, because of what it is, and not simply because of what it does, of wishing to work for its good, for a common good, rather than for individual reward, is no more a Thatcherite concept than "public service," "public duty," or "public responsibility." It is the evacuation of terms such as these, rather than simply poor pay, which has brought about what is often called a "loss of morale" in professions such as teaching or nursing.

In the place of the notion of society, of the public world, Thatcherism puts the notion of the market, and in the place of the notion of service to the common good the notion of service—i.e., work—rendered in exchange for payment at the market rate. That rate has to be determined by competition, and by hook or by crook competition has to be introduced into those areas of the national life that were previously regarded—not always, it is true, with any obvious justification—as non-commercial. Yet there is a manifest limit on the power of competition to ensure that a service is adequate to the demands of customers when the service is of a highly complex kind, and that limitation is the size of the market. The fewer suppliers the market can support, the more imperfect will competition be. In these circumstances some regulatory body is needed to ensure that the monopoly, or near-monopoly, suppliers maintain an adequate standard, and the definition of this adequacy will not and cannot be provided by market mechanisms. To that extent Thatcherism cannot succeed in reducing the social fabric to the market-place. What of course it can do, and to a certain extent has already done, is to reassign the regulatory function away from autonomous institutions such as the Council of the Stock Exchange, local education authorities, or the governing bodies of universities and vest it in legislation, given effect by statutory bodies, ministerial *fiat* ("school teachers shall have contracts in the following terms"), or parliamentary commissioners.

British society is thus at once polarized and homogenized. The great institutions that gave it depth and complexity fade away. Instead we have on the one hand the undifferentiated mass of individual "consumers," and on the other hand the legislative and executive power of central government organizing those same masses, but as workers, into employment and unemployment and enforcing its will, in the last analysis, by the power of the police. The prominence of the police in British life has increased greatly since 1979. The forces of social control represented by family life, church authority, professional morality, or corporate loyalty have all been losing effectiveness, either because Thatcherism is directly concerned to displace the institutions which were the vehicles of those controls by "the market" and by legislation (the professions and autonomous corporations), or because, though not consciously hostile, it is unable to insert them into its vision of British national identity (the family and the Church). The record of Thatcherism in respect of the family is surprisingly bad: the reform of family law is given the usual low priority and no attempt is made to shield the family from the forces, which in recent years have of course greatly strengthened, pressing both partners in a marriage to become wage-earners, separately active economic units. The poll tax, the tax which differentiates as little as possible between the units composing the population and which logically requires, for its efficient administration, the introduction of numbered identity cards, is a useful indication of how Thatcherism envisages society. We are approaching the state of early nineteenth-century Russia, as Hegel described it: "one mass, consisting of serfs, and another, of those who rule," with nothing in between.

Of course Thatcherism believes that, by personal equity plans and home ownership, the entire nation—except for that fraction of it which is being screwed into poverty as an incentive to the rest to do better—can be made middle class, in something like the sense of fifty or a hundred years ago. But the boom in house prices, which helps create the illusion that everyone who has bought a council house will soon be a millionaire, ensures that, however much incomes increase, enough will always have to be spent on this necessity of life to prevent a significant accumulation of capital in private hands which could form the basis for such a genuinely "middle" class. We can't all be middle, though we can all be homogenized in and through the race to become so.

As it happens, we have an example of the social structure at which (though on a higher level of affluence and with a far more hectic degree of economic activity) Mrs. Thatcher is aiming: the condition of the inhabitants of Prague. Many of them have two homes, share, of course, in the ownership of their national industries, have more money in the bank than most British people and, like the population of other Eastern European countries, are living, if in considerably deprived material circumstances, the middle-class life of fifty years ago. The intermediate social institutions (the church, for instance) are either suppressed or a hollow sham, constitutional issues do not exist, and life is intensely private and devoted to the satisfaction of the consumer's desires, whether through the official or the black economy. In social and political (though not of course economic) terms, Thatcherism rather resembles the socialism it abhors. But with this we touch on the historical position and historical illusions of Thatcherism.

The Cunning of Reason

The end of the Empire has been the most traumatic event to befall Britain after 1945 or even 1918—literally so, for the patient is still traumatized, unable to recognize what has happened to him. He seems hypnotically determined to forget, not that all those limbs have been cut off, but rather that he ever had them. Of course there are the occasional waves of nostalgia for the far pavilions but what we do not see is any appreciation of the profound influence of the Empire on *British* society for a good two hundred years, nor of the crisis that its end necessarily meant for *us*. We are the product of those two centuries, and of the historical rupture that has cut us off from them, and we have plunged that fact into total and pathological oblivion.

From the middle of the eighteenth century Britain conducted its relations with the continent of Europe with the left hand—the principal object of its attention lay elsewhere, on the other side, or sides, of the world. And from that same time Britain's own internal development diverged from that of other European states. As the modern sense of nationhood came to be established, Britain found its national identity and purpose not through internal constitutional conflict leading to revolution—the European norm— but through acquiring and running an overseas Empire. After the Seven Years' War—the real first world war—France lost an empire and Britain gained one, and France had a revolution, and Britain didn't. Throughout the nineteenth and twentieth centuries the possession of an empire had a stabilizing effect on the British political system and a conserving, even embalming, effect on British society. British society had room to move; home politics, even home religious conflict, lacked that last claustrophobic desperation that leads to revolution.

Because Britain could tread the path of reform rather than revolution as it adapted to an industrial economy, it took with it into the new age many of the medieval institutions that elsewhere perished as new nations were born. In 1945 the institutional fabric of Britain presented a quite absurd, Heath Robinsonian, contrast to the rationalized mass-societies of the other warring nations. And we have only to look at the history of religious thought in the eighteenth and nineteenth centuries to see that the Enlightenment passed

England by: though by 1740 it was established in Scotland and threatening England, it then faded away. As the imperial and industrial adventure gathered momentum the English had other things to think about than critiques, whether of the Bible and theology or of the institutions of the Middle Ages.

Organizing an entire society to run an empire, or at any rate to live with one, meant changes and new institutions too. And, though not directly connected with the Empire, all sorts of new developments necessary in an increasingly complex and specialized industrial society took on their peculiarly British character in an imperial atmosphere and were partly influenced by the continuing presence of medieval models: most notably the newly founded public schools and the reformed universities and civil service. It seems unlikely that that great Victorian achievement, the county council, or the new professional organizations, or even the trade unions, would have been granted so great an exemption from central government control had central government not felt that it had wider responsibilities than local home affairs. But the most pervasive influence of the Empire on British national life was that it reinforced, if it did not actually create, a uniquely British phenomenon: what the mid-twentieth century used to call "the class system"—the endless variations on the fundamental polarity of officers and men: gentlemen and players, church and chapel, the natural party of government and the loyal opposition.

In the thirty years after 1947 the political, economic, and military base for this entire structure was dissolved. It ought to have been immediately obvious that structures do not remain standing when their foundations are removed, and that there were some hard times ahead. For various reasons it was not obvious, and Britain's decision in 1945 to collaborate with the forces of mid-twentieth–century modernity was not in intention a revolution, or was only a revolution on the cheap. Having just won a war, the British did not wish to give up all that they thought of as making them great, and indeed British. Instead, the peculiarities of their society were to be maintained, but its privileges to be made available to all. The next thirty years were an age of having things both ways, of having an imperial society without the burden of the Empire, and a modern society without the controls of the modern state. It was as if, having done its bit and laid down its strenuous but conscience-pricking imperial task, Great Britain could now honorably and comfortably retire.

But history knows no pensioners. By the time Mr. Foot's closed-shop legislation was on the statute-book the cushion of empire was gone. The British nation could have avoided putting a price-limit on its welfare state, and could have maintained the principle of doing everything for everybody, if it had also been willing—and able—to maintain an empire which it could have exploited to pay for its own comfort. For thirty years the illusion was sustained that though the cushion was not there, this need not make any difference. Insistently, however, the voice of reality made itself heard—as inflation. And there was no more room to move. The conflicts all had to be resolved at home. Everything that the Empire had created or sustained was an anachronism by 1979, and when Mrs. Thatcher got her one-vote majority of no-confidence in Mr. Callaghan the revolution delayed since the middle of the eighteenth century had begun and Britain had started to become a genuinely modern European state at last.

Not, of course, that Mrs. Thatcher saw or sees it that way: she certainly does not think of herself as carrying to its logical conclusion, unfettered by imperial memories, the British people's decision in 1945 to opt for the modern centrally directed form of society, even though that is what she is doing. For her the "Thatcher revolution" is only a manner of speaking. She is no more aware than the rest of the population of the end of the Empire—but by golly she can act on it. That is the cunning of Reason. Reason—let us call it the logic of history—dictated that the post-1947 illusions had to come to an end and that with the Empire the fruits of Empire had also to wither away. Even without Mrs. Thatcher, and without a Conservative victory in 1979, it would still have happened, but it would have been brought about by hyperinflation rather than by government decree. It would have been messier, and some of the victims might have been a bit different. People might have been shot in Downing Street instead of burning themselves to death there or sending suicide notes to the Home Secretary. As it was, Mrs. Thatcher took opportunity by the forelock and it has been the Conservative party that has bobbed along on the bow-wave of history, rationalizing British society as Napoleon (frequently invoked in the discussion of the Education Reform Bill) did France, or as his twentieth-century socialist and national-socialist successors (not usually mentioned) did Germany and Russia. The imperialist and reactionary gestures that accompany this process have the function of concealing from the party, and no doubt from the Prime Minister too, the nature of the government's main project. The gestures are calculatedly marginal—defending a few rocks in the South Atlantic, persecuting homosexuals—and do not affect the Government's serious interest. The USA is allowed to invade the Commonwealth state of Grenada. The return to Victorian values does not entail a return to the Victorian restriction of political activity to men.

The Real Revolution

Nevertheless, though Thatcherism is putting an end to the ambiguities of the post-war years, seeing that bodies which receive government money are either firmly integrated into the central administrative mechanism or, with their subsidies cut off, thrust out into the market-place, this clarification is not what it seems. For the market-place is no liberal hurly-burly where anything goes and there is not a policeman in sight. The supposedly "free" market is rigorously controlled. This is done by government legislation against "restrictive practices," i.e., against that freedom of association through which genuinely non-governmental corporations, such as business cartels or trade unions, come into existence. And it is done, more fundamentally, by government control of the supply and price of money. Conversely, the newly defined and concentrated realm of government administration is not remote from the din of trade and calmly devoted to the rule of law, the preservation of order, and defense of the national interest. Here too, we are told, the disciplines of the market must prevail (except in respect of the restrictive practice that 40 percent of the votes gives you 100 percent of the power). So wherever we look we see both the right hand of government and the left hand of the market—could it be that each really does know what the other is doing?

In the modern, totally mobilized state, all of both sexes, save the old, the young, and the infirm, are or ought to be workers (and ways are always being sought to reduce the number of exceptions). In Marx's sense—that a proletarian is one who lives by selling his labor—we are all proletarians now, down to the last yuppie. We have seen that Thatcherism has no serious intention of recreating a leisured capitalist class living by the work of others. Thatcherism sees the whole function of society as the process by which the labor of the entire population, regarded as an undifferentiated mass of individual workers, is directed to meet the desires of that same population, regarded as an undifferentiated mass of individual consumers. This vision is not fundamentally different from that of the Marxist states, in which however the converse process obtains: consumption is directed to accord with production. Neither vision contains a conception of society as encompassing a plurality of functions, groupings, or interests, or of a public, political realm as a place where these different elements are accommodated to each other in a principled and rational way. (There is no way of describing, either in Thatcherist or Marxist terms, a forum such as the public inquiry at which a developer, a residents' association, a conservation group, and a planning authority are all represented: for that is neither an extension of the market, nor an extension of the planning agency, but a true expression of the *polis*.) There is no room in the Thatcherist view for any social units larger than the individual, and the individual has his identity only as a unit of consumption or of labor, not as one who shares in the life of any institution—not even of the institutions of government. Because government is thus reduced to the force that either satisfies my needs or directs my work it is indistinguishable for me from the market. The organs of state—legislature, executive, judiciary—are simply part of the market mechanism. They do not, as they did under the Empire, express my feeling of belonging: of being British. They do not represent to me the dignity of free beings living in association under the law—for I am not myself invested with such dignity by the Thatcherist view. The freedom the Thatcherist state protects is the only freedom it knows: the freedom to have what I want, not the freedom to be what I choose; the freedom to have precisely what I want precisely when I want it, not the freedom to associate with others in giving up what I want (e.g., immediate treatment by the Health Service) for the sake of something else that seems to us more important (e.g., accessibility to health care for all). In the Thatcherist view there is nothing else, beyond the satisfaction of desires. There is not even identity: government does not express it and individuals do not possess it. Let me explain.

In a socialist society people's labor is cheap; in a consumer society people's labor is expensive. This, however, does not mean that in it people themselves are of worth. As people become more expensive—because they are more educated and their skills represent a greater investment, or because payment in status and security becomes less important than payment in purchasing power, or because work is more valuable when there are more satisfactions that it can buy—so it becomes necessary to ration the use made of them, and account closely for it. Like expensive computing time, people must be used to the full when switched on and be either instantly transferable to another function when one job is completed or else simply switched off. In the language of Thatcherism: people—that is, workers—must be flexible or unemployed. They must not be tied to a place, but prepared to move to follow employment. They must not be tied by time, but prepared to work all hours and days of the week, especially Sundays. It follows that they must not be tied to any particular group of people or community: that they have families, even, is of no social significance since it is of no significance in the market, except as distracting from their flexibility. Above all they must expect to retrain, to work to satisfy quite different needs several times in their working life. They are in short to be dismembered, reduced to a series of functions that they exercise in accordance with no principle of continuity of their own choosing but only with the demands of the market. For only in this way can they meet the increasing and changing variety of the desires of the consumers. But who are the consumers? None other than the workers themselves. The assumption behind the demand for flexibility in the workers—which denies them the continuity of a fixed identity—is that as consumers too they will have no fixed or limited desires, not give themselves an identity by voluntarily renouncing any of those desires (e.g., to buy furniture on Sundays or to receive forty channels on their TV set) for some more general—and therefore non-marketable—good. In the Thatcherist society we each become a Faust, whose endless and innumerable desires can all be satisfied provided only that he gives up his identity, his soul.

Let me give two examples of this form of Thatcherism in action, the first concerning my own profession. The abolition of academic tenure is an obscure part of the Education Reform Bill which causes little public emotion. Tenure is assumed to be an unjustifiable individual privilege and a shelter for the inefficient (though few are aware that in West Germany, not noted for its inefficiency, all public servants have tenure). But two aspects of abolition make it a revealing measure of where British society is going. First, the terms of the Bill make it clear that government is concerned not so much about sacking idle dons as providing for the redundancy of academics who have been *judged* surplus to requirement. The government, through its agencies, is to have power to intervene suddenly and with immediate effect in the affairs of individual universities, by closing or trimming departments for its own reasons, whereas hitherto tenure has prevented that direct molding of institutions to ministerial wishes. With this tendency of Thatcherism we are already fully familiar. Second, however, remember that being a don is not simply a matter of having acquired certain skills. It is a matter of a continuing accumulation of knowledge and understanding. A research project, in the arts at any rate, is a lifetime affair; and only those who put their whole lives into it get anywhere. The assumption behind tenure is that being an academic is a vocation. The assumption behind abolition is that there are no vocations for anyone any more; society is not composed of people who have lives which they commit in this or that particular way but of functions to be performed only for as long as there is a desire to be satisfied. Lives are uncomfortably distinct and finite things. Like institutions, they are essentially restrictive practices in the otherwise free flow of the market and of government directions. Better to hire not people, but a measurable quantity of their time and work, and then you can forget about them after you have had what you wanted.

The second example is a graphic illustration of Thatcherism's reduction of humanity from lives to material. It is the case of the Westminster cemeteries sold to a development company hopeful that one day it might get planning permission for them. And why, on Thatcherist principles, should it not? The cause of flexibility requires even the dead to retrain—their modest fixity in time and space, a reminder of the limits on desire, is restrictive of the property market and the efficient use of local government resources, so they must accept direction into new employment as the foundations of office-blocks. What, after all, is a human being when he or she is not performing a market function? So much matter, so much soap. There is a clear parallel to Thatcherism's mobilization of the

Westminster dead in its willingness to allow the economic exploitation of the unborn, "fetal material" as they are called, humanity without the inconveniently inflexible vested interests of individual identity.

This is the real revolution: the organization of society in accordance with the principle to which Heidegger gave the name of "technicity," the reduction of being to efficient functioning. In Hegel's more political terms: society is made no longer to consist of "particular people" who have both a fixed role of their own and a notion of how that contributes to the common good; it consists only of "individuals" and their desires, and the state no longer represents a sense of collective identity but is reduced to a "system of needs." This revolution has taken place in Europe and America in various stages over the last two hundred years. In its final, most refined and civilian stage, direction is apparently left in the hands of the market. In fact, however, the central power remains omnipresent, having as its one task the maintenance of "flexibility" throughout the system. Britain, like a rather gentlemanly sleepwalker, went through all the stages in the thirty to forty years after the end of the Second World War. By little more than a historical accident it fell to the Conservative party to introduce the country in the 1980s to a form of modernity that was by then world-wide. The force that made the step inevitable, whoever was in power, was the force of international competition. The international market was so established that, unprotected by the encircling Empire, Britain could no more resist its demand for flexibility than an ailing steelworks could resist Mr. MacGregor. In order to regain power the party of the one nation, of Church and Queen, became the instrument of commercial internationalism. In this contradiction there is perhaps a glimmer of light on the path forward.

Saving the Inflexibilities

Thatcherism is by its nature an internationalist creed (as is shown by the Prime Minister moderating her nationalist objections to the Common Agricultural Policy so as not to delay the deregulation of the European market in 1992). But this market internationalism leaves a national central government in an anomalous position, as the least justifiable of restrictive practices. The Thatcher government is in a cleft stick. On the one hand it cannot commit itself to realizing a European community—not just because it cannot commit itself to any institutional ideal which might imply that men and women are citizens, and not merely consumer-workers, but because this particular institution threatens to take away its powers of direction of the British economy. On the other hand it cannot commit itself to a distinctively national stance since this would require a protectionist attitude to the sterling exchange rate and to key national—or even nationalized—industries, as well as larger subventions for the standard-bearers of nationhood (such as the foreign service, the British Council, or the external services of the BBC).

Thatcherism's inability to envisage European co-operation as a significant political process—and not simply another step in the expansion towards infinity of the market and its "discipline"—is a blind spot symmetrical with its blind spot, in internal affairs, for constitutional issues. In both cases that question of national identity arises which, though first posed by Indian independence in 1947, has remained unanswered and unaddressed by all British governments since then. And it may be that two blind spots make an Achilles' heel. Heidegger thought that the power of technicity could be resisted, though only through giving weight to "insignificant things." But things that are insignificant in the infinitely flexible market—things such as nationhood, political liberties, a collective purpose, a sense of morality, tradition, or responsibility— are not necessarily insignificant to voting citizens armed with the power of choosing an alternative to Thatcherism if the political parties will offer them one. Not all the inflexibilities in the market can be eliminated by the *fiat* of the British government, and it is Thatcherism's profoundest weakness that it either thinks that they can or has no way of explaining, let alone of appreciating, the fact that they can't. Some inflexibilities are simply facts of life: however big the market, even were it the size of the world, it would still be finite, the possibility of competition limited, and the need for regulatory intervention inescapable. Some are anyway too big even for Mrs. Thatcher to deal with: the necessity, for example, of coming to negotiated agreements with European partners and embodying those agreements in supranational institutions. And some inflexibilities people will, if they are allowed, inflict on themselves, sacrificing material advantage for the sake of a freely chosen character:

being the nation that has a health service for all, or that publicly observes Ramadan, or that gives its citizens a constitutional right of access to official information about them, or that requires them to build nuclear bunkers under their homes.

Thatcherism is simply the local British form taken by the global process of the flexibilization of human material; the Thatcher government is simply the local political solvent applied to British society not just by multinational companies but by the entire multinational currency and capital markets whose degree of global integration was briefly and embarrassingly glimpsed on Black Monday in 1987. To call the unification of the European market in 1992 the Thatcherization of Europe is a comical *hysteron proteron*: the truth is that Thatcherism was from its beginnings the Europeanization of Britain. The forces of which Lord Cockfield is the transitory agent set out towards their goal a century or more ago, and Mrs. Thatcher is but one of the ripples they have pushed before them. Nationalist, even jingoist, gestures are simply devices for concealing from the British nation what is being done to it, loud assertions of the opposite of the truth, which is why they so often turn out to be insubstantial or self-contradictory: the government that proclaims the territorial integrity of the United Kingdom signs the Anglo-Irish Agreement; petrol consumption continues to be measured in miles per gallon, but petrol itself is sold by the litre. If Mrs. Thatcher does not believe in society, but only in individuals (i.e., consumer-workers), *a fortiori* she does not believe in nations.

It follows that the opposition to Thatcherist technicity must concentrate first and foremost on constitutional issues and those of national identity. To do otherwise, to accept the primacy of economic over political life, is to sell the pass and to accept a doctrine which is shared equally by Marxism and by Thatcherism because it is for both of them the means for imposing a *political* tyranny. Against the Thatcherist-Marxist consensus that the wishes of central government are to be identified with the wishes of the market there needs to be asserted the political freedom to choose a particular national moral and historical character, the freedom at times to be economically inflexible. It may be that the British people do not want to make that assertion. Maybe they wish to keep their political debate at the level of shadow-boxing between the protagonists of government-directed stagflation and the protagonists of government-directed unemployment. But it will be a sign that Thatcherism is beginning to lose its hold, and that they are no longer willing worshippers of the golden calf and its iron priestess, if they, and the political parties that speak for them, begin to address themselves to the real issues that face Britain today: the (proportional) representation of the people; devolution (the end of the residually imperial relations between the constituent parts of the United Kingdom); reform of the second chamber (and effective limitation of the powers of the first); a Bill of Rights.

The British Constitution as we know it today is essentially a creation of the Imperial period and it could remain unwritten for as long as British society was cushioned and structured and given purpose by the existence of the Empire. With the passing of the Empire the British state has degenerated into an untrammeled autocracy in which legislature and executive are virtually identical. The left wing of the Labour party opposed Lord Scarman's Bill of Rights as vehemently as Mrs. Thatcher's government and for the same reason: they like things the way they are. We have recently heard Mr. Ridley deploying against any amendment by the House of Lords of his Poll Tax legislation the arguments that we used to hear from Mr. Foot and Mr. Benn: victory in a general election gives a party a "mandate" to implement everything in its manifesto, and an unelected, and therefore unrepresentative, second chamber has no right to frustrate the will of the people represented by the House of Commons. When "the people" cease to tolerate the hypocrisies and sophisms of the power-hungry on left and right, and take up instead, like practically every other civilized nation in the world, the un-British task of reflecting, in a written constitution, on who they are and how they wish to arrange their lives, the ghost of Empire will have been exorcised at last.

In recent months there have been signs that the hypnotic spell of Thatcherism is waning and that a new and more fundamental debate is beginning, within, between, and outside the political parties. That debate will alter nothing if it does not focus on the constitutional issue which Thatcherism has made critical. A new definition is needed of the public realm and the legitimate public interest, distinct from the desires of individual consumer-workers on the one hand and from the ambitions of the current central government on the other. What is the modern British *polis*? What is the proper dignity, and what are the proper limits, of the state power? About what are the British not prepared to be flexible? How is the new Leviathan to be tamed?

It is no accident that the churches have been prominent in bringing about the present discussion. For two millennia the Church has been the institutional opposition, sometimes overt, sometimes covert, to the claim of Caesar to own his subjects body and soul, and has forbidden—of course, for superficially varying motives—sacrifice to the Emperor, whether Nero, Barbarossa, or Henry VIII. If in Britain the Reformation sold out to Caesarism, it has nonetheless since 1979 been the Church of England that has shown itself more willing to provoke disestablishment than a Catholic Church still pursuing the respectability that eluded it during the Imperial era. Yet theologically speaking, as the abortion issue shows, it ought to be the Catholic Church that has the fullest resources to combat the moral atomism, the belief in the primacy of individual desires, and the readiness to reduce human lives to material, which paved the way for Thatcherism and still give Thatcherism a deeper hold over the British mind than any merely liberal opposition will ever understand. The Catholic Church in Britain has spent much of the last four centuries in direct conflict with the ideology of British central government; it holds that vocation in the form of a lifelong commitment expressed by solemn vows is still possible, and indeed an obligation; the relative social and economic independence of its celibate clergy and religious has enabled them, and could still enable them, to stand as a sign of contradiction to the pretensions both of the state and of the forces of cupidity that the state has unleashed. But as yet British Catholics seem reluctant to earn themselves again that charge of treason which, in periods when a British identity seemed narrowing or ungenerous, was their reward for loyalty to a wider, transnational community of charity. For the present it is the Church of England that is drawing the principal theological lesson from the attempt to understand Thatcherism: that, in the end, only the Rock is inflexible enough.

2 After Thatcherism
Who Are We Now?

In the summer of 1989, a year after the publication of the previous essay (which foresaw none of it), British house prices had reached, or passed, their highest level ever and the queues of Trabbis stood long at the Austrian borders—two different aspects, no doubt, of the last and extreme peak of an economic boom, though on the whole it is the Trabbis that the future is likely to remember. Little more than another year later the Cold War was over, the Russian Empire was going, and Mrs. Thatcher was gone. Three years on and the British recession was so deep that a further Conservative administration seemed highly improbable. Thatcherism, in a sense, had had its day. Certainly the Walrus and the Carpenter would never again discuss why house values alone in the universe were exempt from the law that what goes up must come down. The simple truths which the government prevented the BBC from broadcasting immediately before the 1992 election have since become common knowledge: that if the British people felt better, economically speaking, in 1989 than in 1979 that was principally because of an inflationary electioneering budget in 1987, which sowed the seeds of later recession; and that during this period the overall tax burden steadily increased. But the claim that the British economy was under new management was never much more than a device from Thatcherism's PR department. The true revolution was social and institutional and as that is imposed on Britain by forces more powerful than the leadership of any political party so it has continued after the deposition of the leader and the discrediting of her reputation for economic competence. In this sequel to what I wrote in 1988, I shall try to take further, in the light of what has happened since, the analysis I then sketched out of the conflicts behind Thatcherism's uniform facade. What is the way forward for a society ever more homogeneously composed only of embodied consumer producers, and why can it not be a way back into any of the social forms of Britain's imperial epoch? Most profoundly these questions seemed to me to be questions of identity, national and ultimately individual. It is therefore obviously necessary to say something about relations between Britain and the European Union, which since the collapse of the Communist Empire have, perhaps rather unexpectedly, come to dominate British domestic affairs, and about alternative forms of identity—based, for example, on religion, nationality, or gender—which are offered to us as escape routes from the remorseless process of globalization. But I have also in honesty to conclude on a more personal note since the assessment by intellectuals, particularly university intellectuals, of the motor forces behind the great events of this century is a major theme of the chapters that follow.

Consumer-Producers

Mrs. Thatcher's dismissal did not deliver her party from the toils of paradox in which she had enmeshed it. Her successor, for example, dedicated himself to the achievement of a classless society—to the historically necessary task, that is, of dismantling the social structure which the British Empire imprinted upon the mother country—and was as right to use Marx's language to do so as to appropriate the name of the great Chartist movement of the English working class for his plan to make all provision of services as auditable as manufacture or trade. (For his successor from the Labour party, the task will be no different, though he may feel more comfortable with the rhetoric.) A profounder contradiction underlay the decision which probably did most to unseat Mrs. Thatcher and to determine the character of the administration that followed: the

decision that sterling should enter the European Exchange Rate
Mechanism at an excessively high parity. Entry into the Mechanism
reflected Thatcherism's desire for a big market, internally free of
government interference; the refusal of a significant devaluation reflected its would-be Gaullist tendency to national self-assertion. In
this incident, however, and in the confusion in which it has left the
Conservative party, one can perhaps see the outline of the deepest
single contradiction which underlay all Thatcherism's paradoxes,
and which will beset any attempt to perpetuate it.

Thatcherism was based on two incompatible assumptions. The
first was that Britain needed to be drawn more effectively into the
global market, to adopt its principles more wholeheartedly and to
abandon all inherited forms of protectionism. This radical espousal
of free-trading was, historically speaking, simply swimming with the
tide, and so seemed to have a mesmerizing irresistibility about it
which many attributed to the personality of the prime minister herself. The second assumption, however, ran directly counter to the
first: it was the assumption that Britain needed to be transformed
into a strong nation-state. In the post-1945 world this goal was an
impossibility, politically, militarily, and above all, economically. You
cannot run a seriously independent line different from that of people with whom you have been allied for fifty years and who supply
your weapons, or different from that of people who own large parts
of your industry, large parts of the products of which are in turn
made in a dozen different countries around the world. The development of the world market saps the foundations of nations as surely
as of empires. From the point of view of the market, any act of a national government is a restrictive practice, an unwelcome act of
protectionism, and national central government itself, the raiser of
taxes, the spender of other people's money, the originator of regulations, the fixer of bank rates and would-be fixer of exchange rates,
is just another vested interest, another unjustified obstacle to the
free flow of capital. Nations are growing obsolete, not as a matter of
fashion or opinion, which could be altered by a determined personality, but as a result of the operation of the same economic trends
that Thatcherism acknowledges and endorses. In swimming against
that tide, Thatcherism, in its nationalist guise, made itself irritat-
ing, embarrassing, or absurd. That fundamental contradiction—
between the free world market and nationhood—expressed itself

even in Mrs. Thatcher's time in bitter divisions within her party and those divisions will continue for as long as the party lives off her intellectual legacy.

"Thatcherism," however, is not a term likely to have a long shelf-life in the libraries of political science. The personality concerned was too specific to a corner of the world too far from the center of events. But in the future, and elsewhere, fiscal, and therefore social, readjustment to a nation's geopolitical decline may well coincide with a revival of nationalism: there is more than one example in the past of this. In the aftermath of the Thatcher years some of the other fallacies in the conventional wisdom of her time have become more apparent, and these lessons of experience may also be more generally relevant.

Recession, for example, has made brutally clear a fact which the vocabulary of consumerism seems designed to conceal: what we may call the proletarianization of the British people. We nearly all live—and increasingly that means women as well as men—by selling our labor to someone else: we nearly all are, or wish to be, employed. We do not live as autonomous professionals or as the managers of acquired or inherited private wealth as a quite extensive class in Edwardian England still did. Even the "self-employed" (the term is revealing) usually pay themselves a salary. The availability of work, and the conditions of work, are quite as important to us as the range of our consumer choice: we are producers as well as consumers, and much more equally both than was ever the case before. In what the Marxists are pleased to call 'late capitalism',[1] the opportunities for the individual accumulation of capital are greatly reduced and the basis for the Marxist theory of class crumbles away: it is no longer possible to characterize whole segments of the population by their relation to the means of production. The property owner is as weird an anachronism as the squire and the ploughman, the clerk and the tradesman; the farmer and the factory-worker, the software-writer and the utilities engineer, are now primarily, and equally, just getters and spenders. Nor is this dual identity of ours a purely private matter, as if it were irrelevant to the market, a mere contingency, that supply and demand proceed from the same physical agents. Consumer demand falters once producers become uncertain of their employment prospects: people who fear for their jobs do not buy a new car, even if they work in the motor industry.

The devices for making us more "flexible"—that is more sackable—workers, introduced in good times, make us that much less confident consumers in bad times, which thereby become even worse. We thus grow particularly aware in recession of how far we are not, after all, individuals whose needs are serviced by an anonymous market but are dependent for much of the content of our lives on our ability to work for others who in turn work for us.

Why, after all, are issues of immigration and asylum now so great, so emotive, and so intractable? Surely the principle of the free market implies also a principle of the free movement of labor? Surely foreigners should be free to compete with us for our jobs as we wish to be free to buy or not to buy foreign products? Immigration controls, passports, and work permits are some of the most obvious instruments of the state power which Thatcherism professes to loathe, yet Thatcherist governments have consistently multiplied them. The truth is that its prospects of employment are at least as important to the British electorate as its freedom of consumer choice, and the state's role is equally important in securing both, whatever ideology may say: as the market grows so will the state apparatus, and there is a market in jobs as well as in commodities. The globalization of the economy implies that world migration is as much a matter for international administration as world trade, and that in the future those supra-national market-places in which labor can move freely will have quite as much political significance as those in which consumer goods can circulate without restriction. In the medium term the consumer-producers of Britain will realize that the European Union is even more important to them as a source of unrestricted employment opportunities than as an impost-free destination for their exports. As the world job-market becomes more regulated, so nations left outside such unions will find in their unemployed a lobby for membership at least as vocal as their manufacturers.

It is a central feature of the social teaching of the Catholic Church that it derives the right to property not from some putative pre-social state of humankind but from the nature of work. In *Rerum Novarum* Pope Leo XIII wrote: "when a man expends the activity of his mind and the strength of his body in procuring the goods of nature he makes his own that part of nature's resources which he brings to completion, leaving on it, as it were, in some form, the imprint of himself. . . . Does justice allow any man to seize and enjoy something which another man has stained with his sweat?"[2] Pope Leo's famous encyclical was to have a profound influence on the Christian Democrat movement which gave liberty, peace, and prosperity to Europe for half a century. As a young seminarian, Heidegger will certainly have known it, and it may have helped him to turn his mind to what about us is essentially productive and directed towards the future. But, of course, to start your understanding of social ethics from an understanding of work was in 1891 already a long-standing characteristic of the Marxist and Hegelian traditions, and it is important for Anglo-Saxons to recognize that this European approach to political economy is not something corporatist, authoritarian, and alien, but —as modern scholarship is making ever clearer[3]—a direct and legitimate development of the thinking of Adam Smith and the Scottish Enlightenment. New Europhobia is but old anti-Catholicism writ small and, in either guise, it involves a refusal to think about the relation between local ambitions and world realities, or between economically defined interests and politically defined order. Recognizing that we are producers as much as, or rather more than, we are consumers punctures the ideology of Thatcherism in two places: what it implies about our identity, and what it implies about the state. And both holes are Europe-shaped.

In the Thatcherist vision (fortunately only partially realized) the Faustian consumer has no abiding identity but simply generates a never-ending series of new wishes, calling for instantaneous satisfaction. But to be a producer is to have a different attitude to time. Unlike consumption, unlike the moment of purchase which ends the productive process, production is not punctual, it is smeared. Production is action which leaves a lasting trace on a pre-existent material, it makes a difference between a shapeless past, before its work, and a formed future. Out of that difference between past and future arise three relationships which are intrinsic to the economic system but which are wholly obscured if we think of the system only as a mechanism for procuring consumer satisfaction: confidence (in the future), solidarity (or mutual trust), and obligation. To produce is to have confidence in the future, just as much as to save or to invest. It implies confidence in an enduring structure, not just of currency but of goods: if I build a house to last 100 years, I expect in fifty years time another generation will still be using it to live in and not—as if it were a Roman villa in the Dark Ages—as a quarry for road-mending materials. Just as to invest implies a trust in others and a certain (not necessarily complete) mutuality of interest, so to make something implies reliance on other makers and service to them, for all production takes the half-finished (not the raw), improves and refines it, and makes it available for further refinement, application, processing. And just as any monetary transaction involves promises and the contractual obligation to fulfill them, so production too involves obligation: not just the contractual obligation to deliver the goods, "to do the job," but the obligation to the production process itself, "to do the job well," to take the matter seriously. There is, for example, the obligation of gratitude, as we might call it, to those who half-finished the material before us ("this is a well-seasoned piece of oak, not to be used for firewood"). There is the obligation of service to those to whom the matter is to be passed on ("you want the best I can do, at the price"). And there is the obligation of honor, to other practitioners of the trade and to the skill itself ("I could do it that way, but this is the best practice"). The whole economic system of activity that delivers products for consumption requires a set of relationships existing through time. Since we as producers are involved in that system our identity cannot be reduced to that of punctual consumers, making contact with the system, like butterflies, only in the moment when we sip from it the satisfaction of our desires. Consumption, as Heidegger might have said had he been able to pun in English as freely as he did in German, is consummation, an end which swallows up all process— production, on the other hand, is the extension of a line, backwards and forwards.

The contradiction in the Thatcherist attitude to the state was manifest even in the mid-1980s. On the one hand it was the enemy whose frontiers were to be rolled back; on the other there was an explosive growth in the powers of central government and the executive. The source of the contradiction lies deep in the nature of money itself.

On the one hand, money is the instrument of accountancy, which atomizes the processes of exchange: measuring always with the same utterly just measure, it first treats us all absolutely equally, and then breaks us down into our absolutely equal component parts, the economic transactions which make up our life-story, all separately docketed and priced. Only where relations are defined in monetary terms can individuals be as free and equal as units of the coinage—though where relations are defined in monetary terms, physical individuals (that is, human bodies) also cease to be significant units of account. Thatcherism—the application of the principles of accounting to the superannuated social structures of Imperial Britain—destroyed the pre-monetary forms of social control: institutional loyalty and self-regulating (i.e., non-accountable, non-sueable) professionalism, along with deference and *noblesse oblige* (the ethos not only of titled landowners but of such late-Imperial institutions as the BBC and local housing authorities). The result was an intoxicating apparent liberation, and a genuine equalization.

On the other hand, however, money, as the promise of future satisfaction, of a future exchange with an unknown third party, is as effective only as the promise is credible. The fourth party, which guarantees that the promises will be kept and maintains the standard by which their fulfillment will be measured, is the state. Individuals die and banks collapse, but the state goes on forever—inflation being merely the index of our suspicion that it will not. The coin bears the image of the Caesar who requires that it shall be accepted, who determines the rate at which it shall trade, and who exacts tribute, all on pain of non-monetary sanctions. The instrument of our economic liberation from a feudal order of personal loyalty, caste privilege, and barter is also, and to the same extent, the instrument of our political subjection.

By extending the role of money in British society, by insisting that traditionally defined services, benefits, and injuries should be given an arithmetical cash value, Thatcherism necessarily extended the role of the state. Public spending as a proportion of the GNP may have remained more or less static, but the production of public paper, of statutes and statutory instruments, grew uncontrollably. The privatization program—essentially a mechanism for changing the accounting and management practices of large undertakings whose monopolistic character remained unchanged—required the creation of a whole new species of regulatory government OFfices (OFWAT for water, OFGAS for gas, OFSTED for education, and so on). The most obvious consequence of the Health Service reforms was an enormous increase in the number of administrators—understandably, since the point of the reforms was that people should write down what they did and be paid commensurately. Doctors were not to be paid according to their professional status—that is, roughly, their skill—but according to their output, like any other worker. And a homogenized labor-force, working by the book, requires an army of auditors to check that the book is being worked by—and, of course, a government to write the book (or charter) in the first place. The proletarianization of the population makes the state, as the regulator of the economic mechanism, more necessary, and more omnipresent, not less.

At the same time the extension of home ownership, and so of mortgage indebtedness, puts a considerable majority of all households into a direct relationship with the central monetary authorities, their family finances varying immediately with changes in the rate of interest. The fallacious insinuation that a necessity of life—a roof over one's head—should be regarded rather as a speculative investment was one of the principal means by which Thatcherism sought to convince us that we were all capitalists, kings of our castle, who could cock a snook at the state. Another was the initially restricted sale of shares in the privatized utilities, which was mostly and rightly regarded as another government hand-out to the deserving medium-rich, and made little long-term difference to the proportion of British industry owned by private individuals. Denationalization turned state capital into quasi-non-governmental capital owned by pensions and insurance and similar funds but it increased the necessity for state regulation of the financial world and did nothing to change the employee status of the great majority of the population of working-age. In one way or another Britain is now owned not by individuals, nor by a class, but collectively, and the system for managing that ownership is the state. Inequality of personal fortunes has declined steadily since the early years of the century, not because the Edwardian bourgeoisie has become more egalitarian but because it has been entirely replaced. And even if it lay in a government's power to restore that old social order it could not do so for, not long after it began the attempt, it would be voted out of office. This not a trivial point, but in order to understand its significance we must look more closely at the relation between the market and the state.

Our behavior is determined on the one hand by what we want to do and on the other by what we are forced to do—"la concupiscence et la force," Pascal says.[4] Part of the appeal of a consumerist ideology is that it can appear to be radically opposed to coercion: if only people can be left free to pursue their desires, everyone will in the end have all that they want. The market, after all, has no powers of coercion: all its transactions are voluntary acts of exchange, and what is called "market discipline" is simply the process of adjustment by which buyers and sellers learn to be realistic about the strength of each other's desires. The state by contrast is in the modern world the unique repository of force, and, strictly understood, is nothing else. It is by the threat of force that the state secures obedience to its laws; by force, therefore, not by exchange, that through taxation it acquires money to spend; by force that it maintains the integrity of its borders. It is no wonder that an ideology which makes us think of ourselves as nothing but consumers should be hostile to a power which seems to exist only to restrict the supply to us of the goods that we want and to deprive us of a substantial proportion of our means of purchasing them. However once we have learned that, unlike the capitalist bourgeoisie of the Edwardian past, we derive our ability to purchase satisfactions not from some mysteriously acquired "wealth" (i.e., the accumulated exploited labor of others) but from our own engagement in the market as producers (i.e., from our wages) we may learn to think rather differently of the state.

In the first place, as producers we find in the state our natural ally. Not simply because the state may use its legislative powers to add, in effect, to our wages, by improving our conditions of work—by forbidding trading on certain days of the week, for example, or employment below a certain age, or without certain safety precautions, or at the cost of cruelty to animals. Seen simply as rises in wages, which imply, all other things being equal, rises in prices and reductions in employment opportunities, such decisions limit our range of options both as consumers and as producers and are not necessarily welcome to us in either role. But they can also be seen as reflecting long-term concerns that are not consumer interests at all but arise only out of our activity as producers: the need for confidence that we are building a worthwhile future for a later generation, and not compromising that by our maximal exploitation of the present; the sense of solidarity, that is, of the rightful interests, as they perceive them, of all those with whom we are in economic relationships; and obligations, which may or may not be expressed in religious terms, towards the natural world, towards others, or towards ourselves. Necessary though an authority may be to ensure that we are consistent in pursuing these long-term goals, it is however possible to deceive oneself about how far one can force oneself to pursue them by acting contrary to one's own desires—it is possible to vote for protectionism, for example, and then to buy cheap contraband rather than dear home products, to campaign against Sunday trading and then to pop down to the supermarket on Sunday afternoon because one has run out of milk. Thatcherism was right to be skeptical about the efficacy of far-reaching state intervention in the market. But it was quite wrong to imagine that therefore the state's role in human affairs is or should be minimal or can be expected to decline as the market grows.

For—in the second place—the market depends on the state for its preservation, even its existence—something of which a producer, or would-be producer, is more quickly aware than a consumer. The more elaborate the system of exchange, and the more refined the arrangements for financing it, the greater is the need for a coercive power to audit, regulate, and protect it, and to resolve the multiplying conflicts within it—to define and defend property (real or intellectual) so that contracts may be made to convey it, to provide the courts where contractual disputes may be resolved, to settle a framework, which will eventually necessarily be international, within which conflicts of jurisdiction can be decided. The bigger and more active the market becomes, the more important is the state's role as banker, as guarantor of a currency and fixer of basic interest rates. Nowhere is the dependence of the market economy on state power more routinely evident than in the state's monetary responsibilities, which have their unique importance precisely because of the state's monopoly of force. For the strength of a currency, the degree to which the state's guarantee is believed, is determined by the state's ability to discharge effectively its other functions, fiscal and legislative, police and military. Why has the ruble plunged towards worthlessness since it became possible to buy it? For the same reason that Russian industrial output in 1994 was 45 percent of what it had been in 1990: that the Russian state has been unable to maintain social order, to establish a legally regulated system of banking and exchange, or, most fundamentally perhaps, to define property rights so as to create confidence in the future. There could scarcely be a clearer object-lesson in the importance of a state-structure in maintaining economic activity. Fantasies of a stateless future for the world ignore that all exchange requires agreements, and all agreement implies, in the extreme case, enforcement.

It is probable that our interests as consumers and as producers cannot be reconciled except by force. (Marx thought it certain, but he did not foresee the extent to which the conflict between classes would be replaced by a conflict within individuals which violent revolution could not resolve.) As consumers we need ever wider choice and ever higher quality and so impose on ourselves as producers ever sterner requirements, to which we become ever more resistant, for better work and longer hours. At some point the state uses its coercive power either to restrict demand (e.g., by legislative control of competition, imposition of standards, prohibition of certain goods) or to enforce supply (e.g., by strike-breaking), and so, for a while at least, the issue is settled, politically, if not economically. The modern world has developed a remarkably effective mechanism for deciding when that force is to be deployed—the vote.

Growing economic activity has broken society down into units, physical bodies, which we call human individuals, in which the functions of consuming and producing intersect. But at the same time political power has been broken down and redistributed over the same units. We have been proletarianized, but we have also been enfranchised. The spread of universal suffrage has been the single most striking feature of world politics in the twentieth century. ("Democracy" is by contrast a nebulous piety.) The principle "one-man–one-vote" has been a measure of modernity for old nations, and of nationhood for new. It has everywhere accompanied— and perhaps facilitated, but perhaps also controlled—the atomization and homogenization of traditional society. The exercising of our right to vote is the point at which we assert the unity of our consuming and producing selves: we weigh up our interests as consumers against our identity as producers (often enough our desire for satisfaction against our need for security) and come to a single decision—one decision for each physically mature human body— about how coercive power is to be applied to the relation between them.

The procedures, collectively known as the constitution, by which votes are turned into executive acts and policies, are therefore of the utmost importance to the character of a modern society. It is the constitution which determines how, precisely, desire and force, the market and the state, are to be reconciled, for the present and in this place. The constitution however was one of Thatcherism's blind spots. It had no theory of the vote. The vote is our identity but Thatcherism spurned it as the building-block of the state and refused to consider constitutional issues, whether electoral reform or the internal structure of the United Kingdom or its external relations. Thatcherism therefore impaled itself on another contradiction when it tried to reassert a national identity, for that could belong only to a state, not simply to a market. How could it both assert a vigorous, confident British state, and at the same time roll back its frontiers and reduce it to a minimal level of activity? So there was a second blind spot in Thatcherist thinking: Europe.

European Identities

The European Union is probably best understood in terms of Christmas trees. The story is that Brussels regulations require Christmas trees to be symmetrical in shape, with regularly spaced needles, identical roots, and the same color.[5] The truth is that no such regulations exist—but that the Christmas Tree Growers Association of Western Europe has indeed drawn up its own *European Specifications for Christmas Trees* "to improve their quality." The moral is that hostility to the supposedly homogenizing tendencies of the European institutions is largely misdirected. It is not Brussels that is imposing an ever more uniform pattern on our daily lives but the market; the mass-producers and the bulk buyers. Nothing as tangible as a group of officials is ironing out national differences, but the complex elimination of trade barriers, and the intensification of international competition and the growth of international cartels. On the contrary, the officials represent, however tenuously, a state power, however nascent, that is endeavoring to give political shape to the economic process. If a European standard Christmas tree is inevitable, I would prefer, personally speaking, to have some minute say in deciding its shape, rather than none at all. At least the officials, if at many removes, are part of an elected structure (the Commission—the Council of Ministers—the national governments—the national parliaments); the businessmen are no part of it whatever. The removes are too many, and too indirect, but those are remediable defects. A European constitution is gradually evolving: the more effective our vote, the stronger will be our European identity—a supranational identity, yes, but then life is supranational, nowadays.

The true ground for the Thatcherist hostility to European integration lies not in nationalism but in anti-constitutionalism. An unfriendly eye, however, soonest sees the unflattering truths. Is a European constitution possible? With the passing of the Cold War a particular plan for Europe's future became obsolete and the forces which might have realized it evaporated. The vision—never, of course, generally shared or officially endorsed—of a centrally administered West European state, the currency, citizenship, and armed forces of which would displace their national predecessors, represented a possibility which might have grown into reality under American patronage and in the lee of the Iron Curtain. Withdrawn from extensive relations either with the Eastern half of the continent, or, in the days of dictatorship, with the Greek and Iberian peninsulas, and protected, at first by the existence of NATO, and by the simplicities of Soviet-American confrontation, from the need to elaborate anything but a purely theoretical defense or foreign policy, a small group of nations might have developed into the central keep of a Fortress Europe. By the time of the Maastricht conference in 1991 any such dream, or nightmare, belonged to the past. The conference, however, prepared too long beforehand, and caught out by the Revolution of 1989, became a series of unedifying attempts to relaunch stranded plans, while all around the tides of history went out faster than water out of a bath.

If the European Union is currently an unhappy entity, that is essentially because it lacks a new political vision based on the new realities of the post-1989 world, and only a *political* vision will do. Europe's problem is not *whether* it needs a political structure, but *which* structure it needs. A Labor government in Britain may be able to contribute directly to a solution. The Conservative British administration was unable to do so because it was committed in principle to denying the necessity of giving any political structure to economic relations. The Labor party has no such prior commitment but may still bow to the inherited authority of the Conservative attitude.

That attitude, in Europe as at home, must encourage the growth of a secretive, unrepresentative, and possibly corrupt bureaucracy, thinking in categories that are already outmoded. Indirectly, though, British-Conservative "obstructionism" (the term has been used by George Soros, who must know more about the world market than anyone) may after all make its positive contribution.

It is, for example, perfectly plain that any future European system must be federal, in the normal sense of that term, i.e., non-centralized. The British refusal to use the word has the advantageous consequence that the compromise term ("ever closer union") avoids the suggestion, which "federal" might imply, that the process of unification can ever be fixed into an unchanging treaty relationship between autonomous nations. Similarly, and more substantially, lasting monetary union is not conceivable without at least as much political union as is necessary to secure general budgetary oversight and, probably, a common defense policy: British objections to any common currency whatever may help delay one-armed and one-eyed schemes until that joint advance is possible. And the British insistence on incorporating new members, especially from Eastern Europe (which would be wholly admirable were it not for a suspicion that Britain wishes to dilute the Community rather than to widen it), must if successful weaken the British power to obstruct and must strengthen the central bodies by increasing the number of decisions they can take by qualified majority.

Even in the conflicts and stalemates of the mid-1990s the outlines of a possible European constitution are visible—that is, a political structure which would give Europe's proletarianized citizens some element of control over the supranational facts of modern economic life. It would be characterized by regionalism, by the operation of a principle of subsidiarity which would penetrate below the level of the national governments (to which the British Conservatives wished to confine it) and would distribute power and money away from the national centers, where the true enemies of our liberties are to be found, towards smaller units. It would have a unified currency once it also possessed the representative and executive institutions capable of inspiring confidence in its ability to manage such a thing. And it would almost certainly have to consist of two or more concentric rings to allow not only for different stages or rates of development within it, but also for an accommodating relationship with the world economy as a whole. It would be a political formation unlike anything history has yet seen—but the European Union is that already. It is unlikely that Thatcherists would play much part in the discussions leading to its construction—but they played next to none in the construction of the Union in the first place.

Yet there could be a distinctively British contribution to the European future which would be of the first importance. It was, admittedly, one form of Thatcherism's fundamental paradox that while its historical task, pursued with zeal, was to rid Britain of empty and decaying structures left behind when the Empire went out of business, it presented itself as a campaign to recover the glory of the Imperial heyday and this convinced no one outside the Conservative party, let alone outside Britain. But the contrast Thatcherism sometimes liked to draw between Britain's worldwide role and the introspection of the European Community was not just bombast or a negotiating ploy. There are genuine assets preserved from the liquidation of the British Empire and, if Britain were to withdraw or distance herself from the Union, the Union would be poorer without them: unhealthier, and a less reliable contributor to world peace. The United Kingdom is the largest representative in Europe of the worldwide body of English-speakers; it maintains political, economic, and personal connections with the Commonwealth and a mysteriously still "special" relationship with the United States; it has the largest foreign exchange market in the world, with a daily turnover considerably greater than its government's annual budget, and is Europe's largest source of invisible earnings; it has, ethnically speaking, the most mixed population in Europe. One reason for the recurrent tensions between Britain and the rest of the Union is that, to a markedly greater extent than the other post-Imperial powers, Britain still has a political awareness of its global interests and represents to its partners the power, and the threat, of the global market.

The same forces that are breaking down the social structures in Britain, and the barriers between the nations of Europe, are breaking down the barriers between Europe and the rest of the world. Money is the greatest of all equalizers: it measures by the same measure the heavily insured and holiday-rich Volkswagen worker in Wolfsburg and his or her counterpart in Kuala Lumpur or Seoul.

The result is a price-differential which protectionism may mask for a while, but only at a political cost. Eventually Germany will have to decide between the interests of its car-manufacturers and those of its partners in Europe or in the World Trade Organization who have given up the industry and whose populations demand cheap imports. The lesson of the past is that, whatever its short-term value, protectionism, which is imposed by the state, can in the long term be maintained only by the means proper to the state—force. Provided therefore that the international economic and political network stays able to put a punitively high cost on the resort to war, a world-scale transfer of wealth from North to South and a gradual equalization of economic conditions (such as has characterized the internal development of Northern states since the start of the century) remains a (very) long-term possibility.

But how strong does the network have to be? In Europe it seems to have become very strong: not only has Europe in the last fifty years not seen a war; it has also seen some enormous socio-economic changes, such as the decimation of the coal and steel industries, which a century or so ago would hardly have been conceivable without a war. Worldwide the mesh is broader and the links are frailer (it is difficult to imagine the network exercising much influence over a conflict between Russian and China about Siberian resources, for example). It is all the more important, therefore, that if the European Union comes closer to a common foreign and defense policy its economic policy yields only minimally to the temptation to regional protectionism. A Europe that reverted to the fortress mentality would be a threat not only to the world's weaker economies (already ravaged, for example, by sugar-dumping) but also to world peace. That part of the British program which maintains the doctrine, as old as the European empires, that Europe should be the market-place of the world, deserves applause (but not of course any suggestion of contempt for the political institutions of the global village, the United Nations Organization, and its agencies).

The process of globalization will not come to an end with the establishment of some supranational European identity. Europe's immediate neighbors have already seen to that. A welcome sign of the gradual strengthening of the global network and of the possibility of—relatively—peaceful economic equalization within it is the historic change misleadingly known as the Islamic revival.

Partly through an accident of geology the crescent of oil-rich territories surrounding industrial Europe from Morocco to Kazakhstan became essential to the Northern economy at a time when the simple use of military force to create empires had ceased to be practicable. At Suez in 1956 for example it became plain that Britain could no longer intervene as she had done in the nineteenth century to annex Egypt and dismember an economy that in those days threatened to compete with her own textile industry.[6] With an atomic balance of power more respect had to be shown to states sitting on reserves of billions of petrodollars than had been usual in the gun-toting Imperial age, and they in turn, as was shown by the banking crisis that followed the price rises of 1973, were dependent on Europe and America to turn their oil into gold. Colonial relationships with different metropolitan powers, or combinations of them (France, Britain, Spain, Russia) were displaced (except, initially, in the Russian case) by the single, market, relationship of primary producer to industrial consumer. Producers who are at liberty to enter into, and to vary, contracts necessarily possess as much legal personality as their contracting partners and the nations of the petroliferous crescent soon had the same international status as their customers. In this their position might seem similar to that of other formerly colonial or semi-colonial territories, particularly along the Asian Pacific seaboard, whose strength in manufacturing and finance has made them, too—and perhaps with more guarantee of permanence—into full participants in the global economic and political network. What makes for the difference, however, is that the end of overtly imperial relations between Europe and its immediate periphery has not established a new relationship of reciprocity so much as it has re-established an old one, last flourishing in the sixteenth century.

The global market has precipitated a European crisis of identity by leveling the wall which the continent built in the age of Empire to conceal from view its immediate neighbors. The shock of recognition has been mutual. As much as a revival of Islam, the last half-century has seen a revival of the Western, particularly secularist, fear of Islam, and the fear has had a formative effect on its object. Once again the states of Christendom are meeting the encircling powers on what are in theory equal terms and as in the medieval, pre-Imperial, age the diplomatic accommodation is accompanied by an intellectual exchange in which disputatious recrimination mingles with tolerant curiosity. But the exchange contains a promise, or a threat, deeply unsettling to both parties: the context provided by a global future leads to the rediscovery of a shared past.

From the seventh century onwards what is nowadays called Europe has been so linked in economic, cultural, and of course military interaction with the Arab-dominated nations of the Middle East and North Africa that one has to ask whether Europe, historically speaking, is not an altogether larger thing than the North Mediterranean peninsula to which the term is usually confined. Certainly the early Caliphates would seem to have as much right to be regarded as the cultural, and even political, successors of the Greco-Roman Empire as the Germanic and Slavic monarchies which, after similar incursions, established themselves in the North. And neither the Christian churches nor the Islamic communities have yet dared to address the explosive issue which must come to dominate theology in the twenty-first century: their shared historical origins. Plainly Islam cannot be dismissed, as a distinguished orientalist dismissed it in 1933, as "a second-hand Arian heresy"[7] — but that is no excuse for totally disregarding either Islam's Judaeo-Christian roots or the forgotten failings of Christianity which made the rise of Islam natural and perhaps necessary. (Arianism, after all, was no mere heresy but a historical movement comparable in importance with the Reformation.) It may even be that the state of Israel, that deep wound inflicted by Europe on its periphery, proves the point at which the antithesis of Christianity and Islam begins to be healed. Israel's claim to be part of Europe is no better or worse grounded than Turkey's, and the Greater Europe, redefined to contain the one, will necessarily also contain the other.

Of course there are those who wish to interpret the "Islamic revival" as a deepening of the antithesis into absolute difference and unrelatedness. This is a common—but nonetheless delusive—reaction to the growth of the global system. The setting up of "Islamic states" and the application of "Islamic law" is often seen—whether by West or by East—as the sign of the growth of alternative or anti-systemic forces and the spread of cultural diversity. The opposite is the case. "Nation state" and "code of law" are not categories peculiar to any uniquely Islamic way of life and thought but are common currency of the present world process, in the course of which former empires are collapsing via nationhood into a global market. In order to become a legislative system imposed by a constitution "Islamic law" has to change its character completely. "Islamic law is not a code. This is why the frequently heard call for its 'application' is meaningless . . . *shari 'a* is a general term designating good order . . . it is a body of narratives relating to precedents to which is ascribed a paradigmatic status."[8] The call however is not meaningless—its meaning is just different from what those who make it intend. What it means is that this or that state shall have its own code of law like any other, but differentiated from others simply by a series of symbolic features[9]—the regulation of dress or diet or commerce, or the name *shari 'a*—selected from various Islamic cultures of the past. That is not Islamic law as it once was—it is secular law, code Napoleon, with Islamic accoutrements. Once upon a time states and their legislation were but subdivisions of Islam, the realm of religion, peace, and civilization. In the modern world the state and the code are the substance, the Islam can only be adjectival, a matter of local coloration. (Similarly, when the Australian aboriginal flag was raised at the Olympic games what was proclaimed was not the autonomy of the various aboriginal cultures, which once upon a time had no flags, but their belonging to the global order in which cultures are the property of nations and nations come bearing flags.)

Nostalgia for a lost integrity, however, is as patronizing as it is pointless: "cultures" cannot be shut away in reservations, whether by well-meaning outsiders or by local fundamentalists, if only because some or many of the free human beings who maintain them will, inevitably, prefer the opportunities, spurious or not, of openness to the global medium. Once the alternative exists, it cannot be taken away. Often enough the only remedy for some violent intrusion by the global network—destruction of hunting territory by an international mining company, for example—is an appeal to other global agencies: the media, or pressure-groups, or international diplomacy. One way or another, the network triumphs over the merely local. The appurtenances of past cultures can certainly survive in the modern world, but only as something they never were: symbols of an option, a freely chosen style. Culture is the form we give to what is inevitable in our life, and what is inevitable in the modern world is our belonging to the global exchange mechanism of production and consumption.

To close the eyes to that necessity is the shared error of the "culturalist" of the ex-imperial nations and the "fundamentalist" of the ex-colonies. The culturalist asserts the diversity of human ways of doing and thinking and their mutual impermeability, so ignoring our economic unity and denying the possibility of a unifying history. The fundamentalist reasserts a defunct vision, which once encompassed all there was to be known, but which died at the hands of imperialism and globalization and now can be maintained only by inventing a boundary pale which cuts off the reservation from the satanic hordes outside. Economic interaction is thought a matter of indifference, irrelevant to the belief, or practice, or ethnicity which constitutes the one boundary which counts. History is displaced by a local mythology in which events lose both their uniqueness and their global context and become re-enactments of archetypes furnished by the original, now delusive, vision.

> Fundamentalism . . . rarely . . . adulterates itself with specifying matters arising in the present . . . it takes the form of a metonymic representation of present realities when it discourses on matters that occurred in the days of the Prophet . . . . As for historical change, it can, according to this model, be described only as privations of this original essence, as adulterations which in no way sully the purity of the foundation, adulterations which are anyway the work of foreigners, malcontents or other subversives.[10]

The true task of the modern intellectual is neither to apologize for fundamentalism nor to surrender to culturalism, but to identify the form we are giving to the global necessities of our economic life—our global culture and our common history.

Alternatives

The fear-filled longing for a less than global identity is the principal obstacle to a true theoretical understanding of our condition and to the practical achievement of peace. Nationalism and sexism too, like religious and ethnic exclusivism, obscure the economic interaction which links the human race into a single material system, and distract political attention from the deep need to articulate and control the system into the shallower tasks of accommodating self-defined pressure groups (which may of course be armed, or of great size, or otherwise considerable). But the reservation mentality (whether it manifests itself as fundamentalism or as cultural relativism) results from the destructive impact of the global market on previous, inadequate, imperialist, attempts at a universal politico-economic order. It therefore revives older truths and interests which the empires suppressed—even though the political form it gives them is misconceived.

The development of the European market, and of the international security system, has revealed, for example, not only the impossibility of a seriously nationalist foreign policy for the United Kingdom of Great Britain and Northern Ireland but the non-existence of a nation that could bear that name and be the object of nationalist emotion. As a result, the forgotten history of English imperialism within the Atlantic archipelago, which brought the present temporary agglomerate into being on 1 January 1923, returned to haunt the politics of the late twentieth century: Thatcherism found itself denouncing federalism and upholding subsidiarity in Brussels, while maintaining federalism and ignoring subsidiarity in London. The claim that the nation-state was the building-block of the world-system was particularly unconvincing when voiced by a political entity struggling to maintain that rank, perhaps still to achieve it, and the feeble attempts to create a national mythology by manipulation of the school history curriculum or the cult of the Second World War only intensified awareness of the different perspectives of the Welsh, Scottish, and, especially, Irish population. Once the pressures of the Cold War relaxed, and it was no longer necessary to maintain control over the Irish ports and the Atlantic supply routes, the way was open for England to abandon her strategic interest in Northern Ireland and the *colons* who had protected it.

Yet it would be a mistake to imagine that Wales or Scotland or even Ireland can provide for their populations an identity that the United Kingdom cannot. England has so obviously been hollowed out and dissipated by the imperial past and the global present that talk of English nationalism can be only the material of comedy. But things will not be very different for the other insular peoples England has unthinkingly used and abused for centuries even if they regain nominal independence: Anglophobia, an uncertain loyalty to a Celtic tongue, and tribal memories of subsistence agriculture cannot amount to a distinctive presence on an international scene where finance houses, and even oil companies, turn over larger sums than governments. At most they will provide the excuse for differing tax regimes, the regional coloration in the patchwork of a federal Europe, in which the new nationals will want to be able to seek employment at least as freely as they do at present.

Similarly the worldwide movement of feminism has been a response to the incorporation of half the human race into the global system of sexually undifferentiated consumer-producers. Those who earn and spend within that system eventually expect to be able to vote in it too. They then use their votes to secure equity in pay and working conditions, even though the result is a general decline in effective wage levels, so that two earned incomes are necessary to bring in what used to be brought in by one—the principal reason, of course, why the market favors women's involvement. In this process of equalization there lies, however, the possibility of a profound transformation of the system of production.

While work used to be organized to reflect the reproductive timetable of the male body, which permits multiple reproduction of the genes throughout the year with minimal effect on the rhythm of work, the increasing dependence on female workers promises a revolutionary redefinition of the time within which work has to be performed. The forgotten, suppressed, and exploited rhythms of the female body, with its monthly cycle, its opportunity of reproducing its genes only once year as a maximum, and its expectation then of a longer period of nursing, emerge at last into economic and so into political significance. The provision of child care, maternity leave, and career breaks, the financial rights of women (pensions, the right to occupancy of mortgaged houses) and a general physical respect for the worker become political issues. Some related benefits for male workers may follow, such as a greater willingness of employers to provide paternity leave and health care, but the main consequence is that work and personal life become more closely integrated. New constraints are accepted on the process of production, which derive directly from the characteristics of the bodies engaged in it. Since the body is the point at which consumption and production intersect, the result of women's participation in the global market may in the long run be that its activity becomes less frenetically abstract, and its socially atomizing effects are muted.

The recognition that the most important things we produce are not things at all but our own kind would then determine our entire social life.

But that depends on women maintaining the reproductive distinction between themselves and men. If women allow their distinctness at the work place to be obliterated by contraceptive hormones, if they accept a male rhythm of sexual activity and the assumption of the male-oriented industrial economy that reproduction is a private matter—a personal, that is, a consumer's choice—which can be allowed only minimal impact on the rhythm of work (why time off for a new baby and not for a new car?), then there will be no economically significant female identity and the market will remain dominated by male chauvinism masquerading as gender neutrality. Any definition of femininity which detaches the distinction of male and female from the process of bodily reproduction will deprive the distinction of its power to force the process of economic production and consumption into a more humane form—will depoliticize it. Being a woman—having supposedly typically female traits of mind or character or even sexuality—then becomes like being Welsh: belonging to what is at best a particular interest-group, differentiated by a few symbolic tokens, which can never achieve the political self-sufficiency of which it dreams, for politics is a matter of more than symbols. Or at worst it is a—possibly all-consuming—leisure activity, real life and real work being allowed to go on elsewhere, and at the hands of others. But being a woman is one of two, and only two, ways of being nothing less than human.

Feminism has turned for too much of its conceptual underpinning to the excessively individualistic—and empirically dubious—psychoanalytic theories of Freud and Lacan. Far more revolutionary—and far more solidly grounded—is the new conception of the body implied by modern genetics and behavioral ecology: as a bridge between reproductive events, and as the medium in which genes are selected for recombination and survival. Male and female bodies play definably different roles in that process, and human beings are not the only species in which voluntarily or involuntarily celibate bodies may also indirectly contribute to it (and not be reduced to mere detritus, waste products of the selfish gene). It is surely here, with the essentially reproductive nature of all bodies, male or female, that any theory of the cultural role of gender and gender difference must begin, and not with such highly derivative phenomena as the real or imagined stages in the construction of the perceptual world of the child (itself too readily thought of as a windowless microcosm).

For some such reasons as these it is doubtful whether the gay movement, in its various forms, will furnish any deep insight into our modern problems of identity. Certainly it has taught us to abandon the puritan pretense that the social affections, culminating in friendship, can be anything other than erotic in origin, and it has taught us, if we did not know it already, that much of any human being's affective life has a homoerotic character, the acknowledgment of which has been, at times and in certain social circumstances, cruelly or absurdly repressed. But identity is a matter not of our own affective preferences but of the necessities, constructed by the choices of others, that build and transform the global system. Sexual preference, once detached from the process of bodily reproduction, loses touch with the necessities and enters the realm of play—it becomes part of the entertainment industry, a choice to be catered for, but not a constraint on producers. Indeed, worldwide consumerism makes use of homosexuality as a means of eliminating the political constraints which regulate our role as producers: if marriage is redefined as a long-term affective partnership, so that it may be either homosexual or heterosexual, the essentially reproductive nature of male and female bodies is no longer given institutional (and therefore political) expression. Bodies are seen as the locus only of consumption, not of production; production is thereby repressed further into our collective unconscious; and producers, particularly women, are deprived of the political means of protest against exploitation. (It becomes more difficult to maintain, for example, that certain working practices are destructive of the family, for "having" a family is treated as the "choice" of a particular mode of consumption.)

As an organization the gay movement is essentially a consumer lobby, a group, like a fan club, united by similar tastes and demanding their satisfaction. It is hard to see why anyone should be discriminated against on the grounds of their tastes, but equally hard to see why matters of taste should be matters of right. A closer analogy might therefore be with a quasi-ecclesiastical sect like scientology, entry to which is also voluntary, by an act of conversion ("coming out") which then gives access to an elaborate social and institutional network. There might well be a right of association in such a body, but that would be the limit of its political role. Like such sects the gay movement also has its fundamentalist wing, maintaining the all-important difference between those inside and outside the reservation—in this case, the difference between the "bent" and the "straight" mind—and deserving a similar degree of serious attention.

In recent European and American literature and philosophy the question "Who am I?" (let alone "Who are we?") has become so unanswerable as to be all but unaskable. In one of the most widely read of modern novels, Umberto Eco's *The Name of the Rose*, there are few, if any characters of a kind that an earlier novelist might have recognized. There are exhilaratingly Rabelaisian avalanches of associative erudition, there is a cast of uniformed monks distinguishable only in the gruesomeness of their deaths, there are one or two embodiments of historical tendencies, and there are two figures in the foreground who, on closer inspection, dissolve into constructs out of literary allusions—like Arcimboldo's seasons dissolving into vegetables. In this parody of a thriller the murderer turns out to be a book and on the last pages we are invited to emerge from beneath a self-sustaining but foundationless vault of interconnected meanings to contemplate absolute nothingness. It is surely no chance that the actors in the story are all men except for one object of brief fornication who is quickly removed to become "burnt flesh." As in an unregenerate industrial culture woman is praised but absent, and so is the reproductive capacity of both men and women.

A similar tissue of indistinguishable names and bizarre, but in this case reversible, deaths shrouds the main figures in another global best-seller, Gabriel Garcia Marquez' *A Hundred Years of Solitude*, a much richer book. Here too, though sexuality is omnipresent, the consummation of bodily existence in the love of parents for each other and their child makes up only a single and pathetically passing episode in the conclusion to the novel. In both these books a human being seems to have become a repeatable cipher, a variation on a structure, rather than a unique bodily locus of social functions. This development is surely a consequence of the worldwide dissociation of our economic and our political identities so that we no longer know as straightforwardly as, say, all the characters in *War and Peace*, that we are—among other things—nationals of particular states. Being international is as much a theme for Eco, and being pre-national a theme for Marquez, as being Russian is a theme for Tolstoy. While English writers have shown little interest in what it is to be non-national, German and American writers, particularly poets, have since the 1950s—at least since Paul Celan's *Wordgrid (Sprachgitter)* in 1959 and Robert Lowell's *Life Studies* in the same year—been keenly aware that biography, and especially autobiography, the writing-out of identity, is the most problematic of literary forms and therefore the one most worth attempting. And the poets have perhaps shown more sense than either the philosophers or the novelists that the root of the problem lies in the realm neither of psychosexuality nor of semiotics but of history, in the task of making meaning out of the coincidence of the public and the personal.

In the end, the question of our identity is a moral question, to be answered by achieving an understanding of our history and our purposes and the repertoire of words and ideas through which we formulate them, rather than a technical problem in political or economic science. "Who are we?" means, in part, "Who do we want to be?" and the only experts in telling us our wishes are the wordsmiths, the poets, in the broader and in the narrower sense. The depth of the crisis of identity in which we now find ourselves may be gauged from the loss of confidence in the power of words to name it and resolve it, and the flight instead into the artificial languages of the computer, in which all possible questions are determined from the start, and all possible questions have answers. Poetry matters because it is the medium in which we face up both to the unpredictability of our wishes (of which no fulfillment may be possible) and to the finality with which we are determined by them (however unrealistic they may be).

Home Is Where One Starts From

"Who are we?" is a question which interrogates those who ask and answer it, even if on behalf of others—the intellectuals, who have had rather different roles in the different parts of Europe and who now above all, when their future is so precarious, need to be clear where their loyalties lie. Evidently therefore, since I have asked the question and do not deny that I am an intellectual, I must say something about my own position before we go on.

It has been my good and possibly unusual fortune that since I was eight I have spent all my life as a member of only two institutions, both formerly monastic, and both refounded by Henry VIII in 1542: a cathedral school in the West Midlands, and a Cambridge college. Their link with their medieval origins was of course tenuous, and in both cases it was with a Middle Ages—whether educational, ecclesiastical, or architectural—seen through Victorian and Edwardian eyes. In the course of forty years the link has dwindled into invisibility. The school—once effectively a Tudor grammar school—has become a successful private fee-paying establishment of a kind created by Mrs. Williams and encouraged by Mrs. Thatcher. The college is still poised uneasily between a similar status and that of the centrally funded quangos to which the noncollegiate universities have unambiguously been reduced. That equivocation results from the college's dependence on both private and public resources, neither of which would alone be enough to keep it in existence, and has made it a good vantage-point from which to view the continuing transformation of British society. The shocks are certainly felt, but they are a little muted, and there is a little extra time in which to absorb them. During those forty years a series of private chances and academic decisions—not all mine— led me into studying the literature and thought of Germany, with which I had no previous contact of a personal or any other kind. My parents' connections were with Ireland on the one side and with the British Imperial presence in the Far East on the other, and in that I imagine they were typical of their generation. Europe was wholly alien soil. But life followed where thought led. I came to the university and was taught by people who had fled and fought Hitler and who yet found nothing more compelling than to read and write about the works of those who had foreshadowed, or opposed, or compromised with him. The necessities of study and research took me to Germany and what had been alien became more familiar than anywhere else that was not home. When I had to answer questions from my children about "the War" and the role in it of German places and people that they knew and liked I discovered that without my intending it Germany had become, by adoption, part of my own fate. I had not lost sight of my roots, such as they were, but I had become detached from them.

University institutions have a duty to their time and place—otherwise no one would pay for them—but at its heart is a duty of detachment. Over the centuries my college has served, nominally at least, many different purposes of which the accountants and auditors of the day approved: housing monks, training clergymen for ill-endowed rural livings, and imparting a veneer of book-learning to the sons of their squire-patrons, teaching classics to imperial civil servants and, latterly, law to those who failed their classics exams. It has provided in an undefined and half-hearted way an approximation to what different ages regarded as the vocational training the college existed for—and always in secret, and whole-heartedly, it was executing its true function of channeling the intelligent and gifted poor through its relatively classless limbo into positions of responsibility in the national administration, which it would be their task not to maintain, but to transform. On the whole the universities managed well, and without the assistance of Education Reform Acts, the transition from theology-dominated to classics-dominated to science-dominated regimes, and they show signs of adapting spontaneously to a coming order dominated by business-related studies. Superficially much remains the same as in the past—the candles in Hall, the geraniums in the courts, some of the older faces with their memories of another era. But superficially also there are changes that point to a deeper shift: electric doors sealing off once draughty staircases, long suites of administrative offices, law is now the subject of those who succeed, not those who fail, even the lavatories are not what they were. In the first part of the present century the college was a poor institution with relatively wealthy members, both senior and junior, and a well-developed sense of private charity for the benefit of those who were not well off. It is now once again what it was originally intended to be: a moderately wealthy institution whose members, dons and students alike, are by the standards prevailing in the comparable strata of society at large, generally relatively poor. Those who remember it in its first twenty-five post-war years must look back on that phase as a lost world: the college was indeed then the fading image of a world already lost, and in being that it was the perfect image of the British society of its own time. With its dominant figures men of at least some private means, who played only a limited role in

university affairs, with its ethos not of the public school, but of escape from the public school, and with its gentle devotion to personal
development within a framework of customs recognizably inherited
from the Raj, the regimental mess, and the Edwardian country house,
it was an after-glow of England's high summer, before 1914. In this respect the college shared fully in the British self-delusion of the period 1945–1970: the delusion, which caused John Osborne to look
back in anger, that with two wars won the imperial life could carry on
as before it was so rudely interrupted, but without the nasty bits. Yet
for those of us who were educated in it in those years it was not in
our experience of the unacknowledged nostalgias of British life that
our education consisted, but in something which the college was
there to make possible and to protect: our experience of the wider,
stranger, and less comfortable world of our academic subject, in
which colleges and Britain and the present counted for nothing in
particular, in which most things were different from home, and
home, thanks to that difference, suddenly seemed fortuitous and
open to change.

It would be absurd to imagine that the character and purpose of
an institution could be defined in complete isolation from the society of which it is a part. An educational institution, however, stands
in a particularly delicate relation to the society it serves, and which
sustains it. The concern of an educational institution is not with society as it is at present but with its future, with the standards and
ideals by which it will seek to change into something better and
with its very capacity for change at all—that is with the people who
are being educated, at all levels, including the educators themselves. Universities do not exist to pass on and reinforce the prevailing attitudes of the world they belong to but to preserve its
potential for becoming something different. They can protect the
world from suffocating in its own self-images only if they maintain a
body of people who know and live with change in its more radical
form—intellectual change, a change in your way of thinking about
something you already know intimately, what is called "research."
The tendency in British attitudes to universities, epitomized by
Benjamin Jowett, has since the early nineteenth century been to
emphasize the universities' subservience to their social function of
education. The German tendency since the Humboldt reforms,
most powerfully expressed in this country by Jowett's adversary,

Mark Pattison, has been to emphasize the independence of research. (In both England and Germany the different established political institutions and traditions tended equally to obstruct a full
realization of the attitudes of the theorists.) The truth is rather that
even independence has a social function, and that a society which
seeks education without research will stifle its capacity for development as surely as yeast poisons itself with its own alcohol. A university, in short, should in its overt educational policy subscribe fully
to the social illusions of its time, in order to protect the detached
spirit of intellectual research which will one day destroy them.

On the face of it it is ludicrous that the management practices of
British industry, whose products fewer and fewer people want to
buy, should be held out as a model to British universities, whose
courses, graduates, and teachers are in demand the world over. It is
evident that the British government's desire to replace autonomous
and self-regulating bodies (not only in the educational field) with
centralized management and elaborate accounting procedures has
more to do with a prevailing attitude (what could unkindly be called
an ideology) than with a dispassionately pragmatic assessment of
strengths and weaknesses. But it should not for that reason be dismissed. Attitudes, like winds, do not prevail at random—they repeat,
often in a distorted form, the pattern of the reality from which they
derive. The root reality of which current British education policy is
the newest and greenest tip was accurately described nearly 150
years ago by a detached observer of the British scene, Karl Marx,
whose critical analyses are ready for rediscovery now that events
have dissociated them from the follies of revolutionary and authoritarian socialism. "The bourgeoisie"—that is, the capitalist class—
Marx writes in *The Communist Manifesto*, "has left no bond standing
between one human being and another but naked interest, unfeel-
ing "cash payment".... It has transformed the doctor, the lawyer, the
cleric, the poet, the man of science into its paid labourers."[11]

The dissolving effect of capital accumulation on all previous social relations (such as loyalty, authority, the non-economic rights
and liberties of individuals and chartered institutions), the maxi-
malization of productivity, the integration of the world market, the
remorseless trend towards political centralization and the conse-
quent virtual identification of the state and the market, these were
all foreseen by Marx. There is nothing new in the enthusiasm of

65

modern governments for replacing the "professional" relationship of doctor and patient or teacher and pupil, or the "authority" of the scholar, by exchange relations between a producer and a consumer subject to audit. Marx believed, probably rightly, that all relations that are not exchange relations contain, if measured by the standards of pure exchange, of "naked interest," an element of concealed exploitation (though he also assumed that exchange relations are necessarily exploitative too). His mistake was to interpret as class conflict what was a universal change in the relation of all members of society one to another. It was Max Weber who realized that there are no villains in the piece, only accountants. Weber understood that the forces shaping the modern, so-called "capitalist," world do not originate in some mysterious material or natural or even historical necessity but in the free operation of the human intellect—in accountancy. Western capitalism became possible, he concluded, only when book-keeping procedures made it possible to define capital, by distinguishing it from income.[12] Capital is not a thing but a definition, and definitions are a proper subject of academic debate. The definitions of accountancy—which in this sense is the only purely academic subject—relate to nothing less than how we are to choose to measure all social relations of the modern world against one another. Research into how *those* principles can or should be changed cannot itself meaningfully be submitted to the tests of productivity, bibliometry and so on, emanating from government ministries and their instruments. Marx saw, through the sadly distorting medium of an embittered sensibility, that there is a greater power for justice, or at least for equality, in the reduction of human relations to countable, monetary terms than in all the political reforms imposed by the mighty with the ulterior motive of preserving their own vital interests. Yet human beings need fraternity and freedom as well as equality, and indeed are so free that in the long run the poets and philosophers can persuade even the accountants to change their minds. The philosopher who best grasped the relation between human freedom and the social—that is, moral, economic, and political—necessities that it creates for itself was Hegel.

Nowadays we need to think above all about the ways in which our world is one and not the ways in which it is multiple—about what is unifying it, and how the contradictions and conflicts it contains are part of a single system and not chance historical confrontations. No one has thought more deeply and concretely about the relation of conflict and unity in the modern world than Hegel. Yet it has been part of the troubled history of Anglo-German relations in the twentieth century that Hegel has for much of that time been treated as an obscurantist apologist for authoritarianism and German nationalism. Maybe it was the semi-detachment of my college from prevailing national orthodoxies that made it possible for me to have a different view of German history and to learn to value Hegel's understanding that political, personal, and religious identity are intimately related. The resurgence of British interest in Hegel in the last twenty-five years is a sign that for the British mind Europe is no longer alien soil and that a dispassionate understanding of the long conflict between Britain and Germany is at last becoming possible. For those of us who still think of ourselves as British that will mean a not entirely painfree reassessment of who we are, as I know from experience.

3 After History
Faith in the Future

A very minor revolution occurred in our national newspapers in September 1989, while the dominoes were falling in the Soviet Empire in Eastern Europe: the face of Hegel (of all people) suddenly and briefly, and surely for the first time, was allowed to dominate the center pages.

The deputy director of the American State Department's policy planning staff, Francis Fukuyama, had published an essay entitled "The End of History" in the right-wing journal *The National Interest*,[1] suggesting that contemporary events were vindicating Hegel rather than Hegel's unruly disciple, Karl Marx; that ideas and ideology were a genuinely motivating force in history, rather than mere economics; that Hegel had seen the ideas of the French Revolution, which Fukuyama identified with modern liberal democracy, as the ultimate goal of history; that we were witnessing the worldwide extension of those ideas through the collapse of the Soviet bloc; and that since no further ideological conflict or development was possible, history had come to an end. In other words—and though Fukuyama did not say it, it was soon enough said—America had won the Cold War and though things would undoubtedly continue happening, nothing much, nothing big, would ever change again. In *The Independent* the much-regretted Peter Jenkins aptly quoted Arnold

Toynbee's childhood memories of Queen Victoria's Diamond Jubilee in 1897:

> I remember the atmosphere. It was: well here we are on the top of the world, and we have arrived at this peak to stay there—forever! There is of course a thing called history, but history is something unpleasant that happens to other people.

It was not very easy to work out what Fukuyama was actually saying in his article, and when you worked it out it usually seemed to be wrong. However the article had what it takes to make a fashion: a good title. And that title, despite its suggestion of aggressive paradox, rightly pointed to two important things about the bewildering state of world politics as clouds of obscuring dust rose all about us from the collapsing tyrannies: one was the feeling that something large scale and fundamental had changed, and that things could not be the same again; the other was that Hegel might help us to explain to ourselves what was going on.

In this essay I want to take up those two points of value in Fukuyama's original article. I will take his phrase, "The End of History," as shorthand for the new world order or disorder which burst upon us or seemed to burst upon us in 1989, and will set out both to analyze what has happened and to ask what this implies for the future of the Church. But I will also take up Fukuyama's suggestion that Hegel is the right figure to guide us on this quest, though for a rather different reason from that which Fukuyama gives. Hegel is not only an immensely broad and deep thinker about mind, politics, art, and history—he is also a religious thinker, a Christian thinker. He saw himself as a modern, that is Christian, Aristotelian or since he was not a modest man, as a modern Aristotle. That perhaps makes Hegel an appropriate guide for anyone who thinks that the legacy of Thomas Aquinas, the greatest of Christian Aristotelians, is not yet by any means exhausted.

Ending the Empires

First then let us turn to the events of 1989, and their aftermath, and ask what sense we can make of them—not initially any particularly Hegelian sense. Just sense. And if we ask that question I think it is immediately clear that Fukuyama's answer does not come into that category. The events of 1989, and subsequent developments in Russia and around the world, cannot be represented as the triumph of the idea of liberal democracy, or indeed of any idea alone and unaided.

The East German state, for example, had long ago ceased to enjoy the intellectual assent of the majority of its citizens if it ever possessed it—but it remained in existence for decades and gave every appearance of being capable of lasting indefinitely, even in the summer and autumn of 1989. The removal of the Soviet military guarantee may have spelled the end of the puppet regimes in Poland, Czechoslovakia, and elsewhere in Eastern Europe, nations which were then free to enjoy their more or less velvety revolutions, but it did not necessitate the end of the East German state. The survival of the East German state ceased to be conceivable at the moment when the free movement of people and money between the two German states was allowed. The wall between the two Germanies and across Europe had been built to safeguard the Soviet-imposed state structure against the threat posed by the free movement of labor and capital. In 1961 Khrushchev recognized that the existence of a single leak or loophole posed a threat to the economic and so the political stability of East Germany, and the wall was completed virtually overnight to staunch the last possibility of hemorrhage through the open wound that was Berlin. The wall as it developed with its death-strips and razor wire and chained dogs and searchlights and sanitized zones deep into the territory behind it, was a monument not to the lengths to which tyranny will go to shackle the free human spirit, but to the absurd and so ultimately unsustainable measures to which the political will is constrained when it seeks absolute control of economic activity.

It is strange that Fukuyama gives no place among the victors of 1989 to the economic factor, even though the presidents from his own party, Bush and especially Reagan, consciously or unconsciously made systematic use of it to win the final round of the Cold War. By intensifying technological competition in the military sphere, above all with the Star Wars program, and even by overheating the Western economy as it entered the boom phase of a cycle in order to exaggerate the manifest difference between Western and Eastern productivity, they put, and perhaps intended to put, intolerable pressure on the Communist governments from their own captive populations. The demand to deliver the—consumer—goods became all the more insistent and all the more impossible to meet as the Western economies seemed to be sprinting away into the distance. In the subsequent slump we have been paying back the debts incurred in that last strenuous effort to unseat the dictators by appealing to the economic interests of their victims.

But of course Reagan and Bush could make use of the economic weapon only because it was there to be used. They could not invent it, they could only magnify, at a politically critical moment, an effect which was already at work and which would eventually have brought about roughly the same results, if not in the present economic cycle, then in a future one. The political will to control, symbolized and effectuated by that monstrous iron fence across Europe, was already being undermined at a myriad points. It was not just a matter of increased tourism bringing an increased black market in second-hand jeans and an increased desire for Walkmans and Marlboros; nor even of the acknowledgment of failure represented by state chains of Intershops selling Western goods for hard currency. It was the brute fact on the large scale that, try as they might to establish a watertight, self-contained, alternative economic system—and only Albania really succeeded in being watertight—the communist regimes could not cut themselves off entirely from the world market: that was where they had to sell their gas and their oil, their sugar and their gold and their other industrial metals; that was where they had to buy their grain in time of dearth; and that was where some of them, notably the Polish regime, involved themselves in the Western financial system by seeking loans. In the area where the technological gap between West and East was greatest—electronics and computing—the communist world was reduced to parasitism and piracy and made no pretense of offering an alternative. And all the while in the background, partly a consequence, partly itself a cause, the telecommunications network was extending itself, and the Comecon countries were entangled in a proliferation of cables, television channels, and interconnected computers. The rising tide of information, as of ever more freely flowing capital, was washing at the subsoil on which the iron fence was founded, and in 1989 the sandcastles crumbled away into the global market.

That global market, that economic interconnection of all human beings across the whole surface of the planet, had been establishing itself manifestly since 1945 and its historical roots lie a good deal deeper in the past. Immanuel Wallerstein, the American *marx-isant* sociologist, dates the final arrival of 'the modern world-system' to the late nineteenth century.[2] Then for the first time in human history a single system encompassed the whole planet: the European states had divided up the surface of the earth and assigned it all to their own empires or spheres of influence. Each imperial power (so we might gloss Wallerstein's thesis) endeavored to set up a self-contained economic circuit within a single political structure, from the colonial primary producers through the industries of the metropolitan territory to the consumers throughout the empire. But the empires also entertained economic relations with one another which were not subject to any overarching political order: a global economy had come into being which was far larger than any of the politically ring-fenced, imperial economies that composed it.

Already by the end of the nineteenth century, telegraph, transport, and trade had brought almost all human beings, including even some of the most remote and primitive, into potential inter-relationship, and it required only the development of the mass-production of consumer goods and durables from cars to Coca Cola, and the arts of mass distribution and mass advertising, to make that potential interrelationship a real one. Since from about 1900 there was no longer any neutral, unassigned territory for them to expand into, those artificially demarcated, sub-global imperial economies were forced into bitter rivalry. The history of the twenti-eth century, from 1914 to 1989 (so we might continue our gloss), has been the story of the disintegration of those imperial political structures thanks to the internal strains and external pressures caused by the intensification of global economic activity which it was not in their power to control. Long before it destroyed the So-viet empire, the global market, as it grew, destroyed the colonial em-pires, notably of Britain and France, which had initially fostered it: even in 1950 Britain was still the largest car exporter in the world— an indication of the power both of imperial preference and of the forces which put an end to it. Nation states are, according to Waller-stein, a twentieth-century invention, the enormously proliferated successor-bodies to empires as the political facade behind which the world economy continues the endless accumulation of capital through the maximum appropriation of surplus value—that is, as he more trenchantly puts it, the unceasing "pressure on the direct pro-

ducer to work more and be paid less."[3] Unfortunately Wallerstein is
prevented from exploiting his analysis to the full by his—not of
course unusual—obsession with a figment called "capitalism,"
about which I shall say more in a moment. Because he wants to
claim that the end of the nineteenth century was historically significant in seeing the establishment of "capitalism" as a world-system,
he overlooks that what was really significant about that watershed
was that it saw the establishment of the one and only world-system
there has ever been:[4] its members were counted, or at least countable, it had no outsiders, and the finitude of its resources had become apparent with the exhaustion of the first and most basic of
all—land. What destroyed the empires was not "capitalism," but
their inadequacy, as subsidiary political units, to the demands of a
global economy. About a hundred years ago the human race entered a wholly new era and since then, as far as most of human history is concerned, we have been living in the Millennium.

1945 was still a turning-point however.[5] In the early twentieth
century there were, or there appeared to be, two ways by which a
world political structure, corresponding to the world economic
structure, might come into being: either war or international co-
operation. Either the existing political units might deploy their coercive powers against one another until only one was left to inherit
the earth. Or a common structure might emerge through negotia-
tion and agreement of all parties. (These alternatives were incidentally already envisaged in 1795 by Kant, the most far-sighted of all
political theorists, in his treatise *On Perpetual Peace*.) From 1914 to
1945 the world took the first path, at a terrible and—as it must now
seem—unnecessary cost: the international organizations were in
these years young, weak, and disregarded. In 1945, even though the
last of the old empires, the Russian, remained intact, and seemingly
at the zenith of its power, a new phase began, soon confirmed by
the establishment of a nuclear balance of fear. The decision to take
after all the path of—relative—peace (also known as the Cold War)
allowed the full consequences of the globalization of economic
activity to unfold in conditions more stable and less militarized
than any that had existed since the world-system was first created
at the beginning of the century. The founding of the GATT was the
first serious attempt to give that global interconnection institutional expression.

The Cold War years then saw a huge growth in the significance of what came to be called first "multinational," and now "global" corporations,[6] a development headed by firms whose business was of its nature international, such as oil companies, but which has come in our own day to embrace such standard forms of industrial manufacture as car-production, which used to be one of the staples of a national economy and, along with an airline—now also internationalized as like as not—a symbol of national pride and independence. But this was also the period of an explosive development of multinational political agencies, whether for defense, trade, or cultural co-operation, some but not by any means all sponsored by the political figurehead of the new era, the United Nations Organization. The UN may be derided as practically ineffectual—though other multinational bodies such as NATO, the IMF, or OPEC certainly are not—but the effect of its existence on our consciousness is immeasurable. It is a very difficult exercise of the imagination to think oneself back into a world without that shared and universal talking-shop, a world in which the biggest conceivable human units were nations and their empires, unequal, no doubt, but absolutely sovereign, engaging in mutual relations only by choice not by necessity, considering the views and interests of allies, if there were any, only occasionally and in the context of some particular and temporary treaty. (What a difference it has made to our national thinking to be in a close military alliance with the same nations for half a century.) In that half-forgotten world such phrases as "human rights," "the world community," "responsibility for the planet," belonged to the vocabulary of philosophy, not of politics.

Since 1945 there has been a shift, deep down, in the way we think about ourselves and our cultural and ethical activities, of which people have seriously become aware only in the last twenty years or so and to which the label "post-modernism" has been attached. But that is something I shall deal with later. For the moment the point which I want to stress is that since 1945 a single overriding economic fact, the development of the global market, has determined not only the economic but the political and cultural life of the human world, and has been responsible for all the most striking changes those years have seen. In particular the development of an integrated world economy has meant the gradual obsolescence of nations as significant economic and even political units in the very years which have seen the foundation of the majority of them. (Note that I do not say the obsolescence of nationalism. Ethnic nationalism is a fear-filled evasion of the hard realities of finance, manufacture, and employment, all of which are now essentially international. Of the hundred largest economies in the world, more than half are not now nations at all, but corporations such as Mitsubishi and Ford. The various forms of nationalism—from harmless Euroskepticism to genocidal Pan-Serbianism—are the cultural myths that keep this disagreeable truth at bay.)

The reluctance of intellectuals to attribute these changes to changes in the economic structure is surprising. Perhaps it is because such an analysis is regarded as Marxist, and Marxism—not entirely adventitiously—was until 1989 closely, indeed criminally, associated with an authoritarian political creed of utopian socialism, from which many quite properly wished to distance themselves. Jean-François Lyotard, in a most influential treatise on post-modernism first published in 1979,[7] attributed many of the cultural features of the post-1945 era to the growth of communications and computing, cybernetics as it was called then, which was to mistake a symptom—albeit a facilitating symptom—for a cause. And Fukuyama ten years later still seems to regard what he calls liberal capitalism as a kind of ideology in practice, something that people choose to do, a system of economic order that people choose to impose on themselves because they are convinced on rational grounds that it is right, rather than as what it is: the way human beings, as economic units, in fact behave, which is always changing and developing. Wallerstein, at the other end of the political spectrum similarly regards what he too calls 'capitalism' as an option, which in his view is forcibly imposed on the weak by the strong.[8] In his case, as in that of other left-wing thinkers (including Marx), "capitalism" is, clearly, given this status in order that a hypothesized alternative to it—a socialism which has never been seen on the face of the earth—should also appear to be an option, variously realizable by choice or force. Lyotard has claimed that utopian socialism is an alibi for capitalism,[9] an imaginary alternative with which we indulge our fantasies, so leaving the status quo intact. The reverse is the case. Capitalism is an alibi for socialism. It is an imaginary object of hatred, whose function is to distract our attention from the will to power of socialists. The concept of capitalism as a unified system, as one possible way of doing things among many others, was invented by an intelligentsia which wanted to assert that it understood the economic order and was able to control it—or at least should be entrusted with the power to make the attempt. But if by capitalism you mean a particular theory or system, capitalism does not exist. Capitalism is not an -ism at all; it is not a theory; it is not a matter of choice. If by capitalism you mean the economic facts of life, then there is, as the lady famously observed, no alternative.

Ending History

"All that is solid, melts into air" Marx says, in the Communist Manifesto, of the impact of bourgeois capitalism on traditional society.[10] Because since 1945 the world market has seriously begun to dissolve protective national structures, the ring fences and Chinese walls that go under the name of national identity, all the smaller structures within nations have begun to feel themselves permeated by some disintegrating fluid. Large and ancient institutions like national churches and monarchies and aristocracies; smaller institutions of varying antiquity such as universities and local authorities; organized interest groups like professions and trade unions, the less organized but similar groups such as national peasantries or other favored occupations (miners, for example), even established commercial entities with a traditionally non-commercial further role— such as banks or building and friendly societies, or even just traditionally "good employers"—all feel the impact of a new demand for what is rightly called account–ability. For it is only on condition that you are accountable, that is auditable, that you are allowed to become part of the global market—and you cannot refrain from becoming a part of it without withdrawing from economic life altogether. If you are paid in money, or in any of the market's products, you will eventually—it is the logic of our age—be subjected to the rule of participation in the market: that your activities be quantified, that they be broken down into measurable units, priceable in money and so comparable with the units into which the behavior of others, anywhere in the world, has been broken down, and that you are allowed no standing in this new world order—for standing itself has to be a quantifiable good—that is not transparently related to your performance indicator, your input-output ratio. The globaliza-

tion of human interrelationships is the strongest of all forces making for their quantification, for, even if they want to, the central organs of a modern—that is, a dissolving—nation-state cannot hold
out against the global market: as the French farmers have recently
learned. More or less gradually, every non-quantifiable, every contractually non-definable, element is leached out of the system of
exchange—the value of solidarity, for example, represented by a
shared day of rest—and is redefined as a free lunch, paid for further
down the line by somebody else.

All these collective sub-national institutions, and nations themselves, used to circumscribe individual lives but also to provide the
context and the markers for individual achievement. ("He never
made much money but . . . he was a good husband / looked after his
employees / won an MC in the war / did a lot for the youth-club /
wrote a great book on beekeeping.") The demand for accountability
either reduces the diversity to the uniformity of different calcula-
tions in the same currency of somebody's costed time, or dismisses
the substantial life these institutions seemed to offer as an
anachronistic tissue of idle privilege, restrictive practices, exploitation, and oppression.

Three consequences follow: First, the political world shrivels. Public affairs hardly seem to exist any more. Privatization, which is the
form in which the demand for accountability affects local natural
monopolies, means what it says: large areas of what used to be the
national life cease to be an area of public discussion. Elected or representative bodies are seen as incompetent to make managerial—
that is, economic—decisions. The affairs of non-economic national
institutions—church, monarchy, judiciary, the national newspapers,
the BBC—no longer seem quite serious as concerns for the central
organs of government. Those seem increasingly taken up with the issues of economic management, which they are increasingly obliged
to acknowledge are beyond their control anyway. What role could
politicians have when what really matters is accountancy?

Second, as the institutions disappear, the definition of an individual life becomes reduced, or clarified, to the sequence of economic roles the individual performs. No longer do we define
ourselves by the church we go to, the party we vote for, or the paper
we read; as there is little any longer in the way of public life, we can
scarcely be defined by our contribution to it, either on the large or

on the small scale. We are at best the series of consumer choices we have made (first an Escort, then a Sierra, then a loft conversion) and the series of jobs from which we have been made redundant—but it is of no great significance to the auditing accountant whether the Escort and the Sierra were bought by the same person, or whether it is only a coincidence that this sales executive and that training manager had the same name. The concept of a vocation, of a job—or task—for life, that defines a large part of what a person is, loses its value, and is actively persecuted. We may still say "she is a printer," "he is a teacher" but what we mean, and what in future we shall increasingly say, is, "she is doing some printing, at the moment," "he is on a three-year teaching contract." The question what "he" or "she" permanently is does not arise: even gender is irrelevant—for the market what matters is the performance indicator that "s/he," the production unit, can show.

So third, traditional concepts of value and truth are changed. In the market, time is compressed into an ever more narrowly defined present. What you have done is an irrelevance. What matters is the choice and the performance *now*—past choices matter only as a guide to present behavior, future choices matter only as the objects of present calculation. The question of what you permanently are, or what permanently is, and is permanently valuable, does not arise. When it is raised, it has a strangely factitious air: when politicians start talking about the values of our society, or even the lack of values in our society, we have a strong suspicion there is humbug around. Talk of values we don't have is being used to conceal values we do have. Despite what the politicians say, we know that our society is coming down with values, that everyone and every activity in it is multiply and precisely valued, quantitatively valued—productivity, efficiency, performance, cost/benefit and P/Y, credit and audience ratings, popularity polls: has there ever been a society which knew so precisely what it valued and how much? And subconsciously we know that and see through the pretense. The politicians know, and deep down we know too, that nobody really does believe very much that the most important things about our *collective* lives are inexpressible in market terms. Certainly not if under the heading of the market you include the communications network. That is now the real repository of truth, as of value. I guess that if you were to ask people—and not only in the West now—what is the best thing you can imagine happening to you and your family, what it would be like for you to live like the gods, most answers would include, alongside being rich and happy, which is only honest, being famous: living, as it were, in the television set, being royal, being omnipresent in the telecommunications network, which is the instrument and expression of the global market. A hundred years ago, by contrast, I suspect a substantial proportion of the answers would have included a reference to heaven. Equally, if you were to ask the present prime minister or president of the USA whose judgment they fear most they would, if *they* were being honest, say: the judgment of their electorate—*their* performance appraisers, *their* customers. But if they were being sententious, they would say: the judgment of History—and what is History for the global market but the television audience of tomorrow, a transcendentalized version of the poll ratings of today? A hundred years ago, however, their predecessors would no doubt have announced, with equal sententiousness, their fear of the judgment of God, or at least of their conscience. Ultimate truth is now not—for most people, really—the word from the mouth of God, but the image on the screen, whether of the television or of the database. Which is why Watergate was a great, real, and truly modern tragedy: Nixon was seduced by the desire for the approval of History into entering as much of his presidency as he could into what was effectively an electronic databank and that very desire brought him infamy. His unforgivable crime was not to burgle the Democrat headquarters, but to cover up: to seek to withdraw from the global information network to whose judgment he had submitted himself. Like Diana, Princess of Wales, he was brought down by the very gods he had invoked.

Of course, there are a lot of people around who think they have what are called "alternative" values: neither the values of the market, nor the values which the market has destroyed. One of the characteristics of the world since 1945 has been the generalization of eccentricity—what is sometimes called pluralism but is really the desubstantialization of *all* values except those of the market. The moral world, like the material world, is supremely represented as a shopping mall: it is now open to us to stroll between the shelves and pick out, or opt for, as the phrase has it, whatever takes our fancy— Buddhism, scientology, environmentalism, feminism, gay liberation, animal rights, Jehovah's Witnesses: in the emporium of pluralism you can have what you want and it is politically incorrect—that is, a restrictive, anti-market practice—to suggest that some commodities should not be put on sale. But the good is not something that we choose to acknowledge—it is something that we have to acknowledge. A true, a substantial value, is not something we have opted for, it is something that has imposed itself on us—as an obligation. And that is why I see the rainbow of minority and alternative cultures or values as a rainbow of delusions, whatever the truth or rightness of the political cause particular groups may espouse. There is not a professor of black studies nor a feminist critic, who is paid, whether by university or publisher or radical protest group, in anything other than green dollar bills. More to the point, they *cannot avoid* being paid and offering payment in that currency: it is what you cannot avoid that are the values you live by, the rest are just—options. We all live in and by the global market and the first duty of the critic is to understand our position and not succumb to delusions. As the lady might have observed, there are no alternatives.

To recapitulate: the collapse of the Communist Empire in 1989 was the last dramatic step in a process which began around 1870 and became the dominant geopolitical process in 1945: the establishment of a global market. The existence of a world economic system threatens, and its development gradually undermines, the autonomy of nation-states. As nation-states become obsolescent, so the institutions of national life lose their hold on the identities and even the interests of citizens, who are more and more determined by global factors, operating from China to Peru. The political world seems an irrelevance, individuality is fragmented, and the past is lost. The old transcendent certainties fade and are replaced by the harsh realities and tangible rewards of the global marketplace in the global village. New transcendent certainties seem to exist, however, if we look for them: the fantasy of a perfect life on the television (which corresponds roughly to what used to be thought of as the life of the soul) and the fantasy of a perfect life on the television hereafter, called History (which corresponds to what used to be thought of as immortality). History, having wholly ceased to refer to the past, and referring now only to this future fantasy, does indeed seem to have ended.

Now I have already indicated that the picture I have painted of what I believe to be post-1945 socio-economic reality corresponds after a fashion to the picture of the cultural and intellectual world to be found in the works of writers who concern themselves with what since 1975 has been called "post-modernism." I should like as the next stage in my argument just briefly to survey the correspondences.

First, there is the question of politics, which seems to me intimately linked with the term "post-modern" itself. I regard "post-modern" as corresponding to what I have here called "post-1945," for I believe that Post-Modernism is inseparable from the development of the global market. This is not an obvious point, for there has been much discussion among those who have taken up the term on whether "post-modern" is a chronological term at all. Most have taken the view that it is not, that what they mean by Post-Modernism is something that runs in parallel with Modernism or is even a permanent possibility of the human spirit—it is suggested[11] that Montaigne, in the sixteenth century, is post-modern, but the brothers Schlegel, in 1800, are only modern. (It is, of course, a Frenchman who makes the suggestion.) As it is part of a Post-Modernist approach to deny—at any rate from time to time—the significance of chronology this is an understandable ploy. Indeed the term 'Post-Modernist' is a good one precisely because "Modernism" in all the arts depended on the belief in an opposition between the present and the past. To be modern was to do things differently. The architects to whom the term 'Post-Modernist' was first applied wanted to deny that opposition and wanted to develop an eclectic style that made free use of any and every past architectural possibility. For the Post-Modernist architect all past styles are simultaneously available as templates in his database.

However, one reason why non-chronological definitions of Post-Modernism are favored is in my view the rather unpolitical nature of Post-Modernist thinkers. They seem to have been infected by the withering-away of national politics which I take to be a feature of the post-1945 world in which, as in Post-Modernist writing, the dominant symbol is the shopping mall. Among the anti-chronological postmodernists we have on the one hand non-Marxists like Lyotard and Derrida who seem to favor an anarchist line, telling us to jump onto the current alternative protest-wagon as it passes by. Their attractive, but implausible, ground is that justice (that is, protest) is the one value that Post-Modernism (that is, the global market) leaves undissolved and indissoluble. On the other hand we have an avowed Marxist like Fredric Jameson who maintains the traditional Marxist contempt for political life, regarding it as a superficial offshoot of the economic process, and happily acknowledging his full agreement in this, and even in all other respects, with the "neo-liberal" right-wing economists, the theoreticians of the market.[12] Evidently, if Post-Modernism is some kind of permanent possibility of the human mind and not historically specific, and so not occasioned by any specific set of circumstances, then it cannot be made the object or motive for any specific and sustained course of political action which seeks to modify or respond to circumstances. It is therefore politically essential to assert that "Post-Modernism" is a chronological term. The loss of a sense of the past, the collapsing of all significance into the present, the refusal to regard the existing market as caused by or developing out of anything is, I believe, one of the most paralyzing features of the socio-economic system that has developed since 1945. To assert the historical contingency of what has happened by asserting the chronological application of the term 'Post-Modernism' is to take a first step out of the trance. To do otherwise, is to collaborate with the hypnotist.

Second, we can see another strange coincidence between Post-Modernist thought and the consequences of the establishment of the global market if we turn to the question of personal identity, the object of some of the most intensive Post-Modernist speculation. The belief that there is no principle of unity in the self, indeed that the self—usually called the subject—does not really exist, is one of the commonplaces in Post-Modernist thought, and it is a commonplace increasingly borne out by post-modern life, in which the external institutions which gave us identity by giving us continuity seem to be fading into the background, in which jobs for life have become, and marriages for life are becoming, the exception rather than the rule, and in which we all seem to be required either to keep running faster in order to stay in the same place or to give up any pretense of controlling our own destiny and allow ourselves to be swept along by events. The question "who am I?" seems ever harder to answer, indeed it seems an ever emptier question as it gets ever less obvious what might count as an answer to it. For that difficulty there are solid social and economic reasons: we do not have to appeal to intellectual developments—whether psychoanalysis, Heidegger, or existentialism—in order to understand why it is growing.

Third, the other great theme in Post-Modernist thought, sometimes called the crisis of the sign—the sign being an element in a system of signification, i.e., a language—corresponds to the shift we detected in the nature of value. Indeed in both cases we could speak of a loss of confidence in the notion of truth and a virtual divinization instead of the media of communication. Just as in Post-Modernist architecture you can now have every style except an authentic one of your own, so in Post-Modernist literary criticism you can have any and every interpretation of a text except the authentic one—and similarly we saw that the shopping mall of values in the pluralist world offers you every alternative to the market except a real one (which would put an end to the shopping expedition). The demand for authentic values now rings as hollow as the demand for a definitive interpretation: deep down we know that what we really believe in is the system, not any meaning or satisfaction that it promises to give us 'at the end of the day', when the work of interpretation, or shopping, is over. For the system—like shopping, interpretation, satellite television, the world's stock and money markets, and work—has no end and no Sunday and goes on uninterrupted twenty-four hours a day, seven days a week.

Hegel and the Church

I must leave to a later essay the question why it should be that Post-Modernist thinkers—most of whom are not evidently conformist characters—should thus willingly present themselves as agents of the new economic order. For the present I had better explain what Hegel has had to do with all of this.

Hegel's *Lectures on the Philosophy of World History*, published in book form after his death, were his most popular and most influential work but they have a rather questionable reputation. They seem to me still however immensely stimulating and profound, especially if they are taken together with the *Philosophy of Right*, to which they are a sort of 400-page appendix. For the *Philosophy of Right* is Hegel's philosophy of the state, and one of the important things to grasp about Hegel's historical lectures is that the term 'world-history' does *not* mean "the history of everything" but explicitly is said to mean something quite narrow: the history of "nations insofar as they have formed themselves into states." So world-history is concerned with the history of the largest political units into which human beings have formed themselves—it is history with a broad brush, certainly, but conceptually we are dealing with something quite specific.

States of course are defined not just by being large collections of human beings—that is what the *Philosophy of Right* is all about. Nor are all states the same. In the *Philosophy of World History* Hegel is concerned with the different forms the state has taken on in the course of time and though he represents these changes as a development, it is important to realize that when one state form is supplanted by a new one it does not necessarily go out of existence but may continue, even up to Hegel's own time, as a kind of living fossil.

And the different forms of states are associated by Hegel with two other things which change in the course of time; indeed for him they are so closely associated that a significant difference in the form of a state is impossible without a significant difference in these other two factors—and *vice versa* (twice over, since we have three variables). The other two factors which change with the state, and with which the state changes, are: the moral self-understanding of the human individuals making up the nation which has formed itself into a state, what Hegel calls "Sittlichkeit"; and the nation's religion, its conception of God.

In other words, for Hegel the political constitution, the prevailing sense of personal identity, and the religion of a state are so intimately linked that all three must change together:

> the Athenian or the Roman state was possible only given the specific form of paganism of those nations, just as a Catholic state has a different spirit and a different constitution from a Protestant state.[13]

The reason Hegel gives for this special significance of religion is that

> Religion is the point where a nation defines for itself what it regards as truth.[14]

A culture's religion expresses what the people of that culture really believe to be the facts of life, what they really take seriously: it is therefore the crucial point of interaction between what is publicly acknowledged to be the order prevailing in the state and what is felt to be the reality of an individual life; for it expresses the truth that is felt to be common to both. According to Hegel then, the State, the self, and the conception of God all vary together, and world history, as the history of forms of the state, is also the history of changing forms of the self and of religion. I shall not now try to exemplify this pattern from Hegel's sequence of state forms—China and India, Egypt and Persia, Greece and Rome, and what he calls the Germanic nations of medieval and modern Europe. But I expect it is already evident that in discussing the new world order after 1945 I have concentrated in turn on the three areas which according to Hegel have to be treated together by the student of world-history: State, Self, and God.

Hegel, however, can give us more help than this in understanding where we are, and in particular, by taking issue with his account of the religious component in world-history, we can try to formulate the role of the Catholic Church in our own time. I should like to look at three of the commonest objections made to Hegel's philosophy of history and try to draw out of them some grounds of hope. For hope is what we need. Only if we look out on the contemporary landscape in the bleakest winter light will we do justice to the pain and disorientation and collapse that is intrinsic to an age of such rapid change. But Hegel is above all others the philosopher who shows how out of conflict and disintegration a new wholeness can proceed, and the Church has the longest possible experience of preaching a similar message.

First, then, it has often been objected, most notoriously by Marx, that Hegel's account of the state, and so of world-history, is idealist rather than materialist. It seems to give priority to human beings' thoughts rather than to the material conditions of their existence. In particular, it gives a prominent place to political institutions and neglects the economic forces which are—according to the Marxists and the New Right economists—far more significant in the molding of society. To the complex questions this objection raises no short answer is possible, but it is possible to point to a misconception which may underlie the objection, and when that misconception is removed much of the force of the objection goes with it. The misconception is the belief that there is an opposition between the economic and political realms, as if economic forces compelled us to act, while politics, by contrast, pretended to be an area of freedom in which we organize ourselves according to our free choice. For Hegel, however—who gives incidentally a considerable, though subordinate, position to the economic system in his account of the state—there is no such opposition. Hegel is a radical humanist and a radical libertarian: *all* our social arrangements are our choice, he believes; all society, in its economic as in its political aspects, is an expression of our freedom. Political institutions—in ideal, stable, circumstances—are merely the most self-conscious and rational expression of the *same* order that we find in our economic arrangements. This is something particularly important for us to take to heart in the present highly unstable and far from ideal circumstances. For the withering away of political institutions in the post-1945 world is essentially a national phenomenon, and it corresponds to a decline in the significance of nations themselves. That decline has been brought about by the growth of a global economic order. The imperative that faces us in the future is the construction of a political order corresponding in scope and structure to the new world market. One thing the chaos in Eastern Europe, particularly Russia, ought to have taught us, is that the economic system is not self-sufficient: without laws of property and property transfer, without protection against violence and confiscation, only the most primitive economic relations are possible. A global economy needs global politics, not just in order to control it, insofar as politics can control economics, but in order to preserve it—against, for example, the threat of war, or sudden changes of national boundaries. And that brings me to the second point.

A second objection frequently made to the *Lectures on the Philosophy of World History* is that they are Eurocentric. Large parts of the non-European world are explicitly excluded from consideration and the story Hegel tells leads with uncanny inevitability towards Europe and Hegel's own place and time. There are some special reasons for this shape to Hegel's story which I cannot deal with now, but the general charge of Eurocentricity is one I am very happy not to rebut. It is one of the rainbow of delusions which have multiplied since 1945 that world-history might have many centers: on the contrary, either it has no center at all, or it has one center and that center is Europe. The delusion consists, as do most of the delusions of alternative values, in the failure to recognize that there is only one economic system and that it is now world-embracing. World-history may once have had many strands—though Hegel would deny this—but now it has only one, and that strand has for much of its length passed through Europe. Specifically, it was in Europe and in Europe's relations with its colonies, in America and Asia and eventually in Africa, that the global market began to be formed, and in its present world-embracing stage it still bears many traces of its European origin—notably the ubiquity, especially at bankers' conferences, of suits and ties. But that is a question of the past, and would be on its own a pettifogging reason for Eurocentric philosophy, and so no reason at all. In the present there is, of course, no reason whatever for asserting the world economic system to be Eurocentric: all the indications are that Europe's relative economic significance will decline rather than increase. But in one respect the Europe which nurtured Hegel still is the growing-point of world-history. It is the point at which political developments are taking place which are literally without precedent, and which are without parallel elsewhere in the world.

The growth of the European Union—long, rheumatic and uncertain though it is—is by far the most complex and advanced political response to the existence of a transnational economic system that the world has to offer at present. The wholly unprecedented nature of the Union accounts for the great conceptual difficulties our politicians have in explaining it to themselves and their electorates. Plainly the European Union can become neither a superstate nor a mere treaty organization of nations, for both prognoses assume the continued possibility of nation states in the post-modern world. The Europe of the future will not be a USE, and it will not be an *Europe des patries* either: it will be *different*, different from any political structure seen before, and that is probably the most encouraging thing about it. The interrelation of the fifteen states is already of a sophistication far surpassing that of any of the merely international organizations which have become so numerous since 1945 and which themselves would have been unthinkable a hundred or even perhaps fifty years ago. The European Union begins to do political justice to the degree of economic interpenetration of nations that the last half century has brought and that has made the traditional national boundaries obsolete. Europe is the testing ground for whatever political structures will in the future have to secure the world economy; the monitoring authority set up under the new GATT agreement, which will bear a faint resemblance to the European Commission, is perhaps a first indication that the European experiment may eventually provide a model for bodies with world-wide responsibilities. This is partly perhaps because Europe has a very long history of the complex interaction of many states, as well as by far the oldest functioning international organization, the Catholic Church, which throughout the Middle Ages gave Europe its unity. Without asserting that the European Union is the faith, one can perhaps say that the Catholic Church's singular success in preserving its transnational activities throughout the nineteenth-century heyday of the nation states suggests that there are in Europe forces making for order and unity even now that those states have gone into decline. But some reservations are necessary and with them we have arrived at the third point.

The third commonly made objection to Hegel's philosophy of history, and the last I wish to consider, is that it has a Protestant bias. Naturally, I think this is an objection with which one may have some sympathy. But the Catholic Church has already accepted many of the fruits of the Reformation and it is not impossible that her future teachers may incorporate so manifestly providential an event in their understanding of the Church's historical character. Hegel's philosophy of world-history is an important corrective to the complacent view, prevalent in many Catholic circles, though rarely publicly enunciated, that Protestantism is defunct and insignificant—say in comparison with Orthodoxy. For in Hegel's account the end of history has indeed occurred, or at any rate begun, but this happened not in the French Revolution, but in the Reformation. Essentially, for Hegel, the Reformation is the beginning of secularization, and secularization, for Hegel, is the supreme religious process, the process by which the divinity of our human world—our human social and institutional world—is at last consciously grasped: the divine is no longer relegated to special churchy institutions or special churchy parts of life, but our whole life, personal, social, and political, is understood as the product of the divine spirit which breathes through our own free actions—the product therefore of us, as divine. Since world-history is the story of the state-forming varieties of religious awareness, and since no further development of religious awareness is possible after its transformation into pure self-awareness, world-history has indeed come to an end with the event which inaugurates the modern secular state, the Reformation. Throughout the post-Reformation period the modern state has of course developed its character, it has grown both in internal complexity and in its coverage of the globe, and it has become all the time more secular and more aware of its divinity. Hegel lived at a time when the global market, modern media, and their divinization, lay some way in the future, but I do not think he would see these developments as anything but confirmation of his view. Secularity is a Christian discovery, as old as Christianity itself but first rendered explicit at the Reformation: insofar as the modern state—which need not be a nation-state—is secular, and not enchained to the service of old gods, it is Christian, specifically, it is Protestant.

My view of the Catholic understanding of the Reformation is that we think the Reformation's fundamental error was not heresy but schism, it was an act of pride. The weakness in Hegel's philosophy, not just his philosophy of world-history, must, from a Catholic point of view, I think be its pride. Unlike Kant, Hegel does not leave room— and emphatically refuses to leave room—for a residuum of the inexplicable, of that which is not accessible to thought. According to Hegel, no significance in world-history attaches to the continued existence of living fossils—but, world-history having ended, perhaps a living fossil such as the Catholic Church may have a part to play once more, and I should like to conclude by considering how the Church may be expected to adapt to, or to influence, the new world order, post-1945 and post-1989. I shall follow once again the Hegelian pattern of collectivity, identity, and truth, State, Self, and God. My guiding principle will be that to be Catholic is to reject the Hegelian assertion of the absolute identity of these three. In the historical world at any rate—eschatology may be another matter—we are not God, we are not the State, and the State is not God; and historically since its earliest days the Church has maintained this position by maintaining an independent institutional existence for the Church separate from that of the State. Only in the countries where the Reformation took hold was the Church's millennial refusal to worship Caesar overthrown as a matter of principle.

I therefore think that, paradoxically perhaps, the Church's status as an international organization is likely to be more problematic in the future than it has been for many centuries. In the era of nation-states, the internationalist aspect of the Church was one of its most obviously noble and appealing features; the Church offered a broader loyalty, and a broader basis for conscience, which could liberate people from stifling nationalism and petty or brutal local tyrannies. Its universality was enough to guarantee its proper role of opposing the State's pretension to total rule over minds and bodies. But in the new order that universality may become the matter of a more serious temptation than the institutional church has suffered since the sixteenth century. For the new order is universal too, and it has certainly not given up its ambition to rule us body and mind. The Church may be tempted to collaborate with worldly powers, flattered that they have at last adopted its global perspective. But the worldly powers have their own motives and purposes, and if one is disturbed when a papal tour becomes a media event it is because it is becoming unclear in such a case who is using, or paying homage to, whom.

Of course, the Church has always, and of necessity, taken much of its institutional character from the political world of its day. The popes have been feudal lords in a feudal era, absolute monarchs in the age of absolutism, in the nineteenth century they became something like presidents-for-life of a kind of international nation-state within the nation-states. It is not to be wondered at if in the future they look a little more like chairmen of IBM or the World Health Organization. The First Vatican Council was a very necessary battening-down of the hatches to face the totalitarian pretensions of the state in the era of unrestrained nationalism: in order to face down the dictators, from Bismarck to Jaruzelski, the Church had to turn itself into something very like the militarized dictatorships it was opposing—Orwell was right to see the Catholicism of his day as a variant of the nationalism he deplored, though he was wrong to imagine that it was the whole, or even a large part, of the Catholic Church. Similarly the Church of the future will act as one global agency among others, and we shall be glad that it is there to do this for us; as our forefathers were glad that the Church had the strength and presence to speak as a state to other states in an age when jurisdictions rarely crossed national boundaries and a man or woman at odds with their country had very few friends. But in those days internationalism of itself gave a certain, almost suprahistorical, aura of moral authority. In the future that will no longer be the case, and if the Church is to continue to be different, to continue to be unassimilated to the secular world which it nonetheless addresses, it will have to draw its authority from elsewhere. I suggest that the Church of the future will need to draw its moral strength not from its international presence but from its claim to represent people as they are locally and distinct from the worldwide ramifications of their existence as participants in the global market. Whatever currents may seem to be swirling temporarily in a contrary direction, the moral authority of the Church in future will lie, as the Second Vatican Council foresaw, with the College of bishops. It will be the bishops, rather than specifically the papacy, which will challenge the claim of the global market to express and exhaust the human world. Lyotard thinks that in the post-modern world history indeed is finished and the grand narrative of the development of the human race, in the manner of Hegel and Marx, is no longer possible; only little narratives can now be told, *petits récits*, which make temporary and local sense of events.[15] I disagree though only partially. Grand narrative continues: on the global scale history is only just beginning, for the struggle to establish a political order corresponding to the economic has a long way to go, and on that journey the Catholic Church has to play, and in the person of the present pope has begun to play, a prominent role. But the little narratives of the victims of the grand process, the stories of what the big new world is squeezing out or ignoring, they will be told on the small scale, and full of details which the new world will dismiss as superficial and inessential. In terms of church structure, the little narratives will be told at diocesan, parochial, or base-community level.

This lesson can be applied to the other areas which to Post-Modernist thinkers seem areas of disintegration. The collapse of an image of the self which was the counterpart to the nineteenth century ideology of the nation-state is for Catholics either stale or positively good news. On the one hand we have always believed that our identity is bound up with that of all other human beings, that we have all sinned in Adam and been redeemed in Christ—and not by the coincidence of a myriad individual choices, but collectively—and on the other hand we have always believed that our life is hid with Christ in God and that our temporary personal self-awareness may be a very poor guide to the state of our soul. In the future therefore I look forward on the one hand to a strengthening of our awareness of global responsibility—of the extent to which we are made up by structures relating us to millions of people we have never met—and so of the need to make individual choices in the context of a global ethic. That will not be a matter just of decisions to boycott

Nestles, to become a vegetarian, or to subscribe to the Catholic Fund for Overseas Development. We may see, I hope we shall see, a new interest in Kant's principle that our personal moral life acquires content and purpose only insofar as it is directed towards the establishment of permanent international peace. On the other hand I expect there will be a revival of the doctrine of the soul, as something quite distinct from self-consciousness or the subject: the doctrine that our identity lies in the good things that we do, perhaps in the virtues that we acquire, something more akin to the notion of karma than of the ego.

And finally I expect that future generations of Catholics will see a great reconciliation with Protestantism. The theology of the spirit, which Hegel rightly saw as the distinctive new impetus which the Reformation gave to human development, the radical following-through of the belief that God speaks in and through us, has more work to do in the Catholic Church than further the charismatic revival. The work of Protestantization—that is the work of Reformation without schism—begun by the Council of Trent and continued by the Second Vatican Council, is not remotely complete yet. We may expect many more idols to fall, many more absolutes to pass away, as the Church takes on its global responsibilities and the accretions of the last 500 years are weighed and sifted. We shall learn to see God in the human world we have made for ourselves now, and not only in some past golden age—in the Christianity of the catacombs, or the Middle Ages, or the recusant period. But at the same time our Catholic belief that we are but creatures, and the creatures of a wholly unknowable God—a belief so firmly upheld by Thomas Aquinas—will I hope continue to safeguard us from self-worship and maintain us in the conviction that nothing we know in this world is ultimate—not the media of communication, nor the system of signs, nor even the end of history.

4 After the Empires
1789–1989

"Thus far consciousness has come" Hegel remarked in 1831, at the end of his lectures on the philosophy of world history,[1] casting those most penetrating of modern philosophical eyes on England, poised to enact the Reform Bill; on France, in the turbulent aftermath of the July Revolution; and on Germany, a loose confederation of semi-autonomous states, with an economic union and one or two central representative and administrative bodies established, and with so close a community of interests that the very notion of "state" was coming to seem inapplicable. If he also chose to see in the condition of Germany that which was most advanced in his present time and so most prophetic of the future, who are we—in a Europe which is a loose confederation of semi-autonomous states, with an economic union and one or two central representative administrative bodies established, and with so close a community of interests that the very notion of "state" is coming to seem inapplicable—to say his prophecy was wrong? Thus far consciousness has come. When at the beginning of the twentieth century the empires, having between them consumed the world, began to ride up against one another and then to crumble, there began to crumble with them the conception of collective and personal identity which they had fostered. In 1989, the year of revolutions, the imperial illusions finally expired, having just had time to celebrate their bicentenary. Haunted by such recent ghosts we find it as difficult now as it must have been in 1831 to distinguish the shadows of the past from the foreshadowings of the future. In what kind of a European home—a term which perhaps should be glossed as "orphanage," rather than anything cozier—have we been abandoned at the end of history, foundlings of the evaporated world-spirit?

In this essay I want to consider three different European traditions of national and personal identity—French, German, and British—in order to discern what is living and what is dead in the ideology which was born on 14 July 1789. What was the hidden relationship in the nineteenth century between the sense of nationhood, the sense of self, and the growth of the colonial empires which paved the way to the global market? Which are the still productive points of tension and contradiction which may now be expected to determine our common future?

France: Original Citizens and Original Sin

When in 1989 the European heads of government gathered in Paris to celebrate the deposition of their predecessors two centuries before, the British prime minister assured the French nation that there was nothing new about their Bastille Day or about the Declaration of the Rights of Man and of the Citizen which their National Assembly had promulgated shortly afterwards. She was, of course, wrong. The French Revolution *was* new. It is a common British illusion, not confined to former prime ministers, that the genuine but partial similarities between the English, American, and French Revolutions mean that the French event was not such a novelty after all. Therefore it is worthwhile to try to define what it is that from our perspective makes the French Revolution the beginning of something new, the beginning, namely, of us.

It is true that in some respects the Revolution of 1789 might seem to be a rather bungled attempt to import into France a British or American model. After the second French Revolution, the July Revolution of 1830, which in a sense concluded the process begun in 1789, it was a commonplace in the French press to compare France's progression towards constitutional monarchy with that of England in the seventeenth century.[2] The public execution of Louis

XVI was set in parallel to that of Charles I; Napoleon was set in parallel to Cromwell; the restored Louis XVIII to Charles II; the reactionary Charles X to James II; and the July Revolution was seen as France's Glorious Revolution of 1688 ushering in what it was hoped (on the whole rightly) would be a period in which the rule of an increasingly prosperous upper middle class would be decently disguised by a politically unambitious monarchy. Moreover, if we turn the clock back forty years we find among the earliest revolutionaries many who, brought up on the political Anglophilia of Voltaire and Montesquieu, prescribed an Anglo-American remedy for France's ills: decentralization; a separation of the powers of legislature, executive and judiciary; a system of checks and balances; a bicameral assembly; a royal right of veto; a form of "habeas corpus"; a free press; and, of course, free trade. Even after the slide into republicanism had begun, the rich merchants of the eastern ports round the Gironde who gave their name to the most dynamic faction among the revolutionary politicians, but who came with a familiar irony to be dismissed—and worse—as conservatives, pursued an economic and social policy modeled on that of their British colleagues and competitors across the seas. The king was already executed when in February 1793 the National Convention, still dominated by the Girondins, voted unanimously against the introduction of price controls, and a month later the death-penalty was decreed for any one who proposed a general redistribution of property and land.

However, to endorse the view of the Girondins, and Mrs. Thatcher, that the novelty they had to offer was simply the introduction of ideas and practices already familiar in Britain and America would be to give credence to the Marxist dogma that the initial stages of the French Revolution were simply a revolt of the capitalists against feudalism—and from that dogma at least we may hope the collapse of state-sponsored Marxist history has liberated us. Hegel, in his lectures on the philosophy of world history, saw clearly what Marx did not: that in the actual course of European historical development the immediate and effective enemy of the feudal order was not the bourgeoisie but the monarchy. European history of the sixteenth, seventeenth, and early eighteenth centuries shows us medieval feudal society being displaced not by omnipotent capitalists but by absolute or would-be absolute princes. Insofar as the French

Revolution was the violent attempt to modernize a feudal state it was a revolution with monarchical tendencies: these could draw on France's own native tradition—the centralizing reforms of Louis XIV—but they also had a prestigious external model in Enlightened Prussia, which we tend to forget was regarded by many at the time as Europe's most advanced—as it was certainly Europe's most artificial—state.

The great Prussian legal reform of 1791–93, the establishment of a uniform legal code (the *Allgemeines Gesetzbuch*, later known as the *Allgemeines Landrecht*), was seen by contemporaries as an achievement comparable with the work of the French Constituent Assembly. Like the frequently heard German claim at this time that the French revolutionaries were simply catching up on the work already done over the last half-century in the Enlightened Protestant or crypto-Protestant despotisms east of the Rhine, this view should not be dismissed as grotesquely unrealistic. The fact is that a great deal of what was done in France in the wake of 1789 looks more like the establishment of an enlightened monarchy than the access to power of liberal capitalism. During the 1790s the importance of the French military and of its associated industries increased enormously, while the prosperity of the big towns and the significance of overseas trade correspondingly declined. The organization of the professions was brought under state control and state officialdom sharply increased; the central administration grew from 700 to 6,000 in 1794, while in the country at large over the same period the number of officials rose from 50,000 to a quarter of a million.[3] These were steps along a path already well trodden by the absolutist rulers of Germany and Austria, as were the rationalization of local government, the codification of law, the abolition of guilds and internal customs barriers, the introduction of a new system of mensuration, and above all the secularization of ecclesiastical property, the breaking of the temporal power of the Church, and the assumption by the state of control over clerical appointments. All of these were measures decreed by the Constituent Assembly while France still had a king. Despite the Marxist theory of an aberration, decline, or betrayal of the revolution, there was no discontinuity with the original revolutionary impulse when at the end of the 1790s France gave itself in Napoleon Bonaparte a monarch no less enlightened and certainly no less despotic than Frederick the Great.

Whatever newspaper editors might have told themselves in 1830, the Napoleonic monarchical system has left its indelible imprint on France, as on Europe, quite as much as the liberal aspirations of the Girondin capitalists (a term which needs to be rescued from the Marxists and given its proper sense of "owners of significant amounts of private capital"). The uniqueness of the French Revolution is that in the context of a nascent mass-society and a proto-industrial economy *two* revolutions occur simultaneously, both of which are essential to the modern European (and now worldwide) form of socio-political life: the establishment in the economic realm of unrestricted individualism and in the political realm of a centralized and unchallenged bureaucratic power structure. We are probably brought up to think that a liberal, let us call it Anglo-American, model of the state, and an absolutist, let us call it Prussian, model are mutually exclusive. Yet the modern European state is neither simply the minimal framework for a nation of free-trading capitalists nor simply a totally unified rational administrative structure—it is rather a fusion of both: both capitalist and dirigiste, both democratic and monarchical (or, as we prefer to say these days, presidential). The fusion of these two models first occurred in what was at the time Europe's largest and most powerful single state, in France in 1789.

Admittedly, the richest five percent or so of the world's population currently think otherwise. For them the eighteenth-century revolution that counts is the British-American planters' declaration of secession in 1776, their historically more remarkable constitution of themselves into a nation by unanimous agreement on a written form of words in 1787, and their less felicitous attempt to append a Bill of Rights to their constitution through a series of amendments which began their passage into law in the autumn of 1789, shortly after the French Declaration. Yet the American example has not on the whole inspired the world's revolutionaries as the French example has done (it was invoked most recently by the white supremacists of Zimbabwe)—perhaps because the American Revolution took place in a pre-industrial, pastoral, and resolutely slave-owning society, with no ambition to overturn the local ruling class, and so was hardly a revolution at all. As a result it was accompanied by surprisingly little reflection on the nature of a modern state, that is, on the necessary mutual accommodation of the economic and political forms of human collective life. In America that reflection was a task for the nineteenth and twentieth centuries, and it is by no means completed even now. If the task continues to be very difficult, that is because of the great strength of what we may call the Jeffersonian strand in the thinking of the eighteenth-century separatists.

Jefferson was a shallow and self-satisfied thinker, obsessed with gadgets, mechanical or institutional, who favored, for example, the castration of sodomites, who proposed to solve the problem of slavery within a generation by separating all slave offspring from their parents at an age when they still represented no significant investment for their owners and deporting them to Hispaniola, and who opined that "the dead are not even things."[4] "Governments," he wrote in the Declaration of Independence, are instituted among men in order to "secure . . . rights"—a proposition which, as history, is certainly erroneous and, as theory, is at least not as self-evident as the Declaration asserts. Jefferson was cool towards the constitution of 1787, the true foundation of American nationhood, but passionate for a Bill of Rights, which "is what the people are entitled to against every government on earth."[5] In the Jeffersonian tradition there is no sense that who we are is to a great extent defined by the collectivity to which we belong, by the community in which we not only consume—that is, enjoy our property—but also produce—that is, work—and of which our forebears and descendants are more than honorary members. For Jefferson we are simply "men" possessed of—or, more sanctimoniously, endowed by our creator with—certain "rights"; collectively we make up only an undifferentiated but (very important, this) countable mass known as "the people"; and the "people," whose "majority" opinion is decisive, are seen as permanently distinct from the "government" and in no sense identical with it. Government is either our policeman or our enemy, absolutely coercive and effective in the areas proper to it, or to be peremptorily abolished when it exceeds them.

There are clear affinities between Jefferson's ideas and those of Bentham and, in our own day, the movement for Political Correctness. In each case humanity is understood as composed in the last analysis of distinct countable units, whether "men" or "persons," and government is thought of as a mechanism charged with securing the "good," or the "rights," of these units. The assertion that "I am left-handed," for example, is thought to define me more nearly, and to say more about me, than the assertion that "I am a citizen of the United States." For the first establishes what is held to be a right (not to be discriminated against by the right-handed), while the second is not the source of a right, but conditional on the (non-)exercise of one (namely "the natural right," according to Jefferson, "of expatriating [one]self"[6]). In each case, too, anarchism coexists disturbingly with authoritarianism, indeed Political Correctness, which appeals both to Right and Left, may be seen as a native American form of fascism. (Jefferson himself prescribed the texts from which political science should be taught in the University of Charlottesville, and forbade recourse to dissenting authors.[7]) But Jefferson's Republicanism—his belief in "a wise and frugal Government which shall restrain men from injuring one another, shall leave them otherwise free to regulate their own pursuits of industry and improvement, and shall not take from the mouth of labor the bread it has earned"[8]—was no more adequate to the task of building a modern nation than his belief in the moral superiority of agriculture to manufacture or his hostility to any proposal for a national bank. Even before his death his party had adopted most of the positions of his opponent John Adams and his Federalists. Jeffersonianism is powerful today precisely *not* because of any contribution it may make towards understanding the national political structures of which it has always been suspicious, but because of its internationalism—its vision of "men" as free-floating entities, joining and leaving states as they please, taking their natural rights with them, of commerce as a surer means to peace than arms, and of a fundamental contradiction between the individual with his rights and property and the government with its permanent temptation to rob him of both.

But contradiction can be creative too. That insight was kept from Jefferson and his American contemporaries by the relative simplicity and transparency of their circumstances, but it became the foundation of the political philosophy of Hegel, as he pondered the complexities of the French Revolution, in which the modern European state was born. Economic liberalism and political absolutism are the twin supports of the European state in its mature form precisely because they are in such profound conflict. Like two beams leaning against each other they stand up because they are straining in opposite directions. At the heart of Europe's most advanced states—and so at the heart of the identity of their members—lies such a creative contradiction: the contradiction between the ambitions of the modern state to absolute control of all its members and its simultaneous need to give, or appear to give, them maximum freedom of economic activity. Throughout the imperialist phase of European development these contradictory forces were kept in equilibrium in a historically distinctive structure: the nation-state with an attached empire. That, contradictory though they are, political absolutism and economic liberalism can co-exist, and indeed must co-exist if a nation-state is to come into being is shown both positively by the example of France, in which, as we have seen, both forces set off their own revolutions simultaneously; and negatively by the examples of Germany and Britain, in both of which one or other of the revolutions was considerably delayed. In France there may not, before 1789, have been as much economic and constitutional liberty as in Britain, nor as much Enlightenment, or as much despotism, as in Prussia, but it was here that the first and typical equilibrium between the two was established. The conceptual device which above all others secured this equilibrium was a redefinition of the identity of the members of the new nation-state—their redefinition as "citizens." Unlike the human being, whose rights were also declared by the National Assembly on 26 August 1789, the citizen is an individual who is also a member of a specific collective, such a collective being denominated in that same declaration of 26 August, a "nation." The nation, as it appears in the Declaration of the Rights of Man and of the Citizen,[9] is clearly a rational absolutist—or, as we now say, totalitarian—structure modeled on the theory—there is little point in arguing about the practice—of eighteenth-century enlightened despotisms: no individual and no corporation, we are told in Article III, exercises any authority, i.e., may lay effective claim to any rights, except by the sanction of the single central power, here called the will of the nation but otherwise known to eighteenth-century theory as the state or the general good. The drafters of this and similar provisions in the Declaration were indeed simply expressing their desire to bring a still largely feudal France into the age of absolute monarchy, when central bureaucracies exerted themselves to extinguish the competing claims to authority of guilds, professions, local corporations, courts and councils, and of course churches. All are to be subject to a single will.

The individual, however—and this is where the uniqueness and primacy of the French revolutionary model emerges—is not defined by the Declaration *simply* as a contributor, through the political process, to the determination of that national will. There is also another quite separate and indeed principal source of individuality formulated by this document. The Declaration defines the individual "man" as the owner, first, of a body, second, of capital, and third of religious views, none of which may be expropriated or trespassed upon even by the general will except in explicitly defined circumstances. The principle of the rule of law—with which much of the Declaration is concerned—is precisely the principle that those circumstances shall be explicitly defined. (This, as we may call it, quintessentially bourgeois ideology was also shared by the Victorian Samuel Butler who once said that the three most important things for a man are: firstly, his private parts; secondly, his money; and thirdly, his religious opinions.) This aboriginal owner, or "man"—so we must read the Declaration of 26 August—enters into the political association that is the "nation," and thereby becomes a citizen. Two months later the entrance qualifications were more exactly stipulated when it became necessary to define the citizens not just theoretically but for practical purposes—the practical purpose of deciding who was to be allowed to vote, and so contribute to forming the general will. Notoriously, "citizens" were divided into "active" and "passive" and the franchise restricted to the former. What the Declaration really meant by a "man" born free and equal therefore was—so France now learned—a male over the age of twenty-five and with enough property to pay taxes equivalent to three days earnings of a laborer. So, to be a free individual, for the National Assembly, meant to be a free economic unit.

The concept of "citizen" therefore conflates two identities for those to whom it applies. There is what one might call the conscious identity of beings who determine their relations to one another by explicit mutual agreement and in articulated rational principles—the identity belonging to a co-responsible member of an Enlightened, total state; and there is the pre-conscious identity, the identity prior to explicit political association, of economic units, endowed for no determinable reason, and before their entry into association, with gender, capital, and probably religious views as well—a non-rational identity, therefore, deriving from a concealed order whose rules the makers of Enlightened constitutions cannot grasp but which all can recognize as prevailing in large parts of contemporary European and American society.

Before I leave the French example I should like to consider two further points about this concept of the citizen: first, why the two forces which it brings into equilibrium need to be understood as in conflict; second, why the occurrence of the term "nation" in the Declaration of the Rights of Man and of the Citizen should *not* lead us to assume that this document is the beginning of the most modern—perhaps we should say, the post-modern—form of ethnic nationalism. These two points are closely interrelated and they will lead us on to consider the example of Germany.

First, then, why should the bourgeois, liberal, capitalist strand in the French Revolution be seen as in conflict with the Enlightened, absolutist, dirigiste, strand? An initial answer might simply be an appeal to the facts—the conflict is patent in the embarrassing compromise between economic fact and political principle which is the distinction between active and passive citizens, or in such paradoxes of the Revolution's development as that the Girondins were able to sweep away the king, his court and his officers but could not advance a new-style centimeter towards their principal goal—a decentralization of authority and a reduction in the importance of Paris. But we need to look a little more deeply.

It is not simply obscurantism to associate the rationalist Enlightened state with the conscious mind and the world of economic interests (and for that matter of sexual difference) with unconscious factors. The truth is that money is the most extraordinarily subtle and accurate invention for defining what people really want—by contrast with what they say they want—and for expressing those wants in terms of other people's wants, even though the other people may be completely unknown to one and stand in no explicit political relation to one. Money is the visible expression of all the social relations of which we are unconscious. The last decade has shown that no realistic theory of economic activity can overlook the importance of money, whatever conclusions quarreling economists may draw from that. Max Weber was surely right to say that the true revolution was not the invention of a "capitalist" mode of production, but the invention of a means of defining capital itself. The banking and accounting revolution of the early Renaissance made possible the translation of all relationships into monetary terms, their analysis into unitary transactions and their measurement against one another. Dante felt himself in the presence of a power destructive of the entire natural and divine order he was celebrating when he met with the autonomous power of money. Accordingly, he punished the usurers in close association with the sodomites and with the subverters of natural language,[10] but for better or for worse we are the inheritors of those usurers. Money as it has developed since Dante's time is the first and so far the only utterly successful universal language, expressing in terms everyone can recognize truths no one can fathom. What do I know of the bankers who lend capital to the shopkeeper who supplies groceries to the laborer who cuts the bananas which end up on Cambridge market for me to buy? What explicit administrative and political structures apart from the money system itself accommodate all those links in the endless chain of economic interrelationship? Yet the connection between me and the remoter links in that chain, links of whose very existence I am unaware, is as real and solid as the conviction of each and every member of the chain that what he or she wants is worth paying a certain, precise, amount of money for. In economic life we very soon run up against the paradox that, although the system is made up of nothing but people's conscious choices to buy and sell, no one person's consciousness does or possibly can comprehend the system as a whole. An invisible hand regulates prices even against our will and no one can say whose arm it is attached to, for it is the arm of everyone, including those against whose will it seems at the time to be operating.

If our individuality then is defined as that of free units in the economic system, links in the economic chain, there will always be something about ourselves that is opaque to us. We will not know quite where we come from nor what all the consequences of our choices are—just as we do not really know where our money comes from nor what it does when we spend it in a particular way—and yet our origins and the consequences of our acts are events and choices in the minds of other people exactly like ourselves: there is no person or factor inside or outside the system controlling it and keeping its secret from us. There is evidently, I think, a serious incompatibility between the identity possessed by such self-alienated and seemingly arbitrary and irrational individualities as the free *economic* units which are "men," as the Declaration of 26 August defines them, and the identity which would be possessed by *political* units operating the political system the Declaration imagines: one in which everybody's decisions are perfectly their own and perfectly clear to them and to everyone else, and are digested through perfectly transparent institutions to emerge as the general will expressed in completely explicit and rational laws. The compromise between these two incompatibles is as we have seen the identity of the citizen—a compromise whose nature becomes evident when the citizen is subsequently divided into active and passive. Compromises are transient—like life, for whose sake they are undertaken. The forces they bring into balance, however, do not go away. Human beings as free economic units, as what the Declaration calls "men," remain incompatible with the political structure into which the Declaration wishes to insert them, the structure which is there called a "nation"—even when nation-states and the empires associated with them have passed into oblivion.

This is the second and concluding point of the French example. The aboriginal owner brings into the pristine nation-state an aboriginal sin—internationalism. To liberal, capitalist, Jeffersonian, bourgeois "man" there is nothing sacrosanct about nationhood. As masters of our own money, our loyalty is to the market in which we buy and sell, not to the political construct whose general will is to impose restrictive practices on our economic behavior, forcing us, for the national good, to buy British rather than cheap. To the true free trader national identity is a meaningless obstruction to the flow of capital. The economic chain is intrinsically international and, as commerce flowers, nation states, the capitalist hopes—must hope—will wither away.

It is not I think true therefore that the most modern ethnic nationalism has its roots in the French Revolution. The term 'bourgeois nationalism', much used in relation to the new states, especially the smaller states, of new Europe, is a contradiction in terms, proceeding from a serious confusion of thought. The bourgeoisie—meaning by that term either the class of the population which lives, or that aspect of the population under which it all lives, from capital and by commerce—is essentially internationalist. Its historical archetypes are the ruling classes of the free ports and free cities of medieval Europe; its modern embodiments are not individuals at all but multi- and international corporations for whom national differences of currency, tariffs, taxation, legal regimes, and so on are an inconvenience and war between nations a disaster. France in 1789 had a bourgeoisie perhaps four million strong. It played a leading role in the early stages of the Revolution, and after being forced into subordination to the central state power by the wars of the later Revolutionary and Napoleonic periods, it re-emerged definitively as politically coequal in the July Revolution of 1830. The distinctive characteristic of the bourgeoisie—its possession of private property—is incorporated in articles 2 and 17 of the Declaration as one of the rights of man and of the citizen. Indeed in the revision of the Declaration in 1793 property was further defined as "goods, capital, income and labor" though a second revision, after the purge of the Girondins, dropped the reference to "capital."

Insofar as he is bourgeois, though, the citizen of the new nation cannot identify himself exclusively with the cause of the political nation's survival or expansion. He is part of a wider community, to which he is committed by the *economic* role assigned him by his definition as a citizen. An exclusive nationalism, which ignores or spurns the wider world, which is internally authoritarian and externally expansionist or even belligerent, is possible only where those who call themselves a nation do *not* include a powerful, bourgeois faction and do *not* make the individual's right to remain in irrational possession of body, mind, and money part of the founding articles of their political association. Do the newly independent states along the Baltic and in the Caucasus, where nationalism and authoritarianism seem likely to be most virulent, have an extensive bourgeoisie? They do not, and indeed do not seem to want one. What they do have, however, as the vehicle of nationalist sentiment, is a class of academics and officials, and it is with this insight that we may transfer from the French to the German example.

Germany: Officials and Nationalists

In 1789 the German states did not have—and Prussia certainly did not have—an extensive or wealthy bourgeoisie. There was efficiency, education, and an absence of the extremes of poverty and corruption to be found in France, but capital was largely in the hands of the state and the higher nobility, most of the population was engaged in subsistence farming and the number of free economic units—what the Declaration of 26 August called "men"—was small indeed. This is the fundamental reason why the French Revolution could not be repeated in Germany—not at any rate in the late eighteenth or early nineteenth century. In the absence of a bourgeoisie there could not be that revolutionary compromise by which a citizen was defined as both a free economic unit and a rationally self-determining political agent. Half of one side of the equation was not there. As a result Germany did not then—nor for nearly another hundred years—become a nation-state. Germany of course had its intellectuals, whose opinions might be revolutionary, but they were rarely men of independent means. The overwhelming majority were salaried officials of the state, among whom must be included university professors and, in the Protestant states, the clergy. When they took up the ideals of the Revolution, therefore, it was with an immediate sympathy for its Enlightened and absolutist tendencies—witness Professor Fichte's treatise on *The Closed Mercantile State*—but with no appreciation of the solidly irrational self-interest of the international class of the economically active which had given the Revolution its impetus in practice.

For those who wished Germany to become a nation as defined in the Declaration of 1789, the place of the bourgeois sense that one is individuated by one's status as a free economic unit was taken by the belief that one has one's identity from the "Volk" or "race" into which one is born. Racial theory and racialist practice are not, as Marxists used to claim, an inevitable outgrowth of bourgeois "capitalism"—on the contrary, they are the symptom of a failure to develop towards the bourgeois model of economic individuation.

Because so many of the manifestations of a racially based nationalism are those of a collective insanity, it is important to emphasize that ethnic nationalism—odd though this may sound—defines *not* a collectivity but individuality. It is the nation that always turns out to be difficult to define, not the nationals. Nationhood is not in the end a matter of geographical boundaries—as the example of Armenia shows—nor of the maintenance of particular constitutional arrangements such as a monarchy or a republic. Nationhood is a matter of the characteristics of the human individuals who are held to make up the nation: who their parents or grandparents were, where they were born, what language they spoke in childhood, what culture they were brought up with. Nationality is therefore essentially a substitute for bourgeois individuality and nationalism is a likely product of the attitudes of those who come from an absolutist state, and would like to attain one of the forms of the modern state, but who are not individuated in the capitalist manner as free economic units.

Take for example the case of two of the earliest German nationalists: Georg Rebmann and Josef Görres both of them ardent supporters of the Revolution. They came to Paris at the ages of twenty-eight and twenty-three in 1793 and 1799 respectively. What they saw of France under the Directory and after Napoleon's coup d'état of 18 brumaire caused both of them to oppose fervently the plans for the annexation by France of the left bank of the Rhine. They both were impressed by a feeling of the alienness of French culture while they were in Paris. In writing about this experience Görres elaborated a distinction between French and German national character on which he based his argument for their political incompatibility.[11] As the early ideals of the Revolution faded so it seemed to Görres that the French had detached themselves from other nations and the "cosmopolitan bond," linking the like-minded in France and Germany, was gone. Görres presents the growth of his awareness of his own German nationality as a reaction to a growing nationalism of the French. In fact, in the light of what we have so far seen, it is surely clear that his sense of alienation and of the differentness of the German national character derives from the impossibility of reproducing in a German context the capitalist, rather than the absolutist, element in the Revolution. And indeed twenty years later Görres publicly acknowledged that the different standing of the Third Estate in France and Germany made any straightforward equation of political attitudes in the two countries impossible.[12]

But the most striking feature of the conversions of Görres and Rebmann to an early form of ethnic nationalism is the personal isolation in which the change took place—in both cases it was the fruit, not of an experience of collective identity and enthusiasm, but of the solitude of the alien in a relatively wealthy and by German standards overwhelmingly populous foreign metropolis. Görres and Rebmann were both decent and moral, indeed moralistic, men, but readers of *Mein Kampf* will know that a similarly lonely sojourn on the Skid Row of Vienna could give birth, in the mind of a man who was neither decent nor moral, to one of the most poisonous forms of nationalism the world has ever known. Unable to find his pre-rational and pre-social identity as a free unit in the economic system, the nationalist seeks his identity instead in the decree of blood and tradition: but whereas the identity of the bourgeois emerges from a real social relationship, albeit one guided by a rationally and politically invisible hand, the identity of the ethnic nationalist is arbitrary and rationally opaque because it is rooted in individual fantasy and the solitude of alienation.

By 1918 Germany had finally acquired a bourgeoisie which both controlled the economic power of the nation and was prepared to give itself a rational political constitution. However by that time the global system was in place and the incipient German Empire was one of its first victims. Metropolitan Germany was plunged into a revolutionary process which ended in 1949 with the emergence not of a modern nation-state, but of the world's first post-modern polity. Nationalism (in any matters more important than sports matches and the Eurovision song contest) ceased to be a significant factor in the sense of identity of those from the Western German territories who now called themselves not "Germans" but "Bundesbürger"—"Federal citizens." The details and implications of this process in Germany will concern us later in this book. For the present we turn to its British version—more genteel, less catastrophic.

Britain: Identity and Empire

The history of Germany between 1789 and 1949 shows us what a partially modern state looks like, in which absolutist political structures combine with a sense of individual identity deriving from nationality rather than economics. The case of Britain, in the same period, shows us what a partially modern state looks like which has the symmetrically opposite defect: a sense of economic identity among individuals, combined with political structures from the pre-modern era.

With the possible exception of Holland, Britain had the longest and most firmly established self-governing bourgeoisie in Europe. The capitalist class achieved this dominance however at a very early stage—well before there was any question of a British industrial mass-society, such as the Parisian melting-pot provided in late-eighteenth–century France—and Britain did not go through the complementary process of establishing a rational, enlightened, absolutist state structure which began in Germany in the early eighteenth century and in France in 1789. Perhaps for this very reason Britain proved during the nineteenth century increasingly unable to harness to its national needs the industrial and technological revolution which it had initiated and in the second half of the century Britain was already manifestly less modern than the late-comer Germany not only in industrial organization and production but also in education and social welfare. Only in our lifetimes—and particularly in the last fifteen years—has Britain seen a truly revolutionary centralization of administration and elimination of all intermediate bodies between the individual and the state apparatus, a sweeping away of the remains of the medieval and feudal order which for a century and a half had been the substance, the charm and the oddity of the British sense of identity.

In 1945, when Germany, for the second time in the century, was looking into the abyss of post-modernity, Britain was in many respects a pre-revolutionary society, the last in Europe. Thanks to the political and economic protection afforded by an encircling empire, acquired early, Britain had survived with its medieval institutions adapted but largely intact. Britons were still not citizens of a state, but subjects of a monarch, a hereditary class still exercised significant political power, the church retained many features of its medieval predecessor, as did other ecclesiastical successor bodies, such as colleges and schools whose inhabitants, like those of prisons, were still regularly flogged. Barristers still ate their way to learning at inns of court and livery companies still administered vast fortunes on behalf of the supposed descendants of fifteenth-century tradesmen. The continuing corporate autonomy of these medieval models had also molded the great nineteenth-century institutional creations: the reformed civil service and universities, the professional organizations, the trade union successors to the old guilds, the county councils, the clubs. Only in the late twentieth century have British institutions learned what it felt like to be secularized by Joseph II or to receive a visit from the roving commissars of the French National Convention. Now the sectional peculiarities and privileges, insofar as they survive, no longer contribute to a collective self-esteem but are the object of impatience and resentment and are passing away forever. We are told, as the Girondins believed, that we are all bourgeois and being made more so—but as in 1789 that is only half the truth, and so not the truth at all. As in 1789, the freedom of the property-owing economic unit, also called "man" (as in "human rights") is invoked to sanction the construction of a centralized and would-be omnipotent state. But this is not the place to go into the ideological and propagandist sleights of hand by which our central administration seeks to conceal from us, and no doubt also from itself, the truth about what it is doing.

In one fundamental respect, however, the present state of Britain, as of Europe, cannot be compared to that of Revolutionary France. It is also the most fundamental reason why national identity has to cease to be a significant category in European politics. The economic order which provided the pre-social and pre-political identity of the citizen in the Declaration of 1789, which gave him a primordial liberty which was not lost but protected by political association—that order has changed. It was open, but it is now closed. There was once room in it for empires, but there is now a single global system. And because there is now a single global system the era has passed, not only of the nation-states, but of the bourgeois class whose defining economic loyalties used to transcend national boundaries and so created the global system in the first place.

The supremely uninhibited expression of the fundamental rights and liberties of *Homo economicus* is probably in Articles 17–20 of the Girondin redrafting of the 1789 Declaration, undertaken in April 1793: there we learn that not merely is it a fundamental right of every man to dispose at his own pleasure of his capital, but that "no form of work, of cultivation, or of commerce may be forbidden him; he may manufacture, sell and distribute products of every kind." The human race was thus recast in the image of a Bordeaux merchant. But have we not also in our own time and place been told to see every human being as a capitalist, with the right, no duty, to become an entrepreneur? There is however a manifest absurdity about the modern rhetoric lacking in that of the eighteenth century. In the eighteenth century there was still terra incognita in the economic world; there were still frontiers beyond which lay wide open spaces; there was still gold in the hills. Bourgeois freedom in nineteenth-century France and Britain could seem limitless ("Liberty consists in being able to do anything . . ." is the opening of Article 4 of the 1789 Declaration)—because the European economy was itself expanding outwards into a void, finding new markets and new resources as fast as its empires laid claim to new colonial territories.

In nineteenth-century Britain and France it seemed so persuasive to say that society was constructed by the free choice of its members because it *was* in a certain sense true that it was open to everyone to leave it—to expatriate yourself and go and try your luck in the colonies or set up your own religious community in America. Because it appeared that anyone *could* do anything, nineteenth-century novelists were fascinated by the way people actually were and what they actually did, for it seemed that in some primal sense it was their choice and not the product of some more powerful causative factor which in the last resort it would always be open to them to avoid by just going away. Mrs. Gamp chooses to be Mrs. Gamp and Mr. Dombey to be Mr. Dombey. It was an illusion of course: you did not leave the European economy by going to the colonies—that was why you could make your fortune there, the currency was convertible—but the dependence of Europe's economy and of a European sense of identity on colonial possessions fell under the regime of a kind of amnesia. It was part of that unconscious, pre-social, pre-political economic order which it is not open to the conscious mind to grasp. America in *Martin Chuzzlewit* is a nightmare, perceived largely through the hero's delirium, and the process by which life in Australia restores Mr. Micawber's fortunes remains unrepresented.

Nineteenth-century France and Britain saw themselves as societies which, by means of revolution or reform, had distributed to the whole of the people the privileges which in an earlier feudal era had been reserved to the nobility—every French citizen took part in the government of his nation, and every Englishman's home was his castle. And in a material sense too the increasing national wealth meant that at least the bourgeoisie enjoyed the comforts, hygiene, and on a suitably reduced scale the houses and gardens of the old aristocracy, and even their cultural pretensions, their conversation, and their leisure. But the belief that a fundamental change in social relations had occurred could be sustained only by a blindness to the shift in the boundaries of society: the bourgeoisie of metropolitan France and Britain might have taken over the privileges of the old aristocracy, but we can see that they had taken over its social and political function as well, once we take into account the forgotten colonies. For if the whole imperial economic structure were brought out into the bright light of constitutional day it would be clear that in the colonies a wholly disenfranchised third estate was still working for the benefit of a metropolitan aristocracy which, rich or poor, believed itself hereditarily, that is racially, entitled to the service.

That Europe and its empires made up a world-system (to use Wallerstein's term) became indisputably obvious towards the end of the nineteenth century. Already in 1848 Marx had seen that the industrial, commercial, and geographical expansion of Europe had logically to lead to the setting up of a global market, a "Weltmarkt." Twenty years later his prophecy was manifestly coming true. The opening of the Suez Canal in 1869 can be seen as a symbolic turning point. In the previous year feudal Japan had embarked on its extraordinarily rapid assimilation to Western models. In the following year the war began which united Germany into a fully industrialized empire. After the huge expansion of trade between Europe, America, and Asia between 1850 and 1880, a number of the fundamental conceptual steps were taken which show the international market taking on a truly global character: the agreement on a standard meridian, time measurement, and the International Date Line, the finalization of territorial boundaries over the land surface of the continents and their adjacent waters, the laying of submarine telegraph cables to set up the first system of instantaneous worldwide communication, and the building of transcontinental railway lines with traffic movements co-ordinated across many time-zones.[13] European populations were swelling as their economies industrialized, and the means had to be created for the disturbed, the displaced, and the ambitious to emigrate in vast numbers around the planet. But once the worldwide political system of empires was in position such movements of redundant producers became a zero-sum—no longer simply a benefit to the exporter, but a measurable cost to some other member of the system—and the political equilibrium of the metropolitan nation-states was threatened. In Britain, in the mid-nineteenth century, Manchester-school free-traders had been able to win their argument against Imperial Preference (and almost achieved the peaceful dissolution of the empire in the process) because the world was still open, and neither British industry nor the

British Empire had a serious challenger. Once the outlines of a global system became apparent to all, with the implied warning that resources were finite and confrontation was on its way, Britain, already seduced into a centralizing theory of empire by its fateful involvement with India, joined in the general slide into protectionism and the last frantic phase of colony-grabbing. The Washington conference of 1884, devoted to fixing the meridian, was followed in 1885 by the Berlin Conference, which carved up Africa. The global market threatened the sovereignty of the principal industrial nation-states—that is, it threatened to make the international economy, not the political will of national governments, the principal determinant of the life, wealth, and happiness of their populations—and they attempted to turn their empires into self-contained, autarchic, trading-blocks. The attempt resulted from a (quite understandable) failure of nerve: the task of finding a political structure to accommodate the relentlessly growing world economy was simply too great. From 1914 to 1989, however, the failure was avenged. Germany countered the British, French, and Russian stranglehold on world markets by developing a matching military and naval capability, with foreseeable results. The USA, pursuing to its logical conclusion the argument against Imperial Preference, twice intervened to defeat a German aspiration to protectionist hegemony, and exploited victory to hasten the dismantling of the nineteenth-century empires in the interests of its own traders. The Russian Empire nearly fell victim to this process between 1918 and 1922 but held itself together by its usual methods long enough to become the principal agent of Germany's second defeat, before succumbing to the pressures which had already disposed of its British and French rivals. Uncountable and unspeakable, the human cost was paid.

The destruction of the imperial order, begun with extreme violence in 1914, came seventy-five years later to an almost pianissimo conclusion. Earth's proud empires have passed away, and with them imperial preference. The greatest single barrier to free world trade, Comecon—in Germany it was literally a wall—has been breached by the rising tide of international capital. We now have a single global market and financial system, sustained by a global communications network, and with the dispersal of the manufacture of single items through many countries even something approaching a global industry. It is true that, as inheritors of the principles of 1789, we—

and our government—still see ourselves as intrinsically and primordially economic beings who enter into a rational political association still denominated a "nation." But free economic units in a single closed global system are a very different matter from free economic units in what appears to be a multiplicity of different systems—or "empires"—each with an indefinite potential for expansion. A nineteenth-century bourgeois identity could seem a mysterious freely self-choosing being, in a relation to society but not a mere aspect of it, because it floated above a bottomless ocean of unknown but presumably infinite economic possibility. Anyone had the right to be able to do anything. But the freedom we are encouraged to have today is the freedom merely to choose, as consumers, from whatever the market offers—while a veil is drawn over what is in a closed system the necessary symmetrical complement of this freedom: our enslavement, as producers, to the demands set us by the market, for the more choice we give ourselves as consumers the heavier the chains we forge for ourselves as workers. In the modern, post-revolutionary world there are no longer any pure consumers, there is no longer a leisured aristocracy—we are now virtually all consumers *and* producers, proletarians, who live by selling our labor.

The great secret therefore which we dare not breathe to ourselves—it would be unfair to blame our politicians, as if they did not say what we want to hear—is that in the post-imperial era the bourgeoisie is no more and the inheritance of the French Revolution is exhausted in the moment in which the British are catching up with it. The economic and political orders could be held together yet apart for as long as it was possible to attribute to "man" a pre-social identity as an aboriginal property-owner. In the age of the global system the economic and the political orders are collapsing into each other. The state concerns itself more and more with the regulation and auditing of economic activity. And economic activity becomes more and more conscious—a matter of rational and political scrutiny: we are more and more aware of the remoter links in the chain of which our own economic decisions are a part—we see better where we come from. We see on our television screens the slave labor on the plantations which grow our tea just as we see the forcible repatriation of Albanian and Vietnamese "economic migrants" so that they shall provide tomorrow's pool of low-waged assemblers of microchips and microwaves. Yet the illusion of a bourgeois existence and a bourgeois identity continues to be dangled before us as a lure. The proletarianization of the nation has even been called embourgeoisement. As small businesses disappear and the proportion of private investors in the stock market shrinks we are told we have become a nation of property-owners because more of us have mortgages which attach our incomes and prevent us from saving.

What is "the holiday"—arrangements for which have come to dominate the working year—but a temporary pretense that we are capitalists, an annual two-week saturnalia during which the waiters in the hotel are allowed to be its leisured guests? Is it not the same lure that we dangle before all the world to draw it on into the global system—"join us and you too can be the tourists, not the waiters," a modern version of the promise of citizenship in the mother country made by our nineteenth-century ancestors and models to their colonial dependents and no more likely to be honored. For the global system is closed not only in the sense that the players in the game are now known and numbered but also in the sense that the system has expanded to and is already constrained by the physical limits of the planet. Certain counters in the game are already numbered too, such as the supply of fresh water, the gene bank, and the ozone layer. It has wisely been said that the earth can certainly support a population of ten billion people but not of ten billion middle-class people.

So Francis Fukuyama was right to say the end of history had come in at least one of the Hegelian senses which that proposition might have: namely that the development of religious and personal identity is no longer dependent on the development of that form of political identity which is provided by the interaction of national states and empires, for the economic and political process is now global and singular. It has been so since the end of the nineteenth century, and it has manifestly been so since 1945. In 1989 the last piece fell into place. But Fukuyama was quite wrong to suggest that some kind of equilibrium has now been reached, that there are no contradictions remaining within the system, and that therefore national, religious and personal identity can be expected to remain indefinitely in what he calls the liberal democratic form. All we can say is what Hegel said—thus far consciousness has come—and there are at least four fundamental contradictions which can be expected to drive future internal change within the global system. Whether it would be right to call that change history is another and subsidiary matter.

1. A contradiction within the structure of obsolescent nation-states, particularly but not exclusively European:

    on the one hand the central government establishes ever closer control over economic activity, defining ever more activities as economic, and introducing ever more detailed and analytical accounting procedures for them;

    on the other hand the development of economic activity strengthens the international basis of economic life and the citizen's sense of a cosmopolitan identity, making the central organs of a merely national state increasingly irrelevant and burdensome.

2. A contradiction within the global system:

    on the one hand there is an ideal of freedom and personal identity which presupposes an open world in which anyone can do anything;

    on the other hand there is the reality of the freedom of market choice between the limited options offered by a closed system.

3. A contradiction between the global system and its physical basis:

    on the one hand the ambition the economic system gives to everyone to achieve a particular standard of living;

    on the other hand the physical inability of the planet to support ten billion bourgeois human beings—ten billion Bordeaux merchants.

4. A contradiction which mirrors all the preceding three in the lives and activity of each of us individually:

    that between ourselves as consumers and ourselves as producers within the same closed system.

It is of course up to us what we make of these contradictions. It is always up to consciousness, or "spirit," what it makes of itself. But in the clarity with which the all-embracing contradiction of our individual existence—as consumer-producers—is emerging now, at the turn of the times, there is great cause for hope. As we become more aware of our economic status as proletarians, as employees of the worldwide employer that is the global system, so our political status as world-citizens becomes clearer and more immediate to us also. With that, the survival and the strengthening of international and worldwide political institutions becomes our own more urgent concern. The bourgeois illusion of infinite economic freedom gave the privileged or "active" citizens of nation-states an impetus to disregard national boundaries which (insofar as it was not simply a product of the process) led to a form of internationalism, to imperialism, and the establishment of the world-market. But the notion that we are all pre-social, aboriginal owners with the world at our feet was an illusion, and its tendency to deceive was not innocent. The belief that one could always expand into new economic territory was the instrument for forgetting the hierarchy of economic relations established and protected within the political structure that was the nation with its attached empire. In a repetition of the process by which the bourgeoisie claimed in its day to be universalizing the privileges and "freedoms" of its predecessor, the feudal nobility, the decolonization movement of the twentieth century has led to a proliferation of what are called nation-states, which are held to enjoy a degree of autonomy that in historical reality only empires have ever possessed. The modern, illusory, "nation-state," with its voting rights at the UN, lacks both an empire and a bourgeoisie, and is therefore a fertile breeding-ground for ethnic nationalism, the most obviously destructive factor in the global system. But the economic interdependence of these political shells is increasingly apparent to their proletarianized populations. We recognize, like the Jeffersonian bourgeois of old, that as economic units we belong to a larger world than our local state, but because, unlike the bourgeois, we see ourselves in the first instance not as property-owners but as employed producers we are aware that that larger world is limited too and is not a realm of infinite freedom. Our economic identity lies not in ownership but in work, and we can work only in the system, not outside it. The system, true, is global, but it is also closed— constrained both physically and by our own demands as consumers. Recognizing ourselves as self-constraining consumer-producers we recognize not only our own finitude but that of the world we inhabit. There is one world and it is not endless and we have to work out among ourselves how we are to live in it together or we shall die in it separately.

Consciousness, having come far enough to recognize the contradictions, must work to resolve them. It is no resolution, however, to treat them as made up from incommensurable fragments, or "aporias," in any selection of which we can choose to live out whatever multi-faceted existence appeals to us. That Post-Modernist answer to the question of our identity overlooks the finite singularity of our physical and economic world. It treats our dilemmas as the arbitrary imposition of Fate rather than the consequences of our own desires and productive acts, retorted upon us by the system of exchange. Post-Modernism, particularly in the form Derrida has given to it, positively obscures from us our collective entry into the post-bourgeois era by continuing to hold out to us the illusion of infinite possibility—an infinity of possible ways of reading the text, whether of the human past or of our own lives. In doing so it makes itself an agent of the omnipresent forces of supply, which are permanently whispering to us that all our demands can be met and that the only true life is a holiday. For all its fearsome appearance of hermetic intellectuality, Post-Modernism—an ivy-like branching growth smothering the sharp outlines of our true situation—is a political movement which serves the interests of a particular class, and it has a political influence, especially through its support of various forms of "culturalism." The only morally defensible and conceptually consistent answer to the question "who are we now?" is "future citizens of the world," yet we are still far from being able to relate that answer to our local and regional responsibilities, whether in theory or in practice, individually or together. Too much in contemporary thinking is an obstacle to understanding that relation between the global and the particular in which the contradictions within the world-system are being played out, and in which our identity ultimately resides.

II
The Politics of Post-Modernism

5 Understanding Germany

Since the Reformation, Germany and the German-speaking world have provided some of the most powerful and influential ideas by means of which the European peoples have sought to understand themselves, after their detachment from the theology and anthropology of the medieval Church. That influence is scarcely diminished, even in the late twentieth century. Marx, Nietzsche, Freud, Wittgenstein, and Heidegger provide between them most of the conceptual ingredients for the Post-Modernist cocktail. German pre-eminence in the physical and chemical sciences and in the historical and philological disciplines had been little challenged for 150 years when it came to an abrupt end in 1933. For considerably longer still, German theology and its secularized successor, Idealist philosophy, have fed the faith and the doubts of the European and American Protestant clergy. Biblical criticism, now a worldwide institution, is still little more than an appendix to the foundational work done by German scholarly deists in the eighteenth and nineteenth centuries and shares their preconceptions.[1] Yet in the Anglo-Saxon countries, particularly Britain, in marked contrast to France, Italy, and Eastern Europe, an awareness of the extent to which the thoughts we think are German thoughts has largely been obliterated by the colossal political and military conflicts of the past century. These conflicts in turn, however, have themselves been interpreted from the standpoint of the nominal victors as the consequence of some peculiarity in the constitution of the vanquished, and not as the expression of crises within the international system to which both parties belong. The extent to which the story of Germany is part of our own story has thus been overlooked, its institutional and intellectual traditions have come to be treated as a local oddity, a subject for specialists. As a result that part of our own identity which has developed in constant interaction with Germany—the Church, the monarchy, the universities, schools, and civil service, the Victorian ethos and the idea of Empire, British socialism, British philosophy, British music—has become incomprehensible or inaccessible to us, assumed to be also a local oddity, another national (if more wholesome) tradition, rather than one band in the spectrum of possible ways of being European. In the children's compendium of knowledge which first introduced me to the wider world (first published in 1948) the section devoted to human geography amounted to eighty pages. The entire entry for Germany ran: "Hiding behind little Holland is the great country of Germany, where the people are a strange mixture of good and bad, with an unhappy knack of picking rulers who lead them to war against everyone else."[2] That sentence implied a quite false notion of what it was to be *British*.

The German contribution to European thought, both secular and religious, is neither alien nor marginal. Recovering the sense that it is *our* thought, and thought about *our* condition, is an essential part of that work of European unification which cannot be separated from the work of redefining national identities. No doubt the Idealist period in German philosophy owed its particular character to local circumstances, but Kant and Hegel between them created a synthesis out of all the most significant strands in the thought of post-Reformation Christendom, and until the latter years of the nineteenth century British and Americans could recognize their achievement. Economic rivalry between Britain and Germany intensified after 1870, imperial and naval rivalry after 1890, and Britain was swept by a tide of hostility to Germany, to the German immigrant community (then Britain's second largest, after the Irish), and to German culture. Bertrand Russell's conversion from Hegelianism to mathematical logic in 1898, an event which has influenced the course of Anglo-American philosophy down to the present day, signaled the changing mood.[3] The age was over which had begun with Prince Albert's hopes for a confluence of German and British traditions and was best represented by the liberal, Catholic, Anglo-German historian Lord Acton. After the First World War the disgraceful policy of repatriation—the expulsion to Germany of hundreds of families settled in Britain for two or three generations—eliminated any public German presence from the cultural life of the major English cities. This ethnic cleansing of the British intellect was not reversed by an influx of (not always welcome) émigrés from the Third Reich, many of whom had no desire whatever to act as ambassadors for a culture from which they were fortunate to have escaped with their lives.[4] Even nowadays, forty years after the Treaty of Rome, when "continental philosophy" has returned to glower across the academic committee-rooms at entrenched "Anglo-Saxon linguistic philosophy," "continental" probably means in the first instance "French." Yet it is not the chance vagaries of personal reading that made Sartre, Ricoeur, or Derrida into commentators on Hegel, Nietzsche, and Heidegger. If we are seriously concerned to understand our (post-)modern condition, these figures cannot be avoided. When Professor Eagleton makes a substantial contribution to literary theory he writes a book, *The Ideology of the Aesthetic*, almost entirely devoted to German thinkers. Yet he never raises the question (surely interesting?) why his subject, unmistakably a concern of the European, and global, mind, should be almost a German monopoly.

Germany and its philosophical and critical tradition are essential themes and contributors for the debate about Post-Modernism—but not simply because of the power and authority of German philosophers of the eighteenth and nineteenth centuries. Germany also entered the post-modern and post-bourgeois era a generation before the other industrialized European states. In the 1920s, stripped of empire and bourgeoisie, Germans were dropped into the world market and left to find an identity for themselves. Writers and thinkers—Heidegger foremost among them—responded with a burst of multifarious creativity which briefly made the Weimar Republic into the cultural focus of Europe. But the pluralist welter suddenly ran out into fascism and it became clear to the more decent intellectuals, such as Franz Werfel, that "we in our modest way first stoked up the fires of the hell in which mankind is now roasting."[5] After the collapse of the Cold War balance of power, the dilemmas of Weimar Germany have been revealed to be general. The need to compete in a world market is undermining social and political certainties everywhere. The most serious threat to world peace seems once again to come from violent sectarian ideologies. And once again it seems doubtful whether the intellectuals of Europe and North America can mount any counter-offensive or whether the Post-Modernists are not unwittingly collaborating with forces that will destroy them. Heidegger's thought of the post-war years only reiterates the themes he first enunciated in the 1920s and 1930s, but it therefore retains its perverse relevance. The decline of the Weimar intelligentsia into Fascism may be seen as the first case of the failure of a Post-Modernist movement to meet the political challenge of globalization. For that reason alone it would be worthwhile for us to start trying to understand Germany.

Some Illusions

The feelings of trepidation and resentment aroused in Britain in 1990 by the imminent unification of East and West Germany derived as much from the disturbance of illusions about ourselves as from any rational insight into the affairs of our most powerful and important neighbor. "Don't mention the War" was a good joke because it precisely identified a *British* obsession: since 1945 a mythologized version of the Second World War ("the War") has stood in as the vehicle of a national identity which neither the twilight of empire nor our ever shabbier political institutions, let alone our industries or our culture, could provide. Germany thus came to function as the counter-image that told us who we are. Yet the perception that the principal adversaries in "the War" were Britain and Germany is shared by no one outside Great Britain (and certainly not by Germans). Britain's part in the conflict was undoubtedly—in so far as such sweeping judgments are possible—an honorable one, and strategically at least as important as that of Serbia (whose resistance delayed Hitler's attack on the Soviet Union and so gave General Winter his chance). But the casualty figures tell their own story. The Second World War was the penultimate stage in an armed struggle for the inheritance of the British hegemony between America,

Germany, and Russia. That struggle began in 1914 and ended in 1989, nominally with an American victory but in fact with the exhaustion of all parties, and with a clear bid for the spoils from Japan. The British contribution to the Seventy Five Years' War was initially (in 1914–1918) significant, if subsidiary to that of France, but by the time of the Normandy landings in 1944 it had dwindled to a sideshow. Yet it is difficult to discard myths that have at some time been essential to one's survival. Alarmed by the prospect of a "reunification" it could no longer prevent, the British government organized for itself a seminar on Germany at Chequers, but later revelations about that seminar showed that even at the highest level at which in modern Britain the political and intellectual worlds can interact (and quite evidently not all of the seminar was conducted at that level) the subject of Germany is peculiarly beset by illusions. The very term "German reunification" is triply misleading.

First, the uniting of the Federal and Democratic Republics is far from being the whole of the issue. Unlike Bismarck's achievement in the years 1866–1871, with which at first sight it seems comparable, it is but one of the consequences of a much larger shift in world affairs: the disengagement of two super-powers whose military strength had polarized the loyalties of most other states, and the return to prominence of a unit older and politically and culturally more mature than either of them—Europe (Christendom, as it once was). To talk of the need to embed a united Germany in a united Europe is to treat as an imperative what is already a fact. The economic forces which made it too expensive for the Russian empire to continue to hold its tributaries in military subjection have already made the states of Western Europe too interdependent for them to be physically capable of waging against each other wars of national aggrandizement in the manner of more primitive nation-states, such as early twentieth-century Germany or contemporary Iraq. Equally, however, the agreeable notion must be resisted that popular revolution has brought down the dictatorships of Eastern Europe: the dictators fell, not because the people voted for capitalism or for union with the West, but because the Kremlin withdrew their cover. Why the Kremlin did so—why the revolutions were not suppressed as they had been before, and as they were in China—is too large a question to answer here, and it is not a part of the history of Poland, Bulgaria, Czechoslovakia, or East Germany either.

Second, as many in Germany pointed out, not least Willy Brandt, "re-unification" is a thoroughly misleading term for a process the end-result of which has been the establishment of a wholly new political unit, with frontiers which have no precedent in German history. Shorn of territories to the West and to the East, some of which had been German for longer than there have been English-speakers in Ireland, it is not a "re"-construction of the Reich of Bismarck, or of Hitler, or of any of their predecessors. It is an end to the pain of much personal separation, but it also has the excitement of a new political beginning.

Third, however, the unanimous conclusion of the Chequers seminar seems to me quite wrong: the Germans, we (some months later) were told, have changed. The forty years of the Federal Republic, economically the most successful and politically the most democratic state in Europe, show that Germans have put their past behind them and, whether or not they are still aggressive, angst-ridden, assertive, bossy, etc., they are not going to repeat the appallingly destructive imperialist adventurism of the first part of this century. That we need no more dispute than a similar proposition about the imperialism of Britain, France, or Belgium. But we can have surer grounds for hoping that the achievements of the Federal Republic are not going to be abandoned than some putative change in national character. Germany has not changed: rather, the particular circumstances of the Federal Republic have permitted the re-emergence of some of the most deeply rooted, and to an outsider most attractive, aspects of the German political and cultural tradition.

"Other" Germanys

The well-meaning friend of the Federal Republic may point us away from the Germany of Hitler and Goebbels, of Himmler and Eichmann, towards an "alternative" Germany, a "true" tradition—that of Bach and Beethoven, Goethe and Kant, and the failed coup of 24 July 1944. In the Nazi period itself, or its immediate aftermath, Curtius and Meinecke, Benn and Hesse did as much. There are, however, many Germanys and, alas, few can be called less "true" than the others. The traditions of the land of poets and thinkers are not so easily separated from the catastrophic political developments of the twentieth century—and not only because, if there is a line from Bach to Beethoven, it presumably carries on to include their self-proclaimed successor, Richard Wagner, while any line from Kant and Goethe presumably passes through Nietzsche and Heidegger too. There is also the fact that poets and thinkers are no alternative to effective politicians, and that to wash your hands of the whole dirty business of politics, as many German intellectuals have done since the eighteenth century, can in practice (and even in theory) mean no more than to collaborate. Washing your hands is after all a tradition inaugurated by Pontius Pilate.

For a similar reason, it will not do, as some revisionist historians have recently proposed, to see the Second German Empire of 1866 to 1918 as just another bourgeois nation-state like England or France at the time, with its own form of parliamentary democracy (including Europe's largest and oldest surviving socialist party), and with markedly better social security and technical education than prevailed further west (the "aberrancy" in German history being thus limited to the period 1918–1945). If it were true that the united Germany of the 1990s is returning to the institutions and attitudes (as it is certainly not returning to the boundaries) of Bismarck's Reich, the other nations of Europe would have grounds for apprehension. Late nineteenth-century Germany differed from its Western neighbors not only in the pervasiveness and explicitness of its militarization, but also in the very cultural attitudes and social structures which enfeebled the opposition to Hitler: the subordination of the industrially and commercially active bourgeoisie to the officer class, and through them to the land-owning, and in some cases still juridically sovereign, nobility; the cultural prominence of civil servants; the consequential tendency to envisage the nation as held together by a unified command structure, rather than by the shared loyalties of otherwise competing, or simply differing, interests; and the increasingly articulate dissociation of Christianity (especially, as the *Kulturkampf* showed, of Catholic Christianity) from the understanding of what it was to be modern, and to be German.

We must tap a deeper vein in German history if we are to identify what has made West Germany after 1945 so different: we must go back well before 1933, before 1866, even before 1648 and the end of the Thirty Years' War. Since the later Middle Ages, in fact, Germany has been, in the literal sense of the word, one of the most civilized of nations: a nation of cities. Visiting England in 1710, two Frankfurt noblemen commented on what seemed to them the extraordinary lack of cities: what called themselves such were simply unusually sprawling villages. The absence of physical walls meant an absence of mental and social cohesion, of local identity. The German towns, the great financial and artisanal centers, whether Free Cities or not, from Nuremberg and Augsburg to Ulm and Strasbourg, the Hanseatic towns and the commercial (and later publishing) centers of Frankfurt and Leipzig, had their heyday in the fifteenth and sixteenth centuries—though some of their characteristic attitudes survived much longer in the Low Countries and Switzerland, after they had gone into decline in Germany itself. If there is an alternative German culture it is here: in the world of Dürer and Riemenschneider, Erasmus and Eck, Sebastian Brant, Hans Sachs, and—one of its last representatives—the seventeenth-century realistic novelist Grimmelshausen. City culture was by definition a middle-class ("bourgeois") affair: the product of citizens who were their own masters organizing things for themselves, often after protracted disagreements. Money talked, but it was evident that there was a public realm—comprising, for example, building standards, or the training of apprentices, or the proprieties of dress—that should not be subject solely to the interests of individual profit. The constitutional privileges guaranteeing local autonomy were jealously defended—"particularism" this decentralized patriotism would be branded by the propaganda of nineteenth-century nationalism. But trade was too important for local pride to become exclusive or introspective: to the North there was Britain and the Baltic, to the South the cities of Italy, to the West Flanders and the textile industry, to the East the spice and silk routes. Autonomy was possible only within interdependence, and what would now be called supranational institutions linked and safeguarded these local centers: the Hanseatic League, the Holy Roman Empire—which preserved this perspective on the German constitution until the end of the eighteenth century—and the Roman Catholic Church. Bourgeois, republican, communitarian, decentralized, and internationalist—that is the truly "other" Germany.

The Origins of Authoritarianism

The Holy Roman Empire was not, of course, simply a league of cities: its elastic structure accommodated also numerous hereditary (and ecclesiastical) principalities, and if the plump cities had the wealth, the lean and hungry principalities had (on the whole) the land and the military forces. In the emperor the cities had a natural ally, for in the princes both had a common enemy. The balance of power between the central imperial authority and the constituent territories shifted decisively with the Reformation, however, when certain of the princely territories arrayed themselves against the Emperor to protect the new religion and many of the cities joined them.

Luther is one of the most fascinatingly ambiguous figures in German cultural history, which is not poor in such ambiguity (Goethe and Brecht are similar cases). The son of an industrial entrepreneur, and in many ways a product of late-medieval German urban piety, he nonetheless threw in his lot with the princes, both in their opposition to the Emperor and in their pretension to absolute authority within their own realms. The Lutheran Reformation was the point at which the assertion of individual freedom from institutional bondage went over into a surrender of institutional protection—whether of the Church, of the Empire, or of natural law—against the one free will that counts in a fallen world, that of the most powerful. New priorities were establishing themselves in Germany.

Whether religious change was a cause or simply an expression of this great shift is probably not determinable at all, and certainly not determinable here: the religious, economic, and political aspects of the new age have remained inseparable for all of its nearly 500 years. The decline of the German towns, which was already becoming apparent by the end of the sixteenth century, may have had many causes: a redirection of trade-routes, a prolonged economic crisis, most fundamentally perhaps the rise of the western European maritime powers as a competing focus of commercial and industrial activity. But a crucial precipitating factor was indubitably the terrible inheritance of the sixteenth-century revolt of the princes, the devastating religious war of 1618–1648—in particular the decision taken by Cardinal Richelieu in 1630 to prolong the war (which as an internal conflict was by then effectively settled) in order to break the power of the empire. The latter phase of the Thirty Years' War was especially destructive, being compounded by plague and famine. The average population loss in the country was 40 percent, in the towns 33 percent. In 1800 the population of Nuremberg was still only half of what it had been in 1600.

More important still were the long-term political consequences of the war: by the time of the death of Louis XIV, who had continued the policy of ravaging western Germany, the empire was scarcely more than a confederation of absolute princes, with little external constraint on their conduct and next to no internal opposition. Whether or not they were nominally independent, the cities of Germany were now relatively insignificant. The main economic activity in most territories was the maintenance of a standing army, and of the local court: capital was concentrated in the hands of the state, the principal entrepreneur was usually the local ruler, with his nearest competitor a member of the nobility, rarely of the bourgeoisie. The republican traditions and chartered privileges of towns and corporations were systematically ignored or suppressed in the interests of a centralized conduct of political and economic affairs by the prince and his bureaucracy. Appeal to the imperial courts was difficult, expensive, and—with an eventual backlog of 16,000 cases—largely ineffectual. Protestant Germany knew no extraterritorial ecclesiastical authority. After 1648 the German bourgeoisie, by contrast with its self-confident counterparts in England, France, and the Low Countries, was economically weak and politically neutered, and had lost any independent cultural role. The arts which now began to flourish were those dependent on courtly patronage: baroque and rococo architecture, opera and orchestral music, and the French-language theater. By 1720, however, a new *modus vivendi* between the intellectual classes and the state power, a cultural compromise unique to Germany, had begun to establish itself.

For if Germany no longer had a capitalist bourgeoisie to compare with that of Western Europe, it had, thanks to its multiplicity of rulers and their increasing enthusiasm for centralized control, an exceptionally extensive class of officials, dependent on the state for their livelihood. The bureaucracy included not merely judicial and financial officials, but schoolteachers and in Protestant territories the entire clergy (appointed not by lay patrons, but through his Consistory by the ruler himself), and it was recruited and trained, and itself considerably swollen, by an unparalleled system of universities (over fifty of them, at a time when England numbered only two). It was this official class which offered social advancement and material reward to the gifted poor, conditional only on their loyalty to the state system which patronized them, and to the person of its ruler. It was also this class which gave birth to the theological, philosophical, and literary culture of Germany's golden age, from the end of the Seven Years' War in 1763 to the death of Goethe in 1832.

The peculiar character of that culture was a reflection of its peculiar social base. Cut off by static and monopolistic economies from the freedom of independent economic agents, and by despotic constitutions from the freedom of independent participants in a political process, Germany's middle class, while overtly accepting their subordination to the princely will, expressed their opposition in their cultivation of the freedom of the mind, and of ethical and religious, rather than political or material, self-determination. "Reason as much as you like," Kant has Frederick the Great say in his essay *What Is Enlightenment?* "and about whatever you like—but obey!" Both Pietism and the rationalist Enlightenment of Leibniz and Wolff, superficially the bitterest of enemies, combined a belief in the internal autonomy of the individual with a belief in the impropriety, or even the logical impossibility, of any transeunt action by the individual on the order of things around him, with which his harmony was instead ensured by prior divine arrangement: "the soul," said Leibniz, "is absolutely sheltered from exterior things." As music began its own venture into the interior, with the ever profounder exploration of key-relationships, the fiction of equal temperament provided an image of that compromise between the subjective and the objective orders by which the eighteenth-century German middle class accommodated itself to the political realities of absolutism. In the latter part of the eighteenth century, Pietism and Enlightenment converged in a process of secularization which generated a series of ever more daring and remote reinterpretations of Christianity: the cult of sentiment, ethical religion, the philosophy of history, critical, transcendental, and absolute Idealism, the theory of the Aesthetic, philhellenic and romantic literature.

The theologians, biblical critics, philosophers, and poets responsible for this extraordinary intellectual efflorescence owed their distance from orthodoxy to more than a fortuitously early ar-

133

rival in the Age of Doubt. Stipendiaries practically to a man of their local prince (the few tragic exceptions, such as Kleist and Hölderlin, whom conscience or circumstance deprived of office, merely prove the rule), they willingly, and often consciously, continued Luther's tradition of investing the state with a spiritual authority they would not accord to the Church of Rome: "the modern" (that is, Fichtean) "philosopher is necessarily a Protestant," remarked Fichte,[6] the author of *The Closed Mercantile State*. Enlightenment in Germany, and its continuation, Idealist philosophy, was the handmaid of the omnicompetent state, and its principal target was "superstition," that is, the intellectual foundations of an independent institutional Church.

Neither the ossified bourgeoisie of the depopulated towns, nor the crumbling imperial structure, let alone the old international Church, had the political or symbolic power to focus German aspirations as the century of nationalism opened. The model, and, some prescient spirits already foresaw, the instrument of German nationhood was to be the absolutist principality, literally deified by Romantic political philosophy, and the clearest and certainly the most powerful example of it was the kingdom of Prussia. The Prussian reforms, begun after Napoleon's overwhelming defeat of the old regime at Jena in 1806, restructured the military, educational, and administrative systems, but not in order to extend elective procedures nor to preserve the ancient German freedoms (which the city of Frankfurt had proudly announced to General Custine's advancing army were worth any liberty, equality, or fraternity the French could bring). The reforms completed the century-long surreptitious revolution by which the German middle classes established themselves as the true expression of the state, and of the German nation to come. But the middle classes that won this victory were not the economically independent members of a bourgeoisie who saw themselves as contracting to live together under certain conditions. They were an officialdom, a salaried bureaucracy, whose first principle was loyal and incorruptible service to a master not one of themselves, to the prince in whom the authority of the general will was held to be vested, and whose absolute right to obedience was in turn communicated to his agents. The officials who carried out this German equivalent of the French Revolution had no need to execute their king, they simply parceled out his divine right among themselves. Thus did the old spirit of autocracy enter into the modernized German constitution of the nineteenth century.

Hegel and Marx

The philosophy of Hegel is the supreme expression of Germany's social and intellectual revolution between 1770 and 1830. With its complimentary remarks in *The Philosophy of Right* about "the universal class" of public officials, who transcend the particular interests both of landowners and of the industrial and commercial classes, and with its approval of a political order said (incorrectly) to resemble that of contemporary Prussia, it has, however, often been seen as little more than a blatant and sophistical apology for the corporatist and authoritarian state of which Hegel, as professor in Berlin, was a servant. But Hegel was Prussian neither by origin nor by upbringing, nor in his sympathies: he came from a corner of south-west Germany with a long history of constitutional conflict with its ducal rulers and the most important single influence on his political thinking was the French Revolution. If the lectures on the *Philosophy of World History* conclude with a flattering picture of contemporary Germany (not Prussia), it is because Hegel—with possibly subversive optimism—is suggesting that it is here rather than in France, torn between a Catholic reaction and a nihilistic liberalism, or in pre-Reform Bill England, with its venal and still essentially medieval Parliament, Church, and army, that the principles of the French Revolution are being most concretely realized.

It may be difficult to recognize the reality of 1820s Germany in Hegel's picture of a collection of constitutional monarchies whose rulers, though hereditary, have little more to do than sign their name, where government is in the hands of officials, but all careers are open to talents, where fundamental rights of property and the person are universally acknowledged, all relics of the feudal system have disappeared, and the stronger states, in guaranteeing the independence of the weaker ones, both eliminate the likelihood of internal German wars and render the very boundaries of statehood theoretical. But this is not a picture drawn by an apologist of absolutism. Indeed, as we have seen, it bears a more than passing resemblance to the European order that has developed as the age of nationalism has faded away. Hegel's classic status as *the* philosopher

135

of the modern world, who has anticipated and comprehended everything from sociology to existentialism and deconstruction, derives from his integration of the perspectives both of Germany's uniquely developed official class and of the European bourgeoisie. Drawing on Adam Smith and Rousseau as much as on German Idealism and Romanticism, his political and historical thought shows the State as emerging from the necessities imposed equally by the natural environment, by unseen economic interrelationships ("the system of needs"), and by deliberate human self-understanding and self-regulation. The bourgeoisie—city-life in the broadest possible sense of the term—is essential to the State but not coterminous with it, and while limiting the independence of the institutions of civil society ("the corporations") the State positively requires for its own health their prosperity and diversity. The principle of co-operation between the different and even overtly opposed elements within the whole State structure, on which Hegel lays great emphasis (by contrast with the adversarial understanding of the separation of powers in the Franco-American revolutionary constitutions) is not merely a reflection of the eighteenth-century compromise between the German middle classes and their absolute princes: it is a resumption of the spirit of co-operation between private profit and public discipline which had for centuries been the ethos of the German cities.

After the European restoration, and with increasing rapidity after Hegel's death in 1831, Germany was overtaken by the Industrial Revolution. Between the failed uprising of 1848 and the final establishment of Bismarck's empire in 1871 the formerly agrarian German economy reached the industrial pre-eminence within Europe which it has never since lost. A huge social upheaval accompanied the change (the population of Berlin grew from 200,000 to 2,000,000), of which the most significant feature was that Germany now acquired a recognizable modern bourgeoisie: a middle class of private entrepreneurs and rentiers and their employees which was independent of the state and was the principal locus of economic power. The political structure of bureaucratic absolutism had been carried over by the German "revolution" into the nineteenth century. But this political structure could now no longer bear the same relation to the national culture as before, for now its patronage had a rival in that of a middle class that was economically increasingly self-sufficient however successfully it was still excluded from the overt exercise of political power. The social basis of German classical culture was overturned, and the new class looked for a culture of its own. It was not particularly successful, but an example of what it found is D. F. Strauss. Strauss started his intellectual life in the 1830s seeking shelter from atheism in Hegelianism; he ended it, after the Franco-Prussian War, asserting that modern men and women put their faith not in God but in insurance companies, and found edification not in sermons but in newspapers. Like the proselytizing materialist Ludwig Büchner, brother of the dramatist, he was a figure immediately comprehensible to his fellow-bourgeois across Western Europe: translated by George Eliot, he might be feared and repudiated by his English contemporaries, but he was acknowledged and understood by them as Kant and Hegel had not been.

The cult of interior freedom, which had been the basis of Germany's greatest achievements in literature and philosophy, and perhaps in music too, began to wither in the warmer drawing-rooms of the *Gründerzeit*. Before dying, however, it drooped: it survived well into the twentieth century but with an ever more problematic and degenerate air, the last figure to promote it with any simple-minded—if admittedly rather coarse and artificial—vigor being Richard Wagner. But Wagner was allowed his peculiar prolongation of the classical German literary and musical traditions by the bizarre historical accident that was Ludwig II of Bavaria, thanks to whom he could masquerade as the protégé of a court patron in a manner at least fifty years out of date. The majority of mid-nineteenth–century German intellectuals, unlike their predecessors in the previous century, could call on private means, sometimes their own, to support them (Schopenhauer, Strauss, Feuerbach, Marx, and Engels, for example). But, as is the way, they were not usually grateful. They hankered after the high culture created by German officialdom, indeed in most cases they hankered after the offices as well (especially the professorships). To men intelligent enough to be aware of Germany's past, the new bipolarity of the national life seemed like a betrayal, and it was with all the resentment of a disestablished clerisy that Nietzsche (then briefly a professor) launched his onslaught on the betrayal by Strauss, and the Bismarckian Germany which he represented, of the cultural inheritance which in Nietzsche's view he had rendered indistinguishable from

Philistinism. Wagner, as apparently the true inheritor, could applaud complacently—until Nietzsche saw through his masquerade and his turn came as well.

Karl Marx may have been no match for Nietzsche in the intelligence of his invective, but he chose his target a good deal more shrewdly: not the cultural representatives of the bourgeoisie, but the bourgeoisie itself. How little of Marx's passion is expended in sympathy with or even (by contrast with Engels) interest in the lot of the poor! His seething energies were directed almost exclusively at his enemy—*his* enemy, for a seemingly inexplicable personal animosity fires his writings, as it does Nietzsche's. What have I done to harm Nietzsche, Strauss wondered, and a similar question must have occurred to bourgeois readers, if there were any, of the *Communist Manifesto*. The answer is the same in both cases: Marx's enemy, like Nietzsche's, had deprived his generation (and perhaps him personally) of the status they could have enjoyed as the rightful sons and heirs of Germany's great officials, perhaps specifically of Hegel, the greatest of them all. Even had Marx been able to have the academic career he originally desired, it could not in the new Germany have given him the role it had given to Hegel.

Exiled after 1848 to the land of bourgeoisie triumphant, Marx devoted the rest of his life, and all his virulence of mind, to one purpose. He sought to understand the force which, having been effectively absent from Germany for two centuries, had in his own time returned with such swiftness and power that by the time he was thirty it had shattered the cultural certainties into which he had been born. It is no coincidence that the revolutionary socialism which is incongruously appended to Marx's immensely penetrating but deterministic and apolitical analysis of the economic and cultural dynamic of capitalist society should flaunt the vocabulary of "dictatorship," should scorn the political freedoms of liberalism, and should over and over again have lent itself to oppression, deceit, and murder in the interests of an omnipotent bureaucracy. Marx's cultural values were those of eighteenth-century German officialdom. (What is the difference between envisaging the withering away of the state, and envisaging, as the Romantics did, a perfect synonymy of the individual and the collective will?) He was nostalgic for the political order that had produced those values, and he added to them only a profound understanding and hatred of the forces that had made them impossible. His sense of public morality was no different from that of Frederick the Great. The lineage of the absolute state passes directly through authoritarian socialism.

The National-Socialist Revolution

It was of the essence of German classical culture that it was Protestant. The secularization of religious thought and language which is its central concern is, according to Hegel, the new principle introduced into world history by the Reformation, reaching its culmination in his own time. Hegel is only being consistent when he identifies the vehicle of the secular—the concrete expression of the religious impulses of the individual—as the particular state to which the individual belongs. The Reformation was after all fought in order to dispute the authority of a supranational religious jurisdiction, and Hegel allows for no significant relation between states other than war. A perspective broader by far than that of the particular state is available through art, religion, and philosophy—but none of these has an institutional embodiment that transcends the boundaries of the state. Yet, just as the German Enlightenment regularly stopped short of materialist atheism and carried its criticism of institutional Christianity only so far as to subordinate it to the prince, so even in the later nineteenth century the German political ascendancy—Kaiser, nobility, army, and officialdom—did not abandon a Christian allegiance. To be a Protestant was to be German (the literature of the time is full of such identifications), but it was to be Christian too. The *Kulturkampf* was a last attempt, after Reformation and Enlightenment, at an elimination from Germany of international Christianity in favor of the national variety.

Fifty years later, when the cultural conflict was renewed with much greater ferocity, it was not in the name of Christianity at all. The political ascendancy—the Führer and the party—was avowedly anti-Christian: one of the few such regimes to come to power in Europe, it reveled in its own pagan religious ceremonial and bogus mythology, and it conducted the nation's internal and external affairs in explicit disregard of the Christian principle (fundamentally important to Hegel) of the equal worth of all human beings.[7] Well over twenty million lives were extinguished as it showed the world that it meant what it said. How did this disaster come about?

Germany after the Industrial Revolution, and especially after the reorganization, as we may call it, of 1866–1871, was a sadly divided polity. Political responsibility and the cultural high ground remained in the hands of the old and decreasingly representative absolutist order, while the new bourgeoisie, which had created the nation's economic power and was now the source of its intellectual vigor, lacked the political education and experience to formulate a role for itself. It inclined either towards a nationalist imperialism in imitation of Germany's western neighbors, or towards a socialism which was simply the old order called by another name but with its benefits distributed to a larger clientele. Its economic success seemed to mark it out as the natural European inheritor of the old imperial powers, Britain and France. But in the trials of strength imposed by the completion of the global system political resources were as important as economic. After 1914 the rickety national structure stood up less well than its competitors to the strains of war, and in the hour of defeat it tottered, like other residually feudal regimes before it, and indeed contemporary with it, into revolution. The twenty-seven years after 1918 in Germany bear a strong structural resemblance to the twenty-six years after 1789 in France. In both cases a constellation of forces, led by a politically unpracticed middle class, combined to overthrow a monarchical system. In both cases there followed episodes of attempted compromise with the past and ventures in constitutional government, punctuated by internal economic crisis, violence, and disorder, and accompanied by unhelpful pressure from without, until a dictator took power who both made the revolution at home irreversible and engaged in megalomaniac schemes of foreign expansion which eventually led to his downfall. If there is a difference of two or three orders of magnitude between the two cases in respect of their recourse to surveillance, delation, judicial murder, and massacre, it can largely be attributed to a hundred years' development of technology and mass industrial society, and to the experience of the mechanized mass-destruction of human 'material' in the Western trenches.

Because of the peculiarly evil ideology of National Socialism, and the unique horror of the crimes it perpetrated, it is easy to overlook the extent to which Hitler, as far as Germany itself was concerned, simply completed a revolution which had been begun by other agents. For all the vituperative hostility to the traitors of

1918 who had stabbed Germany in the back, there was no more question of Hitler restoring the Hohenzollerns than of Napoleon restoring the Bourbons. His Reich had no Kaiser, and no nobility either, except for decorative purposes. His *Gleichschaltung* swept away all traces of the feudal world, the multiple jurisdictions into which it had divided Germany. (A personal friend of mine used to recall how as a boy before 1918 he performed the feudal service of harvesting for a reigning count.) Under the Nazis Germany became, for the first time in its history, a classless society.[8] Had it been such in 1919 the Weimar Republic might have survived. But in the 1920s there were still too many competitors for the loyalty of a nation that had with unexpected suddenness been genuinely enfranchised and made into the master of its own destiny. The social structure had been largely untouched by the abdication of the monarchy: the political horizons of untitled Germany, from the industrialists, who subsidized Hitler, to the shopkeepers and artisans, who voted for him, were still limited to the options laid down in the old empire—nationalism, socialism, and authoritarianism. Hitler wove all three together and, exploiting both the novelty of the modern media of mass-communication and the political inexperience of the new German public, made himself into Germany's first successful mass-politician. There lay ready to hand in the old culture the elements of the religion of the (German) state and the critiques of Christianity, culminating in that of Nietzsche. There was no longer any need to accommodate them to the established Protestant religion of the hereditary ascendancy, for that was swept away. Gone too, in the appalling economic mayhem, originally of inflation and then of mass unemployment, was the bourgeoisie that had fumbled its way to revolution in 1918. The mass-politician had a mass-society to work on—the first in Europe, thanks to the ravages of defeat. Of the *ancien regime* there remained only the officials who had served it. Imbued with the principle of loyalty to the state power, they continued to do what they were told, and kept the wheels of absolutism turning after the demise of the princes. The secularized Christianity that had sustained them for so long reached its final dilution as the empty principle of obedience to the leader, whatever claptrap or wickedness he might mouth.

Perhaps such a humiliation could have been inflicted on that noble tradition only by an ex-Catholic such as Hitler. Conversely, the true opposition to National Socialism is not to be found among those who organized the conspiracy of July 1944, who—whatever moral outrage they may also have felt—were politically motivated by their loyalty to the pre-revolutionary norms of the old empire, nor among those who chose the route of "internal emigration" into the army (where nonetheless some independence of the Nazi movement survived), nor again among those who dissociated themselves spiritually from what went on around them and whose intense but inactive suffering was praised by Hermann Hesse. The true opposition was that which appealed to an external authority. In other words, the opposition which emigrated to the countries at war with Hitler; which remained loyal, like Thomas Mann, to the unregarded principles of the Weimar Republic; which protected—as brave lay people, priests, and bishops did—individual victims of the racial laws; and which denounced the state's atrocities as contrary to common decency, to the word of God, and to the teaching of the universal Church.

The Return of the Other Germany

The devastation to which Germany awoke in 1945, paralleled in its history only by the Thirty Years' War, was not inflicted simply by the Allied bombs that burnt its cities, nor by the Russian soldiery who had terrorized its countryside: it was also the result of a twelve-year social revolution in the course of which the mechanism of an absolute state had turned on and destroyed itself. Had it not been for the ghastly memories of what had been done in that time Germany could have felt relief. Four centuries of gathering despotism had come to a cataclysmic end, Germany and the world had paid dearly for Luther's stand and Richelieu's intrigues, but the German people was suddenly on its own: the kings and princes and emperors and leaders were gone, as in 1918 they were not, and in 1949, with 100 marks apiece, everyone started again on (theoretically) the same footing. It was a moment like that in Goethe's *Hermann and Dorothea* (a poem with no role, nor even a mention, for aristocratic rulers) when Hermann's father and mother meet in the hot ashes of their burnt-out town and pledge themselves to each other, to the future, and to hard work. It was also a moment such as none of the victor powers could experience. Their ambiguous reward has been to have time to adjust to the discovery which in Germany was instantaneous: that in the transition to the global system all that was solid in the old order—imperial, national, and bourgeois—melts into air.

What has happened in the Federal Republic since has been a return to the only thing that was left, Germany's oldest and deepest traditions. The federal structure, a compromise with the much more elaborate historic subdivisions of Bismarck's state which is largely borrowed from the Weimar Republic, has proved its worth, not merely in limiting the power of central government, but in preserving that regionalism and local republicanism which from the Middle Ages onwards never wholly disappeared from view until 1933. The traditions of the old cities are particularly noticeable in the acceptance that, although it is essential to preserve competition in some areas, certain others are public rather than private responsibilities. Obvious examples are the urban transport and municipal facilities (that every former town of princely residence has its own theater and opera-house is one of the happier legacies of the absolutist period). Also, though, one notes the, by Anglo-Saxon standards, remarkably restrained and co-operative attitudes of trade unions, a result no doubt partly of the much greater prevalence of democratic and consultative procedures in the work-place. The most famous example of a public institution too important to be used for the sectional advantage of competing interests (in this case politicians) is the German currency, its integrity entrusted to the independent Federal Bank. A certain mystique still attaches to the caste of "officials," but they no longer represent a state power in conflict with the capitalist class. The social market does not seem to be a *conceptual* problem in modern Germany. Germany's willingness to co-operate with other Western states, and its eagerness for the European idea, are not simply consequences of the immediate past—a desire to be loved, or to lose its former identity, or to find a new and acceptable field for imperialist sentiments. They are also part of a return to an internationalism which has always been natural to Germany, thanks to its central geographical position.

The accident that the Federal Republic has been the only predominantly Catholic state to call itself Germany has marked it off decisively from its predecessors and contributed as much as any other factor to the obsolescence of the classical culture. That culture's social and political base was a conflict which was as old as the

143

Reformation but which, as a peculiarly German phenomenon, is over. The energies generated by the conflict produced a literary, philosophical, and musical tradition which in the first third of this century was *in extremis* and which after 1945 has found no successors. Only in socialist resentment of what Germany's resurrected cities have achieved have the traditions of the nationalist and Protestant past lived on. It is the writers who have both accepted the new world and who have also possessed the intellectual power to relate it to the past (Grass, for example, Böll in some of his earlier works, and especially the poet Paul Celan) who have had something to say to non-German speakers. Music, theology, and philosophy (with the notable exception of Habermas) have been confined to a few scavengers in the ruins.

All this, of course, applies only to West Germany. For forty years the Russian forces of occupation kept in existence in the East a petrifact of the national socialist version of the German absolutist system. (The indistinctness of socialism and national socialism, except in respect of socialism's Christian inheritance, was here particularly evident.) Indeed, with a weird ingenuousness the government of the Democratic Republic used to boast of its continuity with the Prussian "legacy" (even though none of its territory was technically part of the kingdom of Prussia until after the end of the Holy Roman Empire in 1806). In 1989, before the moral, administrative, and economic hollowness of the old regime had been fully exposed to comparison with the West, it seemed as if a reformed GDR still had the makings of an identity of its own, or at least of a distinctive contribution to a new German state. Immediately after unification it became clear that all the GDR had to offer were the contents of its museums and its crèche service for working wives, and its best hopes for the future lay in as complete and rapid an absorption as possible into the Federal Republic.

If the new state is looking for a historical ancestor, it could do worse than look to that which its new boundaries suggest: the Holy Roman Empire, freed from both Prussian and Austrian hegemony. It has already been given, in Christo's wrapped Reichstag, an extraordinarily potent cultural symbol: the world's first post-modern political unit was immediately recognizable in this absorption of a deeply compromised national past into the polythene abstractions of the global market. The legislative assembly that had the self-knowledge to permit so humane an act of vandalism has proved its moral right to point us the way into the European future.

For the rest of Europe, indeed, few grounds for anxiety need remain. There will, of course, be a marked cultural change in the Federal Republic through the sudden and very considerable rise in the representation of Protestantism, atheism, and socialism. It is, however, only the strengthening of socialism (the one surviving form of the worship of the German absolute state) and of its associate, neutralism (a left-sounding label for German nationalism), that is obviously problematic. Already in the Nazi period German Protestants had learned that to survive as Christians they had to identify themselves not with the state but with the opposition, and in the last years of the GDR this commitment became as significant politically as the anti-Caesarism of the Catholic Church in Poland. With the end of the real political basis for the Catholic-Lutheran divide we may actually hope to see progress towards healing the schism in the land in which it originated (and so also a much-needed strengthening of the reformist wing in the Roman Church). After all, Luther's original reforms, and much of the secularizing Enlightenment that developed out of them, have been gradually accommodated by the Catholic Church as inescapable features of the modern world.

Even Germany's classical inheritance now takes on a new aspect. Since in the post-imperial, post-bourgeois, and post-modern world we all live by selling our labor, and most of that labor is sold directly or indirectly to the state, the bourgeois culture of early nineteenth-century France and England is in some respects already as opaque to us as the culture created by German officials was to their European contemporaries. For the proletarianized functionaries that we all now are, the literature and philosophy of secularized Lutheranism, which at their best integrated both an official and a bourgeois perspective, have a continuing relevance. What is definitively past is the nationalist obsession with the absolute and unitary state that was built into German culture in the moment of the Reformation schism. In the post-war economic order nations of that kind no longer exist. It was Germany's misfortune, between the seventeenth and twentieth centuries, to have developed to an extreme certain essential features of modernity—bureaucracy, intellectual secularization, and Lutheranism—in isolation from the institutions which might have moderated them—elective government, a popular culture, and the universal Church.[9] The re-Catholicization of German culture will prove in the long term to have been one of the most important innovations of the (West) German Federal Republic. (It has certainly been one of the foundation-stones of the reconciliation with France.) In politics and literature Catholic institutions and Catholic memories have recovered an equality of respect with the products of Lutheran secularism, dominant in Northern Germany since the demise of the ecclesiastical states at the end of the eighteenth century. It is now possible to imagine the currents which for two hundred years or more have swept German intellectual life along a course of its own being redirected into the broader stream of European Catholicity. That was the historic vocation of Germany's greatest twentieth-century philosopher. Heidegger failed the test, however, and despite living on for nearly thirty years in the new Germany, he took refuge in a parochial understanding of what his nation had achieved. But, provided it is adapted to a more international perspective, as now it can be, the German classical tradition still has much to teach the world. It may even have something for participants in Chequers seminars. Now that no account of human political life can possibly ignore the supranational economic and institutional order, the prospects for a Catholic Hegelianism have never been so bright.

6 After Enlightenment
Hegel, Post-Modernism, and the State

One sign that the inter-imperial tensions of the years between 1870 and 1914 have at last been resolved, and that ways of thinking have grown up which are more adequate to the global realities that were then created, has been the remarkable resurgence in English-speaking lands, since about 1960, of an interest in Hegel. Cultural Germanophobia has lost its political impetus and thinkers with a wide range of concerns have rediscovered the breadth and power of Hegel's vision. The American philosopher David Kolb, in a close and inspiring study, *The Critique of Pure Modernity: Hegel, Heidegger, and After*, sees Hegel and Heidegger as between them offering a full range of possible answers to the most fundamental question of all—what is selfhood in the modern world? The collapse of Marxism-Leninism as an effective political creed—which post-dates Kolb's book—has naturally returned interest to Marx's Hegelian origins. In Francophone philosophy Hegel never lost his standing as one of "les maîtres penseurs" (A. Glucksmann's phrase) and Derrida has devoted a whole volume (*Glas*) to a series of ironical glosses on Hegel's *Philosophy of Right*. Yet Hegel's Germany was pre-industrial and pre-imperial, and in his day the world-system which for over a century has determined the lives of all of us had yet to be established. How was it that he could grasp principles which over a century after his death would still be of profound practical relevance and would continue to irritate the complacencies of the Post-Modernist? And, given that he was emphatic that his was a Protestant philosophy, is there a link between what in a Catholic perspective must seem its limitations and those respects in which it has after all, been outwitted by the later stratagems of the spirit of world-history? To answer these questions I propose a circular tour, setting out from our present situation and returning to it, and considering first the relation between the global market and the Post-Modernism which tries, more or less resentfully, to shrug off its Hegelian leading-strings; then the nature of the Enlightenment, the critique of the Catholic world-view, of which German Idealism from Kant to Hegel was the culmination; and finally the relation between Hegel's political system, his German circumstances, and the changed circumstances in which we find ourselves now.

"Genealogism" and Consumerism

It is a strange paradox of the post-modern world that although many of the intellectual tendencies to which it has given birth are intimately connected with the rise of the global market, very few of those who have nurtured and promoted those tendencies give any public support to their local market-oriented political parties—the revolutionary parties which, in the double-speak which is no longer confined to totalitarian regimes, call themselves conservative. Deleuze and Lyotard are not notable Gaullists nor have Chomsky or Jameson done much for the Republicans. Another manifestation of the same paradox is that, except for an occasional temerarious architect, virtually all the representatives of Post-Modernism are employed in universities, and their discourse seems often hermetically academic, yet what they say, in both its content and its method, is quite likely to be directed against traditional categorizations of knowledge, traditional canons of texts, and traditionally authoritative interpreters and interpretations. Indeed, one of the principal arguments against giving Derrida an honorary degree of Cambridge University was that "M. Derrida's doctrines . . . undermine the fundamental grounds which provide a place in the scheme of things for intellectual enquiry in any field; and so for the very existence of universities in society."[1] The same argument could perhaps have been advanced against Socrates, Hume, and Nietzsche (who all had to manage without Cambridge honorary degrees), though that does not make it any less cogent. But it remains odd—given this main argument *contra*—that the main argument *pro* was Derrida's enormous, and undisputed, *academic* influence.

In his 1988 Gifford Lectures, published in 1990 as *Three Rival Versions of Moral Enquiry*, Alasdair MacIntyre expressed the fear that the possibility of discussion, or even communication, with the Post-Modernist followers of Nietzsche (whose form of inquiry he called "genealogism," after Nietzsche's *On the Genealogy of Morals*) was so restricted that the humanistic departments of the university had ceased to be a place for the rational investigation of the good and so could provide no rational self-justification when asked to do so by their paymasters. "Insofar as the curriculum . . . is no longer a whole, there can be no question of providing a rational justification for the continued existence and flourishing . . . of the university as the whole that it once was. . . . When . . . external critics of the university . . . have proposed measures by which the achievement of contemporary universities should be evaluated . . . the official spokespersons of the academic status quo have with rare exceptions responded with stuttering ineptitudes."[2] MacIntyre treats at length two features of "genealogism" which are either agents or symptoms of the process which has brought the post-modern academy to this pass. More generally, "genealogism" has subverted belief in the unity of knowledge by subverting belief in the unity of the object of knowledge: there is "no single world" which knowledge could be of or about and therefore there is no unity possible in knowledge itself (and therefore not in its academically institutionalized forms either). Instead there is a "multiplicity of perspectives and idioms," possible ways of looking at the world—idealist, empiricist, sociological, psychological, religious (57 varieties), scientific (ditto)—which will prove, on genealogical investigation, to be multiple particular manifestations of the will to power. It would be sheer superstition— another willed, but unacknowledged, perspective—to imagine that one could allow for the perspectival distortion and that, to quote Nietzsche, "a world would still remain over after one subtracted the perspective!" Perspectives have no justification or ground—except in the will to power—they cannot be made part of any larger scheme—their most appropriate literary expression is therefore the aphorism rather than the article or the book, though genealogists may sometimes write parodies of articles or books or whole encyclopedias in order to make what is in the end a single aphoristic point—and one perspective cannot be made to yield to another by considerations of argument, authority, evidence, or even plausibility: perspectives are incommensurable. Those who speak different idioms in the (post-)modern pluralist academy cannot talk to each other, and usually do not want to. No wonder the spokespersons in the administration buildings find it difficult to explain to the inquiring outsider why they are all *there*, and that in the most literal sense: why these windowless professional non-communicators need to be housed side by side on the same, no doubt expensive, humanities campus.

MacIntyre analyzes a second, more specific, Nietzschean subversion, to which Freud and Lacan (and for that matter Jung too) have also contributed. Foucault in 1970 praised Deleuze for conceiving the self as multiple and fissured,[3] and the disintegration of the subject has become one of the commonplaces of Post-Modernist thought, yet MacIntyre sees here a serious problem, both practical and theoretical. If it is no longer possible to give "any account of the identity, unity, and continuity" of the self, how can we assert the moral accountability of a person for his or her earlier actions? Is there indeed no relation between the Paul de Man deconstructing texts in Yale in the 1970s and the Paul de Man writing in support of Nazi ideology in Belgium in the 1940s? The question is not just *ad hominem*, but has a theoretical dimension too: all "genealogy," all unmasking of intellectual and moral perspectives as derivative from the will to power, involves a disowning of past illusion. But you cannot tell the story of your emancipation from deception and self-deception unless there is an "identity and continuity of the self that was deceived and the self that is and is to be."[4] *Who* is doing all the unmasking? "Can the genealogical narrative find any place within itself for the genealogist? . . . Make of the genealogist's self nothing but what genealogy makes of it, and that self is dissolved to the point at which there is no longer a continuous genealogical project."[5] Nietzsche, we may add, showed himself aware of this problem, in one phase of his writing at least, by attributing his destructive vision not directly to himself but to a steely mask called Zarathustra. The coherence of the process of deconstruction, whether of the self or of a text, is secured only by granting a special status to the self of the deconstructing author. The "genealogist" remains exempt from the devices he or she applies to others and is still permitted to claim the privileges of identity, continuity, intention, authorship within the text, and all that goes with them outside it—such as copyright income, a personal list of publications, and honorary degrees. Ann Jefferson, an expositor of Derrida, acknowledges her difficulties when she writes with rueful irony: "What I have tried to say—namely that writing is not governed by the subjective intentions of its author . . ."—and goes on to add that this self-contradictory project "has (inevitably) been partially contradicted by the manner in which it has been said"[6] and not just by its manner, we would add, but by her own claim to have an intention and be a self. The paradox which occasions this irony is not explained, as Dr. Jefferson thinks it is explained, by invoking the malign but all-pervasive and irresistible power of "logocentrism," which is the name Derrida gave to the erroneous belief (as he thinks it) that there is something outside texts to which they refer—the belief, we might say, that language, or at any rate some statements, have a cash value. Rather, the paradox is best explained as a variant on the paradox with which we began: that the intellectual classes seem willing to go to any length of self-conscious self-contradiction in order to deny their task of understanding and being understood. That they are seeking to remove themselves from the normal systems of human interchange is best exemplified by the very notion that "logocentrism" is an error. For there is one thing that is quite certainly outside the text, one thing to which language quite certainly refers: namely, everything that money can buy. From that, however, our latter-day clerics bashfully avert their virginal gaze.

It is really rather extraordinary that the belief that there is "no single world" for us to have knowledge of, that there is only a boundless and bottomless plurality of mutually untranslatable idioms for speech to occur in, should have gained such ground at a time when the unity and boundedness of our planetary existence has become more concrete, and more visible, than at any previous time in the history of the human race. Never before have all human beings so obviously been part of a single system as in the days of the worldwide financial, information, and communications networks that sustain the global market. Never before has so much of each individual human being's needs and activity been convertible into terms so universally comprehensible and measurable: the relation between the cost of a Japanese video-recorder in Zambia and the hourly wage of a plumber in Poland can be expressed in terms immediately meaningful to an oilworker, or even a carpet-seller, in Kazakhstan, terms which translate directly into cans on the larder shelf. Meanwhile, MacIntyre tells us,[7] rights theorists cannot talk to contractarians in North American departments of moral philosophy and, Derrida tells us, there is nothing to talk about anyway. The impression of incommensurability among the multiple perspectives—academic, moral, or ideological—of the post-modern world is created insofar as they fail to direct their attention to the one world that we know we all occupy, the world of money and work and consumption, and its physical basis, the third planet. Insofar as different perspectives do refer themselves to that single world order—as for example do some Marxists, some ecologists, some Heideggerians, and some traders in commodities futures—they are in principle capable of talking to each other about something. Insofar as that reference seems in principle to be excluded, the innocent inquirer is asked to share the same tunnel-vision as that of the Persil salesman for whom the only issue in life is the difference of his product from Brand X. True, there have never before been so many different wares on offer in the world market and if there is to be competition maybe brand-identity has to be maintained; maybe the contractarians and the rights theorists need to stay as incommensurable as Coca and Pepsi, as IBM and ICL, lest the difference between them be thought to be indeed only a matter of words, or even of letters.

The belief that there is, not a single truth and a single world, but a multiplicity of mutually untranslatable perspectives, is strangely analogous to the belief that the market is a boundless medium within which perfect competition is possible between an infinite number of discrete commercial identities. Both beliefs founder on the rock of what we may call globalization: the increasingly apparent economic integration of the whole world within the ever more insistent constraints imposed by its physical limits. "Pluralism" is these days a popular word, and a comfortable idea, in many more or less theoretical contexts, but it is something of a mystification—an appearance of variety in the adiaphora in order to conceal the unity in what counts, a velvet glove round the hidden hand. But what makes the mystification so necessary and so persuasive? Why is collaboration with *this* concealment so attractive, even to those professionally committed to the understanding which removes masks? A clue lies in the second subversion MacIntyre identified.

The fragmentation of the self, which the "genealogist" asserts, is paralleled by a fragmentation of "genealogical" or deconstructive writing into aphorism, marginal annotation, questioning, and irony. The import of that stylistic fragmentation is however fundamentally contradicted by the aspiration of "genealogical" thinking to constitute a coherent project, and ultimately by the appearance of "genealogical" writing as a book, that is, as a product, originating in an author, and circulating in the system of human interchange. *That* system is not comprehended by genealogism, though it is a system that is unitary, universal, and well worth trying to understand. The fragmentation, or deconstruction, of the self is used to deny the possibility of authorial continuity within a text, of continuity between the authorial persona within the text and the moral, legal, and economic personality who is the author of the book, and so ultimately of continuity between the text on the one hand and human social and economic life on the other. Yet if it seems plausible to say that the self is really something fragmented and multiple, that is because certain developments in contemporary social and economic life seem to be bringing that result about. But that causal connection is precisely what "genealogical" deconstructive thinking not only cannot represent—it denies it exists. In so doing it plays the game precisely as the global market wants it played. For the fiction by which the global market commends itself to us and encourages our participation in it is that the human self is purely a consumer. The only purpose of the market—so the fiction runs—is to give consumers choice, and to match products to consumers' wishes: to furnish the nearest approach to the goods I want to consume at the nearest approach to the price I want to pay. The market does not concern itself with whether my choice is rational, whether it is identical or consistent with choices I made yesterday or may make tomorrow, nor does it concern itself with any purposes I may have in making my choice, or any consequences of my choice insofar as these do not themselves involve further market decisions. Indeed, as far as the market is concerned, I exist only in the moment of making a single commercial choice: other choices are made by other selves. And so things are for the genealogical-deconstructive thinker too: interpretations of texts and perspectives on the world are matters of momentary choice, requiring no rationale and implying neither consequences nor continuity—one self for one purpose, one for another; the self indeed is little more than a formality, the name we give to the principle that consumes options, the transient locus of interpretation. There is nothing outside the text, just as there is nothing outside the market— or so it appears to the consumer.

For the market seeks to conceal from us—lest it inhibit the arbitrariness and frequency of our choices in it, that is, of our purchases—that it has another, a shadow, side. It is not only the place where needs are satisfied; it is the place where orders for work are given. The market not only serves consumers; it disciplines producers. And in the contemporary world, where we are all—more or less—equally both consumers and producers, the market has to conceal from us that we shall eventually come to feel the consequences of our consumer choices in the form of constraints on our productive activity. (If we work in the British motor industry but regularly purchase cars made in Japan we shall eventually have to work harder for less money.) Wider still and wider must the bounds of pleasurable consumption be set, and so ever more unmentionable must our productive part become, ever darker the privacy into which it is sunk, ever more impenetrable the membrane separating the moment of enjoyment from the lifetime of consequences. It is, as we saw when reflecting on Thatcherism, in the nature of production that it takes place in time, that it takes time. In the unsleeping fluorescent glow of round-the-clock commerce, consumption is as instantaneous as the signature on the contract of sale, the electronic transfer of funds from account to account, the emptying of the supermarket shelf. But behind the doors marked "Staff only" lies a world of time, and so of life, the market's Unconscious, repressed by a contraceptive culture. Behind the market scenes lies a world of people who have "been there" a long or a short *time* (as opposed to the shoppers who have "been there" few or many *times*), who have seen changes, who have expectations or worries, who are on the job (which is not an instantaneous matter, but smeared through time). It is they who feel the consequences of the consumer choices out on the exchange-floor, who meet the deadlines and implement the development strategies, changing from part-time to full-time, working shifts or overtime, trying to do the job well this time, trying out ways of doing it differently next time, trying always to stave off the moment after which there are no more times, and in which the producer dies, the moment of redundancy, in which it becomes clear that for the consumer making his or her choice the producer is a wholly redundant consideration. The fear and the trauma of redundancy are the immediate proof that being human is not just being a punctual self making consumer choices, whether between different commodities or between different interpretations. Being human is also, as Marx objected to Feuerbach, taking part in the process of production by which the world is changed—made different from what it was before, so that (since difference necessarily implies *some* continuity) through production history becomes possible and, with history, time. It follows that we human beings are continuous with our earlier identities and accountable for our earlier actions not because we are, or possess, selves which have made various choices, but because as producers we necessarily exist in time and there has been in the world a series of changes which bear our mark, makings of things, effects we have had on other people, the passings on to children of our genes or the imprint of our personalities, most basically, perhaps, the alterations, willed by us or others, that have been made to our own bodies. "What I do is me" and essentially we are not substances but participants, participants in the process of doing. Any anthropology is manifestly defective which does not take account of the fact that our identities start as those of children and, through making and self-making, and being made by others, grow only gradually into maturity. St. Augustine's presentation of his own identity starts with his behavior on his mother's breast, but the self as presented by Descartes or Fichte, or even by Goethe's Faust, has no childhood. If de Man decided to forget the sins of his youth, that was a sin of his old age and not the worst inconsequentiality of the individualist school in which he had enrolled. The eye of Zarathustra does not even have a body, let alone a beginning.

Repression of the knowledge of the world's unity and singularity is therefore repression of the knowledge of our own (re-)productive activity through time, in the interests of *jouissance* and consumption. The illusion that we can all consume and none need produce is the illusion that all the world can be Girondin bourgeois, that we can all live off our capital. It is of course possible for *some* to do nothing but consume while others do little but produce, but a society which acknowledges and accepts that fundamental differentiation of roles and identities is called feudal. If we want to understand where "genealogism" comes from, and its strange relation to the market ideology of consumerism we must attend to the transition in European society from a feudal to a bourgeois mentality. That transition took many centuries. Eventually, in its later stages, it learnt to call itself the process of Enlightenment, but by the time it had achieved this degree of self-consciousness it had already taken on two very different forms, with two different ways of concealing the social importance of production and, for that matter, two different literary traditions as well. There were two Enlightenments, and because Hegel united, and in a sense terminated, them both, he was able to think thoughts about the interdependence of consumption and production within the one world-system which are still relevant to our own post-bourgeois age.

Two Enlightenments

As soon as the fiction is voiced that all equally are called exclusively to consumption we are in the presence of a mentality that can properly be called bourgeois. I believe we first find that fiction in the erotic mysticism of the *devotio moderna* of the fourteenth century, at a time when the economic relations which gave rise to the bourgeois class were first establishing themselves in the city-states of Italy, Germany, and the Hanseatic League. Those relations were characterized above all by the development of a system of monetary exchange—of banking and of book-keeping practices which permitted the distinction between capital and income. Money is the great leveler: cash from a prince is no better than cash from a pastry cook. All are equal in the eyes of the florin. A new tension therefore enters thought: that between the ideas of the new, but politically unemancipated bourgeoisie on the one hand, and on the other hand their feudal rulers and the great structure of medieval theology and anthropology which gives conceptual expression to the feudal order. That tension is provisionally resolved in the creation of a new concept, or fiction, of detached personal identity. Suddenly human beings are no longer apprentices maturing their way through life, learning as they go, but selves born complete and mature into the world, endowed with capital, they know not from where, ready to make consumer choices without having previously produced. For money is the medium in which the value of goods and the value of work are notionally equated—consumption and production of different goods are reduced to a common term. The establishment of a money-economy thus makes possible the first step towards forgetting that we are, necessarily, producers, and so not detached identities at all, but episodes in a larger story. The mystics were perhaps the first to conceive detached personal identity as a universal possibility and to imagine a state of consumption without production that was not confined to a particular class in the feudal order but was in principle accessible to all. The mystic has glimpsed a fulfillment of humanity which is outside time, that is, outside the productive nexus, and best imagined as boundless, but personal enjoyment. Conversely, but at the same time, systematic thought takes a newly hard-headed turn, an "epistemological turn," as MacIntyre calls it, which is of fundamental importance in differentiating modern from medieval and ancient philosophy. "What do I get for my money?" the canny businessmen of thought ask after William of Ockham; "how sound is the credit of these entities asking me to invest my belief in them?" All the world's a market, the fifteenth-century morality plays suggest to us, and most of the stallholders are frauds, tempting us to squander our precious self. The self-sufficient, all-testing, all-judging, all-valuing, and so selectively purchasing-and-not-purchasing self which is the fictional consumer put before us by modern apologists for the market is clearly recognizable in the omnivores of the Renaissance: Rabelais' Pantagruel, surely the greatest consumer in literature, is at once an emblem and a parody of the world-swallowing, self-obsessed, humanism of a Michelangelo. Montaigne, intoxicated with his own power of judgment is an even more ambiguous figure: his chosen means of being curious about everything is to doubt everything, and he is left with the single certainty of his permanently fluctuating self: life as window-shopping, endlessly turning over in your pocket the unspent coins. Both Montaigne's method and his conclusions were bequeathed to Descartes who gave culminating expression to the "epistemological turn." Descartes recentered philosophy and theology on a self which is created by isolating the thinking consumer so completely from the "extended" producer that only the pineal gland is there to mediate between them.

But Descartes is an ambiguous figure too: half swashbuckler, half brooder, he was, like Ignatius before him, deep in the shadow of the Reformation, the final outgrowth of the *devotio moderna*; yet, as the strange story of the pineal gland shows, he was determined not to accept Luther's radical division of each human being into the subjects of two different kingdoms, one earthly and the other heavenly. (What is commonly called "Cartesian dualism" belongs more properly on Luther's doorstep.) France in his time went through a revolution which was to determine its social and political structure for 150 years or more, and since the outcome of that revolution was virtually the opposite of what happened in contemporary England this was a time when a deep divergence in the intellectual and literary traditions of both nations also began. The French revolution of the mid-seventeenth century saw a (relatively) enormous growth in the power of the monarchy and a subjugation or assimilation to the central bureaucracy of the independent bourgeoisie. Descartes stood on both sides of that divide and hoped perhaps to hold them together. His vorticist theory of the entire physical world is Gargantuan in its ambition and as materialist as could be wished by any cloth-merchant or Harpagon, with both feet on the ground and both hands in his neighbor's till. His theory of the thinking self, however, never seriously commended itself to English philosophers for it emerged from a social context which as time went by was increasingly un-English: from the frustrations of the *noblesse de robe*, the politically tamed and powerless bourgeois, forced out of economic autonomy into the dependency of governmental or quasi-governmental office, whether as tax-farmers or presidents of *parlements* or as lesser officials. For them Descartes' picture of a mind which retained its independence while surrounded by a physical world quite beyond its control was a picture painted from life. In the German principalities where, after 1648, the pattern of the French revolution in government was repeated and carried to an extreme, the Cartesian consolation was presented in a subtle local variant by Leibniz.

Eighteenth-century Germany was, as we have seen, a society almost devoid of a politically significant commercial bourgeoisie but increasingly dominated by a bureaucracy recruited from the upwardly mobile middle class and the lower ranks of the nobility (the higher nobility remaining dedicated to their traditional tasks of war, government, and consumption). This class of officials was not peculiar to Germany and it was as old as the *ministeriales* of the medieval emperors (Ockham was one of the first of them to make an intellectual mark), but it developed in a fuller and purer form in eighteenth-century Protestant Germany than anywhere else in Europe. For these servants of the secular, or secularizing, state Leibniz' theory of the monadic self offered a Cartesian model of identity unencumbered with what appeared to them Descartes' regrettable counter-tendency towards materialism. Although it was a theory for political eunuchs, in a society where all power of decision lay with the one absolute ruler, it was not a feudal theory, for it was based on that complete equality of identities that only a money-economy makes possible. All monads are equal for Leibniz, for all are representations—or representatives—of the divine monarch. All relations between things, in fact, are reduced by Leibniz to "representations" or "perceptions" and so in a sense he makes the epistemological turn absolute. "Absolutely sheltered from external things," the monad contains *within itself* the seed of its development in time, the rule for all its growth and changes: it is windowless, it never breaks out, not even through some cerebral gland, into causal action upon an extended world, but that is the price it willingly pays for its invulnerability to any interference from outside, from extension. This ring-fenced self, with its hot-line to divine omniscience, and with its productive capacities prudently enclosed within it as the material of a purely private enjoyment, is identity as the official knows it. The official (always male) consoles himself for his lack of material and political independence with the thought that he is the immediate agent, the point of delivery, of the divine— that is, the monarch's—plan. He may not be able—he thinks—to take part in the rough-and-tumble of commercial production, in which material bodies mark and are marked by other material bodies, indelibly—the process of industry and trade by which the bourgeoisie of France and England were vastly increasing the wealth of their nations but which in Germany remained sluggish state monopolies. He is however able—he reflects—to produce within himself the series of internal changes wholly independent of external circumstances by which the germ of his identity, that image of the godhead, grows, develops, and flowers—the process of "Bildung," as by the end of the eighteenth century it was called, the process of formation, education, and "culture." The industrial and political revolutions of England and France were paralleled at this time in Germany—economically backward but administratively advanced —by a cultural revolution, above all in the realm of philosophy.

Intellectually speaking, then, the way to these two different revolutions was prepared by two different Enlightenments. Both had their ultimate origin in the decay of the feudal order which set in as the monetarization of social relationships began, and the High Middle Ages passed the peak from which Dante surveyed a perfectly just universe. On the one hand there was the bourgeois Enlightenment which criticized the feudal estates—first the clergy, then the nobility—for their inability to justify their existence and their privileges by their contribution to the circulation of money and the growth of capital. The liquidation of property during the Reformation and the English and French Revolutions was preceded and accompanied by a spate of political and philosophical polemic directed against the property owners. Whether urbane and humorous (Erasmus or Mandeville), or passionate and ideological (the Diggers or Tom Paine) or just painstaking and remorseless (Locke or Voltaire), this essentially empiricist critique, with its appeal to what to a banker, merchant, or master-craftsman would seem equity, common sense or observable fact, culminated, in the eighteenth century, in the new science of political economy and the work of Bentham, in both of which human beings are, as a matter of principle, made as equivalent and uniform as units of the coinage, and neither nobility nor clergy have a great part to play. But at the same time we find the remnants of the medieval world being criticized from quite a different quarter and from a quite different first premise—the primacy of collective order. This monarchical or bureaucratic Enlightenment, as we may call it, was principally the work of officials of the crown—the main political beneficiary of the collapse of feudalism—seeking to eliminate the independence of historic institutions, including such third-estate anomalies as free cities and guilds, and to subordinate them to a single administrative will. Sometimes benign in its earlier versions (More, Bodin), sometimes ruthless (Machiavelli, Hobbes) the attempt to see in society a centralized structure, corresponding to or deducible from the structure of the human mind, became the systematic project of generations of philosophers in eighteenth-century Germany from Leibniz and Wolff to Fichte and the Romantics.

Let us for a moment try to characterize these two different traditions by looking at their consequences in literature—the different ways in which the bourgeois mentality got written down. Philosophy did not fare so well in England as in Germany. Indeed after about 1740 the English largely gave it up and left it to the Scots, who, being deprived of their political autonomy, and finding themselves in much the same relation to the English as the German officials to their own sovereigns, had the leisure to seek similar intellectual consolations. But this was an age when the English had no leisure, except insofar as others worked to provide it for them. While the Scots had an Enlightenment the English founded first one empire and then another. At the same time they founded a new literary genre. For the benefit, initially, of women and domestic servants, whose reading time was paid for by the productive labors of the wage-slaves of the head of the household, busy scribblers invented a new form of prose romance in which the bourgeois order ever more confidently reflected and admired itself. Spreading, like industrialization, from its English homeland the novel eventually became the most subtle means of representing extensively in language what it was to be human in the "modern" or "bourgeois" period of Europe and the Western world which ended (at the latest) in 1945. It thus provides the fullest and most persuasive images of what a human identity might be that is called only to consumption: its heroes and heroines make their way through the imagined world only as consumers of its delights and horrors, as if supported by some hidden capital. A Girondin could think of all men (rarely women) as endowed with universal primordial rights only by both postulating that they all possessed capital and forgetting that some must therefore nonetheless be workers. In the same way the principal figures of the great novels, from Tom Jones and Fanny Price to Esther Summerson and Martin Chuzzlewit, experience the rich world their authors describe, and they experience it *in time*, but, for a reason which seems to lie in the nature of the genre, they cannot be shown engaging in productive labor. This strange feature of the realistic novel—that it can represent anything except work—does not change, however diverse the languages and cultures into which the genre spreads. There are of course many representations, from the picturesque to the melodramatic, of the work*place*, of characters in an industrial landscape; what is missing is the sense of the lifelong identity of what we are and what we do. The English novelists prefer to guide their characters to a happy ending by means of a secret endowment—gradually or suddenly revealed—with inherited wealth, noble birth, or virtue of a degree which can be suitably rewarded only with the perfect marriage—with romantic emblems, that is, of the emancipation from work. Stendhal is more ruthless in showing the life either of the man who really does possess the fruits of the work of others (Fabrice) or of the man who really does not (Julien Sorel) and who is uncompensated by any device of romance. (Dickens too, though, in the original version of *Great Expectations*, strikes the note of tragic bitterness as he dispels the grand illusion of consumption without production, and confronts the guilty Pip with the true benefactors on whom he has battened.) When Levin, in *Anna Karenina*, gives up the attempt to join in the labor of the harvesters he is not only acknowledging that his own moral development has taken a false turn—he is also embodying a limitation of the kind of book Tolstoy is writing. Work, it seems, in all these cases cannot be *both* talked about *and* shown, as a character can. However it is not absent: it manifests itself silently and all the time in the work done by the writing author, in the narrator's rendering of the imagined world, in the linguistic achievement that is Tolstoy's evocation of a dog's eye view of a shoot or in the painful progress of Balzac's pen from blotch to blotch of the reeking wallpaper. It is omnipresent but it is unrepresented, the forgotten basis for the continuing, temporally extended, identity of the characters. That is why the characters are perfect analogues of what we may call the imperialist or capitalist self—an identity based on the illusion that, in a world where all are equal, we do not have to work in order to be.[8]

That illusion is not shared by the official; but the production which is essential to his monadic self is wholly internal. Inheriting the Lutheran subservience to Caesar he inherits also the Lutheran dualism, in an extreme form which denies the very possibility of externality: work is work of the soul upon itself, not of bodies on matter, or other bodies. With supercilious envy, the world of industry and commerce, from which the official is anyway excluded, is dismissed as mere appearance: the reality is the command issued by the monarch, God, or Reason. The kind of novel which expresses this belief, the German "Bildungsroman," is a pale and half-hearted affair, undecided between two worlds. Philosophy is different, though. In late eighteenth-century Germany, philosophy, the principal form of secularized theology, was the vehicle of an attempt to grasp the world both as consumed and as produced which in range and energy and impact, if not in variety, was the equal of the achievement of the great novelists. After 1781, when Kant's *Critique of Pure Reason* was published, the movement of German Idealism gave a new topicality and intensity to epistemology, the science of the detached self which makes all things into the material of knowledge and, by internalizing it, treats even production as a form of consumption. The official class was gaining a firmer grip on political power, particularly after the destruction of the Prussian old regime at the battle of Jena. The example of the French revolution and the Napoleonic reconstruction and, for the prescient, the prospect of industrialization, all made more urgent the need to define the relation of officialdom to the bourgeoisie, which elsewhere in Europe was asserting so successfully its right to rule. The political philosophy of Hegel is a synthesis of both the major self-interpretations of the post-feudal European middle class: as economically and politically free "men and citizens" (but is the recipe really as universal as the declaration of rights pretends?) and as individual embodiments of the state power (but is that really freedom, as the learned and salaried professors claim?). Hegel brings together both the imperialist self and the monadic self, both an empirical, libertarian, English (and Scottish) tradition and an idealist, bureaucratic German tradition. He is heir of both Enlightenments and his theory of the state owes as much to the bourgeois and empiricist Scottish economists as it does to the rationalist and Idealist officials of the German academy.

As Hegel came to maturity the largest feudal institution in Europe finally crumbled into nonentity. In 1796, a series of separate peace-treaties between the French Republic and various German princes put an end in all but name to the Holy Roman Empire: Hegel was twenty-six and was starting to write extensively on theological and political issues. The Empire lingered on for another decade, by the end of which Hegel had completed *The Phenomenology of Spirit* and the ground-plan of his entire system. In Germany, the twenty years up to the so-called Restoration of 1815 saw more than the collapse of the *ancien régime* however: they were also a period of very active state-formation. The geographical boundaries, juridical basis, and internal organization of all the German-speaking territories changed very greatly, and more than once. For a brief period, from 1815 to 1819, the chaotic institutional nebula of the old Empire seemed finally to have condensed into a federation of small to medium-sized sovereign German states, each with a written constitution of a markedly liberal nature. It was the spectrum of political possibilities created in these honeymoon years after the Congress of Vienna that Hegel analyzed and presented in his *Philosophy of Right*: because it was visible for so short a time and was soon overshadowed by more sinister developments in Austria and Prussia, it is often forgotten altogether. Hegel's political philosophy is then treated as abstract utopianism or, worse still, as a glorification of Prussia (which usually means not even the Prussia he knew in his lifetime but what it became after his death). Hegel did not move to Prussia until 1819, when his political system was virtually complete, and the nearest thing to an exemplar of the state he describes in the *Philosophy of Right* was probably not Prussia at all but his native Württemberg as it would have been if the amendments he proposed to its new constitution had been adopted. Even as they were, the new German states had systems of government that, on paper at least, were more modern and—as a later age would call it—democratic, than the corrupt and shambling and still largely medieval political structure of pre–Reform Bill England. But the new constitutionalism had a fatal weakness. Everywhere, in Württemberg no less than in Prussia, it had not grown naturally, it had been imposed—by external *diktat*, by the will of the sovereign, by the high-minded ingenuity of reforming officials. Power was never transferred—at best it was generously lent. After the student unrest of 1817 and the Carlsbad Decrees two years later, reformism lost its sway, the loans were called in, the promises were broken, and the officials dutifully set about administering a police state instead. Hegel was aware of this weakness and in one major, indeed crucial, respect his account of the modern state is based not on the German reality of his time but on principles he saw operating in the wider world of Western Europe, and perhaps America too. In the *Philosophy of Right*, in direct contradiction of the political circumstances actually prevailing everywhere in the German-speaking world (except Switzerland), he gives the central role in the construction of the state not to the official class of state employees but to the economically active bourgeoisie whose interrelationships in the process of production and consumption, which he calls "the system of needs," make up the fabric of "civil[9] society." The Enlightenment of the economists is largely given priority over the Enlightenment of the idealists: the State does not depend on the monarchy of reason, it is built up from the activities of its citizens. It is an extraordinarily far-sighted abstraction from the perspective natural to an eighteenth-century German intellectual—W. H. Bruford found that in 1820 in Weimar, a small town but still a capital, there was virtually no middle class at all[10]—but to it is due Hegel's continuing and immediate relevance to the problems of (post)-modernity.

The Hegelian State and the World System

The *Philosophy of Right* is of peculiar interest today because it so clearly raises the question: What is the relation between the economic order of civil society and what Hegel calls "the political state," the organs of government? Are there questions about our collective lives which cannot be answered simply by leaving the matter to the market, in which supply and demand are adjusted to each other? Are there decisions to be taken which are not in the end decisions of consumers or producers to buy or sell? Do we have a political as well as an economic identity?

It is fundamental to Hegel's treatment of this issue that he does not regard the political state as something additional to civil society, something that one might have or might do without, as a town might or might not have a municipal museum, or the United Kingdom might or might not include the Isle of Man. Hegel divides his discussion of social behavior (Sittlichkeit) into three sections devoted to the family, civil society, and the state. All the individual members of a given population belong, in principle, under each of these three headings. Even a member of the supreme cabinet or council of ministers which advises the Crown will also be a member of a family and will also, at least as a consumer, be a link in the chain of buying and selling that constitutes civil society. Conversely, there is a political aspect to the existence even of a child who is still a minor, for example, as the object of laws relating to children's welfare, or by association through its parents with an interest group (a "corporation") pressing for political advantage. Even the activities peculiar to the political state are not, in Hegel's scheme, as numerous, nor do they generate as many autonomous institutions, as we might now expect. Many tasks that we rather loosely think of nowadays as the responsibility of "the state," come for Hegel under the heading of "polity" (Polizei), which is a (sophisticated) part of civil society. Maintaining public health, providing for public education, regulating the standard (and price) of basic foodstuffs, relieving poverty, servicing the physical infrastructure of commercial life (e.g., streetlights, a favorite example of Hegel's, which may stand for all the other public utilities that were unknown in his time and place)—all these have a clear economic significance with calculable costs and benefits. They are services which collective self-interest will always—eventually—find necessary, and there is nothing philosophy has to say about the way in which they should be provided. The state institutions in the strict sense are only three in number: the Crown, which normally does no more than sign the papers preserved to it by the government and thereby gives the form of an act of will to the government's decision about what is desirable; the bureaucracy, which makes the will of the Crown effective; and the representative and legislative bodies which formulate the decisions which the Crown endorses. (The government is formed out of the upper levels of the bureaucracy and the legislature.) The legislature however is nothing other than the public voice of civil society. Hegel is so anxious to preserve the principle that the economic and political orders are identical that he criticizes the idea that suffrage is simply a matter of one man–one vote on the grounds that it is inadequate to economic, that is, social, reality: the interests of those who live off the land (in 1821 Germany's biggest industry by far) are different from those engaged in trade, and the interest groups, or corporations, that form within civil society—guilds, professional bodies, unions, friendly societies, and perhaps also church and educational institutions—are also constituencies that deserve direct representation and should not be reduced to the status of being merely personal concerns of individual voters. This syndicalist tendency in Hegel's thought is less dated than it appears (it is reflected in the role of the life-peerage in the British House of Lords and in the representation of regional interests in the second chambers of federal states such as Germany and Australia, as well as in the function of modern political parties as coalitions of interest groups) and it is anyway less important than the principle it embodies. The state is not, according to Hegel, a branch of public administration dealing with certain areas thought of as especially significant. The essence of the political state is not administration at all but representation—the representation of all the members of civil society to themselves and *as a whole*. In civil society a group of people live together in a system of reciprocal needs and satisfactions; in their representative legislative institutions they become aware of that system and all their interrelations as a limited whole. They see it, affirm it, modify it insofar as it is capable of being modified by law, and so constitute themselves as a particular state. A state is a civil society seen, by its members, as a whole. Politics—the state—is the self-awareness of a community.

Insofar as they are aware of themselves as political beings, as citizens of their state, the members of a community have reached, Hegel believes, the highest possible degree of individual self-awareness. We can say there is such a thing as a state when there are individuals who have towards it an ethos (Gesinnung) of patriotism: they recognize their society as something they have a duty to die for, if necessary. Patriotism, however, is, Hegel says, an everyday virtue: not the humbug of occasional ostentatious emotionalism, but the confidence with which one walks the streets in security at night, "the fundamental feeling of order, common to all."[11] It is an identity of one's awareness of oneself with one's awareness of the order in one's state, which is both the source and the expression of one's existence as a being with rights and duties. (It is one of the absurdities of contemporary conservatism that at one and the same time it seeks to revive patriotism and to instill contempt and distrust of the state: if you can't be patriotic about your state, you can't be patriotic at all.) We do not need to consider whether Hegel envisages this patriotic self-awareness as actually achieved in one or more of the states of his time, or as possible in them, or as possible and therefore in some special sense actual. What matters for our purposes is that Hegel offers a representation of the self which is radically different from that characteristic either of the bourgeois or of the bureaucratic enlightenment and which has been made possible by a theory of political society which carefully balances the claims of the two contending factions within the middle class (§297). Bourgeois society, in Hegel's scheme, generates two sets of institutions which are forerunners of the state: as producers, the members of the "system of needs" create interest groups, perhaps even cartels, known as corporations—in their ambition to direct everyone's affairs in accordance with their own interests the corporations create the forum in which discussion of the general good, and so representative institutions, can grow; as consumers, the same set of people identify needs that are best met collectively and set up the services comprised under "polity." Once the state is in existence however it needs a "universal class" of officials to defend its general interests against the particular ambitions of bourgeois society. So the principal internal tasks of the state bureaucracy are moderating and superintending the activities of corporation and polity so that they correspond to the general will expressed by the legislature. The self of the mature Hegelian citizen reflects this entire circular structure. It is neither the bourgeois-imperialist self dependent on its private capital—that is, on the repressed and forgotten work of others—for its illusion that it is free to consume without producing; nor is it the bureaucratic self dependent on the crown monopoly of force—the veiled power by which laws are maintained and taxes raised—for its illusion that, outside the economic nexus of human needs, it can produce (bilden) its own private and asocial identity. It is neither like a character in a realist novel, nor like the agent, or ego, in idealist and post-idealist philosophy. It is a self which knows itself fully in the political institutions which represent it, because those institutions emerge directly from the economic facts of social life.

Persuasive though this vision of a modern self is, in one vital respect it belongs too polemically to its particular cultural tradition to have the universality which it claims. It is a Lutheran vision, and the self, and so the state, which it envisages is too enclosed and too solitary. No role is given to our economic relations with members of other states, and so no allowance is made for a civil and ultimately a political identity which might transcend state boundaries. The boundaries of the state are the boundaries of political life: international relations are a purely arbitrary matter of agreements between absolutely sovereign partners which may be revoked, with complete moral propriety, at any time. International political bodies are an impossibility, a contradiction in terms. No citizen's identity can be fractured or left incomplete because of some conflict of loyalty to different public jurisdictions.[12] The claim of a church to be institutionally anything more than a corporation subordinate to the state is roundly rejected by Hegel in a long footnote to §270 of the *Philosophy of Right*. Yet this is all untrue to our post-modern experience, determined as it is by globalization. If we drag our eyes away from the punctual and all-consuming self, in which market ideology assures us we can find a completely satisfying identity, to the realities of production, it is clear that most of us live caught between national and international authorities, between the local market in which we want to buy our satisfactions and the world market in which as sellers we have to compete, between the national and international legislations which regulate these markets, and between political attempts to define ethnic or similar communities on the one hand and universal causes, religious, sexual, or humanitarian, on the other. Hegel is surely right to claim that there is a political dimension to our lives as well as an economic one, that it is not alien to us but is the expression of our sense of self, that without it the economic sphere cannot function effectively, and perhaps not at all (as we shall see in a moment), and that the essence of life in a state is the freely chosen regulation of the interaction between political force and the economic system of needs and satisfactions. But his understanding of the forms states might take, and of the possibility of state-like bodies mediating between bodies, that are almost but not quite states, or not states any longer, is limited by his historical perspective—and so therefore, is his understanding of the selves which states express. With the passing away in 1806 of the Holy Roman Empire, and in 1815 of Napoleon's Catholic Empire—which in Germany seemed in some ways a prolongation of its predecessor—Lutheranism acquired in Germany a political autonomy which it had never possessed under the settlement of 1648. It was no longer bound, by what was effectively a supranational constitution, to recognition and even a limited toleration of Catholicism, of which it was the junior partner. Once the constituent territories of the old Empire had been given complete independence, Hegel was free to take as far as he wished the Lutheran readiness to identify church and state jurisdictions and Luther's rejection of the suprematist claims of Rome. In the case of the Holy Roman Empire Hegel, uniquely, allowed his historical judgment to be colored by the emotions of his early manhood, when the Empire was at its most pitifully ineffective and seemed only an inert obstacle to the great Revolution in France, and he always dismissed notions of an international political order, particularly those of Kant, as marginal or illusory. Kant was not a subject of the emperor, and was even further from Catholicism than he was from orthodox Lutheranism, but he belonged to an era when the basis of Europe's political structure was still in theory feudal rather than nationalist and when the concept of world-citizenship still deserved serious analysis. Much in his philosophical system can be seen as an earlier form of Hegel's fusion of two Enlightenments, but in his account of international relations he was further-sighted. And since, in the German tradition, concepts of the state and of the self are inseparable, this may also mean that Kant can offer us the modifications to Hegel's picture of human identity that we need in an age that cannot yet be described as post-Hegelian. Although both thinkers maintain an equilibrium for as long as they can, Kant, in the end, in his critical philosophy, favors the bourgeois, empirical Enlightenment, embodied in what he calls the faculty of "understanding" (Verstand), Hegel in the end, for all his concern to do justice to the creative power of the bourgeoisie, inclines to the unifying monarchical power of reason (Vernunft), the Enlightenment of the crown officials. It is for Hegel as certain that our thinking must amount to a unity, now, as that in a state there can be only one monarch at a time. It is this absolute assertion of the unity of systematic thought which has been the main stumbling-block for modern interpreters of Hegel. Maybe Kant, for whom the unity is only ever a future ideal, can show us how to modify Hegel without abandoning him, and political thought seems the right place to start. For political thought is not only the flower of Hegel's system, it is also thought about the real circumstances which were its roots. So let us ask how Hegel's political scheme relates to the historical reality that Kant too has described. How does Hegel think a state comes into existence?

In one sense, the question is misleading, if it is meant to imply that for Hegel a particular civil society could exist before, and without, being a state: it is precisely being a state that gives a community a particular identity. You can't have a national identity without having a state (we might think that Jews or, say, Kurds, show that you can, but if we then consider the difference between being a Jew and being an Israeli citizen we shall think again). Hegel repeatedly emphasizes that the political state (whose institutions may be embryonic or vestigial, but it will not for that be any less a state) is not only the goal of the process he is describing but also its presupposition—identity is always, for him, a matter of becoming what you are. The question "How does a state come into existence?" is not therefore fundamentally different from the question, "How does a particular civil society come into existence?"—nor should we expect anything else, given the importance to Hegel of the fact that in both cases the population of individuals we are dealing with is the same. In purely natural terms human beings grow into groups larger than families either by the process of reproduction, or through being forced together by military power, or by mutual economic interest (§181). But how do a number of economically and socially interacting people come to constitute a particular whole? Hegel's answer is: by limitation. At different points he mentions three limiting factors that are necessary for the growth of a state identity— whether, alone or together, they are sufficient is not clear. First, there are the physical, or geographical, factors unique to a particular case—a state must have physical boundaries. For as long as the American frontier is fluid, indefinitely open to the west, Hegel said in his lectures on world-history in the 1820s, America cannot form a state.[13] Second, a state is something that proves itself, ultimately in war, against other states: it shows that, like other states, it is something its members are prepared to die for, and that can be shown only if they do die for it and so equate the limits of their lives with the limits of their state. Third, however, the state, as a collective self-awareness, comes into existence as a limitation of civil society upon itself. In Hegel's time it was already an old notion that government has a role as soon as resources are scarce and priority in distribution has to be determined by something other than ability to pay. Hegel gives the notion a more sophisticated and dynamic form: it is in the nature of civil society, the economic system, to create a permanent and permanently intensifying apparent shortage of resources, that is, permanent and increasing (relative) poverty. Over-production increases competition and so both depresses wages and furthers the division of labor. Poverty grows, and so also do the divisive pressures on the fabric of civil society itself, especially on the producer-led institutions or "corporations" which are the sources of a sense of belonging and of self-respect. For a while civil society can avoid these problems by creating colonies and markets overseas to soak up its excessive products, but if this cannot be done or the colonies become independent, the day comes when "the turmoil of this situation can be reduced to harmony only if it is brought under control by the state" (§185, Zusatz). It has been said of Marx that his most indisputable insight was into the runaway nature of the capitalist process. Hegel had this insight before Marx, though, and did not need the word "capitalism" to help him. When the state steps in it does not, and in Hegel's scheme cannot, put an end to the processes intrinsic to the system of needs, no more than it can alter the fundamental facts of geography, or the fact that sooner or later we all die: the state cannot stop the generation of poverty. What it can do is to prevent the decline of the poor into a "rabble" who feel themselves excluded from civil society, increase its polarization into ever richer and ever poorer, and may eventually destroy it altogether. The state cannot make the poor rich but it can ensure that they continue to have rights, and to feel they have them. Even the poorest Englishman, Hegel notes, still feels himself to be an Englishman and to have rights and freedoms of which he can be proud (§244)—he still has the "ethos" of a member of his state. Hegel is not proposing—as Marx at least pretended he thought Hegel was proposing—that the state is a convenient fiction, a propaganda trick practiced by the haves on the have-nots, to keep them from revolution. Hegel is making three linked assertions. First, it is impossible for the system of needs to make everyone (relatively) rich: there will always be rich and (relatively) poor and this distinction will tend to grow more marked not less. Second, political and economic values are quite distinct: being free—that is, being a self-determining member of the self-determining whole that we call a state—is a different matter altogether from being rich or poor. Only a charlatan will claim that making people free will also make them rich (a fallacy much propagated in the 1980s and 1990s). On the contrary, in a free state there will be rich and poor, and an increasing difference between them, as in any economic community. Third, however, the state, through the operation of commonly agreed law, and of the force which is its sanction, counters the tendency of civil society to self-destruction at least for a while: on the one hand it takes such measures as it can against the increase of poverty, on the other hand it provides its members with a sense of self which transcends their role as elements in the system of needs and work, consumption and production. A certain range of inequality within the system is acceptable to me for as long as I feel it to be *my* system. I may, for example, accept that a government legislates to deregulate my profession if I feel that I—or fellow-citizens in whose good will I believe—elected the government, or if I feel that, in principle or in certain circumstances, the government cares enough for my well-being to intervene to save my job; that is, I will accept my economic disadvantage for as long as I feel that the community which inflicts it is *my* state. When I cease to feel that, I drop into the alienated "rabble," without state or full selfhood—the "underclass," as it is now called—and when the rabble grows large enough it will overthrow the state and cause civil society to regress at the cost of great dislocation and suffering for all—as the French Revolution put back the development of French civil society by at least thirty years, and the Russian Revolutions of the early and late twentieth century inflicted even greater reverses on the Russian people. A subtle and resourceful state however may maintain the—intrinsically unstable—equilibrium for a long time. But states are no more immortal than the people who compose them, and Hegel is quite clear that in time—in history—all states come to an end.

Limits, in short, make a whole, and when a civil community recognizes and affirms its limits it makes a self-conscious collective, that is, political, whole—a state. Hegel's theory of the state transcends the political theories of both the bourgeois and the official enlightenments with their different partial, and partially illusory, conceptions of the self. If we want to follow his example in an age when the global market has largely eradicated the distinction between bourgeoisie and officialdom and has created the new, and peculiarly illusory, conception of the punctual self (always only the locus of consumer choice and never the agent of production)—if we want, that is, to find out the truth about our selves and where in the world political identity and political action is still possible and necessary—then we should pay attention to the limits on our collective economic existence.

At first sight there do not seem to be any physical limits on the civil community to which the populations of Europe, North America, and the Pacific littoral belong. In the age of mass air travel, rivers, mountains, seas, and even distance do not present noticeable obstacles to the flow of goods, information, or people. London, Frankfurt, Paris, New York, Tokyo are closer to each other than to many parts of what is nominally their national hinterland. (True, it is difficult for the inhabitants of an island to appreciate how much of their historic identity they lost once the only difference between flying Brussels-Paris and Brussels-London was that in the second case you got a demonstration of how to put on a life-jacket. But on the screen that opens on to the Internet even these stylized icons of a physical frontier are absent.) However, there is another sense in which we are fully aware of physical limits defining our community as a unique system of human needs: only so much fossil energy, extractable mercury, fresh water; and every month brings some newly discovered constraint on the chemical manipulation of our environment. The most significant—that is, the most symbolic—day of the twentieth century was the 16th of July 1969: the landing on the moon signified the end of giant steps for mankind in any direction. It was the day on which the human race finally and with great effort ran its head against the wall. NASA's *tour de force* demonstrated not only the emptiness of the great out-there—no New Worlds for stout Cortes, merely dust, darkness, and deadly radiation—but the enormous difficulty of getting to it. Since it would take longer to fly from the earth to Mars than to walk from England to Australia a new tyranny of distance was confirmed and with it our enclosure in our own local biosphere (of which any conceivable interplanetary extension, whether a space station or a bio-engineered Venus, would be only a peninsula). There are no longer civil societies forced by physical constraints to define themselves as the occupants of particular areas on our planet's surface, as was the case in Hegel's day: the physical constraints we now feel force us to define ourselves as united by our occupancy of the third planet. Our civil society is one and global.

In the political arena, in which environmental summits take place, we are already beginning to accept that we are a single world, with a unique natural body which does not extend to infinity. Equally unwillingly we also recognize that our economic activities now embrace all human beings but have serious, indeed fatal, intrinsic limits. There is a problem of poverty in the modern world quite as insoluble as that which Hegel diagnoses, but it is a problem not for individual nations but for the whole international economic order. Individual nations may make themselves wealthy, just as did the individual families who prepared the ground for the nineteenth-century state as Hegel understood it. But they can do so only by exacerbating competition and so driving other nations into a poverty which threatens the cohesion of the wealth-creating system. The gap, we know, between rich and poor gets only wider. And the poor can be expected not only to laugh at the environmentalism of the rich, but also to turn in desperation to the weapons of terror, nuclear if possible. Indeed, as national boundaries melt away, so the process of impoverishment becomes visible again even in areas of the world which were once uniformly privileged. Cardboard cities, banished to the colonies in the heyday of imperialism, have reappeared on the streets of Cosmopolis, and the middle-class families of Europe and North America, feeling the impact of Far Eastern expertise and pay-rates in such fields as computing, finance, and industrial manufacture, see their income stagnating and the nightmare of pauperization being realized in the generations to come in their drug-dependent children and their grandchildren born with congenital AIDS. In the painful adjustment, therefore, of trade deficits and surpluses round the world, in the fight against pandemics, terrorism, and international crime, and—more charitably if less persistently—in the coordinating of international aid and development, there is coming into existence a world political structure to ameliorate the worst consequences of our economic interaction, to persuade us all to carry on in the common endeavor by giving us universal ("human") rights, and to stave off for the present the inevitable but indefinitely postponable end.

So it might seem that the global process is heading for a world-state. Increasingly, when we say "we," "we" means the human race. Increasingly, "we" are aware of ourselves as a finite natural unity, with finite natural resources. (Hegel would say, our "we" has the "moment" of individuality). Increasingly, "we" are aware of ourselves as a community which has to find ways of reincorporating those whom the economic system, the system for satisfying our mutual needs, threatens to exclude. (Hegel would say, our "we" has the "moment" of universality). What "we" do not and cannot have, however, is that identity which comes to a community through defining itself over against others of the same kind. (In Hegelian terms, our "we" lacks the "moment" of particularity). For all practical purposes we are alone in the universe. We cannot constitute ourselves into a world-state, in the full Hegelian sense of the term "state," because there is, and can by definition be no other world-state in war with which we would feel under a duty to die for our own. World-citizens could not have a sense of patriotism: they could not therefore have a sense of complete identity with the political institutions that represented them, however directly these emerged from global economic life. Of course, economic and political relations with an extra-terrestrial state would make possible a planetary state whose citizens could feel patriotic about belonging to the Earth. But the question would then arise whether there could be a super-world-state incorporating both ourselves and our "alien" counterparts, and whether we could feel patriotic about *that*.

The obsession of our collective fantasy with extra-terrestrial encounters (usually leading to war) is a symptom of our uncomfortable awareness that the ever closer economic (and so political) union of the human race must create a structure which will be unlike any we have known before, which in particular will not be able to give us a secure collective identity. Dreams of Earth's involvement with alien empires are wish-fulfillments, born of a hankering after past certainties: the process of ever closer union is acknowledged, but it is imagined as terminating in a planet-sized nation state. The reality, however—which the dream is trying to deny—is that, unlike the other state-forming powers of physical and economic limitation, the limiting power of particularity is on the wane, diluted by the same internationalization that is strengthening the other two powers. As we all become less different from one another, we all become less certain of our identity. Patriotism, the readiness to die for an *existing* state, is virtually extinct throughout the world. (Perhaps the Swiss possess it.) The cynics who ask how many are prepared to lay down their lives for Brussels or the UN should be more cynical: how many *more* are prepared to lay down their lives for the land of their birth? Of course there are many prepared to die, and very many prepared to kill, not, however, for states but for causes and ideas, for religions, for groups (including animals), and for what is called nationalism, that is, the erection or consolidation of states which are at present non-existent or only partially established. That is not patriotism, as Hegel understands it. Loyalty in life and death to a "feeling of order common to all" has little to do with current events in Serbia, Armenia, or Algeria. The world political unit, in which our search for collective and personal identity could finally be satisfied, in which we could be freely self-determining citizens, is an idea or cause too, not a state. It is not, and cannot become, completely real, for against whom could it wage war?

Not that major wars have ceased to be a possibility. It is, for example, a very serious question whether China will be able to claim its share of world resources and the world economy without a Third World War. And if we envisage such a war, or the steps that would be necessary to avoid it, and the tectonic plates into which that military or—preferably—political process would break up the human race, then it is clear that particularity has not lost all its power. There are potential large-scale political units in the world—units, that is, of a size commensurate with the global economic process— which are capable of developing into something like states in the Hegelian sense, with limited interests of their own and capable of giving their citizens the opportunity to choose their identity freely for themselves. The development of the political institutions in both China and the European Union over the next decades is a matter of as much importance for world peace as the future of such global bodies as the United Nations or the World Trade Organization. Under the pressure of economic globalization the political world is developing two sets of structures whose future interrelationship will determine how many human beings are still alive at the end of the twenty-first century: regionally supranational bodies capable of developing into something like Hegelian states, and world institutions, coextensive with the global market but lacking the authority that comes from fully representing their constituents' sense of who they are. Hegel has still much to tell us about the mutual dependency of selfhood and statehood in the regional units into which the world order is coalescing, but to the global entities our only philosophical guide is Kant. Hegel did not have Kant's understanding of the possibility of a world political system that would be unified but something short of a state in the full sense of the term. Kant believed that you could not understand the past unless you had a vision of the future, that the only coherent vision of the human future was that all states should bind themselves into treaty relationships which would prevent war between them, and that in the end only those states which had "republican" (as we now say, "democratic") constitutions would be willing to enter on such treaties. Kant's analysis may be said to have been given at least negative confirmation by events, since the two most destructive wars of the twentieth century were launched by his own nation when it was autocratically ruled—on the second occasion by a tyrant who in 1934 demonstrated his contempt for consensualism by withdrawing Germany from the League of Nations. Kant certainly did not think that a world of democratic and peaceable states was a probable future for humanity or even perhaps a goal attainable within a specifiable period of years, but he did think that the only foreseeable alternative is mutual mass-destruction—the "perpetual peace" of the cemetery—and that we need such a goal to define the direction in which we are going, to make sense of our moral lives, that is, of our personal and collective history.

The notion that we could at the same time conceive of a goal and know that we cannot attain it—what Kant called having "ideals"—was anathema to Hegel. Yet this refusal of the future and of what we might call the incompleteness of human life is the weakest point in his system and the source of all in it that seems unrealistic or objectionable. More than any other of the great philosophers, except perhaps his models Aristotle and Spinoza, he aims to make us feel at home in the world. But the evidence of the century and a half of world history since his death is that though we have a city to build here it is not an abiding one, and that our life has direction rather than a definable purpose. The states that have grown up since the French Revolution cannot be revered, as Hegel requires, "as something divine on earth" (§272), because they are plainly transcended by political or nearly political structures, secular international bodies or supra-national religions or other causes, which do not themselves amount to states, but which point us towards an ideal of ever closer cooperation. Similarly Hegel's unparalleled understanding of the extent to which we create the world of meanings that we inhabit needs to be complemented by Kant's understanding that all our knowledge is in the end dependent on things as they are in themselves, that is, as they are created and given to us, in a manner—or by a power—which is necessarily beyond our knowing. And equally, for all Hegel's insight into the unity of the manifestations of the world-spirit, Kant understood that self-knowledge cannot be absolute or perfect but that selfhood always has to be projected or extrapolated from "the series of [our completed past] actions" (§124) into a future of what we hope or ought to be. Hegel marked himself off both from Kantianism and from a Catholic understanding of the modern world by his radical rejection both of the theology of creation and of any philosophical concern with the future. These defects in his system could be remedied only by a new analysis simultaneously of Being and Time. For that Germany had to wait for another hundred years.

7 Martin Heidegger and the Treason of the Clerks

In the nineteenth century the task of bringing together the Hegelian and Kantian streams of German Idealism was
left largely unattempted. The philosopher who came nearest to success in it was Nietzsche, who had only limited knowledge of the
work of either of his forerunners. The academic tradition of Neo-
Kantianism remained alive however, and in constant conflict with
various forms of the dominant Hegelianism. In the early twentieth
century, it issued in the movement of Phenomenology, which presented the task of reconciliation to the man called to perform it
both by his innate ability and by his social origins—Martin Heidegger. Through his influence on Derrida in particular, Heidegger has
been the most important philosophical progenitor of the Post-
Modernist movement. He also provides one of the earliest examples
of that strange paradox of the twentieth-century intellectual: the
coexistence of a radical theoretical critique of the bourgeois concept of selfhood with a practical political stance hostile to the
global market which has made bourgeois selfhood obsolete. In his
case, living out that paradox led to a veritable pact with the devil.

A Process of Assimilation?

After Hegel's death in 1831 the modern state, whose outlines he had
discerned in the halcyon years of German constitutionalism from

1815 to 1819, was ever more imperfectly represented by German political reality. True, after 1848, and with Bismarck as the chief magi-
cian, Germany was gradually transformed into a simulacrum of
other successful European nation-states. It acquired a unified political structure, an industrial revolution, with capitalist bourgeoisie
to match, and even a respectable little colonial empire, scattered
across Africa and the South Seas. But it differed from its Western rivals by what, in the quarter of a century leading up to the First
World War, they came to call its "militarism."

Of course there was plenty of hypocrisy in the charge: military
attitudes and interests, uniforms and physical discipline, pervaded
British and French society in the age of Stalkey and Baden-Powell
to an extent which would nowadays seem intolerable, and which already seemed ridiculous in the post-war perspective of Graves and
Orwell. Germany really was different, however. The fondness of
Kaiser Wilhelm II for his soldier's uniform was more than the expression of a neurotically operatic personality—as which it made
Thomas Mann bite his lip in embarrassment[1]—and more even than
a reflection of a society in which military service was universal and
military rank was, for the untitled, the key to precedence. The public gesture claimed a continuity with the traditions of the eighteenth-century Prussian kings which was genuine and which had a
greater influence on the political character of the German state
than its modern economic sub-structure. Because in 1849 the king
of Prussia, Friedrich Wilhelm IV, was too proud to accept the German crown offered him by a parliament of burghers and professors,
and German unity was in the event achieved by force, the political
institutions of the state established between 1866 and 1871 were
still those of an absolute monarchy and not—or not yet—the self-
expression of German civil society. The brilliant act of imagination
by which Hegel had thought his way beyond the circumstances of
his time and envisaged a state in which a Western-style bourgeoisie
and a German-style bureaucracy would, through representative institutions, reciprocally control each other, was left suspended as an
unfulfilled prophecy. For the young Wilhelm II to dismiss the head
of his government in 1890, by dropping the pilot Bismarck, was an
act of arbitrary rule which had not been possible in England for
two centuries. In the new Germany, and particularly in Prussia, the
Crown remained the ultimate source of political power and pres-

tige and its appointees remained the culturally dominant class: the military and the administration, the university professors—at the height of their international esteem between 1848, when Acton went to study in Munich, and 1914, when T. S. Eliot went to Marburg—and the Protestant clergy. Their position was increasingly threatened by Europe's most rapidly industrializing system of needs, by the ever more numerous and self-confident representatives of German capital and German labor, and they defended it as a beleaguered élite usually does: by cultivating contempt for what lay outside it—for civilian society and for money—and by reinforcing the obstacles to joining it—multiplying the demands for paper qualifications and insisting on the purity and autonomy of native German traditions.

The official culture of the Second German Empire is an unappetizing alliance of the military with the aesthetic and of the mandarin with the racist. To paint or write about city-dwellers in ordinary clothes with money worries was tantamount to declaring yourself a—proscribed—Social Democrat. The most deadly charge in academic debate was that of being "unscientific," closely followed by that of being unsuited to educate German youth—both of them were deployed by the establishment philologist Wilamowitz-Moellendorff in his assault on Nietzsche's professional reputation, that is, on his suitability to occupy an official post. The extraordinary outburst of literary and philosophical productivity in late eighteenth-century Protestant North Germany, which Nietzsche rightly saw as the symptom of a tense and desperate search for meaning, was implausibly canonized as a "classical" achievement which it required a doctorate in literary "science" to appreciate and which was appropriated as the national heritage of a state unknown to any of the writers concerned, and to which few of them would have wished to belong. Orthodox Jews, though nominally given equal rights with other citizens in 1871, were by a silent conspiracy excluded from the upper reaches of the army, the administration, and the universities until the revolution of 1918, and so on the whole chose to find their way in the "free" professions as self-employed lawyers and doctors, or remained confined to the ignoble activities of business and finance which had been their special preserve since the Middle Ages. Nor was the situation of Catholics very different, indeed it was transiently worse since throughout the 1870s the new state waged a bitter war against the hierarchy, religious orders, schools, and institutional structure of the Catholic Church (the "Kulturkampf"). Poles (the greater part of modern Poland lay in the territory of the Second Reich) were anyway virtually certain to belong to one or other of these excluded groups but were also the object of ever severer legal measures aimed at suppressing their language and expropriating their land. In its cultural policy the empire of Bismarck and Wilhelm II continued the homogenizing and rationalizing tendencies of the bureaucratic Enlightenment just as in its state structure it continued the tradition of monarchical authoritarianism.

All the time, however, the leviathan was growing that must inevitably burst the flimsy cage in which the monarch and his officials tried to contain it: by 1910 the German steel, chemical, and electrical industries were all larger than the British and not long afterwards the German bourgeoisie started, for the first time since 1848, to take charge of its own political fate.

Heidegger was born (in 1889) into a disadvantaged and disregarded class. In a village still divided by memories of the Kulturkampf the Heideggers had stayed loyal to Rome, though privilege lay with the Old Catholics who had broken with the papacy and taken the state's shilling. Nor could the altar-boy, and later seminarian, expect much more than condescension from the wider world in which he first felt his philosophical vocation: Protestants did not take Catholic faculties of theology wholly seriously—they had "a faint air of 'dubious scholarship'"[2]—and Catholic chairs of philosophy were few. Yet Heidegger's ambition, he wrote in 1915, was "to devote his academic career to making available the intellectual deposit of scholasticism for the future intellectual struggle for the Christian and Catholic ideal of life."[3] In the same year he concluded his study of (as he thought) Duns Scotus with the hint that he might now move on to Hegel's "colossal historical system" in which "all previous problematic themes of fundamental philosophy" were absorbed.[4] Integrating or at least confronting Catholic medieval theology with the supreme intellectual product of Lutheranism might have recovered the true spirit of the Hegelian system by modifying it in precisely those areas which now seem its most serious weaknesses: its neglect of the transcendence of God and of the independent individuality of things (its neglect, we might say, of the doctrine of creation), its tendency to Caesarism or state-worship, and its lack of a future-directed sense of morality and politics, especially international politics. Had that really been Heidegger's next step he would have challenged the cultural narrowness and self-deception of the Second Reich far more fundamentally than Nietzsche did. Instead, as the Reich crumbled in defeat and revolution, he accepted the offer of recognition and social opportunity which his parents had always refused and—already married to a Lutheran wife—announced in the first days of 1919 his rejection of "the system of Catholicism" (though not yet of Christianity or metaphysics).[5] In Freiburg he now moved from the department of Christian Philosophy to General Philosophy and close dependence on Husserl, who soon extracted from the university a special post for his brilliant protégé. At the same time Heidegger felt greatly drawn to the figure of Luther, who had also had to reject the system of Catholicism in order (in the German-Hegelian view) to found a new epoch of the spirit, and when he was appointed to a chair in Marburg he could move as an equal in the circle of Rudolf Bultmann who thought him "*the* Luther expert here."[6] He could also be received in the house of Frau Geheimrat Hitzig who was rumored to be a blood-relation of ninety-one living German professors.[7]

But Heidegger's was no ordinary story of emancipation and assimilation into a majority culture—not least because in the moment when he joined it the foundations of that culture had shifted, or rather, they had been removed altogether. True, throughout the economic upheavals of the twenties, "salaries will continue to be paid," as Thomas Mann, not himself an official, sardonically noted in his story *Disorder and Early Pain*, and the procedures by which, for example, the state appointed university professors did not change significantly after 1918. But the monarchical center, which gave the bureaucracy its purpose and its authority, had gone. Who were they now there to serve, all those public servants, and with them the army, the academy, and the Protestant churches? Surely not the capitalists and the trade unionists whom they had been keeping at arm's length for generations and who had now mysteriously succeeded in claiming for themselves the right to rule? Anyway, the German bourgeoisie had taken its uncertain hold on the new republic in circumstances which virtually guaranteed its own destruction: not only were there the ruinous impositions of the Versailles treaty to meet, but the empire had been shorn away, overseas, in Poland, and in Alsace-Lorraine. The owners of private wealth did not inspire confidence as the pillar of the new order. The extreme severity of the two great economic crises of inflation and depression, which leveled German civil society to the ground, both reflected and accentuated a crisis of political identity, and so of political control. Who now were the Germans and who was to tell them what to do? Where was the German state? There were very many, particularly from the armed forces, whom revolution and the end of the war had dispossessed or deprived of station, who could feel patriotic only towards a state that no longer existed.

An extensive state apparatus remained, but it seemed to float free of any economic or social ties. From the first years after the revolution its members found different ways of claiming for themselves the mantle of monarchy. In the army, in religion, or, the relevant professors proclaimed, in art, sociology, history, literature or philosophy could be found the key to the human condition and (therefore) to what was wrong with Germany. The preachers neglected only whatever they had in common with their fellow-citizens who thought differently—for it seemed to them a trivial matter to be a citizen of *this* republic. The babel of competing, groundless, and mutually incomprehensible ideologies which made Weimar Germany an intoxicating, and dangerous, place, resulted from the coincidence of several factors which were originally independent of one another: the collapse of a central identity and authority; the survival nonetheless of an authoritarian bureaucracy with a long tradition of hostility to the bourgeoisie; and Germany's unusually early arrival, thanks to the upheavals of 1918–1924, in the post-bourgeois era. The defective culture of the Second Reich, in which patriotism was possible only as a theatrical outburst (as when the war began in 1914) and not as "the fundamental feeling of order common to all," was inadequate to the political and economic crises which followed the end of empire and emperor. The Weimar Republic eventually voted itself out of existence because its members did not believe themselves to belong to it. It cannot be said that its intellectual officials, among whom Heidegger took an increasingly prominent place, did much to convince them otherwise.

Heidegger and Jünger (i): The Rediscovery of Production

Seen from the end of the twentieth century, Germany between 1918 and 1933 looks like a prophetic pre-enactment, on a smaller scale though for that reason perhaps more frenzied, of much with which we have all had to become familiar since the end of the Second World War. The international conflict which resumed in 1933, like other and older processes, did not come to an end until 1989. It is not therefore surprising that we can still learn from the thinkers of Weimar Germany, however unlikely, or even unsavory, provided we understand their context. Many of them survived well into the post-war period and continued their original lines of thought—among them Heidegger and the man whose influence on his political philosophy is still not properly appreciated, Ernst Jünger.[8] Jünger could celebrate his hundredth birthday, on 29 March 1995, without remorse for anything he had written because, in enough respects to quieten most people's conscience (admittedly, that need not be many), he had been proved right. What is of crucial importance to us of course—given the continuing relevance of what he has to say—is the point at which he went wrong.

Jünger himself was a free man. The success of his war memoirs, eventually prescribed reading for National Socialist schoolchildren (though he was never a member of the party), gave him financial independence. With that went a detached clarity about the social changes he was observing, though not about his own status as a bourgeois *littérateur* whom the changes would necessarily make obsolete. Having by willpower and miraculous good luck survived four violent years as an officer on the Western Front, he found in that experience, as did others, a paradigm of civilian life too. But Jünger's account of "the Front" is utterly devoid of self-aggrandizement or self-pity (or indeed pity—which is almost all that it has in common with Hitler's tabloid rant on the subject). He sees in modern war an organized process of the destruction of men and *matériel* which is a simple continuation of the organized processes of production and deployment that have led up to it. While for Tolstoy the military class was still blessedly unengaged in the system of needs, enjoying "a state of obligatory and unimpeachable idleness,"[9] for Jünger modern war and peace are both equally and primarily *work*. Modern soldiers and civilians move equally in vast numbers but as highly

disciplined individuals, mechanized and depersonalized, redistrib-
uting huge concentrations of energy.[10] Urban traffic is as precisely
controlled by signal lights and the threat of sudden death as an in-
fantry advance; physical fitness is equally imposed by military drill
and voluntary sport; faces give way to masks whether in the operating theater, at the cosmetics counter, or in chemical warfare. Just as
modern total war knows no distinction between soldiers and civilians, between the enemy's military and economic strength, but seeks
to annihilate both, so modern society even when at peace has to be
understood as striving for a total mobilization of all resources
whether human or natural, the making of all things available to be
worked on, the total submission of life and leisure to the regime of
work. This is a "revolution *sans phrase*" (*Arb* 275), that is, in all but
name: property is not overtly confiscated or nationalized, we continue to think ourselves owners of our house, for example, but "the
total [i.e., financial and legal] setting in which property is inserted
has changed fundamentally" (*Arb* 283), ownership is now only one
aspect among others of a working life, and what we own we own
more as a fief than as a free-hold. (This probably means that property is now seen simply as a realizable asset, is subject to detailed
regulation by the state, consists increasingly of industrial products
and so on.) "Mobilization," moreover, is now planetary, Jünger
thinks. At the end of the Great War (which he believes to have been
only provisional, *Arb* 157) the "global bourgeoisie" ("Weltbürger-
tum") may have appeared to be victorious everywhere (*Arb* 156, 153),
but it has succeeded only in making universal the factors which, as
Germany's example shows, must necessarily undermine its rule:
technology, competition, overproduction, the arms race (*Arb* 159,
169, 172, 191). The subject peoples of the victors' empires can also
wield the weapon of "the right to self-determination", which has
been used to dismember Germany and Austria (*Arb* 242–243). In the
conflicts which are to come the old collection of nation-states pro-
fessing liberal principles, but practicing colonialism, must pass away
and a world-wide unity and order must take its place, for "the
worker", the agent of "mobilization", is not bound in principle to any
one place or people but everywhere fulfills what is essentially the
same role (*Arb* 187, 192, 291). "The collapse of the bourgeoisie and its
world-view"[11] means furthermore the advent of an entirely new form
of art, reflecting the new sense of a collective human task but with-

out the liberal belief that the human community is destined to make infinite progress. The "bourgeois" art which concentrates on rendering "uniquely personal experiences" is obsolete and tedious (*Arb* 127–128, 221): its place will be taken by an art whose object is the entire planet, understood as the limited whole to which we are confined (*Arb* 163–164, 210, 217). The art of the future will be the planning of town and country on the world scale and subject to the recognition that the world is not endless (what is now called environmentalism). Jünger published these insights in 1930 in an essay called "Total Mobilization," and in 1932 in a substantial book, *The Worker.*

By 1930 you were already more likely to see certain truths about modern, particularly German, society if you were not a Marxist, encumbered by the need to account for the supposed success of the doctrine in far from modern Russia, and unwilling to accept that virtually a whole nation could be proletarianized without a socialist dictatorship. For it is, and was, easy to be misled by the continued prominence of great families, the Krupps, the Mendelssohns, the Rathenaus, and of the cartels with which they were associated, and to underestimate the extent to which Germany after 1924 was becoming a post-bourgeois society of consumer-producers. Agonizing changes were taking place that had little to do with the stylized class struggles envisaged by international communist orthodoxy. Hyperinflation had destroyed the savings of the middle classes and had swept away several generations' growth of private, charitable, and learned foundations which had depended on investments. No armaments industry was permitted, by which the economy might have been stimulated and harnessed to the building of the new state. There was no empire to which to export unemployment or which could provide cheap land or new opportunity. All the problems had to be solved at home, and by hard work, and in competition with other nations, better placed thanks to their victory. There was no room for the comforting illusion of the infinite depth of the bourgeois personality, cushioned by the forgotten labor of others and the ever-present background possibility of escape to the colonies. Jünger rightly saw that the units of the new society emerging around him were, uniformly, workers, and he rightly made this term refer to all, and not only or primarily to manual workers in industry. He was also right to see that the new "type," as he called it, would necessarily have a different sense of self from the "individuals" of the old world, best represented he thought by the poet-geniuses of the nineteenth century. The modern technical mind has, he says, little interest in those refined consumers of the pleasures of existence, and those who try to follow in their footsteps are forced into expressing "an unprecedented intensification of *suffering.*" "You sometimes almost have to pity these intelligences, for whom the production of the unique experience is an ever more ungrateful task, when you think that in the present context such an achievement is at best perceived as a kind of sentimental saxophone solo" (*Arb* 264).

Heidegger too had responded, far more profoundly and dispassionately than Jünger, to the creeping revolution *sans phrase*, and in *Being and Time* (1927) presented a wholly new analysis of what had once been called "the self" and "personal experience." He was still enough of a Catholic, and a scholastic,[12] to be suspicious of the Romantic ego, and the most immediately striking feature of the book is its resolutely third-person treatment of matters from which, since the age of Descartes, it has seemed the first person cannot be excluded (for example, sense experience, identity, meaning, conscience). "I" and "we" are largely banished and their place is taken by "existence" (Dasein), itself one of the special ways the world has of being.[13] The stylistic ploy was not in itself original: it is already frequent in Hegel, and Heidegger clearly learned something of this sort from the contemporary late poetry of Rilke, a superbly sensitive *grand bourgeois* who knew that the pleasures of his existence were being undone by the explosive—and to him alien—power of work. Heidegger's style however reflects a conceptual revolution: he has seen the opportunity of dethroning both the principal postmedieval forms of the self—the all-consuming bourgeois self with its illusory infinity, and the ring-fenced autonomous official self, producing and forming itself within its monadic cage. What has been called the self, he argues, cannot be thought in isolation from a world in which it already is, which colors its moods, and is the object of its concern. Indeed, prior to any constitution of a separate "self" is the revelation of the cared-for world as a shared world. Because we know the world before we know ourselves, and because we know the things of our human world as, in the most basic of economic relations, supplied by or made for others, it would be true to say that we know others before we know ourselves (*SuZ* 117–119).

Neither in the 1920s nor later did Heidegger admit that social change in his own time and place had made it possible for him to undertake this revolutionary analysis: his philosophy never allowed for its own derivation from a material world. Nor did he like to think of himself as the Reformer only of post-feudal philosophy: he claimed, rather fancifully, to be correcting a misapprehension that had begun among the Greeks. But only in the aftermath of the Great War, and only among those undeluded by the intoxication of victory, could it be appreciated that an era in economic history was coming to an end, and with it an era in human self-understanding. And maybe only someone familiar with the thought-patterns of the era that had preceded the one which was now dying could find new words for the new world that was to come after—whether or not he correctly understood his historical position.

At all events, there are two further vital respects in which *Being and Time* draws on the legacy of medieval Catholicism. Heidegger's insistence that life is absolutely and essentially finite (*SuZ* 258–259), that authentic existence is possible only if we recognize, without evasion, that we are to die, was the basis for what he sometimes, and his followers more often, called atheism. Seen historically, however it was in the first place a rejection of the fantasies of immortality, and continued spiritual activity after physical death, which had become common in liberal Protestantism after Leibniz and had found their way into Catholic piety too. In that sense, Heidegger was returning to the materialistic rigor of a Dante, according to whom we have only this life in which to act, and after that the judgment (the moment of death being decisive). Like Nietzsche's doctrine of "the eternal recurrence of the same," with which it is conceptually connected, Heidegger's doctrine is an attempt to restore a sense of the infinite importance of limited life which has been gradually fading since the Reformation went over into self-conscious Enlightenment. But Heidegger's philosophy of death is important above all, not for its theological implications, but for leading directly to his formal characterization of a way of existing which Jünger could describe only vaguely and intuitively. For, Heidegger argues, a world limited by death is necessarily a world in time—past, present, and future. In the "vulgar" or everyday understanding of time however (as Heidegger calls it), the most important limit time puts on our existence is thought to be that we have to exist in the present. The present is seen as a bottleneck through which an endless future streams into an irretrievable past. This view of time as "consumption in its most abstract form" (*SuZ* 431)— of which he thinks Hegel provides the most radical expression— Heidegger rejects. The most important feature of an existence in time is, he says, that it is stretched out towards an approaching future (*SuZ* 329): it not only has, but is, a project, and we show that we know our mortality in the "care" inspired in us by and for the world in which we find ourselves. The notion that our very being involves us in dealing purposefully with the world is the most generalized and fundamental form of the truth that we have to live in the world as workers, which Jünger thought destined to be the dominant truth in the modern age. Depersonalization, finitude, and a temporality in which the future is primary are the themes in *Being and Time* in which Heidegger is most obviously, and most creatively, modifying and modernizing the intellectual inheritance of nineteenth-century Germany and the Hegelian and even Lutheran elements still active within it.

Heidegger and Jünger (ii): The Neglect of Consumption

The closer Heidegger came to direct intellectual and practical involvement with contemporary affairs, however, the more decisively was he influenced by the process of assimilation on which he had embarked in 1919—and the more willing was he to submit his immensely more powerful mind to the journalistic opinions of Jünger (and others). "It is one of the supreme and cruel pleasures of our age," Jünger wrote, "to take part in the demolition work [that is . . .] the treason of the spirit against the spirit" (*Arb* 40). The stylistic corruption of this remark—the deliberate indulgence of mischief-making metaphor, and the pose of a hope that it may become reality—is repellent enough, and unhappily typical.[14] (Admittedly, it can also be found in left-wing writers of the period.) More important though is the precise form of Jünger's act of intellectual high treason, for it is the form of Heidegger's too (cp. *Arb* 66).

Taking his cue from Oswald Spengler's essay of 1920, *Prussianism and Socialism*, as perceptive and preposterous as *The Decline of the West* itself, Jünger denies that economic factors can be invoked to explain the developments described in *The Worker*. Spengler and

Jünger agree that to believe in economic causation, or even influence, in human affairs is a part of the collapsing "bourgeois worldview" (to which, consistently, Marxism is assigned). How then does it come about that "the worker" is now rising to such prominence? By a historical change too profound for explanation, Jünger replies; by the growth of a new "type" (the term pretends to derive from Dilthey), a new set of human possibilities. In other words, he has no alternative to an explanation he is nonetheless not willing to contemplate. It might seem extraordinary that Jünger brushes aside economic considerations when he has talked so persuasively about electricity grids, road networks, and armaments, about the obsolescence of protective tariffs, and changes in property rights—these he merely lumps together as "technology," the means by which "the worker" seeks to achieve "total mobilization." But of course, if he were to allow an economic perspective on the Germany he is describing he would have to revise completely his picture of the historical relation between the "worker" and the "bourgeois." By denying the central role of the economic nexus Jünger prevents himself from seeing that the figures he has characterized as workers are consumers too, and that if the whole world is being mobilized— and if they are being mobilized with it—that is only in order to provide satisfactions for everyone's desires, theirs among them. Jünger is thoroughly typical of the right-wing political thinkers of the Weimar Republic in having no theory of consumption.

In Germany, this coyness about the link between production and consumption has a quite specific historical significance: it is the *proton pseudos*, the life-lie, with which the bureaucracy defends itself in its long struggle with the bourgeoisie. Insofar as Jünger suppresses the fact that his "worker" is necessarily also a consumer, his new "type" is simply the bureaucrat rebaptized for a proletarian age, and that is why, from the start of his treatise, Jünger opposes the figure of "the worker" to that of "the bourgeois." The German official class sees itself as external to the system of needs, and their satisfaction through labor: their own labor, they claim, is disinterested, and produces value that is not negotiable and perhaps not even consumable. Altogether, they think, the importance of sale and purchase in human affairs can be exaggerated. They certainly discard Hegel's notion that the state proceeds out of "civil" (or "bourgeois") society and keeps the economic system in existence by providing the forum within which its conflicts can be resolved. The treason of the German clerks, between 1918 and 1933 was that, for the sake of their own survival as a class, they ignored or abandoned the representative institutions generated by the system of consumption and production, whether at the national level (the republican Parliament) or the international (the League of Nations was an object of particular contempt). Rather than accept their new status as fellow consumer-producers in a mass-society—a step in which they could see only a surrender to their historic enemy, the bourgeoisie, even though it was withering before their eyes—they preferred to put themselves in the hands of a resurrected, and safely non-commercial, absolute monarch.

The National Socialist German Workers' Party claimed precisely to represent every aspect of the new "type"—except its economic reality. The intellectuals prepared the way for that claim. Spengler argued (largely correctly) that the positive and constructive political program of authoritarian socialism (as distinct from Marx's purely critical theory of class war) was identical with the Prussian tradition of enlightened monarchical absolutism. Both aimed at constructing a "state of officials" ("Beamtenstaat"),[15] in which every worker would be an official, rather than a salesman of his own labor (*PuS* 70). Work, for an official, he says, whether in Frederick's Prussia or the socialist state of the future, is not an economic matter but a matter of duty—as if officials worked only for their consciences and not for other people. "The official class is not an economic but a functional unit" (*PuS* 71)—as if all officials did not have in common that they owe their economic existence to the same single paymaster. Prussianism and Socialism are at one, Spengler thinks, in facing "the decisive question, not only for Germany but for the world, and it has to be resolved in Germany for the world: is commerce in future to govern the state, or the state to govern commerce?" (*PuS* 97). Spengler in 1920 sees the issue with (almost) as much clarity as Hegel a hundred years before him, but by comparison with Hegel's his solution is disastrously unbalanced: a socialist (that is bureaucratic) Germany, headed by a restored monarchy. A society therefore which would contain two of the three elements that had made up Germany's ruling class before 1914, but which would be purged of the third disruptive, revolutionary, creative (and wealth-creative) element, that the others had failed to contain, the bourgeoisie.

Ten years later Jünger saw that the German capitalist and imperialist middle class which had flourished during the Second Reich
no longer existed, and that a restoration of the old monarchy was
out of the question. But he retained Spengler's faith in the salvific
role of bureaucracy, and its corollary—a disbelief in the power of
economic relations to create social solidarity. In the present "tragic"
crisis, he wrote in 1932, only "the remains of the old hierarchy of
soldiers and officials . . . seek to maintain the traditional concept of
duty" (*Arb* 252), but once "the seizure of power" (*Arb* 257) has taken
place a "worker's democracy" will come into being which will be
"more closely related to the absolute state than to the [present] liberal democracy, from which it seems to emerge" (*Arb* 255) and in
which authority will be given to a specially trained "cadre of officials, officers, captains and other functionaries" drawn from the il-
legitimate and the orphaned, and so free of family bonds (*Arb* 281).
He envisages the possibility that this constitutional change will
come through the actions of "a strong man," or through a popular
vote (*Arb* 255–257), but does not consider that many of the people
are likely to be voting, not for one political system rather than another, but for a continuity in basic consumption which economic
disorder denies them. Jünger's flirtation with the vocabulary of National Socialism always stops short of overt endorsement (he makes
use of the term "race" in a private sense of his own, but ridicules the
theory of eugenics, *Arb* 145, 281) but it corrodes the structure of his
argument. For he has from the start conceived "the worker" as a
"planetary" figure, and he admits that total mobilization is quite as
opposed as liberal democracy to the protectionist measures by
which German nationalists want to pursue the goal of economic
"autarky" (*Arb* 273). As soon as he ventures on to economic terrain,
Jünger is carried away by the logic of his case towards liberal and
Hegelian conclusions from which he can rescue himself only arbitrarily. Restrictions on the international market in goods and labor
and on the international financial system are as alien to "the
worker" as war, he allows (astonishingly) (*Arb* 273, 291). In the long
run "the worker" will prefer to settle conflicts by "wars without pow-
der" within regional and federative structures that override national boundaries. But in the short run the totalization of life will
be established locally and local powers will test themselves against
one another in war (*Arb* 273, 277). The paradox that the total, plane-

tary, rule of "the worker" cannot by definition be tested in war is not raised, nor is the question whether that rule is already so far advanced that local, autarkic, totalization is anyway impossible. Plainly Jünger is more interested in aligning himself with the war party than in pursuing his argument to its natural end.

From time to time in *The Worker* Jünger hoists a Heideggerian flag—as when he refers to the advent of the new "type" as an "ontological (seinsmäßig) revolution" (*Arb* 104, cp. 77). But the philosopher needed little seduction. He was already personally committed to the class which Jünger was covertly claiming most fully represented twentieth-century humanity. He had transferred from an under-class into officialdom in the moment when it lost its monarch and was exposed to the temptation of thinking it had inherited the divine right to rule. Officialdom had its religion, to which he also transferred, and the spirit of Augustinian Lutheranism blows at times through the pages of *Being and Time*, assorting a little unhappily with the ontology, which is of Catholic and scholastic origin, and clearing the way to Heidegger's own intellectual fall. Heidegger later came to feel[16] that in Being and Time he had given too much prominence to our own "existence" (Dasein) and left the "Being" (Sein) which is revealed to us as the context for our "existence" too much in the background: *Being and Time* was still, we might say, too subjective, too much a product of the epistemological turn which gave birth to modern philosophy. Despite the depersonalized vocabulary, his masterpiece still narrates, and dramatizes, the story of a self finding itself in the world and proceeding to action—a story of fall, reflection, conversion, and resolve. It was able to contribute to a Lutheran and individualist tradition—the Protestant or atheist existentialism of Tillich or Sartre—because it derived from that tradition.

This Lutheran affiliation is most obvious in the division of all life and thought into two opposed camps: the inauthentic realm—of nature, as it were—superficially comprehensive and internally coherent as far as it goes, but unaware of the deepest truths and so fundamentally flawed; and the authentic realm—of Heideggerian grace—where a full understanding reigns both of itself and of its adversary, which is not given to all. Of self, existence, truth, conscience, time, for example, both inauthentic (or "vulgar") and authentic interpretations are possible, and there is a touch of Jansenism in Heidegger's insistence that inauthentic living has its own (corrupt) logic, which is worth dissection. For the true Aristotelian, whether Thomist or Hegelian, there is only one Reason running through all human knowledge and affairs, but Heidegger shows his closeness to the narrower and more provincial tradition of German Pietism not only in separating off territory where an ultimately false understanding holds sway, but in assigning to it the world of social and linguistic interaction, insofar as he subjects that public world to the most rigorous analysis of which he is capable. He does have a theory of authentically shared life but it is to be found in the last two chapters of *Being and Time*, particularly in the fifth chapter on "Historicity" (Geschichtlichkeit), where his concentration seems to be laxer. His creative and satirical attention however is really held by the world of "das Man," of "what people say" and "what people do," in which inauthentic lives are led amid chatter and curiosity and do not rise to a true existence. Human society—the "sphere of association"—is most powerfully and influentially presented in *Being and Time* in a negative light, and with no anthropological or historical breadth.

However the chapter on "Historicity" was of great personal importance to Heidegger. When his pupil, the Jewish philosopher Karl Löwith, met him in Rome in 1936 and suggested "that his commitment to National Socialism was a natural consequence of his philosophy, Heidegger gave his unqualified agreement and explained how his concept of 'historicity' was the basis for his political 'engagement'."[17] But the weakness in Heidegger's account of the historical aspect of our existence is precisely the intrusion into it of the voluntaristic—some would say, in allusion to the theories of the National Socialist jurist Carl Schmitt, the "decisionistic"[18]—element implied by the word "engagement" ('Einsatz', a faintly military term, of a kind favored by Hitler's party).

The general purport of Heidegger's argument resembles Hegel's, though it is less differentiated: history is a moral, not a chronological, phenomenon, a form of being with others, a fate that is by its very nature shared. You can't be historical on your own. In his exposition, however, Heidegger loses sight of that primordial involvement with others on which he laid weight in analysis of the relation between "self" and "world," and presents history as an "inheritance" or "tradition" that "existence" decides voluntarily to accept. In order to explain how "repetition"—it might be less misleading to say

"continuity"—and so the possibility of history, comes about, Heidegger writes the fateful words "existence selects for itself its hero"
(*SuZ* 385). He is so concerned to link his theory of history to his future-directed and purposeful theory of time that he falls into the
trap he laid for himself when he gave his book its Pietistic and, ultimately, epistemological structure: he treats the material of history
as the medium in which a non-historical self expresses once and for
all its commitment to living its mortal life in a particular way. Heidegger thus neglects the sense, obvious enough in all conscience,
in which history comes to us as a given past, not as a corollary of a
projected future.[19]

A very deep-seated prejudice is at work here. Heidegger properly
emphasizes the future-creating limitedness of a being directed towards its end in death, but overlooks, and indeed tries to argue
away, the past-creating limitedness of a being reflecting on its beginning in an act of parental (or, for that matter, divine) generation.
It is true there is an allusion to our sexual origins in the term Heidegger uses (*SuZ* 179) to describe the state in which we open our
eyes on the world, "Geworfenheit"—usually translated "thrownness," but the word has the further association of "whelpedness."
But that is contemptuous Manichaeism. It is not just a moral and a
theological but a natural truth that Being is given by an act of love,
and for so great a truth ontology must surely find a place. Our personal "existence" involves us in passive reception—grateful acknowledgment of the limitedly given—as well as active projection.
Behind Heidegger's reluctance to see historicity as a gift, and not
only a construct, lies a general—but, as his analysis of the presuppositions of selfhood shows, not necessarily fundamental—hostility
to givenness.

And that is perhaps simply another form of the neglect of consumption in favor of production characteristic of many of Heidegger's contemporaries. To consume is to accept something made *by*
another, *for* us: we become their future, they become our past. Consumption is the pleasurable transformation into our own existence
of the productive labor of others. At first we are simply passive re-
cipients—whether of God's work during the six days of Creation, or
of our mother's labor in giving us life, or of her production of our
first food—later we join the system of (equitable or inequitable)
economic exchange. Like Jünger and Spengler, however, Heidegger

can see only one half of the cycle by which what one consumer produces another producer consumes. That the purpose or project of
our existence must necessarily appear in another's existence as
something to be received and consumed, and that therefore in our
own existence too there must be an irreducible element of the alien
received and transformed, plays little part in Heidegger's theory of
historicity. But whether or not we can choose our heroes, we certainly cannot choose our parents. For most of us it is as difficult to
acknowledge that we could have been born of no other parents
(and were born of their act of love) as to acknowledge that we must
and shall die. The *reductio ad absurdum* of Heidegger's position is
Jünger's view that the ideal soldier or state functionary would have
no parents at all. Denial of the past is the typical act of authoritarian Enlightenment. A theory of politics which sees our life together
as emerging not (as Hegel thought) out of mutual care and the mutual satisfaction of needs but out of some individual fiat—whether
of assertion or submission is immaterial—is a theory for officials.
For officials are always tempted to see themselves as embodiments
of the monarchical "I will," rather than servants of civil society, and
perhaps especially so when the monarchy has just been abolished.

"The Self-Assertion of the German University"

Heidegger regarded his commitment to the political "Movement"
(as the National Socialists liked to call their party), in the spirit of
the Nietzschean Lutheranism which in *Being and Time* came to over-
lay the original Catholic ontologism, as one man's resolute choice
of his fate, as his choice of the specific manner in which he was to
live a shared existence. In reality, it was his personal contribution to
an act of class treason by the German bureaucracy and military
against the revolution of 1918. The treason consisted in a stubborn
refusal to join in the task of finding political structures to accommodate the economic forces which had made the revolution and
imposed on Germany the end of empire, and in a reversion to the
political hierarchy of the Second Reich, minus its embarrassing and
inconvenient head of state. This "engagement" was the final step in
Heidegger's betrayal of his philosophical vocation—to unite
Hegelianism and scholasticism, and to reconcile Germany's Protestant and Catholic traditions—a betrayal which had begun with his

conversion to the pre-revolutionary Establishment in 1919. It was not an acceptance of racism, irrationalism, or a personality cult, but it left him armed with no moral or intellectual weapon to combat them and prepared, as Löwith pointed out to him, to sit down at the same table as Julius Streicher in a committee dedicated to making these the fundamental principles of German law. Between 1930 and 1933 Heidegger read *Total Mobilization* and *The Worker* and thought Jünger's ideas worth discussing in detail "in a small circle" with his (Jewish) assistant Werner Brock.[20] In his later account, he seems to imply that Jünger's thinking was of decisive importance to him in the events that followed.[21] On 27 May 1933 Heidegger, who in April had been elected Rector of Freiburg University as a result of a National Socialist cabal, and who on 1 May had very publicly become a Party member, delivered his inaugural address, *The Self-Assertion of the German University*. A notable feature of this address, if we compare it with that of Ernst Krieck,[22] Heidegger's rival in the Party and in philosophy, installed four days earlier as Rector of Frankfurt, is its freedom from overt references to National Socialism. Krieck states in so many words that as "Führer of the University" he will cooperate with "the leadership of the NSDAP" (Krieck 14/331), that "as a matter of principle the university will in future be an organ and element of the state" which "under authoritative leadership will have to carry out its educational work within the context of a racial-political (völkisch-politisch) basis and goals" (Krieck 12/329), that it is unnecessary "to think up artificially the fundamental idea and purpose" of the university since "destiny has imposed them on us by the 'völkisch' revolution [i.e., the "seizure of power" by the NSDAP]" (Krieck 10/327), and that the new generation of academics will be "the intellectual wing of an elite which will be a pillar of the State, an SA of the mind" (Krieck 8/325). Heidegger makes no allusion, explicit or otherwise, to Hitler or his party and refrains from using the pass-word "völkisch," substituting a term of his own, "volklich." The Baden Education Minister Wacker, immediately after hearing the speech, accurately described it as "a kind of private National Socialism" (*Selbstb* 30) and criticized the absence of any reference to the party's fundamental doctrine of race—the description of course fits Jünger too. Heidegger was doing precisely what Krieck thought unnecessary: developing a theory of the university out of the theory of knowledge (Wissenschaft), and that out of a theory of Being, from all of which it would follow that one should join "the Movement"; he was not accepting as primary the Party's dictates and developing from them a program for "The Renewal of the University" (the title of Krieck's address). The practical result was much the same in both cases. But Krieck's prevarications are the common currency of administrative tyrannies. The indirection of Heidegger's address reveals with utter clarity the self-deception of an entire class, which may not have been able to penetrate his style, but which to a greater or lesser extent shared his illusions. Krieck made no bones about the statism of the new order and the role even of students as functionaries carrying out the Führer's will (Krieck 12/329). Heidegger holds out the illusory prospect that he and his fellow-officials can become the supreme determinants of the nation's will (*Selbstb* 15). His title is revelation enough. In the moment in which, by the process of "Gleichschaltung," all institutions are publicly and avowedly to be transformed into organs and elements of the state, he proclaims the proud autonomy of what for three hundred years had been the institutional heart of the German bureaucracy. By its devotion to the philosophy of Being, the university is to become "the place of intellectual legislation" (*Selbstb* 18). No longer is it to be the servant, let alone the training-ground of servants, of the state, except perhaps in the sense in which Frederick the Great claimed the rank of servant: it is to be the educator of the masters, of the "leaders (Führer) and guardians of the fate of the German people" (*Selbstb* 10). Two elements of collective life disappear completely from this vision: the economic and the political. There is no suggestion, at a time when seven million were unemployed, that "the fate of the German people" has an economic component in which the university is involved and which it has a duty to understand. Of the careers which Heidegger mentions for his students only two—being a doctor and being an architect—might lead to work in the private sector; the others—"statesman," teacher, judge, pastor—are the classic roles of the German state functionary (*Selbstb* 16). And anyway "knowledge is not at the service of the professions, but vice versa." There is no mention of university finances. As for politics, Krieck at least reminded his institution, ominously, that it had lost its independence and that he would be working closely with the Party and the local administration. For Heidegger issues of representation, decision making, and the division of powers seem not to arise. The "self-assertion" of his university is a contextless will to its own existence, which proves to be no more in the end than the will to conduct philosophy by asking the Heideggerian question: "What is Being?" The German university was once the supreme agency of monarchical enlightenment. It gave birth to systematic idealist philosophy as a secular, state-centered substitute for religion, in which all society could be understood as rationally related to one controlling authority. After 1918 the authority had gone but the philosophy remained, carrying on enlightenment in a political void, its substance dwindling as its arrogance rose.

The void was a deliberate and artificial creation. Between 1918 and 1933 Germany and the world did not lack political problems of great depth and urgency. But Spengler, Jünger, and Heidegger, and the many who thought like them, persisted in seeing the problems in the categories of the defunct Second Reich. To them parliaments, workers' councils, and especially the League of Nations, were lies, farces, and "inauthentic," because representative institutions had indeed been precisely that in the still essentially absolutist constitution of Bismarckian and Wilhelmine Germany, especially when they had been seen from the perspective of the absolute monarch's uniformed and civilian servants. To see representative institutions otherwise, to see them for example as serious attempts to give the power of choice to the post-revolutionary masses, would have meant abandoning that perspective and admitting that the privileges of officialdom were a thing of the past. Heidegger, for whom those privileges were hard-won, seems not to have noticed that "the Movement" to which he adhered succeeded only because it directly and in practice addressed the new social, economic, and political issues, whatever its pretense of archaism. (Of course it was a pretense: had it not been, Hitler's first act would have been to restore the monarchy, if not the Hohenzollerns.) National Socialism was a mass movement, which correctly understood the proletarian nature of post-imperial German society, which saw the possibility, perhaps necessity, of using public investment to alleviate an economic crisis, and which in particular realized that it had to master parliamentary politics if it was to succeed in its purpose of destroying them. Heidegger fixed his eyes on the hope of a (kingless) restoration contained in the promise to undo the revolution of 1918 and overlooked, for the present, the genuinely revolutionary modernity of

National Socialism. The political upheaval outside the university is mentioned by him only once, in the last lines of his speech, and the way to participation in it is said, as in *Being and Time*, to lead through a personal decision by his academic audience about its own identity: "We are willing our selves" (*Selbstb* 19). It may seem a comical, if grimly comical, hubris that Heidegger imagines a nation at whose pinnacle stands an authoritarian university all of whose faculties are organized to ask, in their different ways, the central question of his own philosophy. But the personal hubris is a small-scale analogy, strictly speaking a metonymy, of the hubris by which, in the dying years of the Weimar republic, the German official and military classes neglected their real duty to their own polity and tolerated its overthrow because they imagined they would then be returned to the Wilhelmine world, whether under the name of nationalists, socialists, Germans, or "workers," or all four simultaneously. "Private National Socialism" destroyed the Republic as effectively as the real thing, probably more so. It felt uncomfortable with the reality of the Third Reich, grumbled perhaps, but remained publicly silent—in Heidegger's case for the rest of his life. It rose, too late, to an opposition, which inevitably was compromised, on 20 July 1944.

Heidegger's tenure of the rectorship was short, inglorious, and not a little absurd. The military vocabulary of his inaugural address and of his peremptory memoranda could not disguise that in administrative reality any notion that the university might "assert itself" was quite incompatible with the new order, or disorder. In the absence of a firm political framework, the Party, the police, the local and the national administration all claimed the right to interfere in the university's affairs—particularly matters of personnel—and in clinging to his illusion of autonomy and resisting demands for arbitrary expulsions Heidegger soon acquired the reputation of being uncooperative and soft on Jews.[23] He was certainly not soft on Catholics. It should be remembered that Hitler's parliamentary strength was initially based on Protestant votes, the Catholics dutifully voting for their own party, the Centre. The rectorship was the period of Heidegger's most virulently anti-Catholic utterances and he actively persecuted the Catholic student body in the university.[24] Perhaps he wanted to demonstrate to himself the connection between his current political engagement and his decision in 1919 to abandon the "system of Catholicism," the intellectual force that most strongly resisted assimilation to the ideology of bureaucratic enlightenment. But unfortunately for him the new regime was anxious to come to a concordat with the enemy and he was overruled. He campaigned in November 1933 for endorsement by plebiscite of Germany's departure from the League of Nations and of a one-party Reichstag, but rumors of his unreliability and even of his mental instability prevented him from achieving the ambition which would have crowned the program announced in his inaugural address: appointment as the head of a quasi-monastic residential academy in Berlin which would have certified the ideological purity of all future university professors in Germany.[25] When in April 1934 it became clear that even in Freiburg his utopian plans for a reorganization of the university curriculum round the philosophy of existence were unrealizable and would be opposed by the Party, he resigned.[26] A classical colleague and Party comrade met him on the street shortly afterwards with the wicked question "Back from Syracuse?"—an allusion to Plato's failed attempt to persuade the tyrant Dionysius to put philosophy into practice.[27] But from Plato's folly only Plato suffered. All humanity has been marked by the tyrant to whom Heidegger gave his enthusiastic, and at the time no doubt influential, support.

The Clerk's Tale: Doctor Faustus

Between 1943 and 1947, in the years of retribution, Thomas Mann, in his Californian exile, wrote *Doctor Faustus*, the novel of Germany's pact with the devil, "a strange kind of transferred autobiography."[28] Mann had supported the Weimar Republic since its inception, rightly seeing in it the continuation of the political traditions of the liberal Wilhelmine bourgeoisie, and remaining true to it even when its institutions were burdened with quite new tasks by an economic revolution. But he came to recognize that in the "humanism" which he so valued, the literature, philosophy, classical learning and music of eighteenth- and nineteenth-century Germany, there was the seed of a poisonous plant; that even he had perhaps unwittingly nurtured it; and that, though he was himself a victim of the Führer's thugs, and wrote and broadcast tirelessly against them, he could not disavow the Germany which had made him. *Doctor Faustus*—his greatest novel, though possibly not his best—is an acknowledgment of the historicity of our being more profound than anything Heidegger wrote or did. At the same time it is Mann's attempt to uncover that original perversity in the inheritance he had to accept. Analysis of the relation between class and state was not Mann's business—he left that sort of thing to his brother Heinrich. With an intuitive rightness of symbolism, however, he chose for the storyteller on to whom his "autobiography" was to be transferred a representative not of his own class but of the officialdom which had contributed far more than the *grands bourgeois* to the culture which he admired and served. The story of the modernist composer Adrian Leverkühn, whose life is (largely) that of Nietzsche, transposed chronologically into the next generation, and whose art is (largely) that of Schönberg, is told as a parallel to the sixteenth-century chap-book story of Faustus in such a way that Leverkühn's period of greatest creativity may be understood either as the interval between a syphilitic infection and final, protracted, dementia, or as the reward for an agreement with a sinister stranger (who may be a hallucination) to sell his soul and renounce love. The narrator who is charged with this *tour de force* is Serenus Zeitblom, a schoolteacher of classics and childhood friend of the Lutheran Leverkühn, though himself a Catholic, who is assumed to begin writing two and a half years after Leverkühn's death, on the same day in 1943 when Mann began work, and who finishes some time after Germany's capitulation in May 1945. The novel is a hall of mirrors, at the far end of which stands an image of artistic achievement bought at the cost of supreme inhumanity and spiritual desolation—at the near end the windows of the narrator's study shake to the rumble of Germany's falling cities, while he writes of the advance of the Allied troops and the opening of the concentration camps. Leverkühn's non-verbal art is known to us only through Zeitblom's eloquent and extended account of it in words; more remote still is the meeting with the devil, presented to us in Zeitblom's indeterminately modified transcription of a report by Leverkühn; nearer to us, in appearance at least, is Zeitblom's narration of Leverkühn's public and personal existence in a social world shared with a welter of intellectual, artistic, and monied characters or caricatures in settings varying from the lecture halls of the Second Reich to the decadent salons of the Weimar Republic: here we feel we can expect more or less coherent and reliable accounts of emotions and motives in lives brought to disaster when Leverkühn yields to the temptation to love. What then is the connection between that distant and uncertain image of a diabolical contract, whose half-hinted associations with all periods of German culture give great density to the text, and the bulletins of war that reach Zeitblom's desk at the same time as they reach Thomas Mann's? Is Leverkühn's "bold life" a metaphor of German history, perhaps of some supposed collective nihilism, redeemed at the last from all the evil it has done by the art it has created or even by the mere energy of its own denial?[29] That would be an intolerable conclusion.

If we stand a little further back, we can see the novel as a whole. And then we see that the most important character in it is not Leverkühn but Zeitblom. Self-deprecating, pedantic, and humanitarian, he has in appearance a certain uneasy detachment from the public insanity and corruption surrounding him—he took early retirement in 1935—and is a frequent and ineffectual wringer of hands. He speaks in the end with a German voice because he has no other, and he acquiesces at the point where the only alternative would be exile. He shares like Mann in the war-fever of 1914 (F 405), though retrospect makes him, like Mann, a little shamefaced; like Mann, who at one time welcomed the sinking of the *Lusitania*, he sees in the torpedoing of passenger-ships a demonstration of German technological superiority and gives no thought to the victims (F 229); for all the sarcasm which he heaps on his nation's leaders, it is the "loss of territory" (F 231) and the jeopardizing of the German heartland which most clearly demonstrate to him that they are bankrupt; on the "Jewish question" "I have never been able entirely to agree with our Führer and his paladins" (F 15). In a sense he is the novel's only character. The conversation between Leverkühn and the Devil shows in miniature—as a homeomery—the structure of the entire book, for as the Devil is to Leverkühn so Leverkühn is to Zeitblom: "You see me, so for you I exist" says the stranger (F 323). Why ask whether he *really* is the Devil? Why ask whether Leverkühn *really* is as Zeitblom shows him—a musical genius, an analogy of the Fatherland, a monster of calculating cruelty who can murder by remote control, simply by holding the right conversation at the right time? For the purposes of the novel the image is enough, whatever the reality. Zeitblom means it in all earnest when he passingly calls himself "Adrian's *alter ego*"

(*F* 595), and Thomas Mann means at least two things when, speaking of his depiction of his two central figures, he refers to "the mystery of their identity" (*F* 740). The pedant sees the composer—he does far more, he conjures him up by words, by devices whose artificiality is frequently acknowledged, and runs to the free admission of sheer invention (*F* 576)—and so for him he is, indeed he is him. Seen from a little extra distance all the mirrored images collapse into a single appalling vision—not the life of Leverkühn "told by a friend," as the sub-title has it, but the mind of Zeitblom exemplified in what purports to be the biography of another. It is that vision which makes the novel into a political parable.

"We have fed the heart on fantasies. The heart's grown brutal from the fare." The analogy of Germany in *Doctor Faustus* is not Leverkühn's real or unreal contract with the powers of darkness but the development of Zeitblom's supposedly humane and classically educated imagination which gradually brings forth that myth of a diabolical pact and gives it ever more nightmarish verbal shape. Just as the cold draught blowing from Leverkühn's strange interlocutor tells us that he is no mere phantom, so Zeitblom's rattling windows tell us that his dream-like absorption in his friend's career is part of a world where all events, even dreams, have their real consequences. In that extraordinary conversation, in which modernity is confronted with the archaic, and culture with desecratory coarseness, it is not Leverkühn who is corrupted, but his biographer, trapped, as he admits, into writing a script for the Devil. The interview—or, rather, Zeitblom's writing-up of the interview—is Mann's symbolic representation of the final step in the treason of Germany's culture-creating bureaucracy: its alliance with forces utterly opposed to its "humanist" inheritance, and contemptuous of it, out of an inflated sense of its own importance. Heidegger took that step, but then drew back. Zeitblom's further development as a writer mimes the development in the mind and feelings of those who carried on. Committed to his "Faustian" understanding of his hero's fate he carries out in his imagination—for he admits it is entirely fabricated— a murder-plot against Leverkühn's homosexual friend. The culminating point of this mental collaboration—the preparatory work of the mind which made possible the ultimate horrors of Hitler's regime and the cataclysm of war which obliterated it—is Zeitblom's account of Leverkühn's affection for his five-year-old nephew. In order to press on us the uttermost consequence of his understanding of Leverkühn—as a man diabolically fated, or re-solved, to kill anyone he loves—Zeitblom undertakes a deliberate and detailed description of the child's agonized death from menin-gitis. "How could you do it?" Thomas Mann tells us his English translator asked him of these pages (F 827), and thereby he prompts us to ask of Zeitblom: "how could he do it?" A man who word by word can torture a child to death in order to demonstrate the meta-physical extremity of his situation is, evidently, spiritually prepared for the Final Solution of any human "problem."

In *Doctor Faustus* Thomas Mann, a writer wholly above any suspi-cion of collaboration with Hitler's movement, has rendered an ac-count of his own identification with his tragic (F 232) Fatherland, to the point of acknowledging what in himself could lead even to its worst crimes. He has done this by creating a narrator-figure from educated middle-class Germany who is close enough to his coun-try's central cultural tradition to be characteristic, but distanced enough not to forfeit all our sympathy. Mann and Zeitblom may be similar, however, but they are not of course identical. Mann, the bourgeois Lutheran, an atypical German man of letters simply in virtue of being a successful freelance, makes the bearer of his trans-ferred autobiography a differently eccentric figure, a Catholic offi-cial. The strength of his novel lies in its representation of the inescapability of their German inheritance for both author and nar-rator, despite their—differently grounded—critical distance. That is what gives their tragic ring to Zeitblom's last words: "my friend, my fatherland!" But it may be that the impression of inescapability is due to an unintentional sleight of hand and to the limits of Mann's imagination. For we see next to nothing of a Catholic influence on Zeitblom's thinking—where are the statues, the confessionals, the sectarian sense that Protestants are strange, which determine the atmosphere of Günter Grass's Danzig stories? where is Modernism? where is Neo-Scholasticism?—and as a result his critical distance, though nominally explained by his religion, has no discernible basis other than the secular and thoroughly German brand of humanism which he shares with Thomas Mann. Zeitblom is almost as assimi-lated as Heidegger. And so the novel lacks that broader perspective which Heidegger also renounced when he turned away from the "system" of an international and ancient church. The "culture" which fades away into darkness in Leverkühn's last work is a thin and self-absorbed affair, which has too long been detached from its economic foundations, and which never represented more than a part of Germany's inheritance, to say nothing of the rest of the world. Other Germanys were possible besides Zeitblom's, and after 1945 some of those possibilities were realized.

8 Crossing the Line?
Heidegger and the Post-Modern University

Heidegger, the German master, . . . came with the best of references; but he was a silent, morose man, not very popular either with masters or boys.

THE RETURN OF SHERLOCK HOLMES

The story of Heidegger's political decline and fall is not a mere biographical adjunct to his philosophy. If it were, it might either be dismissed as an irrelevance, or be regarded as practical disproof of his system, whatever its merits in theory. But Heidegger's failure as a man is inseparable from the circumstances that made both for his strengths and for his limitations as a philosopher. The most important of these circumstances were not peculiar to Germany, though for some decades they may have appeared to be: now they are revealed as the circumstances to which we are all having to adjust our thinking and our living. For that reason the story of Heidegger is a fable for our times.

Heidegger rightly sensed that the modern, post-bourgeois, self is not an owner but a producer, defined from the start as working in and on the world, and so always projected towards the future. However, because he accepted an old prejudice in German academic culture, which associated production with the bureaucracy rather than with commerce and industry, he overlooked that production is necessarily part of a system of exchange. He overlooked therefore that our self has always also to be defined as consumer, and a recipient of goods from the past. He not only failed to free himself from the prejudices of the old order, he sought assimilation to it, and threw in his lot with the obsolescent class of academic officials whose bid for intellectual and political leadership he articulated in his rectoral address.

Since Heidegger and Jünger first outlined the principal features of the post-bourgeois world in the late 1920s it has become evident that they were not describing a purely local, German, crisis. It is all the more vital that in accepting their analysis where it is strong we do not also take over their limitations. The temptation is considerable to admit, even to revel in, the "deconstruction" of the self as it was known to a bourgeois and imperialist age, but to except from the general dissolution the self of the academic official, who is seen either as alone capable of understanding the process or as alone capable of resisting it. Either route, Heidegger's example shows, leads down into the pit. For in either case we underestimate our own involvement in the revolution brought about by the internationalization of economic life, we lose sight of the necessary complementarity of economic and political structures which was already clear to Hegel, we turn our backs on the international political institutions in which our more than economic identity is beginning to be expressed, and we take refuge instead in some direct manifestation of the local state power, such as arbitrary legislation, collective emotionalism, or, ultimately, violence.

Both Heidegger and Jünger continued their analysis of the world-order in which the new Germany had to find its place well into the post-war period. Heidegger's thoughts and attitudes have had great influence in Germany, France, and America and latterly, and more indirectly, in Britain too. But being essentially continuations of lines laid down before the Second World War was over, they have offered little indication of how the contemporary academic intellectual can avoid the fate of the German intelligentsia of the Weimar Republic. Strange to say it is Jünger who—however diffusely and fitfully—has suggested a truer assessment of our present situation.

Technology and "the Stand"

During the later 1930s, when he was the object of the increasing suspicion of the National Socialist authorities—being charged simultaneously with nihilism and crypto-Jesuitism—Heidegger seems to have found Jünger's thought increasingly useful in explaining to himself how he came to be involved with the Party. In 1935 he delivered a lecture course under the title *Introduction to Metaphysics* which included the remark that "what is nowadays touted as the philosophy of National Socialism . . . in fact has nothing whatsoever to do with the inward truth and greatness of National Socialism," a phrase which, when he published it in 1953, he glossed with the words "(namely with the encounter between technology on a planetary scale and modern man)."[1] The gloss has been much criticized, but there is no reason to assume that it fundamentally misrepresents Heidegger's political views immediately after his resignation: the current state of world affairs and the task which National Socialism ought to perform, but probably now will not, have been better understood by Jünger, whose vocabulary the gloss uses, than by non-entities like Krieck. If in 1953 Heidegger also wished to imply that in 1935 he had been seriously alienated from his party, that of course was disingenuous. In 1936 when he met Löwith in Italy he wore his swastika with the same unaffected unconsciousness of its effect with which, had his life-choices been different, he would have worn a Roman collar. It is true that in 1939–40, at a time when Jünger was under a cloud for publishing the novel *On Cliffs of Marble*, a polemic against a psychopathic tyrant, Heidegger held a seminar on *The Worker* which he was ordered to discontinue. But the evidence of his wartime teaching is not, as has been claimed,[2] that he violently attacked the National Socialist regime, but that, at best, he assumed the ironically detached attitude of one with a deeper historical insight than the statesmen of the day.[3] In these years Heidegger steeped himself in the poetry of Hölderlin who also had been disappointed in his age, expecting from the great Revolution of 1789 a new epiphany of the Greek gods, and being granted only Napoleon. From the vantage-point of this improbable, and to some of us offensive, self-identification, Heidegger could see his "engagement" of 1933 as proceeding from the mistaken belief that the NSDAP would somehow counter the planetary advance of technology—e.g., by favoring the philosophy of Being—whereas it proved to be merely another of its instruments.

Both Jünger and Heidegger published important essays on world-civilization in the immediate post-war years, when they met personally for the first time and exchanged ambiguous compliments and dedications. Both of them continued to develop some of the main themes that had preoccupied them before the war but the lines of their thought began seriously to diverge. For Heidegger, as he told the audience of his lecture-course *What Does it Mean to 'Think'?* in 1952, the Second World War had decided nothing in respect of the "essential fate of humanity on this earth." Europe's conceptual landscape was, for him, unchanged since the period 1920–1930, when it was "already . . . obsolete and inadequate to what was coming. What will become of a Europe that tries to put itself together out of the stage-props of that decade after the First World War?"[4] Nietzsche, Heidegger argued, had already felt in his own time that an epoch was ending, and that his contemporaries had to ask themselves whether they were "metaphysically prepared" to "rule over the earth as a whole" (*D* 64). Sure that they were not, Nietzsche had announced the necessity of a Superman capable of "thinking beyond the . . . crumbling . . . nationalisms" and taking part in "the government of the earth," and like Nietzsche in 1888 and Jünger in 1932, Heidegger in the 1950s clearly still thought that only a completely transformed human being, a new "type" would be capable of "facing the decisions that are to come" (*D* 66–67). Jünger himself however was more prepared to learn from experience. In "Crossing the Line" (Über die Linie), written for the Festschrift presented to Heidegger on his sixtieth birthday, Jünger suggests that after the Second World War, in the era of the atomic bomb, "total mobilization has entered a stage even more ominous than the previous one," after the First War,[5] and that nihilism, in literature "the great theme for the last hundred years" (*L* 261), has reached a moral and political extreme (though like Heidegger he tends to see this extremity as so far exemplified in the sufferings of Germans, rather than in the sufferings Germans have inflicted on others[6]). However, in the words of Heidegger's favorite quotation from Hölderlin, "where there is danger the means of rescue grows too" (*L* 265): at the extreme, opposites touch. 1945 differs from 1918 in that a point zero has been passed, a median or equator crossed, and a new calculation has to begin (*L* 271–273). A global civil war is taking place in which—as the scale of the mass-destruction threatened by the new weapons shows—the future of the planet is at stake, not the future of particular nations or empires. And that means, Jünger believes, that the framework has been created within which a world-state, dimly envisaged in *The Worker*, has become a distinct possibility. Such a global order need not be achieved by force: it may come about through treaty-arrangements, particularly if the two super-powers are joined by a third, for example a united Europe; or maybe, Jünger remarks in 1950, thirty-nine years before the event, the strains of competition will cause the peaceful collapse of one of the contending parties. Ten years later, in "The World-State. Organism and Organization," Jünger expressed his conviction that "the planetary order is . . . already achieved. It remains only for it to be recognized. . . ."[7] The advent of the world-state is manifest, he says, in the worldwide absorption of such "natural markers" as day and night, or the seasons of the year, into "the abstract working day of twenty-four hours," and in the ironing-out of distinctions of race, class, and—particularly—sex, for the sake of uniform working practices. Even the division of the world into two or three super-states and the opposition of East and West are less potent facts of modern life than "the figure of the worker," the new type of human being to whom they will eventually succumb. When however the Worker's State reaches its maximum spatial extent and is recognized as truly global it will cease to have the character that states hitherto have had: being unique it will not need military force to protect itself against competitors, and war, we may hope, will be obsolete.

Jünger's assessment of the post-1945 world is remarkable not only for his percipience but also for his recognition that whatever the continuities there has been a decisive change since the 1920s. "[A] conservative attitude . . . can no longer arrest or divert the growing movement, as still seemed possible after the First War," he wrote in "Crossing the Line" (*L* 273).

> For conservatism always has to find itself a base in parts of the terrain that have not yet begun to move, such as the monarchy, the nobility, the army, the land. But once everything begins to slip there is no longer a point of support. . . . All we own [unser Bestand, one of Heidegger's favored words] is moving as a whole across the critical line. . . . One can no longer scheme to preserve a house, some item of

personal property, from the fire-storm. . . . On the contrary, possessions that have been thus rescued have a whiff of the absurd about
them, at best they are museum pieces.

If these remarks, and the allusions to the overcoming of "nihilism"
(a label early attached to Heidegger's philosophy), were intended as
a covert critique of Heidegger's increasingly public refusal to think
about the modern world except through reflection on Hölderlin,
the Greek and German philosophical classics, and the simplicities
of peasant life, Jünger received a devastating riposte in Heidegger's
contribution to his own sixtieth-birthday Festschrift in 1955. In "On
the 'dividing line'" (Über "Die Linie," later retitled "On the Question of Being," "Zur Seinsfrage") Heidegger rejected any application
of the term "nihilism" to his thinking (and of course any suggestion
that it might be "overcome"), praised Jünger's works of the 1930s,
but argued that it was impossible to give any conceptual content to
his new image of "crossing the line," and subjected Jünger's vocabulary to a searching and far from friendly analysis.[8] Jünger appeared
as a typical specimen of the "technical" age he described in *The
Worker*: with a careless, impatient, and purely instrumental attitude
to the use of the words which it is, by contrast, the modest task of
philosophy (such as Heidegger's) to preserve and ponder (*ZS* 253).
The world wars which mattered so to Jünger seemed to Heidegger a
superficial affair, "the more technical their armaments the fewer the
issues they can decide" (*ZS* 252). Jünger had made the mistake of
telling the sage what the sage meant, but for all the looseness of
Jünger's writing it is difficult to see his essay as the obtuse misrep-
resentation Heidegger makes it out to be. The image of "crossing
the line," of the momentary passage through a zero state into a new
world, the reverse of the old, or incommensurable with it, has powerful antecedents in Rilke,[9] on whom Heidegger drew all his life,
and it plays a crucial role in a short lecture series of 1949–50 which
under various titles was one of the most influential of Heidegger's
post-war writings. *Technology and the Turn (Die Technik und die Kehre)*,
as it eventually became, is also more indebted than Heidegger ever
acknowledged to Jünger's *The Worker*.

In the first place, the technology which is said to give modern
civilization its historical character is for Heidegger not merely an
instrument, but the way in which the whole world is made manifest

to us, the way in which it "is."[10] (Rather as Jünger's "worker" is not an instrument of some other historical cause, but a "type" or "figure" of a fundamentally new humanity.) The specific characteristic of this way of manifestation of "being," is that it involves making demands: Everything that "is" is for us a reservoir of disponible energy. We "order" (bestellen) everything to "stand to" (auf der Stelle sein)—to be ready and available to do our changing bidding, to be part of our "stock" (Bestand) of material (*TK* 15–16). This universal reign of instrumentality—in the sciences and technology, in social, personal and religious life, in art—Heidegger calls by the untranslatably multivalent term "das Gestell"—roughly, "the stand" (*TK* 20). The word suggests variously an artificial structure, the whole business of putting things in place, and the military language of conscription. As an image, therefore—and for some practical purposes, as a concept too—the word is clearly related to Jünger's phrase, "total mobilization," coined in 1930. "Technology is the manner in which the figure of the worker mobilizes the world," we read in *The Worker*, ". . . mobilizes the whole stock (Bestand) indifferently" (*Arb* 145). In the suggestion of "structure" or "scaffolding" the word "Gestell" may also contain a reminiscence of Jünger's description of the "work-site landscape" (Werkstättenlandschaft) (*Arb* 150) of the modern world, the permanent provisionality of a present which exists only to construct the future. It is true that Heidegger no more took over Jünger's other dominant image, the figure of "the Worker," than he took over Nietzsche's figure of "the Superman," destined though the Superman was to "government of the earth as a whole"—his thought had become far too impersonal for such dramatizations. But "the Worker" was an indispensable middle term, between Nietzsche and 'the stand," showing how the essentially moralistic and individualistic concept of the "will to power" could be applied to the industrial and organizational aspects of modern society (cp. *Arb* 67). Jünger's writings of the early 1930s provided Heidegger with some of the most important elements in the vision and the vocabulary he used to diagnose the condition of humanity after 1945.

Second, however, in *Technology and the Turn*, Heidegger accepted not only much of Jünger's account of modernity, but also its principal limitation: his assumption that the issue that primarily required understanding was the role of technology, and his neglect therefore of the economic nexus within which technology is deployed. The processes which Heidegger thinks characteristic of modern technology in no way differentiate it from that of the ancient world or from basic technology at any time. It may be true that in a hydroelectric power-station on the Rhine we see the energy hidden in Nature being (as he says) opened up, transformed, stored, distributed and reapplied (*TK* 16), but the stages are no different when solar energy is made available through the growing of corn, is given a new form by threshing and is stored in barns as grain, is distributed through being fed to horses, and is reapplied when the horses are led to work.[11] The difference between life before and after the imposition of "the stand"—of total mobilization—does not lie in basic physical or technical procedures. Heidegger writes: "The forester who measures the felled wood under the trees and to all appearances walks the same forest paths in the same fashion as his grandfather, is today stood to (bestellt) by the wood-processing industry, whether he knows it or not."[12] But he does not seem to notice that what makes for this difference between the generations is not the increased technological sophistication of saw-mills but an economic and social change in ownership and organization, so that while grandfather was the lifelong retainer of a local landlord at the Schloss, grandson has a contract of employment with an international paper combine. Moreover, if "the stand" were a set of economic relationships it might make perfectly good sense to say that one was subject to it "whether one knew it or not"—but can there be manifestation of being ('Entbergen', usually translated 'unconcealment') "whether one knows it or not?" The consequence of assuming that the outstanding characteristic of the modern planetary order is its technicity (rather than the existence of a global market) is that an unnecessary stress is laid on the relationship (treated, possibly correctly, as radically distorted) between the individual and "things." Jünger's crucial error in 1932 was to overlook that work has no point and cannot indefinitely be sustained unless what it produces is consumed and paid for, and that therefore the exchange relation between producer and consumer—i.e., the economic nexus—is as important to understanding who "the Workers" are as their "total mobilization" of the "material" on which they work. He saw his "Workers" as officials or soldiers who work in response to their consciences or to orders and not as producer-consumers who work to satisfy their needs by satisfying the needs of others. That error is still present in Heidegger's writings on technology, the essence of which, "the stand," turns out to be a structure of apparently unmotivated commands. The error also leaves its mark on the cryptic pages he devoted to "the turn," the "means of rescuing" us from "the stand," his solution therefore to the whole problem of how to live a modern life.

History and "the Turn"

A "turn" of a kind was already implicit in the structure originally announced for *Being and Time*. (Heidegger uses the simple and slightly uncommon word 'die Kehre': the root, clearly recognizable in such compounds as 'Bekehrung', 'conversion', has mostly the strong sense of an "about-turn," to face in the opposite direction.) After an analysis of our existence which concluded by revealing its essential temporality, Heidegger intended to reconstruct an understanding of Being itself which started from the foundation provided by Time. After the Lutheran existentialism, we might say, was to come the scholastic ontology. The book was never completed, though after the first half had been published Heidegger's thinking seems to have attempted to take the intended turn. In the lecture of 1950 called "Die Kehre," the notion of a sudden reversal of direction is associated with the "danger" which is, or is instantaneously revealed to be, "the means of rescue also," in order to suggest how the apparently universal reign of "the stand" need not after all be ultimate. For even if the instrumentalization of relationships is so complete that all "things" and we ourselves seem to be turned into mere functions in a world system, and the very existence of the system and indeed of the world seems to be concealed from us in case we should be distracted from performing our functions, nonetheless this state of mind and being, which makes possible such concrete phenomena as the planetary rule of technology or the scientific conception of the physical structure of the universe, is not the end of thinking and being. In its own mysterious way it is a manifestation of the world. It is a manifestation *because* it is a concealing, a revelation *because* it is a veiling. Because technology and science exclude any question of what things are, apart from their functional role in the system (what they do), what everything is is made mani-

219

fest as that which technology etc. conceals. It is a mystery, yes, but one that presses in on us on every side. Like the Reichstag, it is revealed by being wrapped. In the theological terms which Heidegger always repudiated, we could say that only when there is a completely functional account of the universe from its physical beginning to its human end are we free to see it in its entirety as God's creation, without the risk of thinking that God is an agent performing a function within it. This is not a conclusion that would surprise Hegel, for whom it is a characteristic of the modern age (by comparison with that of the Greeks) that we must live our non-identity with ourselves and in that find our identity; or, as T. S. Eliot put it at much the same time as Heidegger, "In order to possess what you do not possess You must go by the way of dispossession."[13] What might perhaps have surprised Hegel is that while Heidegger presents technology in a historical context, as something that in the course of time takes over from an earlier, "more original" (*TK* 28), mode of being (or "unconcealment"), he explicitly denies that "the turn," the negation of negation, can be historically located. It may be, he says, adopting the Hölderlin posture, "that we already stand in the shadow cast by the advent of this turn" (*TK* 41), but what he is writing cannot (by contrast with a famous diagnostic text by his now alienated friend Karl Jaspers) be a description of "the situation of the age" (*TK* 46). Any attempt to understand our future as a projection from our present—any attempt to calculate the future effects of present causes, to predict catastrophes à la Spengler, or presumably world-states à la Jünger—would be only "technological attitudinizing" (*TK* 43), when what is at issue is the supersession of technological thinking altogether. It is therefore obscure whether "the turn" is a mystical insight, a change of attitude in the individual thinker "here and now," who tends the "little things" of life in the growing light of the hope of rescue (*TK* 33; "Now and here" is Jünger's epigraph for an essay of 1951 with the Heideggerian title "Taking to the Woods"); or whether rescue will come as some wholly inscrutable and incalculable future redemption, a new historical order for which we have to wait in darkness.[14] This dilemma has been bequeathed by Heidegger to Derrida and his deconstructionist school, together with the strangely asymmetrical attitude to history on which in part it rests: our age is historically located insofar as some of its features ("logocentrism," "the stand") are held to be a fall from grace some time in the Greek period, but as those features, paradoxically, include the tendency to think in terms of causes and consequences, or past and present, our age is caught in a self-sustaining illusion, and no future for it, and no escape from it, is conceivable, or at least none is expressible. History has ended, and the rest is silence.

Small wonder that Jünger was reprimanded in "On the 'Dividing Line." Jünger would not endorse Heidegger's insistence that analyses first made around 1930 required no modification in the light of subsequent events, and did not act on his suggestion that he should republish *The Worker* unaltered. However perfunctory and ephemeral they may have been, Jünger's later essays on the situation of the age were in one respect more clear-sighted than anything Heidegger wrote on the subject. Jünger recognized that by 1945 a historic crisis had been passed, a process had been completed and a new order begun, in which all things would have to be rethought. He was not able to identify the process as the establishment of a global market and the withering away of the bourgeoisie, but he understood that whatever it was it had been the driving force behind the literary and philosophical developments of the last hundred years, particularly in the German-speaking world, to which he gave the name of "nihilism." That degree of historical self-understanding Heidegger did not possess. Unlike Heidegger, Jünger thought that the new world had arrived, and that it was possible to say something about it. He also thought it important to raise the question of its political structure and realized—as he had realized when he first described the birth-pangs of the new world in the 1930s—that the question was not an invitation to utopian speculation but related ultimately to changes in the life-style and sense of self of every individual on the planet. To that extent Jünger is a true modern representative of a Hegelian tradition.

In at least three respects, by contrast, Heidegger shows a quite un-Hegelian incomprehension of the historical context of his own understanding of history. First, there is the poor and skimpy affair that Heideggerian history was from the start and always remained: a pre-Socratic idyll when art and poetry reigned, and then the gathering clouds of technology, "the stand," and forgetfulness of Being. This Graecocentric schema is a variant of one popular in the German Enlightenment since the middle of the eighteenth century (though for Hölderlin it was as threatening and ambiguous as it was seductive): ancient Greece is called upon to provide the example of the natural religion, in a natural society, uncontaminated by Christian (sometimes, by Jewish) influence, which the Enlightened intellectual is now preaching to his contemporaries. As the radicalism of the thinkers increases, and as the interpenetration of the Judaeo-Christian and Hellenic worlds becomes more obvious to scholarship, so the moment of corruption has to be pushed further back and the idyll, which for Goethe lasted until Julian the Apostate, becomes more archaic. For Heidegger, brought up on an Aristotelian Christianity, even Plato was suspect, and the account of temporality in *Being and Time* is as explicitly opposed to Aristotle as it is to Hegel. The dispassionate historian however notices that this Graecomania is a peculiarly German phenomenon[15] and that its origins are likely to lie as much in modern German circumstances as in the magnetic qualities of ancient Greece. The appeal to the distant Greek model relieves the modern thinker of the task of consciously relating his thought to its more immediate forebears, the movements from which it really derives, especially the Reformation and medieval Christianity. In Germany that relationship is particularly fraught, since the movements both of Reformation and of secularization were heavy with political significance for the official classes and the universities in which they were educated. Directly confronting ancient Greece with modern Germany in one's imagination excludes from one's mental perspective all genuinely historical questions about how one came to be what one is. And much of what is excluded can be named with a single name: Rome. In the eyes of the Philhellene, antiquity ends with Alexander. The Roman Empire, Roman law, the Roman Church, the Romance languages—for the loyal apologist of a Protestant prince, in the years of the German literary and linguistic revival and in the dawn of German nationalism, these are non-history, mere absences from the foundations of a modern identity. The ideological meaning of the omission is manifest—its personal meaning for Heidegger will concern us shortly. Hegel once again shows his exceptional position in the German intelligentsia by his endeavor to give Rome its due. In Hegelian history the Greece of Pericles is an important episode but it is multiply remote from us. In the Heideggerian history of "technology," or the Derridean history of "presence," we find no sense of the increasing distance set between us and our human predecessors by such landmarks as the French Revolution, the Reformation, the establishment of the feudal order and the medieval offices of Pope and Emperor, or the Islamic, Roman, and Alexandrian Empires before that, most of which figure prominently in Hegel's construction of the modern spirit. But then Heidegger thought world wars trivial, while Hegel's exposition of the historical relation between politics, economics, and religion, between state, civil society, and personal identity, was part of a programmatic political statement which was largely ignored by later German generations, and by Heidegger's in particular.

Second, then, the origins of the historiographical dilemma bequeathed by Heidegger to deconstructionism lie in what is said about historicity in the last chapters of *Being and Time*, that is, in the considerations which prompted him to his political "engagement." Heidegger rightly felt the lack of a sense of futurity in Hegel's account of history, which seemed to him too centered on the present, but the correction he proposed was so excessive, treated the future as so fundamental, and so ignored the independent contribution of the past, that he made it impossible to think concretely about the future at all. In 1927 Heidegger believed so firmly in our power to make our future that he made it the source of historicity. We make the continuity, and so the history, of our existence by choosing our hero, choosing a tradition and inheritance that we have in common with others. We create our past in the image of our future, of the projection of our existence forward to its limit in death. We have a fate (Schicksal) because, like Nietzsche, we are a fate. Out of the contingencies of that "fate" Existence chooses its particular destiny (Geschick), the events it willingly shares with "its collectivity, its people." The flaw in this account is its ignoring the extent to which our "destiny," the historicity of our existence (and indeed existence itself), is a gift from others, and the extent therefore to which the temporality of existence derives from pastness as well as futurity. In *Being and Time* Heidegger rises at best to acknowledging our necessary "co-existence" (Mitdasein and Mitsein) with other people and things, and our necessary "being-in-the-world." He does not consider that we are not just *in* the world but *part of* it, and that other people do not just co-exist with us, but have made our existence possible, as we do for them, or others, in our turn. The nexus of economic exchange is not mere co-existence, and it is astonishing that

223

Heidegger downgrades to an element in our 'thrownness' (I pre-
sume, for I do not think he even mentions it explicitly) the determinant of our existence which is at least as ineluctable as its mortality:
its derivation from other beings (Seiende), namely our parents. He
seems to have overlooked that only sexually reproducing beings can
die (beings that reproduce asexually just carry on, or mutate) and
that if our existence is a Being-to-death it is necessarily also equally
a Being-from-our-parents'-act-of-love. A specific yet wholly uncon-
tingent pastness is built into our existence: a gift that can never be
the object of choice or acceptance by our future-oriented resolve.
Yet instead of the real pastness constituted by our receiving from
others, Heidegger creates a phantom pastness constituted by our
choices about our future selves. And so the history he creates is not
real history either. Self-induced and simple-minded fantasies of to-
getherness and myths of national identity take the place of history's
real components: the laboriously constructed political units, which
we recognize as our own because they create a common order out
of that system of needs in which we consume what is past, exchange
in the present, and produce for the future. Because, like Jünger,
Heidegger was not willing to accept the whole of that nexus, but
wanted to reduce it to the single principle that made up the rationale of an official's existence—pure production regardless of consumption, pure futurity regardless of the process by which what is
future for me engenders what is past for my children—he could see
neither the social, nor the political, nor therefore the historical
character of the regime to which he gave his allegiance in 1933. He
was briefly used and dropped by men with not a tenth of his intellect, but he then compounded the problem by his own obstinacy
(or consistency) and his refusal to rethink the thoughts that had led
him into the desert. He continued to regard his "private National
Socialism" as a true insight into the needs of the time, to which, in a
tragedy comparable to Hölderlin's, his fellow-Germans had failed to
respond. And even as his philosophy "turned" he continued to en-
tertain the possibility that the need he had identified in 1933—the
need for a new humanity to master "technology on a planetary
scale"—would one day be recognized and met by a worthier agency
than the National Socialist party.

   In one respect, however, Heidegger's development from a philosophy of Existence to a philosophy of Being might seem to have

brought an advance, and with it a new definition of historical "destiny." In *Technology and the Turn* he says that "the stand," like any way of being ("unconcealment") that might eventually replace it, is "a destiny" ('Geschick' again), sent us by "that which gives" (or "grants"). He has already established a chain of etymological association between the German words for "grant" and "essence," and so can claim that the essence of technology, if we attend to it properly, will, like all essence, appear to us as a gift. Once we can understand the element of the given even in something as opposite to giving as the utterly "demanding" character of our technological age, we shall understand that even in this the means of rescue may be growing. Here then, surely, is the sense of gift missing in *Being and Time*? But who or what is the giver? Certainly none of our fellow-creatures, present or past. *Being and Time* lacked a sense not only of givenness but of the specific dependency of existence on other existences, and that lack is not made good by Heidegger's later invocation of "that which grants." Maybe that phrase is the nearest Heidegger chooses to come to speaking of the ineffable Divine. But he who cannot receive from his brother, whom he has seen, cannot receive from God, whom he has not seen.[16] Superficially, there may appear to be a great difference between what *Being and Time* says about historicity—that we give continuity to our existence by making our history into part of its project—and Heidegger's later view—that the continuity of things is granted us in a giving which cannot be spoken of in historical terms. But is a "destiny" which we make ourselves so very different from a "destiny" given by a power beyond history—once we remember that in the first case "we" are a power beyond history too? Twice in his life, in very different circumstances, and with what purport to be quite different intentions, Heidegger defines history (Geschichte) as destiny (Geschick), but the pun is the same on both occasions and the two definitions cannot really be distinguished.

The continuity in Heidegger's thinking is personal as well as intellectual and there is a third and personal sense in which he gave no public expression to the historical context of his thought. His political utterances developed in strict parallel to the structure of his thought in general. His "engagement" corresponded, as he acknowledged, to the culmination of his analysis of Existence; his subsequent silence about the working out of the "destiny" chosen by him and his people, about the "situation of the age" after 1945, and about historicity itself, corresponded to the turn, always intended, away from Existence and towards Being. Behind this consistency lies a deeper obstinacy than that which kept him from disavowing his political commitment of 1933. If his later work, in particular, his rejection of Jünger's belief in a concrete mid-twentieth–century turn in human history, leaves the impression not only of unfinished personal business, but of an unsatisfactory metaphysical analysis of the relation between Being and historicity, that is because he never deviated from his original life-determining decision of 1919 to abandon "the system of Catholicism," in which his parents had brought him up, and to enter the system of German official philosophy. The task he then set himself was still effectively a task in Christian theology: to unite a scholastic ontology with a Lutheran account of the life of faith. But he had deprived himself of the means of carrying it out. Had he not cut his links with the Church he would have been able, or forced, to draw on the most extensive corpus of thought on the relation of Being and historicity that the West has to offer: Catholic Christology and ecclesiology. Intrinsic to both is a theme remarkably unprominent in Heidegger's thought at all stages, bodies: the natural and risen body of the incarnate Lord, and the bodies of the faithful, sexually generated, destined to die, and sustained in life by their participation in the economic nexus. How these bodies have become or are to become, the Mystical Body, the temples of the Spirit, is the question in theological anthropology Heidegger decided in 1919 he was not concerned to answer.[17] In his maturity, he thought his principal vocation was to demonstrate the historicity of existence (*SuZ* 235), but since he had chosen to say so little about history as an interrelation of bodies he was in his final years unable to respond to questions about his or our historical situation with anything but a silence that was variously mystical, messianic, and morose.

Heidegger's silence has become—rightly—one of the most contentious features of his life and thought, and it is intimately connected with the inability of Post-Modernist thinking to relate our (collective or individual) future to our (collective or individual) past. Paul Celan, Germany's greatest poet of the post-modern age visited Heidegger on 25 July 1967, in the mountain-hut that had been his retreat since the 1920s, expecting, perhaps hoping for, "a word that was to come" from Germany's greatest living philosopher on the most terrible period in Germany's history.[18] The only word that came was his own poem, telling of his expectation. Heidegger, then as always, had nothing to say of the most plainly psychotic act of the regime he had in his small way helped to power, the bodily destruction of six million of his Jewish fellow human beings, in an administrative program deliberately conceived yet lacking even the shreds of rational purpose—political, military, or even economic— which apologists have claimed for Stalin's otherwise similar crimes.[19] Heidegger kept the silence of Zarathustra, of the exempt genealogist, alone aloof from the operations of the will to power which his pitiless eye has penetrated. Nietzsche did not claim this exemption for himself, but like Hölderlin—and Thomas Mann's Leverkühn—sacrificed himself to the divinity he had conjured up: he destroyed himself, mentally and physically, in seeking to speak to others, in his own person and in his own time, of what he had seen. Heidegger, and other Nietzscheans, such as Paul de Man and Heidegger's French deconstructionist successors, have preferred the role of Zeitblom, dreaming the world-dream, like the Red King in *Through the Looking-Glass*, but saying as little as possible, to others and, no doubt (though we cannot know), to themselves, about their own part in the story they have to tell. But behind the mask of the modest functionary, the humbled mystic, the good-hearted but simple scribe, who loyally delineates a world gone mad and fallen prey to logocentrism, forgetfulness of Being, or diabolical nihilism, there lies a hugely arrogant claim: to be exempt, to have clean hands, to be the one just man in Sodom, alone capable of intellectual coherence in his account of the incoherencies by which deceitful interests reveal their operations. That claim is the besetting and original sin of the officials in their struggle to regulate the activities of the commercial bourgeois and subordinate them to the collective political will. The officials of course have personal interests too, but they are secured not by the willing and mutual deceptions of trade but by their lifelong devotion of themselves to the legislative and executive State, the unashamed wielder of explicit force—they have a "vocation" (Beruf), that is, tenure. And as in the extreme case the liberal capitalists pass over in silence that the system in which they and their friends satisfy each other's needs keeps whole nations in poverty in some distant continent, so the conscientious officials ignore that the state power to which they have committed themselves, which maintains them in office, and which by its nature acknowledges no higher authority than its own will, is capable of abusing infinitely its monopoly of the right to inflict death. Officials are always tempted to think themselves, like the state they serve, above every possible fray, even the fray of being human. If liberal capitalists tend to forget that other bodies have to toil in order that theirs can be fed, officials tend to forget bodies altogether. The bodies of others become material, to be delivered at the appropriate rate to the front, to the factory, to the camp. The officials' own bodies become inexplicable and irrelevant adjuncts to their existence. The first answer (there may be others) to the question "what is the relation between de Man in the 1970s and de Man in the 1940s, between the Heidegger of 'the turn' and the university Rector of 1933, between the fictitiously fragmented author of the genealogical text and the single recipient and disburser of the copyright income?" is obvious enough to any but officials. The same mortal body, the same child of the same parents, acted and thought then and now, wrote the words and receives and spends the proceeds. An anthropology which cannot give that first answer is a mask for an unavowed political or economic interest (an interest, that is, in the manipulation of the bodies of others). Heidegger's silence about the historical character of the age he contributed to making has its counterpart not only in the absence of bodily parenthood, and so of inter-human giving, from his first attempt, in *Being and Time*, at an account of "human Being," but also in the reluctance of present-day deconstructionists to consider the economic function of their ideology. In each case we are dealing with the unavowed "self-assertion" of the same moribund class—the official intellectuals, the state-salaried agents of Enlightenment.

Two Steps to Fascism

Heidegger in 1933 fell victim to what Jünger later diagnosed as the error of "conservatism": the belief that, in the total change that was coming over the world, it was possible to hold on to some element from the past which had remained intact and entire, somehow insulated from the global fire-storm, and build the future on it. A less kind term for the error, which there is no need to avoid since Heidegger himself could not possibly have repudiated it, is "fascism." Fascism is the attempt to give a political embodiment to the new global economic reality by rescuing obsolete forms from the old society which the new forces have wrecked—to make the new economy palatable by artificially restoring autocratic monarchs, military cadres, peasantries, clergies, officialdoms, or, especially, nations. These by definition cannot be what the people really want, though in their desperate sense of lost identity they may imagine they want them. What they really want is the global market in which, one way or another, they have chosen to participate (for *that* is the revolution that has destroyed the old society). The only political form that can reconcile them to the suffering the global market inflicts as the corollary of its benefits must proceed from their new economic relationships. It cannot be a leftover from a world they abandoned because it no longer satisfied their desire. Fascism is therefore by its nature always oppressive, always in conflict with its own people's real desires (expressed in what they are willing to work and pay for) and it must always lead in the end to war, to the futile attempt to maintain by force an order that the world as a whole does not want either. Yet a great imaginative and emotional effort may be the price if an old-established, perhaps partially feudal, society is to accept with full awareness the new economic realities: that all have to work, and may consume only insofar as they can produce, within the increasingly competitive, that is, egalitarian, supranational system of exchange. The reluctance to pay the price may express itself in resistance to the political institutions that in the course of the twentieth century have ever more clearly shown themselves to be intrinsic to the new, global, form of the system of needs: mass democracy and internationalism. Against these overt forms of modern irreligion, rather than against the new post-bourgeois economic relationships, which enter less into public consciousness and with which it is anyway in alliance, fascism opposes its fetish.

Many in Germany around 1930 sought their talisman among the components of the Second Empire: its army, its civil service, its autocratic monarchy, its vestigial feudal nobility. Heidegger looked to its universities. Because like most of his fellow countrymen he was unable or unwilling to understand the worldwide changes, he was unable or unwilling to see that the new institutions of the new Republic offered—to his people and to the world—the best hope of mastering the crisis without its turning to catastrophe. The changes, manifest in Germany as the loss of empire, monarchy, and much territory, could not be denied. But to understand them two separate intellectual steps were necessary and there was no politically coherent group in Weimar Germany capable of taking both steps. The Marxists—socialists and communists—might be able to see what the right wing refused to admit: that the upheaval was essentially economic. But dogma forced them to conceive what was happening in obsolete terms inherited from the previous century: as a conflict between a capitalist and a working class within discrete national economies. The true features of the great change— the establishment of a world market, the disappearance of the class of private owners of significant quantities of capital, and the proletarianization of society (the hegemony of "the worker")—were apparent only to a non-Marxist like Jünger who, for reasons peculiar to his own German intellectual inheritance, disdained economic explanations. Like others on the right wing who shared his disdain, he created a phantom causality of "technology" and "the type"—the National Socialists appealed to "race," Heidegger to "destiny"—to take the place of the concrete desires and labor of physical individuals, cumulated and mediated in the system of needs, as the motive forces behind social developments.

Heidegger and Jünger were therefore as incapable of taking the second step as the Marxists, for whom it would have involved a repudiation, to a great extent, of their own origins. For the next step was to accept the key insight in Hegel's philosophy of the state: that the economic system generates the political institutions which both keep it in check and—by making what appears to be an impersonal system, arising from the interacting limited interests of its members, into an expression of collective identity—prevent it from destroying itself, at least for the present. In practical terms that meant, in the Germany of the 1920s, accepting (but no doubt also reforming) the institutions that had come with the half-spontaneous, half-imposed Revolution of 1918: universal suffrage, an elected government, and membership of the international organizations gradually emerging to express and control the world economic order; it meant, that is, accepting the realities to which Germany submitted only in 1949 (in the West) and 1989 (in the East). Thomas Mann, like Jünger a non-Marxist, could reinterpret his German intellectual inheritance—

somewhat implausibly—as leading him to these practical conclusions, though it also prevented him from grasping that the true continuity of his stance, before and after the Revolution, lay in his
socio-economic position rather than in his devotion to the ideal of
"humanity." However, his loud and explicit campaigning for the new
Republic, from its earliest years, is far more important than any personal ambiguities, or the uneasiness of his relationship with the established political parties. It cannot be laid to his charge that
Germany between 1918 and 1933 failed to create the forum which
might have gathered into a coherent force those elements of a true
understanding of the nation's position which we find in his work and
Jünger's, or in that of Hermann Hesse and Max Weber. That was a
failure of those who in Germany had been professionally charged
with maintaining the coherence of the nation's intellectual life, a
failure of the universities. Heidegger's fall was paradigmatic. In the
crucial years after the Revolution the universities failed to analyze
Germany's past and present so as to encourage realistic reform and
to discourage fantasizing. Instead they succumbed to fantasies of
their own—especially of their own all-importance—which were essentially regressions to the creed that had sustained them through
the centuries of absolute monarchy which were now suddenly over.
Professors of German literature, of sociology, or jurisprudence, or
philosophy, tried out the roomy mantle of Frederick the Great instead of seeking to explain and assist Germany's transition to a post-
bourgeois society under a republican constitution. If that moment of
regression did not put them in the fascist camp, it disarmed them for
any struggle against fascism, whether in its phase of blandishment or
its phase of violence. The end of monarchy was not regretted: it
seemed to open up the flattering prospect of a permanent and politically untrammeled task of Enlightenment for preceptors of the people who overlooked that when the king is gone the courtiers too are
redundant. Heidegger's vision, expressed in his rectoral address, of a
university as disinterestedly devoted to knowledge as any Humboldt-
ian university of the Second Reich, yet speaking the language of National Socialism, educating the "leaders" but taking no orders from
them, was a mirage of a kind which seduced many who thought they
could ride the tiger. But it was not simply muddle-headedness which
caused the official wing of the German "educated middle class"
(Bildungsbürgertum) to prefer mirages to a commitment to post-

bourgeois society and its peaceful political development.[20] It was a class interest, the surrender to which was most crisply symbolized, in an individual life, by Heidegger's abandonment in 1919 of the "system" of Rome. Two steps suffice to recognize the global political process and its derivation from the global economic process. Two steps in the contrary direction constitute the intellectual's road to fascism, the treason of the clerks, whether in Weimar Germany or in other times and places.

Is there currently, for example, a crisis of signification, as the genealogists assert? Surely this is quite as much a case of a phantom causality, invoked or invented to conceal the workings of the global market, as Jünger's "technology" or Heidegger's "stand'"? To the lay observer there seems to be more, and more effective, communication between more members of the human race, and novel sign languages abound more, than ever before. It may be that the self which, if the evidence of literature is to be trusted, had so richly extended a life a hundred years ago, has been reduced to a punctual locus of consumer choices. But that is more immediately and simply explained by the need, in a competitive market, to maximize the rate and minimize the time of return on investments than by any appeal to the subtleties of linguistics and epistemology (or ontology or Diltheyan "types"). Indeed genealogism seems, like the market, to have so little nostalgia for the dethroned monarch and to rejoice so much in the new multiplicity of options that it seems more concerned to exploit our present situation than to explain how it came about. There is in the air a whiff of collaboration, which started us off on our present inquiry. Have we now run it to earth? When Germany became the first fully industrialized European nation to be stripped of its empire and forced to compete unprotected in the world economy, its intellectual classes saw in the corrosion of its social structure a unique opportunity. Karl Mannheim, the sociologist of knowledge, wrote in the year of crisis, 1929:

> It is an absolute imperative of the moment to exploit the twilight illumination which now prevails and in which all things and positions reveal their relativity, in order to see once and for all that all the structures of meaning (Sinngebungsgefüge) that make up a particular world are historical and moveable scenery. . . . In this historic moment, when all things are suddenly becoming transparent and history is actually unveiling the structures and elements of which it's com-

posed, it is our task to measure up to the situation in scientific (wis-senschaftlich) thought.[21]

Mannheim—who, with Heidegger, must count as one of the inventors of the term 'deconstruction' ('Destruktion', 'destruieren', in German, with the sense of "dismantling")[22]—was assuming that, for the time being at least, the professionals of "scientific" thought were not part of the moveable scenery. Salaried or privately financed ("free-floating"), the intellectuals would in their physical existence be exempt from the historic upheaval which was conceived as affecting structures of meaning rather than bodies. The clerks, Heidegger reassured his colleagues in 1933, would continue to offer the German people "the service of knowledge" (Wissensdienst). In the seventy-five–year struggle to replace the empires by a global market, which began in 1914, the powers which for most of the time were the military victors have had to suffer social readjustment as great as that in Germany, but it has been gradual rather than abrupt or catastrophic, and is not complete even now. The intellectual classes of America, Britain, and France have therefore had rather longer to respond to their crisis than the Germans of the 1920s and the response has had a more international character, but it has been similar and has to some extent consciously modeled itself on the earlier German example. Dimly aware that the new economic reality has destroyed both the two possible foundations for the material existence of an intellectual in the age of Enlightenment—as a bourgeois with private means or as a salaried official—they have sought an accommodation with reality by recourse to fantasy. The market, after all—the system of needs—has recourse to fictions too, to protect itself from the growth of the state, the political structures which will control and limit it. If we are persuaded to think of ourselves only as punctual consumers we shall forget that we are also producers and neither allow our act of consumer choice to be affected by the interests of producers nor seek a state structure that will protect them. But such a view of ourselves—as consumers who are not also producers—is sustainable only if we can draw on private capital. As the new economic reality makes this increasingly unlikely we may say that the market view of ourselves as nothing but consumers with no need of the state, the view propagated by the oddly named "conservative" parties, is based on fantasy—the fiction that we are all pre-1914 bourgeois. Similarly, though for different motives, genealogism tries to persuade us that we are nothing but punctual consumers of intellectual options—a view of ourselves that forgets our bodies and would be sustainable only if our material existence were secured for us (in the absence of private capital) by a vocation, an official's job for life provided by the state. The self-image of the genealogist is therefore also based on fantasy—the fiction that we are all professors, paid to undertake self-cultivation (Bildung) rather than production for others.

"Scientific thought" can, it turns out, collaborate with the consumer revolution that has revealed all structures of meaning to be moveable scenery, that is, fashions. Epistemology, the characteristic form of reflection by politically trammeled officials about the non-laboring, all-consuming self they have never been allowed to be, seems to guarantee jobs forever for universities conceived in the old mold—endless possibilities of repackaging the Western intellectual and literary tradition within factitiously insoluble problems ("aporias") requiring an endless multiplication of sub-departments to teach and "research" them. In the same way the free market is held to guarantee of itself the perfect satisfaction of an ever-expanding array of self-justifying wants. The illusions fostered by the "conservative" parties are found persuasive by their electorates until recession reveals that no one any longer possesses the significant amounts of private capital on which they are tacitly predicated; the illusions of the genealogist intellectuals are found persuasive by their university colleagues and administrations until the funding dries up and it becomes apparent that the nation no longer has an omnipotent monarch commanding the propagation of Enlightenment (that is, the critique of Church and bourgeoisie) "for its own sake" (that is, in the interests of the state).

Both sets of fictions have in common that they conceal the simple socioeconomic truth: that the global market has proletarianized us all. We are simultaneously producers and consumers in a new world with room neither for the bourgeois nor for the state officials of the nineteenth century. Rather than face that truth the intellectuals of Weimar Germany invented a battery of non-economic explanations of their plight and took refuge in potentially or explicitly fascist fantasies of a preserved or restored officialdom: "workers," officers, a new clerisy to suppress and replace the old.

But it is only with the second step down the road to fascism that we arrive at the door of the real thing. Heidegger's most unequivocally fascist act, his clearest betrayal of his people and his mind, was his public declaration of support for Hitler in the plebiscite on a one-party Reichstag and withdrawal from the League of Nations. That was the moment when he explicitly rejected the constitution of the Republic and its chosen international identity. He thereby implicitly denied any faith that the local and global political institutions were so rooted in the system of needs—i.e., in the human race's most immediately perceived interests—that they had to be better able to control the system and safeguard the just rights of all than some group of wisely or unwisely selected, or self-appointed, *condottieri* or "leaders." That (allegedly) 95 percent of the voters in the plebiscite shared in this betrayal of themselves and one another does not affect the quality of their action, or Heidegger's, nor does the probability that for many an overwhelming motive must have been the promise of work for seven million unemployed breadwinners. The experience, or just the fear, of redundancy tells us as surely as pain that we are not simply consumers, endlessly exercising our momentary right to choose, but producers too. Unemployment—as Keynes saw—reveals the necessity of politics. But political decisions can be rational or deluded, prudent or self-defeating. The task of discerning and developing the nascent institutions which can control the accelerating process of globalization, while preserving it from local or general breakdown, requires patience, a sense of justice, a willingness to accept the compromises which maintain the hope of growth in an unpredictable future. The fascist turns instead to the illusions of certainty offered by a past which has already been overtaken, to anachronisms which can be imposed only by the arbitrary use of government force—by decree and eventually by violence—and to a denial of the global reality which will inevitably reassert itself at last, probably through a catastrophe such as war. Tyranny and xenophobia are two sides of the same coin. Poujadism, isolationism, socialism in one country, the monstrous reigns of terror in Ethiopia and Cambodia, had in common that they sought to seal off the nation from what was represented as a corrupting outside world and could do so only temporarily and only by calling, willingly or unwillingly, on the powers of central government to stop people from doing what they have done for longer than they have engaged in industry or agriculture—exchanging goods with one another by way of trade. The bugbears of fascism in the twentieth century have been the two pillars of the modern world order, the two beacons of reason and mutual self-interest which alone offer any promise of peace and prosperity in the future: the multi-national company (often alleged in the first half of the century to be a Jewish conspiracy: much in anti-Semitism was a fearful reaction against the growth of the global market), and the international treaty organization, with its dependent agencies. Even now a resentment of international business and cosmopolitan culture is noticeable in Heidegger's intellectual successors, who have not yet adopted a position from which they could consistently disown his campaign of 1933. Obviously Lyotard is no fascist, but it has to be asked whether we are not being disarmed for the struggle against fascism by the argument that the grand narrative, the world-historical perspective of Kant, Hegel, or Marx, has ceased to be an intellectual possibility and that the great economic and political systems that encompass our lives are beyond rational understanding and no more than instruments of oppression. It is difficult to be too emphatic in asserting the contrary: ours is a time when we all face the question how the full integration into the world economy of the Chinese third of the human race, and of other highly populous nations, and so the relative decline in the standard of living of the G7 countries, particularly the USA, can be managed without an economically triggered nuclear war on the pattern of the First World War; when economic collapse and aggressive nationalism threaten Russia, the Ukraine, and other parts of the former Soviet empire; and when movements directly derivative from the fascism of the 1930s and 1940s are seeking to take charge of an otherwise welcome revival in the Islamic world of the awareness that religion has a political dimension, and politics a religious dimension. It is hardly a time to be concentrating on "les petits récits." Not only are great issues now raised of economic development, political organization, moral principle, and the nature of self and personal purpose, but the interrelation of these issues is becoming clearer than it has been for 150 years or more. The only possible perspective for a contemporary intellectual ought to be global, the only possible narrative macro-narrative. To assist the growth of local pockets of irrationality, of non-global thinking, to accept, or even demand, the narrower perspective in which fascist or proto-fascist arguments are, if not defensible, at least not refutable, is to collaborate, like our predecessors in the 1930s in bringing on disaster—only local perhaps, but for those affected none the less complete.

Post-Modernism and the University

The contemporary academic intellectual runs the risk of perpetuating the central error of Thatcherism: the belief that the development of the market economy, necessarily accompanied, as Hegel saw, though not the Thatcherists, by the growth and sophistication of the state, is a process containable within the political framework of a single nation. The process, however, is world wide, and the implicit terminus of the state-building impulses within it is not in a national, but in some kind of supra-national political order. Individuals now feel larger than the country that claims them as nationals, and the political entity that would express what they feel they are does not yet exist. To overlook this development is a natural error for an academic to make for, in continental Europe at least, and since the Reformation, the universities have had a peculiarly close relationship with the national identity. As some of the oldest state-funded secular institutions, they have been the principal organs of monarchical Enlightenment, of the critique of Church, bourgeoisie, and the "corporations," in the interests of rational, centralized, government. (In England they acquired this function only with the reforms and new foundations of the nineteenth century.) The rise of the global market, however, makes monarchical Enlightenment as obsolete as monarchs, or as national governments. Critique of local social conditions—whether historical, sociological, philosophical, or literary—and the implicit appeal to a local, rational political authority which is in principle able to rectify them, and with which the individual can identify, have lost their power to convince: they no longer seem the best that the mind can do. It is asking too much of the officials of an aging nation-state to expect them to project themselves on to the supra-national plane where the mind is young again. In the post-modern academy therefore the mind turns to the critique of itself, seeking to fix in "scientific thought" the moveable scenery to which the national structures of meaning have been reduced. However, it avoids considering—as the official mind has always avoided considering—the institution which makes it materially possible for thinkers to spend time thinking and which has been deprived of its purpose by the same global process which has given their thoughts this turn.

What is the purpose of the universities which give us a living? is a question, as MacIntyre noted, which post-modern thinkers find singularly difficult to answer (though it was asked by Heidegger in his rectoral address of 1933, a fact which the scandal aroused by his National Socialism has tended to obscure). At first—and especially if there is a boom on—the loss of a central national purpose can be a great relief, as it was in Germany in the 1920s. To swim with the tide of consumerism is pleasurable for universities too, and while the tide is rising there is no need to think about the old landmarks it has obliterated. Hence the surprisingly congruent thinking of market apologists and avant-garde academics who otherwise inclined to bureaucratic socialism (for reasons adequately, if unwittingly, made clear by Spengler). The "conservative" parties encouraged us to fragment ourselves into a series of consumer choices, while ignoring the material basis of these choices in the bodies which have to labor to get the means of making them, and they interpreted social change as evidence of a moral crisis rather than the consequence of the economic and political process they were furthering. The deconstructionists fragmented the subject into a multiplicity of options while ignoring the material origin of signs and texts in bodies whose productive activity is all the continuity a subject needs, and they interpreted intellectual change as evidence of a semiotic crisis rather than the manifestation of their own economic and political obsolescence. The "conservative" parties took the step into Thatcherism when in political theory they turned against the supranationalism of their economic practice, opposed an artificial and anachronistic patriotism to the already partly internationalist thinking of their electorates, and averted their eyes from the overthrow of national sovereignty by the global market. The post-modernists took the step into what we might call myopianism when they proclaimed the end of the grand narrative from which they derive (Lyotard is a Kant scholar, Derrida a maverick Heideggerian), proposed to a generation aware of global warming and world poverty that we should concentrate like Heidegger on the little things of life and accept the inherent ungraspability of the very large processes, to which as economic agents we contribute, and averted their eyes from the overthrow of national cultural institutions by the global market and the global communications network. But consumerism loses its appeal in times of recession and when the funds run out and redundancy threatens even the deconstructionists notice that they are producers also, and even the myopians are forced to take the larger view. At this point the risk of fascism is at its most acute: the global perspective has been so long neglected that the nation whose identity quietly passed away during the last orgy of consumption may make some antiquated gesture of pointless self-assertion. So may the university, though its claim to "leadership" is less likely to be taken seriously or to have dangerous consequences.

Richer governments may be tempted to wave their nuclear weapons about or to depart noisily from the international conference-chamber. Areas of the world that have arrived more recently in the global market, and are disappointed by their first taste of the costs of membership, may revert to autocracy, clericalism, or bloodthirsty tribalism. Nietzschean academics may be hard put to it to explain why they should not, all manifestations of the will to power being equally free of value. Alternatively, like Derrida faced with the tyranny of *apartheid*, they may simply abandon their view that justice is merely a narrative convention, which at least is decent.[23] The dilemma of the clerks may not seem of great significance to any but themselves, but it is the terminus at which officialdom arrives when it does not have the courage to admit that intellectual authority has passed out of its hands into the international sphere, and that people now generate the ideas by which they live not in separate national classes or traditions but in worldwide agencies, companies, or movements. They are left entertaining themselves with phantoms, some harmless, some not. Meanwhile, the political structures which have fallen victim to fascist episodes will either sink into hopeless and interminable war and brigandage which will eventually destroy their economic base, or they will return to the global fold as the economic climate improves.

Yet in the period of retrenchment which has now begun it is not inevitable that nations, or universities, should flee from reality into self-important illusion. When the system of needs rides up against its limits the political questions can no longer be avoided and the state-building process begins—on the international level, as once on the national. In the intellectual world the sifting effect of competition will be felt on the once endless multiplicity of options. The incommensurability of perspectives may be expected to reduce as a common interest and a common theme is found—the future and purpose of the humanities departments of universities. Boundaries between subjects, and not only the most recent, will become permeable and as general arts courses grow more common and cease to be regarded with disdain it will become apparent once more what is the relation of all their components to the queen of sciences, theology, from which, in the long history of enlightenment, they have gradually been derived. Indeed, a model for the post-national university, whose day is already upon us, may perhaps be found in the pre-national university of the Middle Ages. A shifting, cosmopolitan community of itinerant scholars, devoted to the elaboration of a new anthropology, would more fully express the mind of the limited whole that the world has become than the market-disciplined deliverers of educational products into which the central administrations of former nations have remodeled their former seats of national learning.

If research is pressing your understanding of an area in which you are wholly competent to the point where your understanding changes completely and so you become incompetent once more, then it is difficult to see how research can be accommodated—that is, paid for—by bodies principally concerned with the sale of measurable quanta of knowledge. Private benefactors and international organizations are the most likely funders of research in the future, not necessarily in new institutions (though the various Institutes of Advanced Study scattered round the world may give an indication of what is to come) but at least in enclaves within existing universities of very different character from their surroundings and in tension with them. Thus, maybe, will that new supranational level of the mind be built up, corresponding to the supranational level of political organization which the global market must build up, if Hegel is right, simply in order to preserve itself. Only from such a vantage point will research in the true sense be possible, the intellectual transcending of the worldwide system of needs, as the nascent world institutions transcend it politically. In that unifying perspective—which will not be just one option among many—we may hope to rediscover our true identity, not just as consumers, but as producers too, with all the consumer-producer's concerns which philosophy in the bourgeois age, whether in its capitalist or its bureaucratic variants, found so difficult to incorporate: time, giving and receiving, generation, death, the state, war, law, constraint, all that lies beyond the market and limits it, even when it has become global.

Can we discern the outlines of that new anthropology, an anthropology for the new "type" which has become real so much sooner than Nietzsche or Heidegger expected (though not Jünger)? As we learn to see ourselves in the context of the one, gradually developing, limited world order, so we may come to recognize what we are seeing not as selves but as bodies. Bodies are individual and material, of course, but they are not just countable units of indifferent matter. Sexually produced, and destined for sexual reproduction, they are genetically unique bridges (unless we are clones or identical twins) between unique acts of generation, and so occupy unique positions in the biosphere, and thereby in the material unity that is our planet. Specifically, however—that is, as a species, collectively—we are bodies that live by exchanging the products of our work with one another (in principle, with *all* others of our kind), by entering, that is, into the economic nexus and the nexus of signs, or language, which sustains it. But signs point to what is absent—what is present needs no sign—and so the system of language points beyond the system of needs and labor, beyond the market, to what limits it. Through language we become self-determining, political beings, and the culmination of that process is the development of a language—which would include such essentially linguistic institutions as conferences, agreements, parliaments, secretariats, and churches of the Word—to enable us to speak of ourselves as potential world citizens. There can be, we know, no world-state. But there can be an increasingly concrete political order of the one world as a whole, which will come ever closer to placing whatever limits we choose on our behavior as economic beings in the world market—an "ever closer union" in the precisely and profoundly correct words of the European Treaties. In that context, we are not selves, but bodily individuals, in whom the collectively shared processes of production and consumption, giving and receiving, uniquely intersect to create time, and who find meaning in what we say and do insofar as we aspire—or know we ought to aspire—to being equal members of that world order which, though ideal, is already in the making. The view of human identity being forced on us by the accelerating developments of our century can be grasped largely, then, in Hegelian terms, provided we allow Kant to contribute some crucial modifications. Kant remarks that however little we may know about the past we know this much for certain about the historians of the future: that they will be interested in us and our age only insofar as we have contributed to the establishment of world peace.[24] In that remark we might find the seeds of a new self-understanding appropriate to the post-bourgeois, post-official, era.

Heidegger was right to turn his attention, early in his maturity, to the mystics and to Luther. They stood near the beginning of a process of which he in a sense was the end. They mark the point at which German theological (and anthropological and political) reflection diverged from the mainstream of Catholic Europe, and he at first believed, also rightly, that he had the ability to bring the streams together again. As an outsider he felt called to resist the culture of the nineteenth-century German bureaucracy which, because of the exceptional importance of the German universities as models for large parts of the world university system, was widely influential in philosophy, theology and the study of history. Had he realized it, he could have found powerful support in Hegel who (like Kant) was far more indebted to the empiricist thinking of the contemporary French and English (and Scottish) bourgeoisie than his German audience liked to acknowledge. Heidegger chose differently, chose assimilation, and the penalty was not only that his thought was cut off from its Catholic roots but that it became marked by the resentment and suspicion of the European bourgeoisie and its literary and intellectual tradition which was characteristic of the officialdom he joined.

For a philosopher who lays great stress on our "being-in-the-world," Heidegger finds it remarkably difficult to locate the philosophical activity in "the world." His literary style obviously links him to Franco-American deconstructionism, yet it also reflects a sense of being "not very reliably at home in the interpreted world,"[25] which has been a continuing theme in German literature since the eighteenth century. He carries to an extreme Nietzsche's habit of arguing from (often dubious) etymologies, from semi- and mistranslations from the Greek, from verbal distortions, amputations and neologisms—as if the words he utters so deliberately and repetitiously could be made to glow with the Being of which he wishes them to speak—yet this concentration on the linguistic medium suggests a lack of confidence in its ability in normal circumstances to be the medium of anything at all. Like Nietzsche too, and like Schopenhauer before him, Heidegger often relies for proof on the authority of some previous literary formulation, as if the adduction of other kinds of evidence raised difficulties that he wished to avoid. One has the impression not of the one World in which we are, but of two sundered worlds—one all words and inter-textuality, the other ineffable. The range of modern literature on which Heidegger draws is very narrow. Rilke and Hölderlin overshadow everything else, even Goethe, even Shakespeare. Not surprisingly, the range does not extend to the European realist novel. Heidegger was an official, and the literature of money—the sign language whose referentiality is never in doubt—was, as the creation of the bourgeoisie, always a suspicious object for bureaucratic Germany.

At a time when Germany desperately needed a mind able to place its cultural heritage in the worldwide context Heidegger clung to what was local and provincial. Along with too many others of his time he rejoiced in the destruction of Germany's indigenous bourgeoisie and did not realize that the same forces would dissolve the old official class too. He showed no insight into the material, commercial, and international nature of the new order and so his thinking illuminates only parts of our post-modern situation: notably, in *Being and Time*, his emphasis on futurity and on what might be called "production in the world" rather than "consumption of the world," and, in his later period, his, admittedly purely formal, analysis of "the stand" and of the "granting" of Being. By contrast with Jünger, from whom much of what is most concrete in his critique of modernity seems to derive, but who was perhaps never an ally, and certainly never a disciple, he had no sense that the twentieth century saw the traversing of a historical watershed. To too many of those who felt the influence of his metaphysical genius he passed on the sensation of living into a cul-de-sac when they were merely living in a period of inadequately analyzed economic and political transition. It is not pleasant to have to admit that the institution, or the intellectual activity, or even the nation, in which you have spent much of your life has passed away or has little future, but it furnishes no grounds for believing that rationality and virtue have come to an end too. There are abundant signs in our own time that human self-interest is capable of arranging the affairs of the race more justly, and perhaps more peaceably, than ever before, and Heidegger's example is a warning to us not to ignore them.

III
Literature and Identity

9 After Realism
Nietzsche and the
"Middle Mode of Discourse"

FOR J. P. STERN

Why study literature? That question is likely nowadays to be met with a hollow appeal to the national heritage, or some such lame and unpersuasive apologia as that literary study is an intellectual discipline like any other, or that it provides convenient material for the acquisition of communications skills, that is, for learning to read and write. Oddly, the question seems scarcely to be addressed by the sophisticated literary theory of which we have a great deal more than we had thirty or forty years ago. But thirty or forty years ago there was a clear answer to it, at least in the English-speaking world. The justification of literary study maintained by F. R. Leavis had immense internal strength and coherence for the very reason for which it is no longer heard in the contemporary university's ever more mandarin and hermetic departments of literature: it shunned literary theory, and on principle. Language for Leavis was the medium (or as his friend Wittgenstein said, a form) of life, and literature was the most reflective use of language for it incorporated all others—literature was about life, and about lesser things, such as thought or imagination or symbolization, only insofar as these were understood as part of life. To engage with the texts

247

of literary theoreticians rather than with the texts with which they purported to deal was necessarily to prefer a thinner and more schematic engagement with life to one which was richer and more subtle. There is something eminently commonsensical about this approach to literature: to reject it one has to say that one does not know what is meant by 'life'.

Well, one can say that. For those of us who think life is a good thing, however, the Leavisite approach had another great merit. It asserted that life, language, and literature are from the beginning and of their nature moral (an insight at which Heidegger's disciple, Emmanuel Levinas, arrived with much greater epistemological labor when he was seeking to distance himself from his master). That is, moral categories cannot be reduced (as Nietzsche and the Freudians variously wished) to stratagems of some life-force, nor are they (as both structuralists and post-structuralists imply) merely linguistic conventions; and consequently, because it is an engagement with life in language, all literature, and not just some sub-sections of it, is open to moral evaluation and strikes a moral attitude. A book always is, or mimics, the utterance of a human being, and a human being is always, willy-nilly, a moral agent. A work of literature is not just a picture of right living nor a means to encourage us to right living, but in the interaction between what it does as writing and what it requires of us as readers, it is itself a form of right living. Literature is worth studying because to read a book that is not vacuous makes us better—not because we have heard a sermon or have contemplated an image of the good life, but because we have kept good company, terrible (or comical) though the things may have been that we have thought about together. To live rightly it is not necessary to understand or be able to describe one's world or even what one is doing, but literature is that way of living rightly in which the detailed observation and honest understanding of the world and of human action is most fully and reflectively and publicly developed.

To a Leavisite humanist it will therefore seem natural to turn to literature in order to learn how to live in the crisis of personal and collective identity which began with the crystallization of the world market around 1870. But three major difficulties will at once oppose themselves to this attempt. First, and most superficially, the development of electrical, photographic, and latterly computing technology has made it questionable whether literary activity itself has a future: not just because the written word has ceased to be the only, or even in some areas the dominant, form of recorded communication, but also because it is in the nature of the computer to treat texts as accumulations of large numbers of rearrangeable basic units, sound-bites of sense (or is it bytes?). The notion that meaning is communicated by single large-scale structures—a tragedy or a novel taken as a whole—is becoming less familiar and self-evident as books are replaced by data bases. Second, though, the technological issue is, as always, the symptom of an underlying social and economic issue. To the ease with which the computer fragments and recombines the units of a text corresponds the ease with which the international economy fragments and recombines the elements of society. And why should the modes of literature remain unaffected by profound changes in the individuals and institutions which it represents, and in which it originates? What applies to literature applies also to literary criticism. The third problem for Leavisite humanism in the post-modern world is that it is itself an aspect of the historical process which began around 1870. The Leavisite plan for the moral improvement of society through literature; its close affinity with the universities and, especially, the school-teaching profession; its derivation from figures such as George Eliot and Matthew Arnold, with links both with popular education and with German culture—all suggest that the movement was the nearest England could come to an ideology of bureaucratic enlightenment of the kind which sustained the German official classes in their struggle for power with the bourgeoisie. In the year in which Heidegger asserted the autonomy and the "leading" role of the German universities, Leavis founded the journal *Scrutiny*, in the more modestly and urbanely formulated hope of creating "a small but critically active public that would have at any rate some centres in universities (and if not in universities, where?)."[1] Has the intellectual cogency of his claims for literature then also passed away as we have advanced—rather later than Germany—into the proletarian age? I believe it has not—just as the cultural theory of German officialdom has retained a certain transmuted relevance, and for somewhat similar reasons.

The Leavisite ambition to give literature the central role among the humane disciplines of the university was a claim to have succeeded theology as queen of the sciences. The intention was that a school of English should "generate in the university a centre of consciousness (and conscience) for our civilisation."[2] The study of secular literature was to foster a personal and social righteousness, in need of no metaphysical underpinning, such as had once been expected from the study of sacred scripture. We were to recover who we are, and were to be enabled for what we have to do, by our interaction with the word of Man enshrined in "canonical" books; and that notion is hardly imaginable without the earlier tradition that such self-discovery and empowerment result from our interaction with the Word of God, spoken to us in a Book which gave us the concept of a "canon" in the first place. In his last great controversy, Leavis found that the only publicly accessible name he could give to what he was opposing to Lord Snow, the BBC, and the "technologico-Benthamite" world was "a religious depth of thought and feeling."[3] It is no wonder that many of his direct and indirect disciples were Catholics. They recognized in the immediacy of the contact he postulated between secular words and moral values a continuation of the belief in the enfleshment of the divine which has been a mainstay of Catholic humanism in many different historical contexts— whether in the ninth or the thirteenth or the sixteenth centuries. In the period after 1945 when the Leavis school was enjoying its heyday, Erich Auerbach showed that the literary realism which it was better able to interpret than anyone else had been made possible by the specifically Christian concept of meaningful history. The Leavisite belief that literature is uniquely able to express our condition and guide our response to it has, then, much older antecedents than British culture of the late Imperial epoch. It need not be thought to be superseded just because that culture has passed away. It was a secularized form of religion and thanks to the religion in it, it can endure. Provided we can rediscover its Christian roots, literary humanism—like Dante's Virgil—can continue to show us at least two-thirds of what constitutes right living, even in the global market.

If the post-modern literary theory which derives from Nietzschean "genealogism" is unable to give us a reason for studying literature (let alone for theorizing about it) that is ultimately because it denies that initial intimacy between word and thing and moral meaning which it was the strength of Leavis to have recognized as something given and not capable of further analysis. 'Realism', it has been noted, is a term that applies both to the way things are depicted and the way they are assessed.[4] That coincidence is not chance but expresses a fundamental truth, and not just about literature. That we live in a world of morally meaningful things is as much an aspect of our finitude as our sexuality or our death. Post-Modernism betrays its collaboration with global consumerism in its insinuation that all these limitations can be opened up to infinity— an infinity of desires and satisfactions, of life in the shopping mall, of possible rearrangements of the system of language. To assert the relevance of a Christian humanism to the post-modern world is to take on the task of tracing and counteracting this detachment from finitude—in the theory of language which denies the unique importance of literary realism, in the universalization of male sexuality which denies the independent significance of the female and of parenthood, and in the obliteration of the thought of death. Nietzsche himself is the best witness to much of this process.

The Language of Zarathustra

J. P. Stern tells us that between the language of poetry with its concern for particulars and the language of philosophy with its concern for the general, between concrete and abstract, metaphor and concept, there lies a middle or hybrid mode of writing, practiced in particular by Nietzsche, which it was Nietzsche's greatest achievement to devise and to bequeath to many successors in the twentieth century, but which has antecedents which include the Book of Proverbs, Pascal, and William Blake.[5] In an unpublished essay of 1873, the young Nietzsche seizes on one of Pascal's *Pensées* as a prime example of the activity of an intellect that has freed itself from the established metaphors and conventional concepts that make up ordinary, contemptible, functional language: "Les rivières sont des chemins qui marchent, et qui portent où l'on veut aller" ("Rivers are walking roads, that carry us whither we wish to go").[6] The description that follows of a de- and re-constructive, paradoxical, zeugmatic, and ironical play with an accepted linguistic and conceptual structure "contains the most accurate account we have of Nietzsche's own future philosophical and literary undertaking . . . of the discontinuities, *aperçus* and aphoristic turns that will come to characterize his writing."[7] The argument of the essay, *On Truth and Falsehood from the*

Extra-moral Point of View, is that language is doubly metaphorical, doubly a metaphysical (rather than a moral) lie. For language consists of words which have only an arbitrary or conventional relation to thoughts, and thoughts have no rational or systematic relation to the physical objects to which they are simply the response of the human nervous system. Whatever the coherence of this argument, Nietzsche draws from it the conclusion that language is a system of self-sustaining metaphors that cannot be firmly bedded down into non-metaphorical referentiality, in short, that linguistically expressed "truths are illusions, whose illusory nature has been forgotten" (III 314). This belief that language is distinct from, can gain no purchase on, "a silent cosmos or world of unworded experiences, to which all utterances are intended—but fail adequately—to refer," is a belief that Stern has shown to be shared by Schopenhauer, Nietzsche, and the early Wittgenstein (*A Study of Nietzsche*, pp. 95, 193). This belief is the premise of all Nietzsche's critical and aphoristic engagement with the metaphysical and moral vocabulary of his time. In 1873 he still thinks it possible that a freely creative, artistic spirit might, even if only through "an intimatory translation, a halting interpretation," mediate between the subject and object he believes to be so completely sundered, though to do this would require "a middle sphere and a middle force of free poetry and free invention" (III 317). In 1888, at the end of a literary career which has turned him (he tells us, with almost metaphysical seriousness) from a metaphysician into a moralist, Nietzsche finds that "middle sphere" of language, however poetically creative, to be self-condemned, in virtue of the very metaphor that denotes it:

> Die Sprache, scheint es, ist nur für Durchschnittliches, Mittleres, Mitteilsames erfunden. Mit der Sprache *vulgarisiert* sich bereits der Sprechende.—Aus einer Moral für Taubstumme und andre Philosophen. (II 1005)

> Language, it seems, was invented only for what is average, middling, mediable. Simply through language the speaker *vulgarizes* himself.—Extract from a theory of morals for deaf-mutes and other philosophers.

What sort of language is written then by the philosopher who can neither speak nor hear the medium through which the herd (III 868) think truth and truthfulness to be communicable? It is a language which, even in 1888, even in *Twilight of the Idols* (to which I shall here give most attention), still conforms to the pattern laid down in 1873 for any language whatever. It is an (in principle) end-less sequence of mutually sustaining, mutually parodying, and mu-tually criticizing metaphors (which is not to say that Nietzsche's total repertoire of metaphors does not *in fact* have a limited and specific character). That principle is given to us *in nuce* when Nietz-sche tells us, for example, that the phrase "peace of mind" may be synonymous with

> der Anfang der Müdigkeit, der erste Schatten, den der Abend, jede Art Abend wirft. (II 967)
>
> the beginning of weariness, the first shadow cast by evening, any sort of evening.

"The beginning of weariness" looks a fairly literal, physiological, phrase (though it need not be—it might have a cultural-historical sense, for example); certainly it looks sufficiently literal for "the first shadow cast by evening" to seem an elucidatory metaphor. Yet the addition "any sort of evening" makes the first reference to evening seem in retrospect to be fully literal, while at the same time opening an endless perspective of further possible metaphorical applica-tions. Indeed, this is but one item in a brilliantly ingenious—and not in that at all unusual—enumeration of different possible more or less metaphorical synonyms for the initial metaphorical phrase. The list accumulates with such ease and rapidity that it seems it could go on for ever, though it in fact ends—if it is an end—in an application to the very work Nietzsche is writing:

> *Götzen-Dämmerung*: wer weiß? vielleicht auch nur eine Art "Frieden der Seele" ...
>
> *Twilight of the Idols*: who knows? perhaps also just a sort of "peace of mind" ...

Any term in the sequence can be seen as "just a sort of" some other term, and each term stands at the head of another potentially end-less sequence consisting of "any sort of" itself. By the end of this reflection the distinction between 'literal' and 'metaphorical' mean-ing has practically ceased to exist. Nietzsche has said as much in the preceding reflection, where he referred to "those natures that need la Trappe, metaphorically speaking (and non-metaphorically)"—"im Gleichnis gesprochen (und ohne Gleichnis)."

Even that—by public convention?—most real world of public, institutional, history is for Nietzsche only one more moral-psychological conformation metaphorically related to many others, whether philosophical, personal, physiological, or mythical, in a sequence whose first, or last, term is likely to be his own work. In *Twilight of the Idols* the section "The 'Improvers' of Humanity" (II 979–982) begins and ends with a programmatic statement of Nietzsche's aims and beliefs. There are, we are told (in italics), no moral *facts*, moral judgments are never to be taken literally, they are "merely sign-language, merely symptomatic." Signs, symptoms, of what? Nietzsche gives a first example taken from the medical, or at any rate veterinary, area to which his word 'Symptomatologie' has perhaps already directed our attention. Instead of the "improvement" of humanity we should speak of its "domestication," its "breeding": "only these technical zoological terms express realities." Not that Nietzsche seriously means that his two words 'Zähmung' and 'Züchtung', which look even less technical than their English equivalents, have a special non-metaphorical status. It becomes apparent from the continuation of his argument that "reality" is simply a part of his own affective and polemical vocabulary, a term which points to the metaphorical—that is, the deceitful—status of the vocabulary of his adversaries. "Domestication" and "breeding" he says are "realities of which, to be sure, the typical 'improver', the priest knows nothing—and does not *wish* to know anything"—but they are also the beginnings of a metaphorical chain in Nietzsche's text which cannot by any stretching of the associative imagination be called "zoological." "Domestication" applies to what goes on in menageries, Nietzsche says, "improvement" does not, so we should not apply "improvement" to the moral history of humanity, which *as history*, as raw event, justifies another metaphor, another sign-language. The early medieval church "was" a menagerie.

It is even more difficult to give a sense to the word 'was' than to the apparent claim that zoology is non-metaphorical. 'Was' is not just a harmless copula in a self-contained witticism. Nietzsche is invoking the real past of contemporary public institutions and he develops his metaphor as purposefully as if it were a historical explanation. Menageries need to be filled with wild beasts—what beast was hunted to fill the early medieval church?—the "blond beast," the Teuton. To be sure, a superb flight of metaphorical fancy sovereignly dismisses any philistine, literal (e.g., eugenicist) notion of what Nietzsche might mean. The captive Teuton, he says:

> stak im Käfig, man hatte ihn zwischen lauter schreckliche Begriffe eingesperrt.
>
> sat in a cage, locked away behind rows of terrifying concepts.

(The further development of the metaphor of the sickness of the caged animal need not concern us here.) It seems ridiculous, after such a sentence, to bother one's head too much about what Nietzsche means by 'was'. But a serious question is still raised by Nietzsche's claim—whether we call it sovereign, or whether we call it heedless—for the truth of one description of human society (the "zoological") rather than another (the "moral") and by his refusal to acknowledge any distinction between the historical and the moral realms—each the object of metaphorical interpretation *ad libitum*. May he not then, in the eyes of those (who may include ourselves) who continue to believe in the more or less distinct existence of a public, institutional, and historical world, appear—when he says for example that human society is a matter of "breeding"—to be asserting a truth about that world, even though he believes neither in the possibility of asserting truth nor in the separate existence of that or any world other than the totality? In the remainder of the section "The 'Improvers' of Humanity," Nietzsche praises what he believes to be the Indian caste system, with its institutionalized contempt for its lowest class, calling it an "Aryan humanity" which contrasts with the Jewish hostility to the principles of "breeding" and "race." Now it is clear, if we accept the totally metaphorical nature of Nietzsche's style, its middle course between all accepted notions of truth-telling, that Nietzsche is here simply drawing on the intellectual vocabulary of contemporary German anti-Semitism to create another extended quasi-historical, quasi-sociological metaphor in criticism of the hated system of Christian morality (to which of course many an anti-Semite might still adhere). As when he asserted briefly the non-metaphorical status of zoological terms, Nietzsche in elaborating this cultural counter-example is concerned principally for the critical and polemical relation of what he says to the positions of his adversaries. But does he not run the risk of appearing—not to use for his own purposes, but—to *adopt* the principles of anti-Semitism and Teutonism? And, more importantly, does he not run the risk—whatever he himself may mean (though of course he does not mean anything at all)—of furthering those principles, in the public, institutional, historical world in which books circulate?

> Quite as much as Wagner I am a child of this time, i.e. a *décadent*: only that I understood that, only that I resisted it. The philosopher in me resisted it . . . For such a task I required a special self-discipline—of taking sides *against* everything about me that was diseased, including Wagner, including Schopenhauer, including the whole of modern "humanitarianism."—A profound alienation, dispassionate, disenchanted, in respect of everything temporal, of the time: and as supreme desire the eye of *Zarathustra*, an eye that from an immense distance can look over the whole human phenomenon—look *down* on it. (II 903)

Nietzsche's dependence on his own time, of course, is a matter of more than Schopenhauer, Wagner, and the anti-Semitism of his own sister and brother-in-law. Stern says that Nietzsche's work "is the biography of a soul but . . . it is a biography that abounds in articulated consciousness of world and time—his time and world, and ours. The work has a broad realistic base." But this extract from the preface to *The Wagner Case* (1888) shows not only that Nietzsche believes his conscious relationship with his time to be essentially, and wholly, negative, but more importantly that he has nothing to put in the scales against the weight of his time and place and culture beyond the picture of himself as the "Aryan" Christ, Zarathustra, at an immense distance of empty space from it all. He has only the power of his own denial, his own contempt, the power to make small—in relation to himself. There are no resources of reference to other times, other cultures, other human achievements, such as those, for example, which build up the shoulders and peaks of Goethe's Olympus. Such references—above all of course to Greece—are absorbed by Nietzsche's metaphorical style and transformed into mere variations on contemporary issues, for historical and cultural distinctions are after all only linguistic fictions. As a result, though negated and diminished, and against his will, Nietzsche's own time continues to speak and operate through his work. We may see this in little matters, such as the assumption that certain issues are important and deserve treatment (such as "the question of marriage" or "the question of the workers" [II 1015–17], or indeed the question of *"décadence"* itself), or even in rare moments of endorsement of contemporary attitudes (as when Nietzsche shows a certain complacent enthusiasm for the first principle of Bismarck's foreign policy [II 966] or speaks approvingly of the military character of contemporary German society [II 983]). We see it in great matters, however, when we consider the reputation of Nietzsche's work in Germany in the first half of the twentieth century, which cannot simply be dismissed as a fortuitous misinterpretation: "More than once [Nietzsche] tells us that communication is not what he is concerned with, that he wishes to be misunderstood. . . . *Zarathustra . . . was* misunderstood . . . yet *that* was a misunderstanding we may be sure he did not wish for" (Stern, *A Study of Nietzsche*, p. 197). But this is to ignore the extent to which Nietzsche's works, and not only *Zarathustra*, offer no resistance to misunderstanding, because the only counterweight to their overwhelming destructiveness, all that they assert beyond metaphoricization, fictionalization, unmasking, reduction, and critique, is either the common, even vulgar, attitudes of his age or Nietzsche's own indeterminate self, indeterminate because deliberately stripped of all determinants of time and culture and interest and loyalty, and reduced at the last to a pseudo-historical mythico-theatrical metaphor—"the eye of Zarathustra." Can we be so sure that Nietzsche would not have wished for the misunderstanding if he had known it was coming? It is all too easy to imagine a concluding fifty-second paragraph in the section "Skirmishes Out of Season" from *Twilight of the Idols*: "Yes, in my *Zarathustra* I gave humanity the profoundest book it possesses. And I rejoiced that it was misunderstood and bestially misused by the National Socialists. For did I not thereby help to bring about the destruction of what I hated most—*Germany*! And did not Germany *deserve* its destruction?—for having *thus* misunderstood me? . . ."

There is perhaps the material for a realistic achievement in Nietzsche's writings. But that material is not made to serve a realistic purpose, it cannot be made to as long as it remains dissolved into the medium of discourse in the middle mode. Stern (*A Study of Nietzsche*, p. 186) isolates a telling, since probably unconscious, "linguistic tic" which at times lends a certain monotony to Nietzsche's style: his over-frequent linking of nouns and phrases by means of the particle 'als', 'as',—"moral judgment as semiotic sign" (II 979), "man as reality" (II 1008), "freedom as something one acquires by conquest" (II 1015), "the world as an aesthetic phenomenon." 'Als' is the representative within the sentence of the theory that language as a whole is disjoined from reality. 'Als' is the universal linguistic solvent through which "a never-ending interchange in the function of words" (Stern, *ibid.*) suspends all images, concepts, facts and arguments in a state of metaphoricity, always only reinterpretations of one another, never pinned down—or abandoned—in the finality of the singular, the historical, or the real.

The process intensifies in the course of Nietzsche's career. Nietzsche is at his finest as a critic of individual writers and thinkers, an analyst of specific phrases. But as time goes on he succumbs increasingly to the temptation to make these individual phenomena signs of something other than themselves, their critique part of some larger scheme. No. 22 of the "Words and Arrows" section in *Twilight of the Idols* deals with a piece of received moral wisdom and inventively sets it in a public, even a political setting:

> "Böse Menschen haben keine Lieder."—Wie kommt es, daß die Russen Lieder haben? (II 946)
>
> "The wicked have no songs"—How does it come about that the Russians have their songs?

Were it not for the series of consequential thoughts laid down by the rest of the collection this question would seem limp. The limitations of a proverb are a subject hardly worth even two lines of Nietzsche's prose. But the representation of themselves as a singing nation is a part of the specifically German ideology (cp. No. 33, II 947). So the Russians are not wicked in themselves but are only called so by the Germans, who fear them—the "sign language" of moral judgment here represents a relationship of "will to power." But in fact the Russians are rightly called wicked *by modern Germans* because the Russian state is built on such different principles from the German. Russia is "the *only* power that nowadays has duration in its belly" because it is "anti-liberal to the point of malignity (Bösheit)" (II 1016).[8] Liberty of course is something that Nietzsche personally loathes (II 1018) because, like the German state, which he has already publicly denounced, it is a symptom of decadence (II 1016). Not that that decadence can be put into reverse (II 1019)— but that should not trouble "us," greatness need not fear infection

from surrounding decadence, for the belief that great men are dependent on their age, are made by their milieu, is another "neurotic" belief with the stench of decay about it (II 1020). Russia is
"the diametrically opposite concept" to the "neuroses" of the other
European states (II 1016), and the great man, the genius, is the antithesis of his age: he is strong, the age is weak; he is necessary, the
age is contingent (II 1019). The strength of the genius consists in his
existing and acting for himself, not for any extraneous purpose, not
for his age or his fatherland or some public cause. Posterity may see
him as its benefactor, but that is "all misunderstanding." The great
man—necessarily misunderstood—is not a beginner of, a contributor to, anything— he is an "explosive" "end," a terminus (II 1020).
Nietzsche's sequence of thought reaches a conclusion outside the
moral and public and political world in which it began, in the con-
templation of a genius figure cut off from his own time and from
posterity by the explosion in him of the accumulated energies of
preceding centuries.

Derrida and Nietzsche

Nietzsche's references to women would not seem to be the most
promising starting point for a study of his thought. In no area of his
writing is the cultural ballast of his age more obviously an unper-
ceived and uncriticized hindrance than in what he has to say about
"das Weib." This, however, is the starting point chosen by Jacques
Derrida for his essay *Éperons. Les styles de Nietzsche (Rap(i)ers. Nietzsche's styles)*.[9] Point indeed, for the reason for Derrida's choice, and
the likely tenor of his argument, are apparent from the moment he
tells us that "La question du style, c'est toujours l'examen, le pesant
d'un objet pointu" (p. 36: "The question of style is always the exam-
ining, the impress, of a pointed object"). The argument—if that is
the correct word for an exegetical structure of such virtuoso ethe-
reality—is that in Nietzsche's texts, particularly *Twilight of the Idols*,
the question of the style is inseparable from, nay, is inscribed into,
the question of woman. The style, or stylus, is not only the instrument of writing, and so of public thought, it is also, as a long, hard
(though in some cases collapsible) pointed object, an instrument of
penetration or, as a stiletto, for example, an instrument of defense,
for keeping a threat at a distance. If "style" may be regarded as mas-

culine, what is feminine then would be veils, sails, curtains, the hymen, whatever may be cut, penetrated, torn aside, or kept at a distance by the style, or even (in the case of a spar or sprit or, for that matter, an umbrella) extended or erected by it. On the basis in particular of the comparison between woman and a sailing-ship in paragraph 60 of *The Gay Science* (II 79–80), and of the parable "How the 'True' World Finally Became a Fable" in *Twilight of the Idols* (II 963), Derrida uses these reciprocal terms to analyze Nietzsche's expressed attitudes to women and to truth. Like Stern, Derrida finds in Nietzsche's thought a tripartite progression, but his scheme is significantly different from Stern's in respect of its last stage. While for Stern Nietzsche's thought characteristically proceeds from the description of an existing phenomenon (*a*) to its rejection (*not-a*) to the reinterpretation and reassertion of what was described, but in a new sense (*A*) (*A Study of Nietzsche*, pp. 160–161), Derrida finds the following pattern: 1. woman is condemned as a figure or power of untruth (Nietzsche "was, and feared, some castrated woman"—the assertion that there is such a thing as truth being psychoanalytically equivalent to the threat of castration); 2. woman is condemned as a figure or power asserting truth—e.g., philosophical or Christian truth—by contrast with the artist-actor who rejoices in masks and deception (Nietzsche "was, and feared, some castrating woman"); 3. woman is recognized and affirmed as a dionysiac affirmative, artistic power (Nietzsche "was, and loved, some affirmative woman," having recognized that the threat of castration, like the assertion of truth, is a phantom) (*Éperons*, pp. 96, 100). Nietzsche's final "affirmation" (the category, of course, is notoriously Nietzsche's own—e.g., II 969) is tantamount to the denial of sexual difference, that is, the denial of the difference between truth and non-truth: the grounds for the original distinction between style and veil, truth-seeker and truth-concealer, male and female (the female being, psychoanalytically speaking, the castrated male), have been eliminated. Derrida concludes (if we except the witty interpretation of Nietzsche's isolated note "I have forgotten my umbrella" as the key to all his writings) with an exercise in Heideggerian epistemology. (Heidegger is taken to task by Derrida for ignoring the phrase "Sie wird Weib," "It becomes female," in Nietzsche's parabolic description in *Twilight of the Idols* of the Christian transformation of the notion of the "true world.") Beyond the distinction between male and female, true and not-true, we enter the "realm of quotation marks," "le régime . . . des guillemets" (p. 106): all concepts that rely on such antithetical distinctions now have only hypothetical, citational, status, and among these belongs the concept—which is not only Heidegger's—of the given, the *datum*, the *donnée*:

> De même qu'il n'y a pas d'être ou d'essence de *la* femme ou de *la* différence sexuelle, il n'y a pas d'essence du *es gibt* dans le *es gibt Sein*, du don et de la donation de l'être. . . . Il n'y a pas de don de l'être à partir duquel quelque chose comme un don déterminé (du sujet, du corps, du sexe . . .) se laisse appréhender et mettre en opposition. (p. 120)

> Just as there is no being or essence of Woman as such or of Sexual Difference as such, so there is no essence of the *es gibt* in *es gibt Sein*, of the gift and giving of being. . . . There is no gift of being on the basis of which something like a determinate gift (of the subject, of the body, of a sex . . .) could be apprehended or set up in opposition [i.e., to being in general].

Derrida leaves it unclear whether this is his position, or his interpretation of Nietzsche's position. Perhaps, in the circumstances, there is no difference.

The most dubious feature of Derrida's analysis is its progressive quality, its own directionality (into the "abysses of truth," to cite one of his subtitles) and its attribution of a progressive dialectic to Nietzsche. This is dubious, first, because Derrida leaves inexplicit the relation between terminus and starting point, for his conclusion has actually annihilated his starting-point. If there is no datum, not merely in the sense that there are no determinate "styles" and "veils" but in the sense that there is no given distinction between "styles" and "veils," it is difficult to see what was the justification for associating men and stilettos, or truth and castration, in the first place, or for distinguishing them from curtains, affirmation, or the coverings of umbrellas. True, Derrida asserts, at the end of his increasingly (as he tells us) cryptic and parodistic text, that in it there "never has been" "*le* style . . . *la* femme. Ni *la* différence sexuelle" (p. 138). Like the early Wittgenstein, having ascended to mystical insight, he draws up behind him the ladder of dialectic, leaving his reader with a text which it is the task of reading to acknowledge as superfluous. But, in all of this, he is simply miming the gestures and presuppositions of Nietzsche himself. Derrida's enactment of the various possible modulations of a belief in the total disjuncture of language and reality (including the only finality—that of self-reference and the total privacy of the great man) is misleading only if the progressive, directional, dialectical mode in which it appears to be couched is taken for more than an expository device—one style among the many styles that are available to the practitioner of the middle mode of discourse.

No sooner has Derrida attributed a progressive dialectic to Nietzsche than he acknowledges how dubious is his attribution. It is not possible, he tells us (pp. 106–108) to determine whether the denial of the distinction between truth and non-truth, style and veil, is not itself another act of unveiling, another act of penetration to the truth: this question, as ("en tant que") question, "reste— interminablement." It is the acknowledgment of the *interminable* quality of Nietzsche's reflections that makes Stern's account of his dialectic preferable to Derrida's—that, and the fact that there seems to be no example of Derrida's third stage anywhere in Nietzsche's work. The third stage of Stern's *a–not-a–A* dialectic returns us, in some sense, to the beginning. Precisely because the "sense" of the return is indeterminate (it is never *really* clear what is the relation between a "value" and a "transvalued value"), the process is not circular—let alone directional —but capable of being indefinitely prolonged. To pursue a Nietzschean concept, such as that of Russian wickedness, through its transformations, inversions, metaphoricizations, and parallelisms until it strays too near the vortex of Nietzsche's self-consciousness and is swallowed up in the metaphor-as-reality of Zarathustra, is like nothing so much as listening to a Wagnerian endless melody, though one that can never give birth to drama.

Derrida rightly sees that there is for Nietzsche a stage beyond the differentiation of male and "female" (= castrated male), beyond the differentiation of truth and untruth, and beyond even the epicene (if elegant, "vornehm") affirmation of illusion. That stage is intimated for us at the end of the parable "How the 'True' World Finally Became a Fable," when both the "true" world and its complementary opposite, the "apparent" world, are equally abolished. But this new state, after the negation of negation, after the abolition of differentiation, is not, as Derrida suggests, one of identification

with and love for the affirmative woman. Nietzsche's dialectic termi-
nates in no such synthesis, and anyway he nowhere acknowledges
the existence of an autonomous femininity. Nietzsche's third stage
is the *reaffirmation of the male:*

> —"INCIPIT ZARATHUSTRA."
> For there to be art . . . one physiological pre-condition is indispens-
> able: . . . the ecstasy of the will, of an overcharged and swollen will. . . .
> Out of this feeling one emits into things, one *forces* them to take from
> us, one rapes them—this process is named *idealization*. . . . Man in this
> condition transforms things until they mirror his power. . . . (II 995)

By "Man," Nietzsche is telling us, he means "man," and in that he
speaks the language of the coming world economy, driven and organized by a male sexuality which excludes female rhythms and concerns. He notes in a fragment "On the Genesis of Art" that,
"physiologically speaking," the "creative instinct of the artist" is
equivalent to "the diffusion of semen through the blood" (III 870).
There is a role for woman in the mysteries of Dionysus but it is a
separate, subordinate, and instrumental role, the role of pain and
childbearing, which exists in order that the ecstatically swollen
masculine will should contemplate and affirm itself into eternity:

> the *sexual* symbol was for the Greeks the archetypal venerable
> symbol. . . . In order that there should be the eternal pleasure of cre-
> ation, in order that the will to life should eternally affirm itself, there
> must also be to eternity "the pangs of the child-bearer." (II 1031)

This is the nearest that Nietzsche comes to an acknowledgment of
complementarity, reciprocity, or relationship in difference between
male and female. We cannot say with Derrida that "he was, and
loved, some affirmative woman." Throughout his life Nietzsche's
passionate desire to identify with someone, to love someone, was
frustrated at every turn by another, a supreme desire—that for "the
eye of Zarathustra"—and throughout his life his "affirmation" remained solitary.

Similarly the delicate interplay in realistic art between truth and
fiction ("illusion") always escapes Nietzsche's understanding. The
realistic novelist and the realistic moralist have in common that
they believe both that things are not quite what people like to think
they are, and also that appearances save themselves, and cannot be

totally resolved into some hidden reality (as, for example, Schopen-hauer thought they could). For La Rochefoucauld as for Stendhal, the appearances, as well as the realities which those appearances rather badly conceal, are equally part of "what there is," the deter-minate datum that "es gibt." Nietzsche sometimes, especially in *Human, All Too Human*, tries to emulate the art of the *moraliste*, ana-lyzing the data of humanity in sentences beginning "il y a des gens qui," "es gibt Leute, die." But his metaphysical prejudice against the "donnée" proves too strong. "To see *what is*," after the fashion of the Parisian novelists (particularly Flaubert and the Goncourt broth-ers) seems to Nietzsche a capitulation, a submission to the alien will of "petits faits," the very antithesis of an imposition on things of the writer's creative urge, and so essentially "anti-artistic" (II 994–995). Not even the joint abolition of the "true" world and the "apparent," not even Zarathustra's dionysiac art, can bring the middle mode of discourse to touch ground. To acknowledge any sort of *datum* would be an intolerable limitation on Zarathustra's will. Were "Being" a *datum*, it would limit his right to the endless metaphoricisation of endlessly interpretable experience—under the "régime des guillemets" "being" is merely that which "interpretation" and "eval-uation" subsume. Were sexual difference a *datum*, it would limit his urge to the erotic transformation of all objects into his own image—under the "régime des guillemets" reciprocal sexual difference, the generative process, merely prepares the way for the absolute monarchy of the male principle. It is not, shall we say, the philoso-phy of a married man.

Reality into Image

"My first transvaluation of all values" Nietzsche, in 1888, called *The Birth of Tragedy from the Spirit of Music* (II 1032), and in style as well as content there is surprisingly little difference between this, Nietz-sche's first published non-philological work, and *Twilight of the Idols*, his last. The controlling belief that, measured against the wordless world to which it claims to refer, language is a tissue of lies is estab-lished from the start. The resultant impossibility of distinguishing literal from metaphorical usage leads on the small scale to the "never-ending interchange in the function of words" that we have already examined, and on the large scale to a general confusion of

literary modes. The question "are Nietzsche's writings works of history, philosophy, or literature?" is as difficult to answer as the question "is this or that phrase of Nietzsche's—about Russian
wickedness, for example—to be understood as literally anthropological, as metaphorically moral-theological, or as hyperbolically journalistic?" and the reason for the difficulty is the same. If in language we can never tell the truth, there can be no control exercised
over what we say that derives, not from the nature of language, but
from the nature of what we think we are talking about—yet our language still has the form of being about something. We cannot apply
to what we say the realist's sole requirement, that it should be relevant to the situation we have chosen to depict,[10] nor can we apply to
how we say what we say the Aristotelian requirement, that it should
have the degree of precision appropriate to the subject matter[11] —
yet the subject matter still seems to be there. We lose even the ability to order our utterances purely by social convention, since those
conventions are themselves formulated and applied in language,
the very medium of lies, and are only metaphors for the conforma-
tions of the will to power. Yet our thoughts remain couched in the
form of communication, in the form of public utterance. Language
remains, interminably—Nietzsche does not himself fall into mystical silence—and with it there remains the *appearance* of speaking to
someone about things. It is reference that is lost, not referentiality,
community, not the form of communication. Though language is all
lies, it is not all meaningless, and through it the philosopher, even if
in total isolation, glimpses "reality," unspoken of course, and unspeakable.[12] That *The Birth of Tragedy* is already the first installment
of Nietzsche's "theory of morals for deaf-mutes and other philosophers" is revealed in that work's refusal (or its inability) to be bound
by such conventional and public distinctions as those between
scholarship and poetry, history and philosophy, exposition and ex-
hortation, fact and fable—in its being "a work of mixed mode" (Silk
and Stern, *Nietzsche on Tragedy*, p. 188).

"The great variety of separate topics that Nietzsche deals with [in
The Birth of Tragedy] give one a feeling of being related, even though
it is not easy to say in what their relatedness consists" (*Nietzsche on
Tragedy*, p. 196). Silk and Stern materially assist the understanding of
Nietzsche's style by identifying what they call "centripetal" and
"metaleptic" imagery as a principal source of that obscure feeling of

cohesiveness. The essence of the centripetal procedure is "Nietz-sche's method of allowing his arguments to be guided and deter-mined by the very metaphors, analogies and myths which are, or are derived from, the material of his inquiry" (*Nietzsche on Tragedy*, p. 338). Nietzsche does not say that the religion of "Apollo, as the dominant force in the Greece of the Homeric period, nullified the threat posed to the Greeks by . . . Dionysiac worship among their barbarian neighbors"; he says instead "the Greeks were apparently perfectly insulated . . . against the feverish excitements of these fes-tivals, though knowledge of them came to Greece on all the routes of land and sea; for the figure of Apollo, rising full of pride, held out the Gorgon's head to this grotesquely uncouth Dionysiac power." Silk and Stern comment:

> It is appropriate that *Apollo* should turn the uncouth power to *stone*, because the Nietzschean Apollo is associated with stone in his capac-ity as god of sculpture. And it is of course especially appropriate that he should be made to do the turning-to-stone in the terminology of Greek myth ("Gorgon's head") to which he himself belongs. But there is no logic to this appropriateness, except for the logic of metalepsis. . . . What is . . . enhanced . . . is the homogeneity . . . of Nietzsche's work as a whole. (*Nietzsche on Tragedy*, pp. 197–198).

We need to add, however, that the "logic of metalepsis" is actually a substitute for any other kind of logic whatever—sociological, theo-logical, historical—and that the "homogeneity of Nietzsche's work" is here enhanced at the cost of the homogeneity of the objects with which it purports to deal. While the mention of "the Gorgon's head" advances the metaphorical cohesiveness of *The Birth of Tragedy*, the socio-economic account of Greek religion, begun in the mention of "all the routes of land and sea," is, by the very recourse to a metalep-tic development of the image of Apollo, left fractured and incom-plete. By the transfer from the historical to the poetic mode Nietzsche draws our attention to the language in which he is writ-ing and away from the object he is purportedly writing about. The crucial step is perhaps the preference of the transhistorical personi-fication "Apollo" to the historically specific "the Greek cult of Apollo." It is made difficult for us to ask to what Nietzsche's primal image of Apollo *refers*, though the assumption of its referentiality remains.

Indeed, to call Nietzsche's method centripetal is to assume that we know what is the center of his inquiry, that despite the mixture of modes we can determine what is the material from which the metaleptic elaboration begins. Throughout the treatise it remains obscure whether Nietzsche is conducting a conceptual argument— an amendment of Schopenhauer, for example—about the relation between music and tragedy, or whether he is conducting a histori- cal argument about the course of Hellenic religion, and then of Oc- cidental culture in general. The retention of apparent historical referentiality alongside a loss of actual historical reference is nowhere clearer than in the case of the primal images of "Apollo," "Dionysus," and "Socrates" (though the case is not fundamentally different with other major images, notably "Euripides," "Italian opera," and "Wagner"). "For Nietzsche Dionysus and Apollo are nei- ther logical entities nor Greek gods. They are cast in a middle mode of language" (*Nietzsche on Tragedy*, p. 338). In other words Nietzsche never decides whether the terms 'apolline' and 'dionysiac' contain a necessary allusion (one imposed by the facts of the matter, a *datum*) to pre-Christian Greek religion—whether they are terms like 'Marx- ism' and 'Gaullism' which require, if they are to be applicable, a his- torical link with Marx or De Gaulle. Or whether any allusion they contain is illustrative, a matter of his heuristic and arbitrary choice, rather like the allusions to Caesar and Machiavelli in the terms 'Caesarism' and 'Machiavellianism', which can be perfectly well de- fined without any specific historical reference. The position is simi- lar with Socrates, whose historical individuality is dissolved away by making him "the very type of Theoretical Man" (I 84), while his his- torical example is the only evidence given us from which we can de- duce in what this new "form of existence," the "Daseinsform" of Theoretical Man, consists. Nietzsche makes no distinction between those attributes of his primal images which are historically—that is, publicly—acknowledged, those for which he is indebted to some source other than his own interpretive ingenuity, and those for which he is himself more or less wholly responsible. *That* is what is meant by a "mixed" or "middle" mode. Nietzsche associates the name of Dionysus not only with the dithyramb (for which there is ample historical support), but also with the doctrine of the ultimate unity of all things (for which the support is more dubious), and with music in general (for which there is no real support at all). Silk and

Stern (pp. 204–209) provide us with these and other examples of the spectrum of associationist possibilities, ranging from the "literal" (or historically authorized) to the extremely "paraliteral" (at the end of a convoluted metaleptic process), by which Nietzsche builds up his primal images or archetypes. The essential common characteristic of these figures is that while they claim some initial— perhaps single, perhaps purely nominal—relation with the "literal"—the historical, the conventionally acknowledged, the determinately real—that relation is not capable of expansion, exploration, or correction through any established public mode of discourse, whether that of historical or "scientific" or of personal experience. And it is of the essence of "the given"—that to which reference is ultimately made, if it is made at all—that "the given" is not some single, isolated "Ansatzpunkt," some privileged datum in consciousness, but is a characteristic of a whole given system which, as a system, is capable of discussion, expansion, and development.[13] The apparent referentiality of Nietzsche's writing is illusory precisely because of the isolation—the privacy and the arbitrariness—of the points at which it touches the world of common knowledge. It is not possible to find more evidence for—or for that matter against—the argument of The Birth of Tragedy. The only admissible expansion of Nietzsche's mention of Socrates for example—the only one that has authority—is that which takes place within Nietzsche's text itself. About this "Dionysus," this "Apollo," this "Socrates," we have to think what the writer tells us to think, and mentions of "reality" are present for their shock value only.

Nietzsche's archetypes belong to a species eerily familiar to the traveler across the lunar landscape[14] of twentieth-century thought and literature. They have meaning, but no determinate meaning, no reference to a shared world of specific things, events, or people, about which it is possible to speak in different and publicly acknowledged modes without dissolving their identity—Hugo's Napoleon is as much Napoleon as Tolstoy's, and we may legitimately compare them in respect of their truth to the man, but Rilke's Apollo is no more Apollo than Nietzsche's, and we may compare them only as visions in the night. In place of realism, even apparently realistic prose offers us, in Nietzsche's term, "idealization"—a transformation into image, reality "repeated" (II 961) and suffused with subjectivity. The writers in whom the process is closest to

Nietzsche's own are his fellow psychologists. The archetypes that stalk the pages of *Totem and Taboo* or *Moses and Monotheism* have the same hectic, cardboard, Wagnerian quality as the dramatis personae of *The Birth of Tragedy*, monsters born of the sleep, not of reason, but of realism. The concept of historicity which underlies the derivation of Christianity from a conspiracy of Jewish priests in *On the Genealogy of Morals* combines the same apparent referentiality with the same absence of assessable reference that we find in Freud's derivation of Christianity from the guilt feelings of "the" assassins of Moses, not to mention the similar feelings of "the" parricidal primal horde. Nietzsche could perfectly well have adopted Freud's justification for the acknowledged arbitrariness of his historical procedure: that it would be vindicated by its success in uncovering the "secret motives" for the "distortions" of the historical tradition.[15] Freud in turn made an even more successful paraliteral exploitation of his cultural heritage than the inventor of "Apollo" and "Dionysus" when he remarked that every one of his neurotics had "been an Oedipus, or, which comes down to the same thing," "had become a Hamlet."[16] It is true that Freud's concern for the "scientific" status of his conclusions leads him to formulate them in a mode in which clear reference to publicly discussible facts does occur and which to that extent is realistic. When Freud tells us of a patient whose neurosis can be traced back to the traumatic moment when his mother threatened him with castration,[17] we are still in the realistic world of tales from the Vienna nurseries. When by contrast he asserts that the difference in the psychosexual development of men and women "corresponds to the difference between a castration that has been executed and one that has been merely threatened"[18] we are in the Nietzschean middle mode of rootless metaphor, the "régime des guillemets," for "threatened" here means (in the majority of cases) "thought to have been threatened," and "executed" means (in all cases) "thought to have been executed," and furthermore—since we are reconstructing the origins of thought—"thought" means "what we may for the sake of our argument call 'thought'." Indeed we may apply to the world of Freudian sex Stern's apt comment about Nietzschean theology: that from Nietzsche's middle mode of language "springs that entirely modern (and depressingly familiar) habit of talking metaphorically about 'God', 'saintliness', 'divine creation', 'sin' and the like without ever quite deciding what non-metaphorical meanings, and what beliefs (if any) go with the talking" (*A Study of Nietzsche*, pp. 199–200). If the "true" world of divine transcendence has been abolished and become a fable, so too has the "true" world of unconscious sexuality. As a Nietzschean post-Freudian, who accepts that "la castration n'a pas lieu," Derrida engages in much presumably metaphorical talk about sexual members, castration, and a "style éperonnant" without any decision as to what non-metaphorical statements about events, actions, or psychological mechanisms are implied by the talking. *Éperons. Les styles de Nietzsche* is written throughout in the middle mode.

The process of "idealization," the translation of reality into image, and the creation among the images of a subjective order (rather than the acceptance of a real order from which the images are abstracted and to which they refer)—that is a literary process that is also "entirely modern (and depressingly familiar)." There is in *Ulysses* a mountain of *petits faits*, as there is in *The Heart of Stone*, but before none of them do Joyce or Arno Schmidt bow in submission; rather the "facts" are compelled into a literary order (or disorder) in which subjectivity appears to have created them rather than contingency. Subtly deprived of reference, by the implication that they are the products of some refined literary or linguistic causality, some immensely diluted "logic of metalepsis," the "facts" in these novels float half an inch above the ground, to which fan-clubs of both authors endeavor to return them by pilgrimages to "the real thing" in Dublin or Lower Saxony. Even the popular novel of the late twentieth century feels obliged to some exhibitionist play with its own fictionality—witness the work of John Fowles, or even David Lodge's *Changing Places*, of which the appeal lies precisely in what it is about and not in what it is. The effacing of the distinction between literal and metaphorical truth, the leveling down of all literary representations into formally equivalent "images," is the most prominent feature of the works of Hermann Hesse, from the hallucinations of Harry Haller in *Steppenwolf* to the alternative lives of Knecht in *The Glass Bead Game*. Indeed it would be interesting to trace the rise in modern criticism of the terms "image" and "imagery," in substitution for the older terms of rhetoric, for these are words whose *raison d'être* is their indifference to the distinction between metaphorical and non-metaphorical writing.

"Seeing the customers in a café someone said to me: "Look how dull they are; nowadays pictures ["images"] are more alive than people." This inversion is perhaps one of the distinguishing marks of our world: we live in the generalisation of the Imaginary. Look at the USA: everything there is transformed into images—only images exist, only images are produced, only images are consumed. . . . When generalised, the image derealises the human world of conflicts and desires, under the pretence of illustrating it.[19]

Roland Barthes acknowledges that in reflecting on photography he is reflecting on a nineteenth-century genre, but he does not recognize that photography is therefore a genre coeval with the great masterpieces of the realistic novel. He recognizes (*La chambre claire*, pp. 146–147) that there is already something archaic about his lament for the passing, in the modern world, of the sense for the "pure contingency" of photographs (p. 52), for the "wholly non-metaphorical presence of the thing" in them (p. 123), the passing of the astonishment he feels at the unmediated confrontation in a photograph with past reality, what he calls "le *'Ça a été'*." Yet he does not recognize that the proper object of his nostalgia is something more, considerably more, than a particular feature of photographs, or that his own belief that photography differs from a linguistic text through its freedom from "reflection" (p. 52) or "interpretation" (p. 165), his belief that language is "by its nature fictional" (p. 134) "never credible *to the roots*" (p. 151), is itself a contribution to the "generalisation of the Imaginary." In photography he still sees—though he knows he belongs to a passing era in seeing it—that pure "Reference" (p. 120) which his own emphasis on the distinction between the signifier and signified has helped to banish from the literary text. It is the loss of realism that is properly the object of his lament, in an age of images, for the loss of contingency, life, and love (p. 147).

Realism, Identity, and Death

Barthes identifies two elements in the structure of photographs, to which he gives the names *studium* and *punctum*. The *studium* is the "encoded"—one might say, the literary—element, the respect in which the photograph alludes to and obeys public conventions about how photographs are composed. The *punctum*—unlike Der-

271

rida's "style," which lacerates veils in the impersonal void—is the element that "comes home to" Barthes himself, an arrow discharged from the picture that pierces his affectivity, a moment of contingency that causes him pain—and others only insofar as their personal relationship to the subject of the photograph is not greatly different from his own. The *punctum* turns out to be of two kinds.

First, there is the chance detail, a conjunction of figures, the position of a hand, a woman's necklace, the straps on her Sunday-best shoes, in which the absolute singularity and contingency of the recorded moment leaps from the frame. In virtue of that one detail the otherwise unknown subject acquires "a whole life outside her portrait" (p. 91), a whole area of hidden ground, "un champ aveugle," is intimated around the picture. In the same way, we might add, the realistic work of literature, if approached without the distrust which Barthes says he can himself never discard (p. 165), suggests that beyond it, between its chapters and before and after, lies *more* of the world, its world and ours, than happens, contingently, to have been articulated. Dickens might have left out a line of his description of Smallweed reading the newspaper, or he might have put in a line more—but, *ex hypothesi* of the realistic mode, Smallweed would not for that have been another man, Dickens would merely have ventured further, or less far, on to the hidden ground. At the end of *Nostromo* there loom both the communists and the North American imperialists, a theme in themselves, though Conrad's principal story is over. Claudius enters in the middle of his conversation with Rosencrantz and Guildenstern—we do not hear what he says before his entry, but we are invited to think that we might have done. We are glad for what the writer has chosen to articulate, we recognize that any picture has its frame, but our mind is projected beyond this particular frame into the one world which we share with the creatures of the writer's fiction and which we know in many modes and from many pictures and many different stories. "How many children had Lady Macbeth?" is a trivial question, and we may not be able to answer it, but it is not meaningless.

In the middle mode of writing, by contrast, there is no "champ aveugle," no "behind the scenes" where things carry on much as they do on the stage until they reach our own experience—behind the scenes in the middle mode there is only non-entity, the acknowledged fiction of "the thing-in-itself," in relation to which what appears on stage is acknowledged as an appearance, is a lie. Because Shakespeare is, among other things, a realist, because his minor characters, like Cinna the Poet, or the Third Murderer in *Macbeth*, simply graze the principal action while pursuing their own unchronicled lives in the hidden ground, Charles and Mary Lamb could write their *Tales from Shakespeare* and Tom Stoppard could conceive *Rosencrantz and Guildenstern Are Dead*. Since however Stoppard emphatically marks off his words and world from Shakespeare's, he writes in the middle mode, and behind the scenes of *his* play there is only emptiness.

The second type of the *punctum* in a photograph is the generalized form, the pure representation (p. 148), of unmediated past reality— "ça a été": this thing, this person, this moment, was, and was real, and is no more. The second form of the *punctum*, then, is the finitude (p. 141) imposed by death, and every photograph bears in itself the sign of my death (p. 151), of the death that puts an end to the love that can only exist between finite and mortal beings (p. 147). It is here that we reach the essential distinction between realistic writing and writing in the middle mode. Realistic literature, literature that has the reference that Barthes attributes exclusively to photography, is alone capable of representing death, and so alone capable of representing love. Nietzsche may deal with "an almost infinite variety of . . . issues" (Stern, *Nietzsche*, p. 199), but he has practically nothing to say on the subject of death.[20] Nietzsche's use of 'was' never has the ultimacy of Barthes's "Ça a été." Discourse in the middle mode is, after all, interminable, it is discourse without determinate reference, and the specificity of a human being (and only a specific, only a photographable, human being can be loved) is determined as much by his or her mortality as by his or her sex. The two types of *punctum* are not so very different: contingency, identity, death, ineluctable determination in time, can all be read, and loved, in a shoe-strap, or a button:

> Thou'lt come no more
> Never, never, never, never, never.
> Pray you undo this button.

Lear's terrible lines are at the boundary of articulate utterance and for Barthes, looking at the photograph of his dead mother, the horrible flatness ("platitude") of death consists in there being nothing to say about it:

The horror is this: nothing to say about the death of her whom I love most, nothing to say about her picture which I look at without ever being able to read more into it [l'approfondir], to transform it. (p. 145)

These deaths cannot be swept back into a cycle of intellectual and linguistic metamorphoses. They mark the point beyond which there is no more to say: they show language to have the finitude of real experience, not the endlessness of metaphoricity.

Yet before we reach the point beyond which there is no more to say, there is a *great deal* that can be said—provided that finitude and mortality are not forgotten or denied. Barthes admits that the agony of loss that he feels before a photograph is sterile—as perhaps is the conclusion of *King Lear*. "If dialectic is that thought which masters the corruptible and converts the negation that is death into the power of work, then the Photograph is undialectical: it is denatured theatre in which death cannot 'contemplate' itself, reflect itself or internalise itself; or again, it is the dead theatre of Death, the foreclosure of the tragic; it excludes any purification, any *catharsis*" (p. 141). This is why Barthes's cultivation of the photograph as the last fading refuge of realistic reference cannot ultimately stand. The dialectic, like determination, is inescapable, and if in the photograph the pain of loss is not transformed, then it will be repeated and preserved—and *thereby* transformed. But not into a *resurrection from* the dead, the true culmination of the dialectic: the undialectical photograph, in which the real past is interminably translated into present image, offers only a *return of* the dead, the resuscitation of a painted corpse (pp. 23, 56)—in Nietzsche's terms: "reality repeated," or "idealization." This is the process, obscure to Barthes, as a result of which the photograph, which has its origins in agonizing immediacy and particularity, nonetheless contributes to the "generalisation of the Imaginary," the universal production and consumption of images, and so to the detachment of experience from reference, and from reality itself. Realism, by contrast, is dialectical: it has reference, and it knows death, but it is fixated on neither, it is an art for "the human world of conflicts and desires," an art of motion, and so of language and (perhaps) of film. Hegel tells us that the death of Nature is the birth of the Spirit.[21] We do not have to follow him into the realm of absolute knowledge to appreciate that having something to say about death is what makes

our discourse human. We are not, as Nietzsche thought, gesticulat-
ing animals drifting at two removes from reality in a sea of
metaphor. We can in language realistically depict and assess our
condition insofar as our discourse is determined, demarcated, by
the knowledge both of death and of death's transcendence. "Le
soleil ni la mort ne se peuvent regarder fixement." "So bleibe mir
die Sonne denn im Rücken." ("No one can look unwavering at the
sun, or death." "So let the sun remain behind my back.")[22] The area
illuminated by that dual knowledge is the area in which work is possible and in which realism has something to say.

In the middle mode of discourse, death, quite as much as God or
sex, is indeterminately reiterable and reinterpretable (as is shown so
well by *Rosencrantz and Guildenstern Are Dead*). The fact of death can
here contribute nothing to the understanding of life, which thus
loses individuality, finitude, and meaning. One of the most ingenious modern attempts to write simultaneously in a realistic and in
the middle mode, Nabokov's *Lolita*, cannot maintain the symbiosis
once it has to relate its characters to their deaths. Quilty is a hallu-
cinatory construct, and his "execution," at once burlesque and brutally protracted, could come from the pages of *Steppenwolf.* The
mortality that counts (and it does) is that of the characters who
count, that is the characters who love—Humbert and Lolita—but
this mortality is related only arbitrarily and formally to their lives:
through the assertion that our reading the narrative is dependent
on their both being dead, and through the details coyly provided in
the Foreword "for the benefit of old-fashioned readers who wish to
follow the destinies of the 'real' people beyond the 'true' story." Yet
in a purely realistic narration we do not have to read about deaths
in order to know that the characters are mortal. When Morten
Schwarzkopf kisses Tony Buddenbrook, leaning against a sandcastle
he has built for her on the beach at Travemünde, love and death
conjoin to define her, absolutely, without release. "Thou'lt come no
more." Tony will be, until a death which Mann will not need to nar-
rate, the woman for whom this possibility, perhaps phantasmal, perhaps juvenile, did not become a reality. The irony in the description
of Morten's gesture towards the sea, when he attempts to say what
he means by "Freedom," may seem to confirm the view that social
forces leave her no alternative. But that does not affect the point,
the realism. The realist is committed only to the absolute, the tran-

scendent, importance of the determinate individuality of human beings, not at all to the view that they are absolutely, or even very much, self-determining. Tony Buddenbrook exists, like her brother, between the possibility, however remote, of a transcendence intimated by Morten's "Freedom," and the certainty of the finite sequence of irredeemable determinations which is called life and ends in death. Because the story which contains her is poised, however ironically, between death and transcendence it is properly called realistic. *Anna Karenina* occupies a similar area of realism, if the limits are drawn less ambiguously and with greater power. The freedom that Anna and Vronsky enjoy in Italy is incompatible with being human, with being determinate, moral, and mortal. It is the image of transcendence abused, of our immortal and absolute worth set against the determinacy of our existence and itself turning into the most inescapable determination of all: the guilt that flows from a wrong that cannot be undone. Or, as the realist prefers to put it:

> For a time after uniting his life with hers and putting on civilian clothes he felt the delight of freedom in general, which he had not known before, and the freedom of love, and he was content; but not for long. He soon became aware that there arose in his heart the desire for desires—boredom. . . . Sixteen hours of the day had to be filled somehow, for they were living abroad in complete freedom cut off from the round of social life which had occupied most of his time in Petersburg.[23]

For those who seek to live beyond determinacy, beyond the human world of conflicts and desires, the return to determinacy, here foreshadowed, can only take the form of retribution. (Which is why Nietzsche *is* responsible for the posthumous abuse of his thoughts.) Others, like Levin, accept their finitude:

> Lying on his back, he was now gazing at the high cloudless sky. "Don't I know that that is infinite space and not a rounded vault? But however much I may screw up my eyes and strain my sight I cannot see it except as round and finite and though I know that space is infinite, I am absolutely right when I see a firm blue vault, far more right than when I strain to see beyond it. (Book 8, Chapter 13, p. 791)

The reward for this realism (and both the literary and the ethical justifications for that term are here equally compelling) is the constant sustaining miracle of transcendence, "the life of the spirit, the only life that is worth living and the only life that we prize" (ibid.).

Post-modern Realism?

Not going to church on Sunday morning has become something of a theme in twentieth-century poetry (though I suspect its first literary treatment is to be found in Goethe's *Faust*). Wallace Stevens, that most Nietzschean of poets writing in English, suggested in a famous early poem on the topic that, if only thoughts of death and of transcendence were banished, finite things would become instinct with all the eternity of which the human mind was capable:

> Why should she give her bounty to the dead?
> What is divinity if it can come
> Only in silent shadows and in dreams?
> Shall she not find in comforts of the sun
> In pungent fruit and bright, green wings or else
> In any balm or beauty of the earth
> Things to be cherished like the thought of heaven?
> ("Sunday Morning")[24]

After a lifetime lived in the middle mode of discourse, however, he confessed that this magical fruit had turned to ashes:

> Life consists
> Of propositions about life. The human
> Revery is a solitude in which
> We compose these propositions ...
> ("Men made out of words," pp. 355–56)

The "middle mode of discourse," it would seem, is the mode *par excellence* of what Heidegger called "the stand," of subjectivity, liberated from all determination, without reference, without public, institutional, or historical sanction, without mortality, and without transcendence. It is a mode of apparent referentiality and indefinitely associable metaphor in which language, the private and solitary medium for the infinitely repeatable shock of confronting death and penetrating differentiation, remains—interminably. It is, we might therefore conclude, realism's negative image. But the question would then naturally arise whether—as is normal—the photograph can be printed as a positive, with the values of the negative image reversed. Might it perhaps be possible for Being to emerge from this universal reign of functionality, for "things to be cherished" to disclose themselves in the "propositions about life"? For the global mind of the late twentieth century, Heidegger's un-communicative insistence that the means of rescue grow in the place of danger might after all point the way to truth. A mode of writing that is purely subjective and manipulative, endless and deathless, is in one respect exactly appropriate to the time: it acts out in words the unceasing, twenty-four hours a day productivity of the global economy for which there are neither mortal individuals nor constraining public institutions but only a world of consumers; it represents to us, as something we can for once enjoy, the purely instrumental and permanently transformable relationships of a world of producers, none of whom has the stable identity of an abo-riginal property-owner, and all of whom exist only insofar as they work. The language of Eco and Derrida, of Rushdie and Marquez, is always at work—it is never simply the passive medium in which things are given. And in that it is true to the global reality which has been dawning on us since Nietzsche's era and which became un-mistakable in 1945.

Too true to it, perhaps—and so not true enough. To be true in a full, Hegelian, sense, post-modern writing would have to mediate one to another all three aspects of our experience: the universal condition of work (our involvement in the global economy); our specific identity as representatives of a particular place and time; and our individuality as a born, sexed, and mortal body. Each, in turn and together, would have to be grasped and shown as ultimate, as the truth. Instead, for the writer in the middle mode there is all too often only one truth, his or her omnipotence as the author who can play at will with the material of imagination, who "transforms things until they mirror his power," who can reshuffle time and place and all specific things into new patterns of metaphor, just as the market repackages them as priced commodities. The temptation to collaborate in this way with the global market is so difficult to re-sist because there is no other market to write for and to pretend anything else is to condemn oneself from the start to dishonesty or mannerism: a writer's first duty is to look the audience in the eye. Yet just as our identity is not exhausted in our market role but is struggling even now to express itself in institutions that mediate between a global economy and national polities, so twentieth-century writing sometimes succeeds in taming that universal process, symbolized by the omnipresent subjectivity of the author, with a sense of the limited and local things that it is displacing and consuming. When that happens individuality and mortality can be recovered too and a post-modern realism can be achieved.

From time to time the hypnotic monologue in Günter Grass's *The Tin Drum* rises to a litany of lament: for Oskar Matzerath's mother, for the Jewish toyshop-owner Meyn, driven to suicide by the "Kristallnacht" of 8–9 November 1938, for the streets and churches of Danzig burnt in the fires of the Russian bombardment. Through the sequence of grotesques, by which that appalling age is made into a fiction, we glimpse lives and things that have been and are no more, that belong in a specific place and time in a geography and chronology that is ours too, and whose loss is as poignant as the *punctum* of any photograph. Oskar's amoral detachment from the horrors he relates parodies the unavoidable indifference to its individual and social cost of those who come after the historical process he lives through, and who accept its benefits: his persona is essential to the universality of the novel's perspective. But he is not proof against bereavement, and because what he loses is not his own creation but a part of the Polish, German, and Jewish past we lose it too and are glad that he gives us words, however bizarre, in which to mourn for it. (As, to be honest, we do not mourn for any of the national disasters in *One Hundred Years of Solitude*.) In a somewhat similar way contemporary writers around the world have found means to embody in their fictions a tension between globalizing forces, which affect how they conceive themselves and how they write, and the local traditions from which they come, and which those forces are—more or less gradually—rendering inauthentic, but which provide their work with its realistic basis. In the archetypal conflict between master and slave, Hegel tells us, it is the slave who, by succumbing, generates the energy for the next phase in the development of the spirit, while the master, enjoying the fruits of victory, fades out of the story altogether. An option for the poor is written into the structure of history, and we learn the truth about our identity from the victims, not from the conquerors.

For this reason, a special place in world culture belongs to Japan: almost alone among non-European nations it has experienced the impact of globalization without the mediation of a specific colonial power. The singularly pure opposition between what is local and what is global, which appears therefore as what is "foreign" *par excellence* (rather than what is characteristic of some colonizing intruder), is the recurrent theme in the work of Shusaku Endo. In his (relatively) early novel *Foreign Studies* the opposition is understood as a confrontation of East and West so intense that it can be overcome only at the cost of the physical destruction of the one who attempts it. Yet the forces making for a reconciliation are mysteriously powerful: a Japanese student feels fated to identification with the dead son of the French family who are his hosts; a Japanese lecturer is so possessed by the desire to share the life of the subject of his research—the marquis de Sade—that he virtually inflicts on himself a tubercular infection, which manifests itself in the moment when he seems fleetingly to have crossed the physical and cultural gulf between them. Christianity appears here as, on the whole, something inaccessibly European, but in Endo's best-known work, *Silence*, its role begins to change, and with it the conception of what it is to be Japanese. In Endo's later books, such as *Deep River*, what is characteristically Japanese is to lack any religious conviction, to be intellectually assimilated to the worldwide secularism of such global institutions as banks, air travel, tourism, and the university. Christianity, in a form so Catholic as to be syncretic and avowedly heterodox, appears now as the worldwide body of the victims of the secular order. It has become one of the mysterious forces pulling together what seemed disparate, a source at one and the same time both of suffering and of the life of the spirit. Endo's moral concern—with faith and goodness, failure and redemption—can conceal the extreme modernity of the global context in which his understated and semi-autobiographical fables are placed. The lives of his characters are rarely epic, their hold on identity is tenuous, their moments of insight, sin, or heroism, are often transient or forgotten, their stories are complementary fragments, like the quiet rain of inconsequential physical detail in his unassuming prose. But here, as in Grass's utterly different medium, we can meet individual death and loss as we cannot in the ingenious repetitive mechanisms of Eco and Marquez, and so we can glimpse what it might mean to be an individual moral agent in a world economy. Similarly, when the Catholic Malayalam author Paul Zacharia tells the humorous story of a starving Keralan's confrontation with the global order, represented by a passing express train which he resolves to hold up with a papaya disguised as a bomb, the gentleness of the would-be train-robber marks him out not—or not just—as a victim, but as a world-citizen too.[25] A marginal form of Christianity often gives Zacharia's figures their—sometimes repellent—individuality but it also gives them their ability to make slight and local incidents significant for a readership which, because it is potentially worldwide, is necessarily involved in the processes shown to be eroding the local life. For many writers, and not only those with a Catholic background, Christianity, even if distorted or heretical, rejected or caricatured, is an irresistible symbol of a world order that is not purely subjective or functional but can relate the global and the local so as to make realism still possible even where the middle mode of discourse holds sway. In the age of the global market only a Christian literature can show us—realistically—who we are.

10 The Idea of Christian Poetry

In memoriam Kenelm Foster, o.p.

Christmas and the Poets

"From the nature of the case," Newman remarks in *The Idea of a University*, "if Literature is to be made a study of human nature, you cannot have a Christian Literature. It is a contradiction in terms to attempt a sinless Literature of sinful man." Unwisely, perhaps, the then rather Leavisite Bernard Bergonzi chose these words to conclude some reflections, published in *Blackfriars* in 1958, on the relation of a Catholic view of certain (principally sexual) moral matters and the presentation of those matters in works of literature, particularly novels. Unwisely, certainly, Bergonzi decided to begin his reflections with the case of Paolo and Francesca (*Inferno*, Canto 5), whom he was persuaded "Dante would surely have liked to forgive . . . were they not already damned." These opening and closing tropes attracted the characteristically circumspect but uncomfortably firm analytical attention of the Dante scholar Kenelm Foster in a letter to the Editor. Bergonzi was convicted of failing to distinguish between Dante-as-poet and Dante-as-protagonist-of-the-poem, and Newman was shown either not to have said what he

283

meant, or to have begged the question. The question, Foster then believed, was this: "can the subject-matter of literature—which, *concedo*, is sinful man—ever be treated, in-*formed*, in a way that may appropriately be called Christian?" The empirical evidence was that it could: the description of Dante, Langland, Hopkins, or Bernanos as Christian writers was a description "that makes sense with respect to them as *writers*—to the way they handle their material (sinful man), to them as producers of literature, in short."

In his reply, Bergonzi effectively conceded both these points but raised a new objection to the term 'Christian literature': its "parochialism." "If literature—whether apparently Christian or not—is good as literature, then its goodness must come from God, and one need not look for further discriminations." Foster however would not let go (did he ever?). His reply to Bergonzi's reply penetrated to what he himself called the crucial question—and perhaps he meant his readers to understand that that was the question of the Cross. The question was not—not at any serious level—whether a writer had to connive at sin in order to depict it. For the human reality which is a writer's material consists not only, in the Christian view, of sinfulness but also of "the appeal and promptings and pressure of grace, i.e. of Christ." So the *real* question is this: "Can a writer be led, 'by faith working through love', so far into his sin-affected material as to handle it with a truthfulness which would not be wholly inadequate to the *total* reality of man which Christianity reveals?" Christian literature is a possibility only insofar as the description *both* of sin *and* of grace is a possibility. The question about Christian literature is a question about Christ. Bergonzi's reference of the goodness of literature to God is theologically inadequate, "for the world, now, is not just God's world, it is Christ's. And we are Christ's, whether we are artists or critics or anything else. And the whole question now is, what is the reach or scope of our intelligence and sensibilities precisely as governed by Christ?" Bergonzi, given the last word by the editor, returned, essentially, to the charge of "parochialism." His concluding concession presents itself as a *reductio ad absurdum*: "I will indeed admit the possibility of a Christian literature *if* it may include *King Lear* and *The Golden Bowl* as well as the *Divine Comedy* and *Paradise Lost*. But I am reluctant to divide the unity of literature as a subject by the application of criteria which, considered in terms of the subject, are secondary."

The unity of literature seems less certain, and less certainly primary, now than it did in 1958. Nonetheless it is perhaps worth taking up that challenge and asking whether Foster's formulation of "the crucial question" does not indeed require that the term 'Christian literature' should apply to more than the "overtly Christian" writers, as Bergonzi called them, to whom—evidently for the sake of convenience in argument—Foster had restricted it, and whether the formulation does not also suggest a particularly precise sense in which even those writers may be said, as *writers*, to deserve the name of "Christian." It is worth asking what was the meaning of the term 'Christian poet' when T. S. Eliot, undoubtedly one of the pre-eminent influences on Foster's intellectual milieu, remarked:[1] "Vaughan, or Southwell, or George Herbert . . . are not great religious poets in the sense in which Dante, or Corneille, or Racine, even in those of their plays which do not touch upon Christian themes, are great Christian religious poets. Or even in the sense in which Villon and Baudelaire, with all their imperfections and delinquencies, are Christian poets." Throughout his intellectual career Foster wrestled with the problems of Christian literature, and specifically of Christian poetry. Several of his early essays, collected in *God's Tree* (1957), touch on the issue, it recurs in various publications of the 1960s,[2] and it runs through the major work of his last years, underlying the preoccupation, both in *The Two Dantes* and in *Petrarch: Poet and Humanist*, with the status that these Christians accorded in their poetry to pagan virtue.[3] The book on Petrarch indeed looks back to an essay of 1963 in asserting the Christian impetus behind early Humanism and so drawing together the two clerkly poets in whom, time and again, Foster saw reflected his own joint concern with Christianity and literature—Petrarch and Gerard Manley Hopkins. The last public talk that Foster gave at Blackfriars, Cambridge, in December 1985, was entitled "Christmas and the Poets."[4]

It was what those who knew him would have called a "typically Kenelm" occasion. His original scheme, preserved on a scrap of paper, was lucid enough: "Virgil, Dante, Herbert/Vaughan, (Hopkins), Eliot, Hill"—many of us might have come up with a similar list, though few would have thought of starting with Virgil. But the original clear outline, a selection of devotional poems on a seasonal theme, disappeared beneath the subsequent growth of elaboration and digression. The speaker had sighted a theological theme and, in his pursuit of that, the obvious appeals of devotion, or even of overt reference to the feast that was the occasion for the talk, were discarded—out went Herbert, Hill, G. K. Chesterton's "The Nativity." Not that the listeners were told in so many words why this shy and hesitant voice was taking them through the *Purgatorio* and *Paradiso*, the versification of various medieval sequences, the vocabulary of the first passus of *Piers Plowman*, and a poem by Alice Meynell. Only later reflection revealed that the common factor was the Incarnation and the Motherhood of Mary. But even later reflection might have been puzzled at being asked to start with Virgil's Fourth Eclogue and to finish with Rimbaud's "Les Effarés," a poem about a group of urchins looking into a bakery at night.

But is this not the key question, posed, if not in the most adequate terms, by Bergonzi? Not: What is the literary status of works with "overtly Christian" themes? But: What is the Christian status of works which do not, or in the case of pre-Christian literature, cannot have such themes? How do they—how do Virgil, and *King Lear*, and "Les Effarés"—contribute to the building up of the body of Christ? This is why Foster began with the Fourth Eclogue, and not simply with the famous prophecy of the child to be born in the returning Golden Age but with a line whose human truth meant so much to him that he more than once incorporated it into sermons on the humanity of Jesus and the motherhood of Mary:

Incipe, parve puer, ridens cognoscere matrem.[5]

For it was this poem that occasioned Dante's own discussion of our question in Canto 22 of the *Purgatorio*. There the poet Statius, whose importance as a model to Dante was second only to Virgil's but whom Dante believed to have been, unlike Virgil, a Christian, explains that to Virgil he owes both the inspiration which made him a poet and (through the Fourth Eclogue) that which made him a believer in the Gospel:

Per te poeta fui, per te cristiano (1.73)

Through you was I a poet, through you a Christian

Quoting this line in the hand-out for his talk, Foster printed it in capital letters. It was the line on which all hinged, the line which expressed the inseparability of Christmas and the Poets, even the poets who say nothing explicitly of the Christian revelation.

Of course Dante is not saying, and Foster was not implying that he is saying, that the works of "the Poets"—be they Virgil or Dante, Shakespeare or Rimbaud—are an alternative body of Scripture, out of which may be read an alternative Revelation. Unlike the word of God, the word of Man lacks a certain irreducible authority and is dependent for its effect on the needs, and indeed the pre-existing illumination, of the reader. Already in ll. 37–42 of the canto Statius has shown how for his moral recovery—as distinct from his spiritual redemption—he has to thank a passage in the *Aeneid* in which he read the meaning appropriate to his circumstances, rather than that intended by Virgil. And in the decisive matter of his religious conversion, Statius first heard the good news from Christian "heralds" and only then did he learn to interpret Virgil's words as consonant with their preaching (ll. 76–81). Only he who is already a Christian can see, and be fired by, the Christian meaning of pagan literature. But for the Christian even the merely human significance of that literature requires to be situated in a Christian perspective and that task is precisely, yet generously, fulfilled in a whole series of cantos of the *Purgatorio*, 22 to 28.

For these cantos, which take us through the cornices of misdirected love, Avarice (and Prodigality), Gluttony and Lust, and up to the Garden of Eden, the Earthly Paradise, are peopled largely by poets. In the company of the pre-Christian Virgil and the proto-Christian Statius, Dante is confronted with his own poetic genealogy, from the Provençal troubadour Arnaut Daniel (canto 26), through the earlier Italian schools of Orbicciani (canto 24) and Guido Guinicelli (canto 26), to Dante's sonnet-writing friend Forese Donati (canto 23). This concentration on literary figures is unparalleled elsewhere in the *Comedy*, and the distribution of poets throughout Dante's three kingdoms may explain why. We meet, I believe, no poets lower in Hell than Brunetto Latini in the circle of the Sodomites (Bertran de Born, in canto 28, being presented and punished simply as a sower of discord), nor higher in Heaven than the troubadour Foulquet of Marseilles in the heaven of Venus. Poets as moral agents, it would seem, penetrate on the whole neither to the depths of "Fraud" nor to the unspotted reflection of divine love. They have rather an affinity—perhaps their art has an affinity—with what is centrally and essentially human, with the perfection of human nature and (as Bergonzi's novelists show) with that human love which, precisely as it approaches the point of its distinction from and transition into divine love, is most clearly in danger of deviating from its proper object. Thus we find them clustered round the gate of the Earthly Paradise, the place of the natural human perfection in which Adam was created, and purging the sins of a misdirected attachment to created things. While the eternal fate of poets, as moral agents, is determined by a response to divine grace which may not at all form the subject-matter of their art, their art itself, being as natural to all of us as our mother-tongue, tends of its own accord, and regardless of the Christianity or otherwise of the artist, towards the representation of the perfection in which human nature was originally constituted. And so, immediately before Virgil leaves Dante and he is handed over to Beatrice, who is the particular aspect borne by divine grace in his individual life, Dante is assured that even as far as this, as far as the Earthly Paradise (though no farther), the ancient, pre-Christian, poets reached in their imaginings (canto 28, ll. 139–141).

Poetry and History

But in respect of Foster's original question, it now looks as if we have reached something of an impasse. A specifically Christian significance *can* be derived from non-Christian literature, but only, it would seem, by an act of hermeneutical prestidigitation on the part of the already Christian reader. The human significance in non-Christian literature which non-Christian authors and Christian readers alike can recognize reaches, however, only as far as the natural perfection of human beings—while the perfection rendered possible in them by the grace which has redeemed them from sin, for Foster the essential component in Christian literature, *that* cannot be unforcedly read out of a literature that does not know the name of Christ. To some extent it is obvious that this must be the case. But if it and nothing else is the case, then to extend the term "Christian poetry" to cover, for example, *King Lear*, or *Les Fleurs du Mal* or "Les Effarés," is either wrong or unhelpful, for it is being asserted either that these works tell us about the specific operation of the grace of Christ (which they do not appear to) or that they tell us simply about the natural condition of human beings (which is, or should be, equally interesting to Christians and non-Christians alike). But may it not be that it *is* possible for poetry to speak of re-deeming grace—that is, of Christ—without knowing that it does so? The example of Dante can help us out of our impasse, provided we make two distinctions.

The first is a distinction between the kind of poetry written by Dante and the kind attributed by him to the ancient, non-Christian poets. The truth expressed by that ancient poetry encompassed, at its furthest margins, the Earthly Paradise. But the Earthly Paradise, we should remember, though made for Adam and Eve, has since their fall had no human inhabitants. Dante and Beatrice meet there before passing up into Heaven, but otherwise this perfect garden is peopled only by allegories. There are no souls here to recall their former lives or to comment on events in Dante's milieu. It has all the charm of the world's first morning but it has remained unchanged ever since and is essentially timeless. The highest truth that non-Christian poetry can represent, then, is an ideal that lies outside history and has in a sense no reference to human beings as, since the Fall, they have actually been. The character of Dante's poem, by contrast, is determined by its *not* making use, outside the Earthly Paradise, of the allegorical mode, its character is determined by what Foster called "that enormous volte face in literary history rep-resented by Dante's peopling his morality play with living persons instead of allegorical abstractions."[6] If the manner of the Comedy is to be allegorical at all, it is an allegory, Foster tells us,[7] after the manner of "the theologians," in Dante's phrase, and from St. Thomas's definition of it "it is clear that in this kind of allegory—the kind that tradition ascribed to the Bible—the historical truth of the literal sense was an essential presupposition."

Dante's great poem, in other words, differs essentially and *in its very manner* from non-Christian poetry (such as the *Eclogues*, or even the *Aeneid*), because of an essential similarity of its manner to that of the Bible, the unique and authoritative revelation: it is about the world of grace, but it is also about the world of history. It is about particular, real, datable, fallen men and women who at particular times and places accepted or rejected the grace of God offered them through and as a result of the bodily life, death, and resurrec-tion of Christ some thirteen centuries before the supposed date of the vision. Moreover, it is for Dante and for the world in which his poem was written the earthly passing-over of the incarnate Word that constitutes history in the first place: that gives direction and purpose to the time which leads up to Christ and an eschatological expectation to the time after him; that divides the ages into a pre-Christian period of signs and figures and a Christian period of fulfillment; that provides the temporal point of reference by which years are dated and people and their activities made singular and unrepeatable. For Dante it is only in relation to Christ that human doings are part of history, and only as part of history that human doings become the subject-matter of his poem. No one has shown better than Erich Auerbach the interdependence of Dante's revolutionary poetic and narrative style—the complex interweaving of utterly individual and eternally fixed destinies—and the "figural realism" of his Christian conception of the phenomenal and historical world: "conceiving all earthly occurrences through the medium of a mixed style . . . as an entity sublimely figural, is Christian in spirit and Christian in origin." When, for example, Dante links two events with the phrase "ed ecco" he is introducing into vernacular poetry, and so into the common conception of what makes for historical continuity, a device whose origins are not Virgilian, or classical at all, but biblical.[8] The *Divine Comedy* is therefore not just *a* Christian poem: it is the paradigm of what Christian poetry is, of what poetry is in the Christian era.

From living in that era not even those who want to can escape—not at any rate without leaving behind far, far more than they may initially imagine. For, as Hegel saw so clearly, the collective self-understanding of modern Europeans, what we call the "history" of their "states," or "world-history," in Hegel's term, is inseparable from Christianity (in which Hegel included the Reformation), and that not simply because of some continuity of institutions, but because of what we modern Europeans (and we are not now by any means confined to a single continent) have come to mean by "history." For as long as we conceive of history as a meaningful interconnection of *all* events, each of which is invested both with individual uniqueness and absolute importance, we are as much within the bounds of a Christian world as if our moral thinking uses the categories of death and resurrection, sin and forgiveness, or if our theology acknowledges the name of Christ. It *is* possible to live outside the Christian world—Homer did, and so did many millions of, let us say, Buddhists, until their first contact with the imperial outriders of the global market, usually Protestant missionaries, bringing with them not only trade and religion but also their own notion of time. But that involved living not only with different theological and moral categories, but with different political and historical categories, with different conceptions of human doings and of their literary representation, from those which prevailed in Christendom—that is, in the cultural unit in which the present world-system originated and which, for all its increasing internal complexity, remained relatively cohesive both in its centuries-old interchange with its Islamic neighbors, and in its distinctness from the Hindu, Buddhist, or sub-Saharan worlds (with which until the establishment of the new system it had little contact). It is a particular merit of Hegel's philosophy of history that it enables us to see European culture since the Renaissance, since the Reformation, and even since the French Revolution, as continuous with the culture of medieval Christendom, as profoundly and distinctively Christian—even though it is also driven by its own inner logic to become secular and global. We do not have to yield to Christopher Dawson's notion[9] that around 1300 the unity that was Christendom disappeared for good. It is true that the form in which that unity of sacred and secular immediately presented itself to Dante—a union of papal and imperial powers—was passing away in the very moment in which he was endeavoring to reflect it. (It is, as we know, in the gathering dusk that the owl of Minerva takes wing.) But simply because from then on the community of the baptized was further divided internally, and divided in new ways against itself, it did not, for that, cease to be a unity: like Guelphs and Ghibellines, heretics and schismatics are still Christians, and the unity which ecumenists seek is that which, without knowing it, they already possess.

It follows that we must make a second distinction. We must distinguish between pre-Christian poetry and secular poetry. Pre-Christian poetry originates in a non-Christian world, a world separated from Christendom either by time, as in the case of Homer or the *Táin*, or by space, as with most of the literature of the Far East, until very recent years. Only by a retrospective interpretation, which disregards the author's intentions, can analogies be found in such writing to the grace which is Christ. The nearest approach to that grace is the Earthly Paradise which both Ezra Pound and W. B. Yeats in their own ways found imaged in the Oriental world (e.g., Canto XLIX or Yeats's "Lapis Lazuli"). Secular poetry is poetry which arises in a Christian context and is fed in innumerable ways from Christian resources, and so tells in all these many ways of the grace of Christ, but yet has acquired the power, as a result of the development of Christianity itself, of rejecting or at any rate concealing, its origins. In the form of secularity, the negation of itself that Christianity has created, Christianity has been spread wherever the global market has reached, and with it has spread, even if negated, the Christian concept of historical time. The challenge of rejection and negation—the constitution of an area of life distinct from the sacred which it thus becomes incumbent on the sacred to penetrate and revivify with a divine presence—has been part of the dynamic of Christianity since the Incarnation, and since the radical secularization of the first Christian missions, which swept divinity out of the world in order that all the world should be reclaimed by God. Sinful, heretical, schismatic, even blaspheming, poetry does not cease to be Christian poetry, no more than sinners, heretics, or schismatics cease to be Christians—indeed it is precisely to them that the Church must go if it is to take up its cross and follow its Master. The romance of *Lancelot* which suborned Paolo and Francesca was secular literature, sinful in its effects and perhaps in its intentions, but it was quite certainly Christian.[10] The love that it invoked derived its seductive power from its being the same love, albeit aberrant in its object, as that which will draw Dante on, through the fires in which so many secular poets of love are purged, to the ultimate vision of the *Paradiso*.

In no writer is the negation of sacred origins at once so all-embracing and so gentle, so diaphanous, as in Shakespeare (who thus deserves perhaps to be called the most Christian writer of the modern age and the only true successor to Dante). For his more metaphysical questionings of human destiny he seems deliberately to select non-Christian settings—*King Lear*, *Macbeth*, *Cymbeline*. The history plays are fairly rigorously secular—the religious dimension of the monarch's responsibilities, omnipresent in Dante, is consciously curtailed, in accordance, one is tempted to think, with the Elizabethan settlement: "every subject's duty is the King's; but every subject's soul is his own" (*Henry V*, Act IV. Sc. 1). Indeed, if *Hamlet* is, as T. S. Eliot thought, unsatisfactory, it is perhaps because it is in the nature of the play's theme that the Christian element in it should be explicit and significant but uncertainly defined—a doubt not only as to the nature of the beyond but as to the extent of its practical influence.

Yet this apparently so non-Christian world is in fact often an inspiringly accurate image of secular experience as experience which only the grace which is Christ can redeem. *King Lear* is Good Friday without Easter, but can we imagine *Cordelia* uttering the fivefold "never" that is in the play the denial of the Christian consolation? Perhaps it is a weakness of the play that nothing in its structure corresponds to Cordelia's implicitly Christian perspective—but perhaps rather this apparent defect is the means by which the play represents precisely the secularity of the "time" into which Christ came to bring redemption (cp. Ephesians 5:16). The disguise of the Duke in *Measure for Measure* is clearly a *kenosis*, yet the play ceases to be a Christian parable at the very point—the Duke's appearance in court—at which its Christian character is about to become unequivocal. To go further would be to make the play a depiction of something other than the world of fallen flesh, in which men, and occasionally women, have power, not angels, and if it is not into that world that God is incarnated then Incarnation has no meaning.

The Christian patterns in Shakespeare's plays (and particularly the miracles of forgiveness and restoration through sacrifice in the last plays) include a deep understanding of Jesus' silence about his own Divinity—an understanding available perhaps only to an age with a developed sense of the distinction between secular and sacred. Those patterns show the Christian reader what it means to have to build the temple of the Spirit in bodies of flesh. No one shows us better than Shakespeare the stuff of which we are made— for he shows it to us as ready to receive the imprint of a grace which he does not depict. Foster occasionally mentioned Shakespeare in his sermons, always with a reverence born of long and close familiarity, and it might have been along these lines that he would have defended this recourse to profane literature.[11]

Shakespeare's combination of realistic writing with assertions about the ultimate fate and eternal significance of human beings and their affairs is Christian in origin, for it is made possible by the uniquely Christian notion of meaningful history. The *Divine Comedy* is neither the representation of a timeless ideal nor a self-contained fiction, but a part of the process of history, which it (partially) depicts—dates measured A.D., and times measured from the meridian of Jerusalem, are no different in Dante's poems from dates and times in the reality outside it. In Shakespeare's work neither the life of Christ nor the historical timescale it makes possible has a structural role, but the conviction that human doings have meanings and that the work of art does not create those meanings but draws on them, and so shares in the process of human living which it depicts—*that* remains. The fictionality of the last romances—of *The Winter's Tale, Cymbeline, Pericles,* and *The Tempest*—is conscious because these works are consciously withdrawn from the Christian timescale— because the historical events through which the grace represented in these plays has become a part of the stock of human meaning on which they draw are passed over in silence.[12] That silence may be attributable to the increasingly heretical and schismatic culture in which Shakespeare lived, but it may also be one, and not the least profound, of the Christian patterns in his poetry.

On the Margin of History

In the early Renaissance, from Dante and Petrarch to the Reformation, as Foster showed,[13] pagan and Christian Antiquity seemed parts of a single historical sweep, "the millennium stretching between, say, Plato or Pythagoras and Gregory the Great, with its centre in the Incarnation of the Word." In the sixteenth and seventeenth centuries, however, the developing distinction between secular and sacred—necessitated by the claim of national structures to complete independence from any international religious order—brought an asymmetry into what was felt to be the relation between the pagan and the Christian past: a meaningful historical development was in this period the exclusive prerogative of the sacred world—only patriarchs or prophets, or apostles, belonged to a historical era that had once been and would never be again—while the pre-Christian past of Greece and Rome became a timeless exemplar of secular humanity, its inhabitants indistinguishable in any important non-religious respect from contemporary men and women. This is the function of figures from pagan Antiquity, indifferently mythological and historical, in the essays of Montaigne or of Bacon and in the dramas equally of Jacobean England and of the France of Louis XIV. But as the age of Jefferson approached, the class of aboriginal property-owners who were to make the Revolutions laid claim to a universality of their own. By the beginning of the eighteenth century the defense of the sacred (for example by Bossuet) and the consolidation of the secular (for example by Voltaire) had substantially eliminated the asymmetry of the pagan and Christian past, put them both on an equal footing and prepared the way for the universal histories of cultural progress which in one form or another dominated the eighteenth and nineteenth centuries and in which the religious impetus was not always as clearly acknowledged as it was by Hegel.

One consequence of the advent of this new era (which may be said to have lasted until the middle of the twentieth century although signs of change were apparent a generation earlier) was a crisis for literature in respect of its subject matter. Historically on a par with their sacred contemporaries, the statesmen and heroes, and even the poets and philosophers, of pagan antiquity came to seem as remote from the modern age as the Hebrew patriarchs of the Old Dispensation had always been. What was a poet to write about now that, thanks to the new historical fusion, the pagan past could no longer function as a model of the contemporary secular order? Some poets (Klopstock, Hölderlin, Blake) drew the conclusion that the modern age, being essentially Christian, required a new sacred poetry based on the new historical fusion. But this left the secularity, which it is the task of Christianity to foster and to penetrate, without literary expression. The eighteenth century, deprived of its secular past, found a new secular material for literature in the present, in itself. And it invented two new means of dealing with that material, two forms that were to dominate literature for two hundred years: the novel, and the subjective (or "romantic") lyric poem.

Both forms can be seen to grow out of elements of the paradigm of Christian poetry that Dante provided for us: the novel out of its physical and phenomenal realism, the lyric poem out of its belief in the eternal importance of individual souls. But those Christian origins (clear enough, in the case of the novel, in *Pamela* or *Robinson Crusoe*, for instance, or even *Mansfield Park*) do not of themselves guarantee the Christian nature of the form that results. Homer, as Auerbach showed, is if anything more realistic than the Bible. But what made for the uniqueness of the Judaeo-Christian tradition was its *figural* realism—its belief that meaning is incarnate in things. Homer, Auerbach magnificently says, can be analyzed, but he cannot be interpreted. There is no *meaning* to the events, he recounts or the things he describes —they simply are themselves. That is, beyond question, I believe, non-Christian poetry, and it has in the last 250 years become possible for literature of a certain—though not perhaps ultimate—profundity to develop away from and out of the culture which gave it birth and to shut itself off in non-Christianity: the novel in *chosisme*, the poem in solipsism (or *vice versa*). But insofar as the novel and poetry pursue the struggle to incarnate meaning in their chosen material they remain essentially Christian. And that implies, if we look back at our paradigm: they remain essentially Christian insofar as they relate their material to meaningful history, history whose meaning, *ex hypothesi*, involves the poet, the poet's subject-matter, and the poet's reader.

We have already seen a little of the ambiguous and uncertain position of contemporary prose writing. Let me now try to say something about poetry in the narrower sense at the beginning and end of the romantic-realist period that stretched from the middle of the eighteenth to the middle of the twentieth century.

Lyric poetry as the first-person expression of secular subjectivity, as the expression of the life of the self in action and passion, knowledge and love, was founded by Goethe. He was its first and greatest exponent, he tried himself in most of its forms, and invented many of them, and his influence was felt throughout the literatures of Europe well into the twentieth century. Though he deliberately abandoned all institutional religion at the age of twenty-one and devoted much of his public life to the fostering of aesthetic Hellenism, he repeatedly claimed to be more of a Christian than some of his contemporaries. He had little or no interest in the new fusion, the new theory of cultural progress which at once secularized the Christian past and sacralized the pagan. As in Shakespeare's case, Goethe's works define a new area of secularity contrasting with what was currently held to be sacred.

Goethe's Faust is a man who has rejected Christianity entirely and with it Christian values and morality, and also the Christian concept of history, the quasi-Christian notion of progress, and the associated concepts of time. His moment of love with Gretchen, a simple Christian woman, is the moment of his redemption, but it is a moment on the very margin of Christian history. Only to the extent to which the post-Christian world of Faust interacts with the

Christian world of Gretchen is the story of Faust a part of Christian history and open to a Christian conclusion. Similarly, in *Part Two* of the play, Faust's marriage to Helen, the resurrected spirit of Greek antiquity, proves to be a moment of the most marginal, tangential, contact with meaningful history. History, in both parts of *Faust*, is experienced only as an unrememberable moment of eternal importance. Such an "eternal moment" is the most reduced state conceivable of the Christian belief in meaningful temporal sequence in the shared life of human beings, a sequence in which the act by Christ which redeemed individual souls, and the rise and fall of the Roman Empire, are, equally, real events. Such "eternal moments" are not infrequently invoked in Goethe's later poetry, but in a sense all his poetry is devoted to them. For all his poems, as he remarked, are "occasional poems," and the "occasions" of them are moments when meaning was incarnate in his life and in his world—fragments of meaning which, because they were found in *this* man's experience, and because he asks us to link them with similar fragments in our own experience, have in them the glint of history. The poem appeals to us, by recognizing its occasion, also to recognize the law of "Nature," as Goethe calls it, which it reveals, the common ground to Goethe's experience and our own, the link between him and us. That bond of like-minded spirits, constituted by moments of insight shared across a desert of meaningless time, is the only history that Goethe acknowledges—he calls it "the communion of saints." That such moments are the extreme or minimal case of a Christian mode of experience is shown explicitly by one of the last of the writers in the lyrical tradition inaugurated by Goethe—T. S. Eliot.

The first half of the twentieth century could already feel the premonitory tremors, and then the spreading shock-wave, from the geopolitical explosion of 1914, which by 1945 devastated bourgeois "European," or "Western," culture and began to transform it into world-culture, with consequences still incomplete and unforeseeable. Many of Eliot's contemporaries—Yeats, Pound, Carlos Williams, Stevens—reacted to their sense of an ending epoch by trying to sever their links with Christian culture altogether and to attach themselves, if at all, elsewhere: to Celtic paganism, to Chinese culture and supra-historical eclecticism, to a mystically non-European America, or to a placeless modernism. Eliot, however, a Southern American by birth, chose consciously and never without a residual artificiality,

to settle among the high places of the English, and Anglican, establishment. (Rather as Goethe, born a citizen of the Imperial Free
City of Frankfurt, chose to remove to ducal Weimar, the quintes-
sence of the *ancien régime*, to which he remained publicly loyal
throughout his life.)

Between 1936 and 1942 Eliot reflected on the significance of this
decision, in the context of a meditation on time and history, in *Four
Quartets*. It was certainly not security, or the wealth and glamour of
empire, that he had been looking for: those passed away in the tempest of the First World War, and, as they left, Pound took his leave as
well. Eliot stayed on, in an England increasingly troubled, direction-
less, and threadbare. *Four Quartets* are full of images of decayed
grandeur, of great but empty houses falling into ruin, or a prey to
modernity—swept away to build a by-pass—or ultimately to the dark
that engulfs us all, animals, men, women, buildings, empires. In *Little
Gidding* he seizes on what might seem the moment of final destruction of the culture he had ostentatiously joined—the London blitz—
and (a deliberate parallel to Dante's meeting with Brunetto Latini)
confronts in that moment "a familiar compound ghost" bearing features of several of his poetic contemporaries (principally Yeats,
though Foster thought Pound was represented as well).[14] Against this
apocalyptic background the ghost reveals the emptiness of a life devoted solely to poetic achievement and unpurified by the fire of divine love. By contrast with the ghost, who left his "body on a distant
shore," Eliot stresses his attachment to England, to England's past,
and (as the title of this *Quartet* suggests) England's Church. And the
nature of this attachment is revealed in the lines that follow: to inherit the English past is not to revive or perpetuate England's political or cultural interests, not to identify oneself with some particular
strand in the English national life, but it is to acquire "a symbol: A
symbol perfected in death." In time, the poem says, all things die—to
that extent the ghost is right—but in belonging somewhere, anywhere, to a particular place and people with their own stories and
loyalties and conflicts, one acquires the ability to live, not in time,
but in history. Historical experience is experience of temporal events:
not, however, of those events as subject to the temporal law of death,
but as symbolic, as replete with a meaning that transcends death.
King Charles seeking refuge at Little Gidding in the night, the All
Clear sounding over blitzed London, a moment in the poet's life

when he hears the laughter of children hidden in apple-trees: these are all events in time that die the death of the elements and are at most the end of a story. But as events in history, in a Christian poet's view of history, they are symbols, symbols in time of that ultimate meaning that conquers time and death. Such a "moment in and out of time" is a reminder and in a sense a re-enactment of the incarnation in time of the eternal Word. It is a historical moment, with all the force that Christianity can give to the word "historical"; and so

> A people without history
> Is not redeemed from time, for history is a pattern
> Of timeless moments. So, while the light fails
> On a winter's afternoon, in a secluded chapel
> History is now and England.

For Goethe, history is now and the moment in which the reader recognizes, as part of his or her own experience, the occasion of the poem—and whatever it is that lies between those two moments and makes them both possible. But for both Eliot and Goethe the "timeless," or "eternal," moment is the moment at which the individual's experience of life as meaningless sequence intersects with, or grazes tangentially, a meaningful universal pattern made up by everyone's experiences. It is a moment of grace and a moment in which grace is accepted, in which the poet's eyes meet the smile of his own Beatrice. For Eliot such moments are explicitly associated with the coming of Christ into earthly life, a coming which every moment in time, being instinct with death, perpetually announces and calls out for. But, for all the explicitness, we are here dealing with a form of Christian experience as consciously marginal as that of Goethe. Eliot's Beatrice was the Church of England, and we may no more doubt his sincerity than Dante's, but if the Christian sensibility of *Four Quartets* is anywhere defective it is in the assumption—derivative, as Helen Gardner has shown, from that minor monument to 1890s Anglicanism, *John Inglesant*—that Little Gidding is an equivalent, and alternative, to Rome.

My Peace My Parting

"What about us? We left all we had to follow you." I have suggested that from 1200 to 1945 European literature brought forth many varieties of Christian poetry, all of which deserved the name insofar as they created new relationships between the source of grace and the secular world, and insofar as the Christendom in which they had their origin had itself become a variety-in-unity. But what of the unity itself? Foster, taking a narrower view of the term 'Christian' than that proposed here, remarked at the end of his essay "Mr. Dawson and Christendom" that *Piers Plowman* was "the most directly *Christian* expression" of the medieval ideal of Christendom, and so, he implied, a more modern expression than that of Dante. For Langland's poem, in which Christ Himself was a principal actor, and in the figure of a working man, was proof that after the sundering of sacred and secular in the fourteenth century "a new Christian culture had been born which could and can survive; but only . . . within that of which it was said:

> And he called that house Unity;
> Holychurch in English."[15]

From Langland onwards, Foster is suggesting, grace is historically visible, not in the whole of human life, but specifically in the Church, and poetry cannot be Christian that is outside the Church. The question of course is: What Church? In one sense it is, and always has been, tautologically true that Christian poetry is poetry of the Christian Church. But Foster's narrower view of the issue requires that we clarify the relation between poetry and the distinct, visible, organizational unit that the Church has been in European culture since the fourteenth century. For there are churches and churches. Goethe and Eliot both find that grace touches history in the "pattern of timeless moments" that constitutes a "communion of saints": they are both churchmen, if with limited congregations. In that, they exemplify a hieratic tendency noticeable among all lyric poets of the romantic-realist era. But these poets' churches are poor stuff. A certain generosity of human scope—which can at times be found in the realistic novel—seems often to be lacking from poetry's exploration of subjectivity as the modern form of the secular, and even lacking from its penetration of this secularity with divine grace. Moreover, the recognition in this poetry of the operation of grace in the world is so much the achievement of the poet alone that there is little space in it for a Christian theme of the greatest importance (and treated accordingly by Dante): the *rejec-*

tion by men and women of grace, of the appeal of Christ, whoever His ambassadors. In an age when the secular and the sacred are divided, the sign of sin and contradiction, of the extent to which the secular world rejects the incarnation within it of the Word, is the Church as an institution—and necessarily, in the age of the nation-state, a non-national, a supranational, institution.

The task of being a fully and authentically—and not just heretically or marginally—Christian poet in the nineteenth century verged therefore on the superhuman. It was necessary *both* to penetrate fully with the grace of Christ the new secular subject-matter of the experiencing self, *and* to give full expression to the necessity of the (Roman) Church's witness against the sinfulness, the hard-heartedness, of the new, would-be omnicompetent, socio-political units into which Europe was dividing itself. The only poets who seem to have grasped the enormity of this task and to have laid out their work on a commensurate scale are Wordsworth and Victor Hugo. Hugo—whose achievement is nowadays sadly neglected—suffered from a certain shallowness of subjectivity, and Wordsworth from the political and religious limitations of his Englishness. One poet, however, who was uniquely well-placed to understand and fulfill the task was Gerard Manley Hopkins, though his output was for various reasons—not all of them accidental—too slender for him to be much more than "a lonely began."

Hopkins's belief, or experience, that "The world is charged with the grandeur of God" was Foster's favorite proof that the unity of Dante's vision could be available to a modern sensibility (in fact, he nearly always misquoted the line by conflating it with the first line of the *Paradiso*). And indeed Hopkins's vision is as distinctively modern as that of Goethe or Eliot: the presence of the divine is found, not in the natural thing on its own, in the trees, the cloud-scape, the windhover, but in the conjunction of the thing and the experiencing subject:

> These things, these things were here and but the beholder
> Wanting; which two when they once meet,
> The heart rears wings bold and bolder. . . .
>   ("Hurrahing in Harvest")

This moment of meeting, of "instress" as Hopkins calls it—often imaged as a flash or glint or spark—is the moment in which the divine significance of the thing, its status as something created by God, is manifest. And because the moment fuses divinity and the created object in a specifically human experience, the moment of instress is a moment in the life of Christ, the God-man:

> I walk, I lift up, I lift up heart, eyes,
> Down all the glory in the heavens to glean our Saviour;
>   (ibid.)

Hopkins's "nature-poetry" is in fact strictly argued theological poetry in which subject and object are as profoundly interfused as in any of Goethe's verse.

The other pole of Hopkins's writing is represented, of course, by the "terrible sonnets" of 1885–89, in which the Christ who in all creation is the "first, fast, last friend" seems to appear as an "enemy," with whom the poet wrestles in a constant temptation to despair. What makes these and other related poems so remarkable a complement to the "nature-poetry" is that we do not merely happen to know, as a matter of extraneous biographical detail, that Hopkins's agony derived from his solitude as an intellectual Catholic convert celibate priest of late nineteenth-century England, but these facts are deeply woven into the texture of the poems themselves. "England, whose honour O all my heart woos, wife/To my creating thought" is not able or willing to be fertilized by his word. He can only pray, as for a distant hope, for the conversion of whole nations ("In the valley of the Elwy"), or think nostalgically of England's first conversion ("To what serves mortal beauty"), or, most urgently, pray for the souls of those he loves whose schism threatens them with damnation ("Henry Purcell," "The Loss of the Eurydice"). The history of Europe—the history of Christian division and militant Caesarism—falls athwart Hopkins's life and twists it out of true: "The Wreck of the Deutschland," which began his mature poetic career, was a response to Bismarck's *Kulturkampf*, explicitly understood as a continuation of Luther's Reformation (Stanza 20). And this rejection, in history, of God's grace, by men and women, is a part of the suffering of the Christ whose beauty flashes off a bird, or a bluebell, or "the features of men's faces," and in that suffering the poet-priest shares, for he is Christ's "friend" in a place and time which will not know Him, in which He "lives alas away." Christ who is "my peace," he says, is also "my parting." Loyalty to Christ separates him from the family, friends, and culture in which he ought most nearly and clearly to see Christ. The greatness of the late sonnets is that the historical source of that parting, of that alienation from his time, is experienced with the same intimacy as the peace of Christ in the union of subjectivity with created things. Indeed, the alienation from the time is experienced as a frustration of the poetic activity itself, and so the tragic theme of his age's rejection of Christ is united with the tragic drama of his own struggle to accept that grace in the crucifying form in which it presents itself:

> See, banks and brakes
> Now, leavèd how thick! lacèd they are again
> With fretty chervil, look, and fresh wind shakes
> Them; birds build—but not I build; no but strain,
> Time's eunuch, and not breed one work that wakes.
> Mine, O thou lord of life, send my roots rain.
>   ("Thou art indeed just, O Lord")

The closer it comes to authenticity, the more the Christian poetry of our age will suffer the "tragic moral tension" which Foster saw[16] as the distinctive feature of Hopkins's work, a tension "between poetry and . . . priestly vocation," a tension—between sharing in the world that needs redemption and sharing in the agency that is to redeem it—which, I believe, is identical with the tension involved in being a Christian in a historical world, that is, with being a Christian at all. Hopkins's "fragmentarily but magnificently" Christian religious poetry had a special importance for Kenelm Foster personally in his own lifelong experience of that tension. But it was also as a sign that Hopkins's example can continue to teach and sustain any believer that Foster took his works with him on his last journey into hospital, as the only worthy companion, in his secular reading, to Dante's *Purgatorio*.

Christian Poetry and the Global Market

Dante and his teacher Thomas Aquinas stood at a turn of the times when, particularly in the cities which gave the bourgeoisie its name, the ordered relationships of feudal society were being monetarized and individualized. In their great intellectual constructs, already old-fashioned in the moment of their creation, the forces that were newly in the ascendant were presented as truly fulfilled in the order that was passing away: in Dante's poem the accommodation of precisely assessed individual existences within a primordially established hierarchy is literal and tangible. By Shakespeare's time the critique of the old order was explicit and had already overthrown its one great international institution, the universal church. By Goethe's time Jeffersonian and Girondin "man" was preparing to call every national institution to account too, and a renewed religious crisis generated both the realistic novel and the romantic lyric. Maybe in the twentieth century we have seen the end of that enlightened and bourgeois era which was born around 1200 and which Aquinas and Dante enfolded in a generous but skeptical embrace. Now that a global economy, and so a global proletariat ("the Worker" in Jünger's phrase), has taken the place of the systems of bourgeoisie and empire, an attitude at once distant and understanding towards those now defunct forces is again called for—hence, no doubt, the revived appeal and topicality in our century of two of the greatest European minds who two hundred years ago personified obscurity and superstition. Can Dante's example perhaps also show Christian poetry the way into the future? Not of course as any sort of model, but as a demonstration that the "crucial" task of that poetry is to "in-*form*" the subject-matter that is the secularity of its own time with the characteristically Christian understanding of meaningful history. By way of conclusion, I shall ask how far the work of three great twentieth-century poets writing in English, none of them British, and none of them in any straightforward sense a believer, can nevertheless be seen as a response to this challenge: Lowell, Yeats, and Seamus Heaney.

Robert Lowell, as fragmentarily and magnificently a poet as he was a Christian, struggled in later life ever more consciously to find a point of junction between the personal, the local, and the historical—the individual, the particular, and the universal, Hegel would have said. In *Notebook 1967–68*, which dealt with one of the most eventful post-war years before 1989, he came to feel he had not succeeded and he later incorporated that collection into two separate books—*The Dolphin* for the more intimate sonnets, *History* for the more public. But the two cannot be separated, not if Hegel is right: having an identity and expressing it truthfully (which since the eighteenth century has been the main function of lyric poetry) necessarily involves a certain claim to universality, to identifying what is shared by the poet, the poet's subject-matter and the poet's readers. To write a modern poem is to give voice not just to an "I," but to a "we," and the medium that makes that "we" possible is what the poem represents as history. No agency, I have suggested, has been able to utter 'we" so all-embracingly as Christianity, for it understands the sacred as the source of the secular and creates a "we," coextensive with "those for whom God died," which its own dynamic is continually forcing it to render more explicitly all-inclusive. The theme, therefore, in which twentieth-century poets (and perhaps novelists too) have been best able to do justice to the new, global realities, to incorporate them in a common history, and so to express a personal and collective identity, has been the confrontation, or interrelation, of religion and secularity (and that is, *par excellence*, a Christian theme).

Lowell took up that theme—no doubt from the poem by Wallace Stevens mentioned in our previous essay—and made of it not a metaphysical meditation but a grand and public utterance, perhaps his best-known poem, which fully deserved its reading at the protest march on the Pentagon in October 1967. In "Waking Early Sunday Morning"[17] the "diminuendo" of (particularly Puritan) biblical faith, the "vanishing" of God's "emblems," is set in strict parallel to the decline from the opening burst of energy in the personal subconscious, from the imperious demand of the spirit for release, to the monotony of a secular "sublime" with which the poem ends: all the Sunday paper can tell us about ourselves is "promotions," "assassinations," and "small wars"—"Only man thinning out his kind/ sounds through the Sabbath noon." "Teach me, my God and King, In all things thee to see," George Herbert prayed in a poem which Lowell travesties with respectful seventeenth-century wit;[18] his poem is a sentimental re-education at the end of which the global process does indeed become visible to the individual whose desires fuel it, but as a godless, meaningless, and historyless circling of celestial bodies "until the end of time." "Pity the poor planet" was in 1967 a prophetic apostrophe of the post-modern era. If however we ask: who are the "we" so prominently invoked in the last line? we shall perhaps uncover why Lowell's *tour de force* does not carry complete conviction and why the link between the individual and the universal eludes him, here and elsewhere. For the "we" of this poem are those who, at the outset at least, strain to spawn like the Chinook salmon and for whom, alas, "All life's grandeur/ is something with a girl in summer. . . ." "We" are American middle-class males, whose apocalypse, however superbly phrased, is not adequate to the planetary generality of the concluding "our." The hubris of the class, and perhaps of the audience, is flattered; the history that overtakes them is—in this representation—too much of their own making. In the reality of the global economy, however, individuals are so alienated from the consequences of their desires that when the consequences return upon them they feel the foundations of their identity are shaken by paradoxes beyond their comprehension. Hopkins knows such paradoxes: what he envisages as his peace nonetheless parts him from the world and from himself, and threatens his ability to write—to establish, that is, a medium shared by himself and his reader anywhere. In Lowell's poem, however, the call to break loose, to be "anywhere but somewhere else," is the affirmation of a local, American, and masculine, culture, which may be bringing disaster on itself and others, but whose destiny is, it believes, in its own hands. Many of the sonnets in *History* recreate the past—even past women—in this image of self-made man. They thus share the defect of Yeats's "Long-legged Fly." For that poem presents history as something made, and uniquely understood, by the minds of exceptional individuals, in a sacred or artistic process on which the vulgar reader may eavesdrop but must not intrude. Yeats's social presuppositions may be those of a leisured rural gentry, Lowell's those of colonial Girondins, but both poems conceal the truth which in the global era it is poetry's task to reveal: that history is not something some few of us make but something all of us jointly suffer.

But in Ireland's time of trouble, between 1916 and 1922, when the violence of historical change swept past Yeats's front door, he wrote, amid the most seductive temptations to heroic illusion, a series of great poems whose theme is precisely the dependence of local and personal identity on forces which transcend its comprehension. The marvel of "Easter 1916" is the sudden revelation that the "casual comedy" of Dublin commerce and society is the material of history and universality. "MacDonagh and MacBride And Connolly and Pearse" are not the stagey demi-gods of "Long-legged Fly." It is only a contingent and incidental consequence of the work and the decisions of the martyrs of the uprising that their names are transfigured. History seizes on them, not they on opportunity—and yet there is nothing to the great event beyond what they are and have done, "changed utterly" into "a terrible beauty." The course of human events has its supreme meaning as the incarnation—the complete embodiment, without any abstract residue—of divine power.

Incarnation is quite explicitly the theme of "The Second Coming" (1919), which is thus a strict parallel to "Easter 1916," but the aftermath of the great European conflict, in which the Irish war of liberation was only an episode, looked like the incarnation not of a god but of an Anti-Christ. In "The Second Coming," however, the vision of impending millennial upheaval is so overwhelming that it largely obscures the actions and responsibilities of individual agents. But in two cycles of 1920–1922 Yeats restored the balance, and his understanding of the anguish of living in the new world disorder attained a clarity and freedom from mystification that he afterwards seldom recovered. "Nineteen Hundred and Nineteen" and, especially, "Meditations in Time of Civil War," struggle to understand, simultaneously, the poet's personal inheritance and bodily posterity, the barbarities of the local fight for nationhood, and the all-embracing perplexities of time, transience, and the whirling cycle of old and new wickedness: "Man is in love and loves what vanishes." The individual's always baffled attempt to grasp the universal order is here made by posing the despairing particular question: How to be a poet for this people in these times? The answer the question receives, at once enraged and faltering, shows that, as in "Easter 1916," Yeats is not posing as the master of history but knows himself its victim. "We pieced our thoughts into philosophy, And planned to bring the world under a rule, Who are but weasels fighting in a hole." The theme is condensed into the limpid symbolism of "The Stare's Nest by my Window," one of the finest of all Yeats's poems and fully comparable with Hopkins's "Thou art indeed just, O Lord," in which he hopes that the honey bees will make their home in the empty nest left by the starling in his crumbling tower, and so will bring sweetness—as it were, of poetry—even to ruin and incomprehension:

> We are closed in, and the key is turned
> On our uncertainty; somewhere
> A man is killed, or a house burned,
> Yet no clear fact to be discerned;
> Come build in the empty house of the stare.

In the three-quarters of a century since these lines were written there have been few places in the world that have not had a chance to prove their truth.

Yet though in "Easter 1916" and "Meditations in Time of Civil War" Yeats recognizes that transcendent meaning, whether glimpsed as a terrible beauty or obscured by "brutal" conflict, has to be incarnate in a particular place and time if it is to be tangible at all, he can in these poems say no more about the meaning itself. "Homer is my example / and his unchristened heart," he later claimed,[19] but the example of analyzable but uninterpretable pre-Christian poetry was not one he could follow: he was, without possibility of escape, a secular poet, the inheritor, that is, of a Christian question, and once the question of interpretation, whether of poetry or of history, has been thought it cannot be unthought. Yeats thought it all the time and with ever greater imaginative wildness as he grew older, after 1917 employing his wife as a spiritualist medium in the hope of arriving at some depersonalized and ultimate structure of meaning. He was silent about the realm of being to which the beauty of 1916 belonged, though the end of the poem suggests, rather disappointingly, surely, that it is limited to "wherever green is worn," so, presumably, to a national myth of Irishry. The mythological and cosmological speculations with which he surrounded his vision of the Second Coming are well known to those whom such things interest. In "Leda and the Swan," of 1923, his refusal of the Christian pattern of meaning began to show its consequences. Without a Christology, the insight that we are the victims of history, not its masters, takes on a sinister coloring. The transformation of our shared life by a god—for example, the inception of the Trojan War, though it might equally be the Dublin uprising—requires, we are told, an incarnation in which the divine is as intimate with the human as one heart beating against another in a sexual embrace. In this insistently pagan annunciation, however, the god remains "strange" and his "knowledge" is not certainly shared with humankind. Without that last and crucial intimacy of knowledge, the terrible beauty which is a divinely significant human existence can be born only as the result of a monstrous act of rape. By writing "Leda and the Swan" Yeats set out on the path that took him not, as he intended, to Homer's sovereign objectivity, but to the Nietzschean disdain of "Long-legged Fly" and "Lapis Lazuli," and brought him under the "cold eye" of the horseman, to whom he addressed his epitaph.

That we can grasp our post-modern, global existence only through the Christian concept of secularity is a conclusion to which I have been helped by reading Seamus Heaney, in whose recent poems Heidegger seems to have played a role not unlike that of Nietzsche for Yeats's, though rather more valuable. It is a more everyday, perhaps less memorable, affair to come under the scrutiny of a pecked hawthorn-berry than of Yeats's mounted Zarathustra, but not in the end less disconcerting. The strength of Heaney's later poetry is that such interrogations are quietly set in the widest context the poet can truthfully imagine. Despite an early tendency to clog every line with turf and burn-water, Heaney is no more a regional poet than Yeats was. Rather less so, in fact, for the presence-in-absence of his Catholic past provides Heaney with the access into universality for which Yeats had to seek artificial and sometimes lurid substitutes. "In Illo Tempore," for example,[20] is not merely an episode of nostalgia for a rustic childhood faith in the old liturgy: the contrasting world of the global media and international literary tradition is also sketched (simply by the line "Now I live by a famous strand"). With his powerfully generalizing analysis of the old order as a reign of "nouns" over verbs Heaney therefore invites us to see his experience as a loss of substance—a loss of the substantive—such as Heidegger thought characteristic of life lived in the pure functionality of "the stand." Yet the poem offers us neither just an individual experience nor just a universal truth, but both at once, and through the medium of a particular life, geographically and historically specific.

Similarly, an impressive series of sonnets written on the death of Heaney's mother takes as its theme the disclosure of being through absence and has the overtly Heideggerian title "Clearances." The finest poem in the cycle is a meditation on that characteristically twentieth-century topic Stevens and Lowell have made familiar to us: not going to church on Sunday morning.[21] In Ireland, however, especially the Catholic North of the 1940s and 50s, that quiet hour is gained by a detachment from the local community ("all the others were away at Mass"). The isolation is not complete, though: in the quietness the son is brought closer to his mother than on any other occasion in their lives by the shared physical task of peeling

potatoes. Later, when she is dying, this moment in the poet's recol-
lection stands in for, but does not obliterate, the religious rituals
of the community from which he is again detached. The absolute
individuality of the shared physical act, and of its negation, death;
the particularity of a place and culture, in turn negated by a hu-
morously detached personal self-consciousness; and the horizon
provided by a universal church, itself modulating into secularity—
these together provide a structure for this rich and moving poem
which Hegel would have recognized as a guarantee of its concrete
truth.

Any poet must have an instinct for the gradations of unsayability:
Heaney combines it with a generous awareness of the multiple contexts of experience. He is thus able to profit from Heidegger's recovery and secularization of a Catholic sense of the priority of being
over thought while avoiding Heidegger's slide into taciturnity (and
worse). For him as for Yeats a new turn in Ireland's murderous struggle for identity seems to have forced on his verse a perspective on
the largest issues of human life together, and it is noteworthy that in
Station Island (1984) he turned to Dante for help in the task. After
1968, the "little destiny" of Ulster has become embedded in the
clichés of global communication ("England's Difficulty," "Whatever
You Say Say Nothing"[22]) and it has become the poet's role to make
sense of that destiny, from the potatoes to the zoom lenses. His
medium, however—that on which and in which he works—is the
English language, which is not merely the instrument of a local imperialism which he has to wrest from the intruders in order to give
speech to a particular colony. It is also the global medium *par excellence*, whose universality it would be self-destruction for the poet to
deny, but to which he has to restore a local significance both for
England and for Ireland. Ulster, Ireland, England, Europe, the world
of television and tourism and lecture-circuit: Heaney seems to know
where he is located within all these circles, his poetry seems to know
where it stands—and how to stand, not sink—on a post-modern,
post-imperial, globalized, secularized, marketized planet. And one
notices time and again how his poems keep their bearings by referring to the universal faith he himself—knowing the typicality of his
fate—can no longer "credit" ("In Illo Tempore"). The tradition of
Christian humanism, even detached from its origins, is old and honorable. The title-poem of the collection *The Haw Lantern* tells how

sometimes the hawthorn with its berry "takes the roaming shape of Diogenes/ with his lantern, seeking one just man."[23] In the global market Diogenes may have a long search. But Heaney's own example shows us how even in our time it is possible to seek oneself to be just, and that in the end is enough identity for anybody.

Afterword

We live in one world. The intellectual fashion for holding that we live in multiple, disconnected worlds is a device of consumerism to prevent us from recognizing our common fate, in case we
are tempted to try to control it. Poetry that tells us who we are performs a revolutionary act, for it overcomes the barriers—between, for
example, the natural and the cultural, the political and the religious—
which obstruct our view of the whole and of our relation to it. The
unity of the human race may once have been only an idea: it is nowadays also material. We are all related to one another through the economic process of production and exchange (and so are gradually
coming to give real significance to our genetic unity). But our interrelation does not end there: economic conflict within the single system,
between consumer and producer, can be resolved only politically;
political choices both create and presuppose political identities, of
groups and individuals; group identities create and presuppose
shared past experiences—i.e., a history—and common future purposes—i.e., a social morality; the medium both of history and morality
is language, whose resources, both for storytelling and for moral
analysis, are perfected in literature. In these essays I have tried to illuminate from different angles the political and historical, moral and
literary consequences of the growth of a closed world economic
structure.

The structure is of course far from complete but it has for well over a century been producing effects in what were once areas of national policy, which national governments, alone or in concert, are no longer able to control. No human life can now be led in total isolation from the ever denser global network and no organized human intrusion from outside it is now possible. Every human being must expect at some time to brush against a tendril put out by a system which is not just international but which—both literally and figuratively—encircles the world. It may at first be no more than the availability—or visibility—of desirable products of mass-producing industry—tools, textiles, and the means of transport—and then the need from time to time to make or receive payments in some—ultimately internationally convertible—currency. But the tendrils grow thicker and do not let go. Governments, anxious to re-duce imports or to meet some other norm set by international com-petition, make their presence felt by imposing (de-)population programs or changes in age-old cultivation practices. Price fluctua-tions in agricultural staples are decreasingly likely to have a purely local cause—as cheap imports to feed growing cities undercut rural producers, for example—and price movements in cash crops and minerals can have devastating and uncomprehended local effects. As soon as industrial production for the international market is begun, competition in keeping down the social on-costs of labor af-fects myriads of urban lives. Radio and television, telephones and transport, maintain awareness of a world wider than the nation and affect language, fashions, and ideas. The more you have in common the more you have to compete about, and vice versa. Among the wealthiest nations, and particularly in their capital markets, which virtually disregard political boundaries, competition and integra-tion are so intense that it is proper to speak of a global market into which new competitors and new areas of competition are con-stantly emerging.

The commercial exigencies which drove our great-great-grand-parents to set up the first planetary grid around 1870 were in the next two generations to prove too powerful to be contained within the political structures which complacently contemplated their equilibrium at the time of Queen Victoria's jubilee. The European nation-states with their attached empires were the products of a period in which continuous territorial expansion made possible the maintenance, though only in the mother country, of the fiction of permanent growth and permanent opportunity for all classes. Capital could be accumulated in significant quantities by a significant number of private individuals—the "bourgeoisie"—without creating the degree of impoverishment and alienation which would lead to social collapse. Over the millennia, of course, mercantile empires have come and gone—most recently the Iberian empire in Central and South America, its demise assisted by the intervention of Anglo-American free-traders in the 1820s. What was unique about the empires founded between the middle of the eighteenth and the middle of the nineteenth centuries was the synergy set up between them and the processes of capital concentration and industrialization in the mother-country. This was not simply a matter of the traditional function (not always efficiently performed) of providing cheap supplies and a captive market, but above all of the management of the social revolution at home: the provision of places of hope, opportunity, and, if necessary, exile for the victims, or the merely restless. After 1914, however, in the course of seventy-five years of the most violent confrontation, the empires have destroyed one another, and so also the sense of an identity, national and racial, social and personal, in which their internal conflicts were resolved.

The end of the empires has meant the end of the class they were designed to protect. A state without an empire, and without a mechanism for large-scale emigration, cannot afford a bourgeoisie which accumulates capital by impoverishing a large fraction of its people. The nineteenth-century states have kept themselves in existence by exporting their poverty to remote sections of the world's population, which they circumscribe with barriers to emigration and persuade to call themselves "nations" too. At home their governments impose tax regimes or engineer long-term inflationary tendencies which between them eliminate private centers of capital. At the same time the increasing activity of the global market ensures that industry's hunger for capital grows beyond the capacity of individuals to satisfy it, and owners and shareholders are gradually converted into the employees of fund-managers, multi-nationals, and governments. The division of the post-imperial world market into directly competing national economies serves a function for as long as it is necessary to press the hitherto leisured classes into work: na-

tional well-being is seen to depend on getting as much of the nation working as possible. Once all are employed (bar the number
who have "naturally" to be left jobless to terrorize the rest) national
divisions cease to be more than obstacles to international capital's
endless endeavor to make us all work more for less.

The function within the world-economy (i.e., the global competitiveness) of industries, and so of the individuals they employ, is more
important to their survival than any contribution they may be supposed to make to the self-sufficiency of the local community, once
denominated "the nation." The transition to the new state-form has
been gradual or abrupt as "the nation" has or has not been forcibly
re-constructed during the upheavals of the Seventy-Five Years' War.
But at the end of the twentieth century we have all, even the United
States, arrived in a society which is not only post-imperial but also
very largely post-bourgeois. It is therefore, increasingly, post-
national. Of course there is still a lot of private money about—in Italy
for example or North or Latin America—but only where there is also
poverty of a degree or extent incompatible with long-term social cohesion. Most of us, in Europe and the USA, as in other industrialized
countries, derive most of our income from the work we do as producers for the market in which we also, though with greater variation,
are the consumers. In Marx's terms, we are proletarians, and from our
role as proletarian consumer-producers in a global market derive
many of the puzzles and contradictions of our political and intellectual life.

When the fundamental facts of our economic existence are
global rather than national, the nation-state is no longer the irreducible autonomous component of the world political structure.
But, as Hegel has shown, the state and the self are inseparable, and
in the global market the individual citizen, or "national," no longer
irreducible or autonomous either, suffers a crisis of identity too. In
a world where we are all employed, even the owners and managers
of capital, the political concepts of the bourgeois age are anachronisms—neither the "state" nor the "individual" is what it was. What
are called "market reforms" are devices for making more activities
(internationally) accountable, and for breaking accountable activities down into smaller units, contractually specified, so that performance can be measured and competitiveness compared: "the state"—
that is, the legislature—once a free association of aboriginal prop-

erty-owners, becomes, now that species is extinct, the local branch of Global Accountants Inc., issuing ever more regulations in ever finer detail to extend and reinforce the proletarian status of those who were once its citizens. A host of "human rights" claimed by this worldwide population of juridically equal consumer-producers are enforced against the old organs of state power, by new international institutions. The principle of non-intervention in a nation's internal affairs grows obsolete, and with it the very idea of a nation.[1] Because the capital extracted from the global market is now on the whole owned by Northern-hemisphere collectivities (an increasing number of them "offshore"), rather than by individuals or classes within individual nations, the significance of the local state bodies is anyway reduced, especially as airlines and the Internet elide geographical difference. Even the "privatization" of previously nationalized undertakings is not what it seems, in the absence of a bourgeoisie to buy up the shares: its principal effects are not to enrich the bourgeois who no longer exist, but to transfer yet more of the local workforce to a global jobs market, and to reduce the sovereignty of the national government by transferring to multinational companies such strategic responsibilities as the supply of water and power, waste-disposal, communications, and transport. Plainly there is something odd afoot if a "privatizing" administration also complains about a supposed loss of powers to extraterritorial political and legal institutions which are at least either elected or directly or indirectly responsible to elected bodies. The unease and xenophobia express a dim awareness of the change in the economic status of the nation, but are directed at the far more visible political institutions which are actually endeavoring to control the changes.

In a similar way, the changes to our individual self-understanding brought about in the last hundred years have been obscured by paradox and unacknowledged class interest. Explicitly theoretical questions about individual identity have tended to be addressed by thinkers associated with the bureaucracy, a sub-set of the middle class with close links to national governments and in perennial conflict with the bourgeoisie. Professional intellectuals have preferred not to notice the process of proletarianization which has eliminated the bourgeoisie and is even now eating away at the position of the bureaucrats. In a world where more and more of us are contracted-out agents of the state through which, directly or indirectly, we sell our labor on the global market, the economic basis for the historic ideological differences between capitalist and official has been largely obliterated. Post-Modernism is the pessimism of an obsolescent class—the salaried official intelligentsia—whose fate is closely bound up with that of the declining nation-state. Pessimism is a form of neurosis, and both the Post-Modernist and the neo-nationalist (or "Thatcherist") show a characteristically neurotic compulsion to repeat a particular emotional stimulus: The Post-Modernist endlessly repeats what he believes to be his parricidal act of shattering bourgeois identity, just as the Thatcherist endlessly laments what she believes to be her nation's parricidal surrender of sovereignty. Both ignore that a more material causality is at work than their neurotic fantasies. Both are unable to accept the loss of their past, so both instead subscribe to a view of the present—as an endlessly repeated moment of consumption—which prevents them from having to consider time at all. In this the Post-Modernists show their derivation from Heidegger, the first systematic philosopher of the post-bourgeois age, who failed precisely in the task he set himself—to construct a philosophy of historical time. If Heidegger's weakness was to devalue the process of consumption, that of Post-Modernism, as of Thatcherism, is to devalue the process of production: all of them detach thought and writing and identity from the socio-economic reality of purposive work, and so in the end from history.

Once, however, we understand ourselves to be both consumers and producers (and in a global market ever more equally both), thought and writing and identity can again be related to historical time. To produce for others is to make a future, and to consume what others have produced for us is to receive a past. The Heideggerian (and so, it has to be said, proto-fascist) tendency, shared by Thatcherists and Post-Modernists alike, is opposed by the Christian belief that our identity becomes visible to us in an act of historical interpretation, in the words by which a past given to us is related to a future of our own making. The interpretive art which we apply in order to create our history, both individual and collective, is practiced and refined in the art of literature. The belief that words can give us realistic representations of episodes from meaningful history was shown by Auerbach to be as old as European vernacular literature, and it is held by some of the twentieth century's most important writers, even if they can present it only negatively and would not necessarily call themselves Christian. From them we can learn what it is to have a modern, that is, a global, identity. The global market has brought into existence a global mind.

No one individual however possesses the global mind. The global perspective is only ever the horizon towards which a particular local standpoint expands. I remember my own standpoint at the moment when this book was conceived. On a streaming wet day in June 1987 I was in the house of I. A. Richards, just before it was to be cleared at last on the death of his widow. The lights were not on, though it was dark under the trees outside. The house had been untenanted for some months and the unnatural disorder imposed by the valuer and the remover—not that of occupancy—had begun to spread over the mementos of two long lives which in some externals at any rate had been entirely typical of my grandparents' generation. Years of work in "the East" were represented by rugs, Chinese cupboards, a few grotesques, a Tibetan hand-bell; grey and white photographs recorded holidays in European hotels and grinning climbing parties in front of Alpine glaciers; less typical perhaps a snapshot of Richards and T. S. Eliot in a court at Harvard, a large framed photograph of the bust of Socrates, and the books—two Cambridges and two generations, linked and separated by countless Atlantic crossings: Ogden and Cornford, Eliot and Lowell, presentation copies still in battered dust-covers, and, the basis of it all, worn-out Edwardian Platos and Coleridges and a recent letter from the stockbroker. Life had brought the books and the lumber together and this was the moment of their dispersal. I felt I was losing a last physical contact with a period in English literature when Britain, on the way down, but with a worldwide scope, met America coming up, with the energy of modernity—a time when the mind was expected to grow deep and individual in an area of freedom which family means opened out on the margin of a serious professional activity, and when poetry was thought to be an image of that freedom. The loss pained me, for I had merely brushed the period with my fingertips, knowing my grandparents hardly at all, and knowing the Richards only in their last years. Just days before, Mrs. Thatcher had been returned for a third term; the university in which Richards had first taught in the 1920s was as gone and almost as forgotten as Aristotle's Academy; and whatever writing and thinking had been in Eliot and Lowell's time they certainly would not be again. What I then conceived was I suppose something of an elegy for the old and a satire on the new, but as I began to write I realized this would not be adequate. There were grave illusions about the past to be overcome, and behind the shoddiness and petulance of contemporary Britain I began to discern a future that was inspiring and not simply ominous.

It is a real feature of modern life, a consequence of the growth of the global market which cannot be wished away, that all that was solid in the coincidence of a self and a social role—vocation, profession, nationality even—melts into air. But that need not be a paralyzing or a nihilistic conclusion. We can and must learn to live (as Kant long ago saw), not as having an identity now, but as intending to have an identity in the future—specifically, the identity of world citizens. Political values and institutions have to underpin the market, even the world-market, and insofar as our lives are directed towards achieving the—always future—goals those values and institutions require, they will have such solidity as mortal lives ought to have. Values that are to be held so universally cannot be matters of mere opinion, mere cultural options added on, if "we" wish, to our other reasons for making this or that purchase as consumers; they must be what enables us to call ourselves "we" in the first place. They must derive from our fundamental role as proletarians in the global market, that is, as consumers who are necessarily producers too. We will show that we have them by our commitment to the very idea of political institutions, as the place where we ourselves decide the conflict between our interests as producers and our interests as consumers. And since we now both produce and consume on a worldwide scale, such conflicts can be decided only globally. Only international institutions, above all those which closely shadow the mechanisms of economic integration, stand any chance of being adequate to the fundamental realities of contemporary life. Much the most advanced and remarkable examples of these, unparalleled anywhere else, are to be found in the European Union—though it is still an open question whether that unique body will continue to show the world the way to effective supranational political co-operation, or whether it will waste its energies on the attempt to create a fortress super-state, a latter-day empire, an attempt which in the global market will most surely fail.

These essays began with political paradoxes and ended with a moral gesture embodied in poetry. That is not because poetry is some kind of refuge from the political and economic world but because that world is not in the end comprehensible without a moral idea which only poetry—only Christian poetry—is subtle and honest enough to put into words. With that proviso, everything said here has a political intent. I have not however been arguing any particular party line—though I think it follows from what I have said that the more flexible the market, the more the party best representing those who work (as we all must now) is the natural party of government. Different party lines are anyway only one of the reasons for choosing between parties. The most important, and the most political, thing I have to say is that the choice between them—expressed not as an opinion uttered, but as a vote cast—is a real choice. It makes a difference, and so shows that we are free agents, not the components of some deterministic economic machine. It is a choice which to some extent—possibly small, but at any rate commensurate with the historical importance of those who make it—will determine with what delay, by how circuitous a route, and with what casualties on the way, we approach the only goal compatible with the rational self-respect of human beings who understand their dependence on each other and on the world that has been given to them: a permanently peaceful global order, freely chosen by all its citizens.

Notes

Foreword

1. See Edward Luttwak, "Why Fascism Is the Wave of the Future," *London Review of Books*, 7 April 1994, p. 3.
2. F. R. Leavis, *Education and the University. A Sketch for an "English School'"*(London, 1943), p. 35.

1 Understanding Thatcherism (1988)

First published as "Understanding Thatcherism" in *New Blackfriars* 69 (1988): 307–324.

2 After Thatcherism: Who Are We Now?

1. F. Jameson, *Postmodernism, or, The Cultural Logic of Late Capitalism* (London, 1991), p. xix.
2. J. Kirwan (ed.), *Rerum Novarum. Encyclical Letter of Pope Leo XIII on the Condition of the Working Classes* (London, 1991), pp. 5–6 (§§ 7,8).
3. See N. Waszek, *The Scottish Enlightenment and Hegel's Account of "Civil Society,"* International Archives of the History of Ideas 120 (Dordrecht, Boston, 1988).
4. Pascal, *Pensées*, ed. E. Brunschvicg, No. 334.
5. See Charter 88, *Citizens* 10 (March 1995).
6. I am grateful to Rushdie Said for this point.
7. Aziz al-Azmeh, *Islams and Modernities* (London, 1993), p. 127.
8. Ibid., 12, 25.

9. Ibid., 26.

10. Ibid., 79, 85.

11. Karl Marx, *Die Frühschriften*, ed. S. Landshut (Stuttgart, 1971), p. 528.

12. Max Weber, "Vorbemerkung zu den gesammelten Aufsätzen zur Religionssoziologie," in *Soziologie. Universalgeschichtliche Analysen. Politik*, ed. J. Winckelmann (Stuttgart, 1973), pp. 340–356.

3 After History: Faith in the Future

A first version of this essay was delivered as a lecture on 28 January 1994 to mark the feast-day of St. Thomas Aquinas. First published as "Hegel and 'The End of History'" in *New Blackfriars* 7 (1995): 109–119, 164–174.

1. Francis Fukuyama, "The End of History," *The National Interest* (Summer, 1989): 3–18.

2. I. Wallerstein, *Geopolitics and Geoculture* (Cambridge, 1991), p. 223.

3. Ibid., 164.

4. Wallerstein thinks—like Toynbee?—that there have been many "world-systems" (Roman, Chinese, Mayan, medieval European, and so on). Taken metaphorically, this usage is perhaps acceptable, if confusing; taken literally, it is patent nonsense.

5. "The second half of the twentieth century will go down in history as a period when humankind took the first serious steps to . . . global governance" (I. G. Patel, "Global Economic Governance: Some Thoughts on Our Current Discontents" in *Global Governance. Ethics and Economics of the World Order*, ed. M. Desai and P. Redfern (London and New York, 1995), pp. 22–38, at p. 22.

6. M. Desai, "Global Governance," in *Global Governance*, pp. 6–21, at p. 16.

7. J.-F. Lyotard, *The Postmodern Condition: A Report on Knowledge*, tr. G. Bennington and B. Massumi (Manchester, 1984).

8. See Wallerstein, *Geopolitics*, p. 107.

9. J.-F. Lyotard, "Le désir nommé Marx" in *Economie libidinale* (Paris, 1974), pp. 117–186.

10. "Alles . . . Stehende verdampft," Marx, *Die Frühschriften*, p. 529. Cp. M. Berman, *All That Is Solid Melts into Air: The Experience of Modernity* (New York, 1982).

11. Lyotard, *Postmodern Condition*, p. 79.

12. F. Jameson, *Postmodernism, or, The Cultural Logic of Late Capitalism* (London, 1991), p. 265.

13. Hegel, *Vorlesungen über die Philosophie der Geschichte*, Theorie-Werkausgabe 12, ed. E. Moldenhauer and K. M. Michel (Frankfurt am Main, 1970), p. 71.

14. Ibid., 70.

15. Lyotard, *Postmodern Condition*, p. 37.

4 After the Empires: 1789–1989

A first version of this essay was delivered as a lecture to the Faculty of Divinity, Cambridge, in November 1991.

1. Hegel, *Philosophie der Geschichte*, p. 539.

2. E.g., *Le Temps*, 31 juillet, 1 août 1831: "après quarante ans comme celle d'Angleterre," "notre glorieuse révolution est achevée."

3. W. Doyle, *The Oxford History of the French Revolution* (Oxford, 1989), pp. 399–401.

4. To Edmund Pendleton, 26 August 1776; to Jared Sparks, 4 February 1824; to Major John Cartwright, 5 June 1824; in *The Political Writings of Thomas Jefferson*, ed. Merrill D. Peterson (Thomas Jefferson Memorial Foundation, 1993), pp. 38, 205–207, 210.

5. To James Madison, 20 December 1787, in Jefferson, *Political Writings* p. 83.

6. "A Bill Declaring Who Shall Be Deemed Citizens of This Commonwealth" (1779) in Jefferson, *Political Writings*, p. 47.

7. Minutes of the Board of Visitors, University of Virginia, 4 March 1825, in Jefferson, *Political Writings*, p. 212.

8. "First Inaugural Address" in Jefferson, *Political Writings*, p. 141.

9. E. Blum (ed.), *La Déclaration des droits de l'homme et du citoyen. Texte authentique avec commentaire* (Paris, 1909).

10. *Inferno*, Canto 17. I owe this interpretation of the episode to an unpublished *lectura Dantis* on Canto 15 by Kenelm Foster.

11. J. Görres, *Resultate meiner Sendung nach Paris* (Koblenz, 1800), p. 84, next quote p. 79.

12. J. Görres, *Teutschland und die Revolution* (Koblenz, 1819), pp. 185–187, cp. pp. 159–163.

13. I am indebted to Paul Connerton for these points, though he would not necessarily approve of the use I have made of them.

5 Understanding Germany

A first version of this essay was published under the same title in *New Blackfriars* 71 (1990): 480–496.

1. See J. C. O'Neill, *The Bible's Authority* (Edinburgh, 1991) and *Who Did Jesus Think He Was?* (Leiden, 1995).

2. Stuart Miall (ed.), *The World of the Children* (London, 1951), vol. 2, p. 254.

3. B. Russell, *My Philosophical Development* (London, 1959), p. 54.

4. Cp. P. Anderson, "Components of the National Culture" *New Left Review* 50 (1968): 3–57.

5. F. Werfel, *Zwischen oben und unten* (Stockholm, 1946), quoted from J. P. Stern, *The Dear Purchase. A Theme in German Modernism* (Cambridge, 1995), p. 380.

6. J. G. Fichte, "Alte und neue Welt," in *Sämmtliche Werke*, ed. I. H. Fichte (reprinted Berlin, 1971), vol. 7, p. 609.

7. J. P. Stern, "Introduction to the *samizdat* Czech edition," in *Hitler: The Führer and the People* (London, 1990), p. xx.

8. "A Social Revolution?" in Stern, *Hitler*, pp. 149–155.

9. It has been a tragic misfortune, but it has not been only that. In the same essay "What is Enlightenment?"in which Kant proclaims the absolute distinction in the Prussian state between freedom of thought and obedience

in political action he goes on to argue that under such a constitution thought will make further and more daring advances than where a greater degree of political freedom (e.g., in England?) trammels thinkers with a prudential concern for the consequences of their ideas. We may, with hindsight, be as inclined to think him right as be relieved that the Prussian state is no longer with us.

6 After Enlightenment:
Hegel, Post-Modernism, and the State

1. Cambridge University *Reporter* 122 (20 May 1992): 688.

2. A. MacIntyre, *Three Rival Versions of Moral Enquiry* (London, 1990), pp. 227, 221. "No single world," p. 36.

3. MacIntyre, *Three Rival Versions*, p. 208.

4. Ibid., 214.

5. Ibid., 55, 54.

6. A. Jefferson, "Structuralism and Post-structuralism," in *Modern Literary Theory* ed. A. Jefferson and D. Robey, 2nd ed. (London, 1986), pp. 92–121 at p. 119.

7. MacIntyre, *Three Rival Versions*, p. 226.

8. The illusion is heightened into hallucination when the narrator's text is removed and the story is dramatized for film or television.

9. Or "bourgeois," the German word for both is "bürgerlich."

10. W. H. Bruford, *Culture and Society in Classical Weimar* 1775–1806 (Cambridge, 1962), p. 62, "little or no real middle class."

11. Hegel, *Grundlinien der Philosophie des Rechts*, Theorie-Werkausgabe 7, §268. Other references to the paragraphs of this edition are given in the text.

12. Whatever Hegel may think the conflict in *Antigone* to be, he certainly does not understand it as a conflict between a national and an international institution, or between one state and another.

13. One might go further and say that the frontiers must be physically proof against immigration, legal or not: if America at the end of the twentieth century is still not a fully formed state, but is still struggling to define the relation between its citizens and their government, that is partly because it has so long maintained its Jeffersonian openness to the free flow of migrating "men" seeking the free exercise of their right to pursue happiness. Insofar as populations desire to defend their conditions of employment against the free movement of migrant workers which the global market demands, they desire to have a state.

7 Martin Heidegger and the Treason of the Clerks

1. T. Mann, "Von deutscher Republik," in *Von deutscher Republik. Politische Schriften und Reden in Deutschland* (Frankfurt am Main, 1984), pp. 118–159, at p. 134.

2. H. Ott, *Martin Heidegger. A Political Life*, tr. Allan Blunden (London, 1993), p. 98.

3. R. Safranski, *Ein Meister aus Deutschland. Heidegger und seine Zeit* (Munich, Vienna, 1994), p. 66.

4. Ibid., 87.

5. Ott, *Heidegger*, p. 116.

6. Ibid., p. 125.

7. Safranski, *Meister*, p. 158.

8. Christian Graf von Krockow, *Die Entscheidung. Eine Untersuchung über Ernst Jünger, Carl Schmitt, Martin Heidegger* (Stuttgart, 1958) is essentially a parallel study, which only to a limited extent discusses the relations between the thinkers. Jean-Michel Palmier, *Les écrits politiques de Heidegger* (Paris, 1968) gives much space to Jünger and concludes in particular that Jünger is the source of Heidegger's understanding of the planetary role of technology. Jünger is scarcely mentioned in Annemarie Gethmann-Siefert and Otto Pöggeler (eds.) *Heidegger und die praktische Philosophie* (Frankfurt am Main, 1988), though see pp. 49 and 52–53. Much the most sophisticated study of the relationship will be found in P. Bourdieu, *L'ontologie politique de Martin Heidegger* (Paris, 1988), pp. 26–30, 36–51. Within its limits—it underestimates Jünger's independence of mind, and the extent to which he changed it—the fine analysis of the paradoxical notion of a "conservative revolution" illuminates both thinkers. However, it is not clear in what sense Jünger can be said to furnish the "matière première" of Heidegger's thought (p. 46), given that *Sein und Zeit* appeared in 1927 and *Der Arbeiter*, "ce livre qui enferme tant de la vérité de Heidegger" (p. 28), in 1932. More seriously, Bourdieu completely overlooks the importance of Heidegger's Catholicism and so fails to see the link between the Lutheran elements in the vocabulary of *Sein und Zeit* and the culture of the German bureaucracy, explaining their presence instead by the influence of Kierkegaard (p. 79). And it is a familiar Post-Modernist paradox (see both our previous chapter, and the next) that Heidegger's words are not allowed by Bourdieu to convey any truth to those in different social and political circumstances, while a similar limitation seems not to apply to the words in which Bourdieu conducts his analysis. The will to power of "homo academicus" is at least as apparent in *L'ontologie politique de Martin Heidegger* as it is in Martin Heidegger's political ontology.

9. L. Tolstoy, *War and Peace*, tr. R. Edmonds (London, 1982), Bk 2, Pt 4, Ch 1, p. 574.

10. E. Jünger, *Der Arbeiter. Herrschaft und Gestalt*. Zweite Auflage (Hamburg, 1932), p. 189. Page references in the text are to this edition, abbreviated *Arb*. Cp. Rilke, *Duineser Elegien* 7, ll. 55–56, "Weite Speicher der Kraft schafft sich der Zeitgeist, gestaltlos / wie der spannende Drang, den er aus allem gewinnt."

11. This phrase is taken from the blurb on the cover of the edition cited in the previous note.

12. See Richard Schaeffler, "Heidegger und die Theologie," in Gethmann-Siefert and Pöggeler, *Heidegger und die praktische Philosophie*, pp. 286–309, esp. pp. 289–297.

13. M. Heidegger, *Sein und Zeit*, 14. Auflage (Tübingen, 1977), pp. 322–323. Page references in the text are to this edition, abbreviated *SuZ*.

14. J. P. Stern attributes it—too kindly—to Jünger's "defective . . . sensibility"; see Stern, *Ernst Jünger. A Writer of Our Time* (Cambridge, 1953), p. 7.

15. O. Spengler, *Preußentum und Sozialismus* (Munich, 1920), p. 90. Page references in the text are to this edition, abbreviated *PuS*.

16. Cp. Safranski, *Meister*, p. 424.

17. Cited e.g., by Käte Meyer-Drawe, "Aneignung—Ablehnung—Anregung. Pädagogische Orientierungen an Heidegger," in Gethmann-Siefert and Pöggeler, *Heidegger und die praktische Philosophie*, pp. 231–250, p. 248.

18. Karsten Harries, "Heidegger as a Political Thinker" in *Heidegger and Modern Philosophy*, ed. M. Marras (Yale, 1978), pp. 304–328, at p. 310.

19. Plainly there is a sense, even if a highly derived sense, in which the history in which we find ourselves is a matter of our choice. But Hegel in his theory of the state gives a much more satisfactory account than Heidegger of the nature of the derivation, that is, of the special sense in which history is a representation of freedom.

20. Safranski, *Meister*, p. 327, cp. O. Pöggeler, "Heideggers politisches Selbstverständnis" in Gethmann-Siefert and Pöggeler, *Heidegger und die praktische Philosophie*, pp. 17–63, esp. p. 61.

21. M. Heidegger, *Die Selbstbehauptung der deutschen Universität. Das Rektorat 1933/34* (Frankfurt, 1990), p. 24. References in the text are to this edition, abbreviated *Selbstb*.

22. Reprinted in Palmier, *Les écrits politiques de Heidegger*, pp. 319–331. References in the text give the original pagination followed by that of Palmier's reprint.

23. Ott, *Heidegger*, p. 256

24. Ibid., 225–276, Safranski, *Meister*, pp. 317–318.

25. Safranski, *Meister*, pp. 325–327

26. Ibid., 315–317.

27. Safranski, *Meister*, p. 324.

28. T. Mann, *Doktor Faustus. Die Entstehung des Doktor Faustus* (Frankfurt am Main, 1967). References in the text are to this edition, abbreviated *F*.

29. These seem to me the interpretations respectively of R. D. Gray (*The German Tradition in Literature, 1871–1945* [Cambridge, 1965], p. 223) and J. P. Stern (*The Dear Purchase. A Theme in German Modernism* [Cambridge, 1995], pp. 376–379).

8 Crossing the Line?
Heidegger and the Post-Modern University

1. Ott, *Heidegger*, p. 294.

2. E.g., by Palmier, op. cit.

3. Ott, *Heidegger*, p. 295

4. M. Heidegger, "Was heißt denken?" (Tübingen, 1954), p. 65. References in the text are to this edition, abbreviated *D*.

5. E. Jünger, "Über die Linie. Martin Heidegger zum 60. Geburtstag," in *Essays I. Betrachtungen zur Zeit* (Stuttgart, 1960), pp. 245–289, at p. 280. References in the text are to this edition, abbreviated *L*.

6. E.g., *L* 259–260, cp. "Der Waldgang," *Essays I*, pp. 291–387, pp. 347–348, and Heidegger *D* 65.

7. E. Jünger, "Der Weltstaat. Organismus und Organisation," in *Essays I*, pp. 495–538, at p. 536.

8. M. Heidegger, "Zur Seinsfrage," in *Wegmarken* (Frankfurt am Main, 1967), pp. 213–253, particularly the passage quoted on p. 229. References in the text are to this edition, abbreviated *ZS*.

9. In particular *Duineser Elegien* 5, ll. 81–86, *Sonette an Orpheus* II 12, 13, and Rilke's last completed poem in German, 'Für Erika zum Feste der Rühmung' ("Taube, die draußen blieb").

10. M. Heidegger, *Die Technik und die Kehre* (Pfullingen, 1962), p. 12. References in the text are to this edition, abbreviated *TK*.

11. Heidegger (like Rilke, cp. n. 10 to ch. 7 above) overlooks that electricity cannot be stored in significant quantities, and that storing energy by pumping water uphill requires only some of the oldest technology humanity possesses.

12. *TK* 17. A similar point is made about the farmer, *TK* 14, for which cp. *Arb* 73, 159.

13. T. S. Eliot, "East Coker," ll. 140–141.

14. Various possible interpretations are well expounded by David Kolb, *The Critique of Pure Modernity. Hegel, Heidegger, and After* (Chicago and London, 1986), chap. 9, "Life in the Modern World."

15. E. M. Butler, *The Tyranny of Greece over Germany* (Cambridge, 1935).

16. 1 John 4:20.

17. Cp. *SuZ* 117: "Allein die '*Substanz*' des Menschen ist nicht der Geist als die Synthese von Seele und Leib, sondern die *Existenz*."

18. Paul Celan, "Todtnauberg," *Gedichte* (Frankfurt, 1975), vol. 2, p. 255; Safranski, *Meister*, p. 486.

19. E.g., E. J. Hobsbawm, *Age of Extremes: The Short Twentieth Century 1914–1991* (London, 1994), pp. 389–394.

20. See K. H. Jarausch, "Die Krise des deutschen Bildungsbürgertums im ersten Drittel des 20. Jahrhunderts," in *Bildungsbürgertum im 19. Jahrhundert. Tl. 4. Politischer Einfluß und gesellschaftliche Formation*, ed. J. Kocka (Stuttgart, 1989), pp. 180–205.

21. Karl Mannheim, *Ideologie und Utopie*, cited in E. R. Curtius, *Deutscher Geist in Gefahr* (Stuttgart, 1932), p. 91.

22. *SuZ* 22–23. Curtius cites this usage of Mannheim's in inverted commas, as a neologism (pp. 95, 96).

23. J. Derrida, "Admiration de Nelson Mandela ou Les lois de la réflexion," in J. Derrida and others, *Pour Nelson Mandela* (Paris, 1986), pp. 13–44. I am grateful to Arnold Davidson for drawing my attention to this piece, and to its significance.

24. Kant, *Idee zu einer allgemeinen Geschichte in weltbürgerlicher Absicht*, in *Werke* 6, ed. W. Weischedel (Frankfurt am Main, 1964), p. 50.

25. Rilke, Duineser *Elegien* 1, ll. 12–13.

9 After Realism:
Nietzsche and the "Middle Mode of Discourse"

The greater part of this essay first appeared as "Nietzsche and the 'Middle Mode of Discourse'" in *Realism in European Literature. Essays in Honour of J. P. Stern*, ed. N. Boyle and M.W. Swales (Cambridge, 1986), pp. 123–157.

1. F. R. Leavis, "Valedictory," in *A Selection from* Scrutiny (Cambridge, 1968), vol. 2, p. 320.

2. F. R. Leavis, *Two Cultures? The Significance of C. P. Snow* (London, 1962), p. 30.

3. Ibid., 23.

4. I. Watt, *The Rise of the Novel* (London, 1957), p. 288.

5. J. P. Stern, *A Study of Nietzsche* (Cambridge, 1979), p. 201.

6. Pascal, *Pensées*, ed. Brunschvicg, no. 17, cp. *Friedrich Nietzsche. Werke in drei Bänden*, ed. Karl Schlechta (Munich, 1954–56), vol. 3, p. 320. References in the text are to this edition.

7. M. S. Silk and J. P. Stern, *Nietzsche on Tragedy* (Cambridge, 1981), p. 340.

8. The sequence, (1) "evil," (2) "not evil, because only called evil," (3) "rightly called evil," is an example of the dialectic described by Stern, *A Study of Nietzsche*, pp. 160–161.

9. Jacques Derrida, *Spurs. Nietzsche's Styles. Éperons. Les Styles de Nietzsche* (Chicago, 1979). The translations here given are my own.

10. J. P. Stern, *On Realism* (London, 1973), p. 108.

11. Stern, *On Realism*, p. 117, quoting *Nicomachean Ethics* I.3.3–4.

12. "Why does Nietzsche refuse to distinguish between 'fictions' and 'lies'? . . . only to one who is prepared to take institutionalized life in the world seriously is this difference of any consequence" (Stern, *A Study of Nietzsche*, p. 188).

13. "[T]he given in experience is always a world or system. . . . The given and the isolated, so far from being synonymous, are contradictory . . . the given is neither a collection, nor a series of ideas, but a complex, significant whole. . . . Furthermore, the given in experience is given always in order to be transformed . . . In experience . . . a given world of ideas is transformed into a world of ideas which is more of a world" (M. Oakeshott, *Experience and its Modes* [Cambridge, 1933], pp. 28–30). Oakeshott dismisses what we may regard as the Nietzschean view of language as an "elementary error" and subverts the Nietzschean primacy of interpretation: "Interpretation requires something to interpret, but when we speak of *it* our language slips under our feet, for there is never in experience an *it*, an original, distinguishable from the interpretation, and consequently there can be no interpretation" (pp. 31–32).

14. Karl Schlechta applies this comparison to Nietzsche's work. See the "Nachwort" to his edition, III, 1436.

15. "Der Mann Moses und die monotheistische Religion" in S. Freud, *Gesammelte Werke* 16 (London, 1950), p. 125.

16. "Vorlesungen zur Einführung in die Psychoanalyse. III. Allgemeine Neurosenlehre," Lecture xxi. Freud, *Gesammelte Werke* 11 (London, 1940), p. 348.

17. "Der Mann Moses . . . ," *Gesammelte Werke* 16, p. 184.

18. "Einige psychische Folgen des anatomischen Geschlechtsunter-schiedes," *Gesammelte Werke* 14 (London 1948), p. 28.

19. Roland Barthes, *La chambre claire. Note sur la photographie* (Paris, 1980), pp. 181–182.

20. Karl Schlechta's *Nietzsche-Index* (Munich, 1965) contains only nine references in all to "Tod," "der Tod," and "ein Tod" (pp. 362–363).

21. G. W. F. Hegel, "Enzyklopädie der philosophischen Wissenschaften im Grundrisse" (1830) §376, *Werke in 20 Bänden*, ed. E. Moldenhauer and K. M. Michel (Frankfurt a. M., 1970), vol. 9, p. 537.

22. La Rochefoucauld, *Maximes* (1678), No. 26; Goethe, *Faust*, l. 4715.

23. L. Tolstoy, *Anna Karenina*, tr. D. Magarshack (London, 1961), Book 5, chap. 8, p. 468.

24. *The Collected Poems of Wallace Stevens* (London, 1955), p. 67.

25. P. Zacharia, "The Train Robbery," in *Bhaskara Pattelar and Other Stories* (Madras, 1994), pp. 34–45. I owe my acquaintance with this admirable collection to Ramachandra Guha, whom it is a pleasure to thank for his enthusiastic advocacy.

10 The Idea of Christian Poetry

A first version of this essay was published under the same title in *New Blackfriars* 67 (1986): 436–454.

1. In the essay "Religion and Literature," contributed to the symposium *Faith That Illuminates* (1935), and included in *T. S. Eliot: Selected Prose*, ed. John Hayward (Penguin, 1953). I quote from Foster's own copy.

2. See "Michelangelo's Failure," *Blackfriars* 44 (1963): 355–363; "Snow against the Poets," *Blackfriars* 45 (1964); 220–226; "The Idea of Truth in Manzoni and Leopardi," British Academy Italian Lecture, 1967; "The Pope and Poetry," *Dante Studies* 87 (1969), an account of Pope Paul VI's *motu proprio* on Dante, *Altissimi cantus*.

3. It is much to be regretted that Foster never addressed himself at length to the problem which he acknowledged to be basic: "How far and in what sense does Catholicism admit the possibility of an *implicit* faith in Christ?" (*The Two Dantes and Other Studies* (London, 1977, p. 154). His treatment of the derived problems in the three-part essay "The Two Dantes" seems to rest on the premise that Dante-the-poet regarded the salvation of Ripheus and Trajan in *Paradiso* XX "as extremely exceptional, indeed as abnormal" (p. 249). Yet Foster's own discussion of the questions in *Paradiso* XIX, to which *Paradiso* XX provides the answer, surely shows that it is Dante-the-character's surprising assumption that "there is no alternative to *explicit* faith" (p. 154) which the eagle is rebuking for the shallowness of its conception of divine wisdom. Foster draws special attention to ll. 85–90 of canto XIX (p. 146), but their implication would seem to me not that "if we judge God to be just or unjust, the criterion itself that we use must derive from him," but rather that if we judge Dante-the-character's *virtuous Indian* to be just we are already assuming in him a—to us perhaps unfathomable—relationship to the divine source of all justice.

4. Arthur Sale recalls a lecture given by Foster to Italian teachers of English on "Three Religious Poets." It dealt with Hopkins, T. S. Eliot, and Dylan Thomas but unfortunately no record of it seems to remain.

5. To profess a belief in the Incarnation of our Lord was to profess at least this much belief in the *theological* importance of His mother, nor did Foster scruple to continue the quotation:

Incipe, parve puer: qui non risere parenti
Nec deus hunc mensa, dea nec dignata cubili est.

Begin, little boy, to know your mother with a smile . . .
Begin, little boy: him who never smiled at his parent
no god invites to table, nor goddess to her bed
(Foster's translation)

6. "Dante: Poet of the Intellect," *New Blackfriars* 46 (1965): 442–446.

7. K. Foster, *God's Tree. Essays on Dante and Other Matters* (London, 1957), p. 32.

8. E. Auerbach, *Mimesis: The Representation of Reality in Western Literature*, tr. Willard Trask (Princeton, 1953) ch. 9, "Farinata and Cavalcante." The link between Dante's mixed style and his unique fusion of history and allegory seems first to have been noted by Schelling, from whom Hegel's comments on the poem, of which Auerbach speaks so highly (p. 167), also partially derive.

9. Foster, *God's Tree*, pp. 108–110.

10. Cp. K. Foster, *The Two Dantes*, p. 30.

11. Certainly he saw the longing for maternal warmth of the urchins in "Les Effarés" "les pauvres Jésus pleins de givre," as an analogue of the general human longing that was fulfilled in the motherhood of Mary, but an explicitly secular analogue, as the poem's comical conclusion emphasizes. I base this remark on Foster's own comments scribbled into the margin of his Penguin Rimbaud, and elaborated in his Christmas talk.

12. Contrast the view expressed by Ann Barton in "'Enter Mariners, wet': realism in Shakespeare's last plays," in *Realism in European Literature*, ed. N. Boyle and M. W. Swales (Cambridge, 1986), pp. 47–48.

13. "'Christ and Letters': The Religion of the Early Humanists," *Blackfriars* 44 (1963): 355–363; *The Two Dantes*, pp. 103, 143.

14. See "Dante: Poet of the Intellect" (*New Blackfriars*, 1965). Helen Gardner lays great stress on the Yeats identification (*The Composition of "Four Quartets,"* [London, 1978], pp. 65–69, 186–189) but acknowledges the presence of other models (p. 185).

15. *God's Tree*, pp. 109–110.

16. Ibid., 1–2.

17. R. Lowell, "Waking Early Sunday Morning," *Near the Ocean* (London, 1967), pp. 13–16.

18. I take it that strophe 5 is a sustained allusion to "A man that looks on glass" etc.

19. "Vacillations VIII" ("Must we part, Von Hügel,"), W. B. Yeats, *The Poems*, ed. Daniel Albright (London, 1992), p. 303.

20. S. Heaney, *New Selected Poems. 1966–1987* (London, 1990), p. 206.

21. "Clearances," Heaney, *New Selected Poems*, pp. 224–232; No. 3 ("When all the others"), p. 227.

22. Heaney, *New Selected Poems*, p. 43; *North* (London, 1975), pp. 57–60.

23. Heaney, *New Selected Poems*, p. 217.

Afterword

1. "Rights discourse must involve a radical modification of state sovereignty" (R. Plant, "Rights, Rules and World Order," in *Global Governance*, ed. Desai and Redfern, 190–218, at p. 204).

Index

335